# JERSEY GENESIS

Charlie Leek, of Lower Bank, said that the Leeks, in spite of their name, had to build boats or become ministers. He preferred boats, and his plant, now managed by his grandsons, has become a multi-million-dollar center on the Mullica River.

# Jersey Genesis

## THE STORY OF THE MULLICA RIVER

*By Henry Charlton Beck*

*New Brunswick*

RUTGERS UNIVERSITY PRESS

*To* SAMUEL SOUTHARD NORCROSS,
*the "Sud" of these chapters,*
*without whose friendship and innumerable "kin"*
*this book could not have been written*

# CONTENTS

| | | |
|---|---|---|
| | Foreword | vii |
| | Foreword to 1963 Printing | xiii |
| 1. | Fisherman's Luck | 3 |
| 2. | Roundabout Islands | 12 |
| 3. | Bishop's Breed | 20 |
| 4. | Cure for Old Age | 33 |
| 5. | Roads Under Water | 45 |
| 6. | Leeds of Leeds | 58 |
| 7. | Leeks in Lower Bank | 70 |
| 8. | Over Turtle Creek | 81 |
| 9. | Captain's House | 92 |
| 10. | Meadow Musk | 102 |
| 11. | Green Bank | 113 |
| 12. | One Corpse to Another | 121 |
| 13. | Pillar of Society | 132 |
| 14. | Snappers and Greentails | 143 |
| 15. | "As Dying—" | 157 |
| 16. | The Adventure of Aserdaten | 166 |
| 17. | Rolling Stones Gather | 184 |
| 18. | The Forum | 191 |
| 19. | Names and Big Guns | 204 |
| 20. | Toward the Port | 215 |
| 21. | Port of the Republic | 226 |
| 22. | The Jersey Devil | 240 |
| 23. | Santa Claus of Lower Bank | 250 |
| 24. | Farewell to Lower Bank | 263 |
| 25. | The Forks | 276 |
| 26. | Headwaters | 289 |
| | Bibliography | 304 |
| | Index | 305 |

The photographs reproduced in *Jersey Genesis* are with but a few exceptions the work of William F. Augustine, who, falling in love with life along the Mullica River long ago, went to live at Atsion, and then, returning from overseas with the end of World War II, eventually built a house at Lower Bank, overlooking the river. The author is indebted to Donald Corvelli, who (except when he was catching tiger beetles at Lower Bank) took time out from his specialty, photographic zoology, to make outstanding contributions, notably the pictures of the last of the salt hay bargemen. The photographs need but little beyond their own eloquence except when their subjects are somewhat beyond the immediate Mullica locale, remaining, even so, an integral part of the half-hidden, unspoiled New Jersey scene. The text, I must say over and over, is the story of a river told by the river itself, almost, or next to it, by the people who have loved it for centuries. It is the work and thought of hundreds of people whose names lie about me in letters, scribbled notes, books, and other material that give evidence of the five-year task—to them all, whoever and wherever they may be, I am deeply grateful.

H. C. B.

# FOREWORD

*"In the beginning . . ."*
GENESIS

I MAY BE WRONG about the Mullica River. I don't think I am. To me the Mullica is the most wonderful of the unrecognized rivers of America.

To awake on a summer's morning, comfortably aware of the sun radiant upon mist rising from cedar water, to look out upon tidal depths moving toward salty reaches of the bay, to watch from a curtained window a doe at breakfast beside tawny grasses of the marsh—these have made the backdrop with which I have balanced waking hours.

"What about mosquitoes?"

This will always be the question when it is known that the scene is New Jersey. I cannot answer that there are no mosquitoes or that I, having gone next to native down the river, am not bothered by them. But I don't think the pests are as numerous as they were in August, 1858, when "horses, covered with blood, laid down in the streets and cattle waded out into the ocean to escape torture." Nor would today's Atlantic City children be like those who "scratched and squalled from the poisonous stings on limbs and faces." There are mosquitoes on the Mullica in season, but we will overlook them.

Perhaps in time we can become like good Parson Woodmansee of Barnegat, who peels off mosquitoes like rolling woolen sleeves down his arms, smiling a little with mingled triumph and prowess. Perhaps we can emulate the calm of the New Gretna real estate man who, they tell me, was entirely unmoved by the question of a prospect: "Are there any mosquitoes in the neighborhood?" "No," he answered, with a straight face, "certainly not! Tell you what. I will give you a dollar for every mosquito you can catch between now and tomor-

vii

row!" Whereupon he presumably became as elusive as he wished the mosquitoes would be until the bargain was completed.

I will have to be more repellent to mosquitoes than I am now before I finally make up my mind exactly where it is along the Mullica I fain would be. The truth is that there is so much to make up for mosquitoes that you rarely let them bother you. Chief delight, of course, is being along the river, long and wide and deep despite descriptions of a dreary, waterless waste. Equal to it is the prospect of being among the river people, far removed from what people mean when they speak of Pineys and shiftless baymen. I have met few Pineys lately for whom these loosely applied distinctions are not, no matter what the implication is, complimentary, and very few who haven't had more in their larders than those inclined to snub them.

At first, I must tell you, I fully intended a novel. "You are missing the main chance," they told me, "when you merely lock these people and places between covers of nonfiction." From almost every aspect that is true. And yet, if this were a book of fiction, its readers might conclude that everything but my backdrop is imaginary. Whatever the book may be, the opposite is true. The more I have lingered by the river, the more I have realized that to imagine anything is unnecessary. The truth is good enough, almost too good. All these things have happened. All these people are real. These villages are as I know them and as these people know them.

I am prepared for argument on this point. Some of my friends who have seen the manuscript or parts of it have said that I have written of places as I have known them, but surely not as the Mullica people know them. I have been polite, I am told, whereas my friends along the river would not be polite. They, it is pointed out, would be honest —and I must agree. I do *not* agree, however, that I have glorified this particular area of Down Jersey just for the fun of it, or that I have looked through rose-colored glasses at anything. Nor do I share the contention that to these people their towns are as ordinary and as humdrum as I find cities.

I have argued that they would not have remained beside the river in such obvious contentment as long as they have if anything about them were ordinary. Through generations they've held on, unspoiled by the world outside, entirely uncontaminated. At this point some-body usually interrupts. Then I wax poetic and say that if a novel is to be written about the river people, it must be when I or some-body else actually lives among them. You can't write about a river from the outside in—I've discovered that. You have to see it with the eyes of one who loves it; you have to be there in all weathers, thrill-ing to frost-carpeted woodlands and the smell of cedar currents—mosquitoes or no mosquitoes.

Joe Robinson, who piloted me up and down the Mullica and who, since then, has been guiding a craft more graceful than a rowboat up the little rivers of Africa, discussed the whole matter before he went away. I told him that by the time I finished the river's story the world would have returned to civilization and that I would be down on my River of Refuge.

"Perhaps it will be in one of those villages," I suggested, "where no one will have had to go back to civilized ways because no one had let them go. In spite of wars and chaos in the world outside, towns and people along the Mullica have maintained their own equanimity, their own refinements, their own essentially American resourcefulness."

Joe chuckled at my vehemence, I remember. "You lie, really," he said. "Maybe you don't know it but you lie. These people—and I love all of them—are more worldly than you think. You forget that the Mullica River was once very much a part of the world and that grandfathers and great-grandfathers of these people had a part in world trade and bustling community life not very different from the industry and living you claim to despise now. They didn't measure up to it, probably," he said, leading me on. "Certainly the world passed them by."

"The world didn't give them up at all," I retorted. "They gave up the world. They discovered they had something infinitely more im-portant than all the world could give them. They decided to hold on to it, to make it serve what they needed from life. There is more of the real America inside and around houses in these villages up and down the river than anybody thinks."

I maintain that even now. The river people have given sons to the world's wars for democracy and freedom, but it has been as if they were humoring an intruding relative who didn't know about the superior democracy and freedom they knew they had. They have refused through more than two hundred and fifty years to quit the land won for them forever by ancestor pioneers, patriots, Tories, privateers, and Refugees. Most of them have looked without longing and with considerable tolerant amusement on the lure of cities —cities for some have been places to gain experience with which to return to the river, by which to appreciate the river more. They prefer for the most part a few fish, a bowl of berries, and a chaw of conversation beside a potbellied stove. In whatever is or isn't to come, I would rather cast my lot with these people than anyone else I know.

Speak of the Mullica to most people, and they wait for you to go on. There must be, their eyebrows imply, a supplemental explanation. You'll find them like that less than twenty miles from the river. There is rarely the rewarding recognition due to a stretch of water that was the key to survival at Valley Forge or even to the roadway to and from a land that found itself only when riches dwindled and world trade sidled away.

"The Mullica?" someone will repeat. Even your most devoted friend is likely to mimic the name. "The Mullica? What is *that?*" Then, with as much restraint as you can muster, you explain many things: That the Mullica is a river rising back of Crowfoot and Long-a-Coming, leading down to what once was the most important harbor of the Jerseys; that for years on end the river's name was the more ambiguous Little Egg Harbor, distinguishing it from the Great Egg Harbor; and that even earlier, to the Indians at least, it was the Amintonck. The river and the harbor and the land about them have provided a kind of genesis for all the world.

It was Joe who told me about the name, Amintonck. Later I made certain about it. There is an Indian deed dated April 11, 1697, recording the transfer of "a tract at the sea-side on the West-side of the Bay, N.W., of the Little Egg Harbour River, called Amintonck, including five islands in the marsh from Mahomecum, also known as King Charles, to Henry Jacobs Ffaulkinburge, of Matinicunk Island, Delaware River." If there was an early fever for changing names, the river surely had it. What is more, the contagion swept quickly from the Barnegat sedges and Mullica swamps to touch the first folk who lived beside it—Henry Falkinburg changed rivers only once but altered the spelling of *his* name almost every other spring.

Henry probably got tired dragging that seven-syllabled title around. Sometimes he dropped the Falkinburg altogether, but that may have been due to an early priority on ink. Henry was a right-living man, the first white settler to settle in what they called Egg Harbor, a neighborhood covering a lot of territory through the years. Those days of Henry's time found the Mullica emptying into brackish coves and salt channels known almost exclusively to waterfowl, cod, rockfish, terrapin, and the Delawares, Indians who used to come down to the shore to make money, a habit that has lured many people ever since.

Pungent cedar waters of the Mullica babbled then without sustained interruption on a pebbly, forest-crowded shore. Henry Falkinburg decided that his success as an Indian interpreter deserved expansion, and the opening of the first real estate agency in Little Egg Harbor came into being. He had managed some heavy deals between pioneering Europeans of Burlington County and the tribal subjects of an amiable Indian queen, Bathsheba, revealing his merits as a business man with professional procedure that proved a precedent—purchasing the best with the least.

Henry Falkinburg's deals were probably no different from others involving property before or since, with the probable exception of the New Gretna transaction involving the reward for mosquitoes. Vast acres of the best land were exchanged for the colorful but worthless trinkets of the primeval peddler, a wanderer called a "scotchman" in early New Jersey. Here remains a land that is peaceful and unspoiled. As for the people, let me quote an entry in Laura Larrabee McConeghy's dog-eared notebook: "Really a primitive people, still with little, if any, fusion." I quoted the entry to Joe Robinson one night, adding, "And she lived in Green Bank long enough to know."

"No fusion!" Joe repeated, laughing. "Plenty of confusion then, I'll wager. And listen: Some of these people of whom you think so much aren't in the Mullica Valley at all! How about Wilmon Ware and his maple chairs? How about the man who weaves baskets of oaken splints down on Turkey Point? How about the bike-riding trapper? How about the man cured of cancer with homemade black salve? How about these? They don't live on your Mullica River!"

I admitted that. They had found rivers of refuge all their own. "They are part of the same pattern," I said, "a vital part of the Jersey scene that's mostly as unknown as the Mullica. These people do things the way their fathers taught them. Their ways have been handed down through generations. They are past masters in the art of making what they have do. They are self-sufficient almost, and so they live in their own kind of civilization."

Joe was inclined to laugh again and so may you. I hope not. For I have made a start with the people I like most, the Fords and Sooys and Cramers and Leeks and Birdsalls and Adamses and Cavileers. I know some of those who have been there always and most of those who went down and couldn't come away. I know the man who says he ignored a berrypicker on the other side of a bush only to discover the man was a bear. I know the man who tells how he lay on his back in a stream, using his boots for decoys to bring down countless ducks with a giant shotgun. I know the man who thought it was fun to nail another man's shoes to the floor of his cabin as he slept; the rascal who cut the tether of a duckboat, watching its sleeping occupant drift beyond the lair of wild geese. "Too many plots, too many characters," Joe said. "A novel couldn't possibly emerge, you see."

And so we come back to the beginning—genesis. "In the beginning . . ."

This, then, is the story of a river, a river of refuge. It is the story of people who live beside that river. In some mystical sense the river and those lives are one. Whatever else this book may be, it will say, I hope, what the Amintonck, the Little Egg Harbor, and the Mullica, ever flowing to and from the sea, have wanted to say for a long while.

HENRY CHARLTON BECK

# FOREWORD TO 1963 PRINTING

As *Jersey Genesis* was completed in 1944, it was virtually impossible to purchase property along the Mullica. Those who made inquiries were repulsed repeatedly by owners who set great store by family ways and inheritances—by houses sometimes weather-black but with plant-filled windows, sphagnum swamps with upland clearings where moss would dry, blueberry patches, scraggly fields, and above all independence born of resourcefulness and ingenuity. Then the war ended, and in its wake came a slow reversal, not infrequently aided by the passing of those who seemed content to go, once their stories had been told or the "invasion" had begun, a reversal often hastened by a new generation that had come home with ideas from "outside." The result is a Mullica River I could not have imagined long ago when I was caught up in devotion to this wonderful stream.

Now there are new and restored houses almost everywhere, in fringes of woodlands that have been cleared as well as on the river's shores; the drone and fumes of myriad pleasure craft in spring, summer, and long after autumn has come; the small talk of folk to whom the aroma of the sedges or cedar water means little and to whom a deer is something to shoot. The late Aunt Hattie's Green Bank store, made spick and span by her niece Shirley and her husband, never can be the forum I knew, any more than can the big boat plant making the celebrated Pacemaker, under the direction of John and Donald Leek, resemble the rambling sheds of their late grandfather, Charlie. The firm name of Charles P. Leek & Son continues recollection of my old friend, lively as a cricket when I talked with him, a patch over one eye making him a genial pirate.

Now you will see that unless I am careful, this new preface will take on a sustained melancholy note. It must not do that. Beauty, after all, is in the eye of the beholder, and much of the charm of the Mullica that was there is still there for me. Furthermore, rarely has it been given to a writer to publish the stories of so many and yet enjoy their friendship through the years; however, that has been true of the men and women who stride across the pages of this book. Perhaps in some measure it was a combination of listening to all they wanted to remember and respecting what they preferred to forget; I don't know; whatever it was, I thank God for it and so much more. Even in the 1940's, it became obvious that I had reached those with valuable chapters to share just in time. Gradually, I found myself much like the pastor of an expanding parish. On one sad occasion I was asked to officiate at St. Paul's Church in Camden at the Burial Office of Samuel Southard Norcross, companion on many a journey down the river.

The Garden State Parkway has brought transformations, but many of them are good in that the traveler can quickly reach the little roads and explore what lingers of what there used to be. Gus Schneider, if he were here, would marvel at the parkway, for it was built in sight of his house on stilts. "Tater" Cramer took it gracefully, even though the new road down the coast junked his drawbridge and made sudden alterations in his life. Rod Koster is on duty in the fire tower at Batsto, for there is no longer a post office in the store at Green Bank. Hollis Koster comes back to the old house at Hermann City, where I miss the familiar face of old Leon, who, it always seemed to me, went downhill after the state abandoned its tree-growing at Green Bank for nurseries at Washington Crossing. Hollis never has had his due as an authority on the flora of the Pinelands.

Among so many, I miss Granny Cramer and a gift apple when I called, as well as the annual Christmas card; Mrs. Bull Miller's green tomato pies, which, as I think she suspected, were a little too hot for me; Jack Updike and his perfect decoys, carved with little more than a jackknife; Lance Cobb, who "fyked" for snappers and hung up a sign when he had any to sell; and Bill Birdsall and his wife, who were horrified at being asked by a passing stranger to "sell Grandfather off the wall."

Not all that was there when *Jersey Genesis* first appeared has vanished, by any means. The house of Chink Simpkins (Sinkins) remains much as it was, although it appeared ready to blow away long ago. Chink went to his reward, and I recall his last days mingled with the unhappy memory of a son killed in the war. The family of Kolektovist Kemble still operates his Beaux Arts Nursery at Lower Bank, but I wonder what has happened to the exotic plants he rooted in unexpected places through the woods to bewilder the experts. Batsto, purchased by New Jersey as part of the Wharton Tract, is in process of restoration as a furnace town and may emerge beyond our expectations when New Jersey truly begins to appreciate its rich heritage of history.

At the moment the transplants, the newcomers to New Jersey, show an interest that exceeds that of those who for so long concluded that everything worth knowing about the state was known. It has been gratifying to witness the increasing pleasure in folklore—the lore of the land that old people remembered, waiting to pass it on to one who would listen. It has been an even greater pleasure to share the satisfaction of those who lived to see their reminiscences in a book. This is the story of a long unsung river that could not have been told except by so many I seem to have "loved and lost awhile."

Henry Charlton Beck

Hillcrest Farm
Robbinsville, New Jersey
August, 1963

". . . For men and women are not only themselves; they are also the region in which they were born, the city apartment or the farm in which they learnt to walk, the games they played as children, the old wives' tales they overheard, the food they ate, the schools they attended, the sports they followed, the poets they read, and the God they believed in. It is all these things that have made them what they are . . ."

W. Somerset Maugham: *The Razor's Edge*

The late Gus Schneider came from headwaters of the Mullica, near the Jackson Road and Bishop's Bridge, but he loved his house on stilts, and all the legends of wrecked or burned British ships said to have gone to the bottom nearby in the Battle of Chestnut Neck. The invaders had planned to put out the forge fires at Batsto and The Forks once and for all.

# 1

## FISHERMAN'S LUCK

*"On those great waters now I am*
*Of which I have been told,*
*That whosoever thither came*
*Should wonders there behold."*

THE MULLICA PEOPLE TO SEE, they said, were the Cramers who once were Cranmers, the Matthewses who now were Mathises, the Birdsalls, the Blackmans, the Fords, the Collinses, the Searses—people who had been there from the beginning. Instead, I found Gus—Gus Schneider.

The name, when I heard it first, meant nothing at all. So I listened as they explained that if ever anybody had gulped down and spouted up great chunks of river history, it was he. Gus Schneider is a wiry little boat mender who can't get any closer to the mouth of the Mullica without living aboard a houseboat. I was warned that Gus was so proud of all the snatches of information he had pieced together that he rarely parted with any of them except in a kind of barter system—fact for fact.

So I armed myself with facts against a meeting with this homespun historian. Groping around for somebody who sounded a little like the descriptions given me of Gus, I concluded for some reason that Henry Falkinburg, earliest wife hunter on the Mullica, was good enough as a starter. Whereas Gus lived in a house on stilts, Henry had lived in a hole in the ground with logs and leaves for a roof. Whereas Henry and his new wife lacked accommodations for a week-end house party, Gus and Mrs. Schneider, I was told, lived in a box and liked it. Later I found out that "box" was hardly an adequate word.

3

Old Henry was the one who had bought for next to nothing those very lands listed in that Indian deed of 1697. Those islands had names then that came with the parchment and had far less crackle —Monhunk and Minicunk. Not long after they were called after the men who bought them from Henry, Osborn and Wills. This was when, long before the first Ocean City appeared on the maps, there were fields almost at the Mullica's mouth, fields that were plowed and sown by Eayre Oliphant, Elihu Mathis, and Joseph Parker.

The only difference between those days and these, when the purchase of certain property in New Jersey is considered, is that then you sped a fast-riding messenger to the Council of Proprietors to have the transaction confirmed, whereas now you send a letter to the Council. In the beginning people were worried about Indians who might change their minds upon discovering moths in purchase blankets or flaws in persuasive beads. Now purchasers who can find acres unspecified in any previous survey in New Jersey follow the identical pre-Revolution routine, seeking out either the Surveyor General of East Jersey at Perth Amboy or the Surveyor General of West Jersey at Burlington. The Provincial Councils of Proprietors meet and act and approve grants as fully recognized today as when their members, subjects of a king, gathered at the end of long journeys by coach. East and West Jersey still continue, formally and without pretense, as if no one is aware that long, long ago a republic was born.

This Henry Jacobs Falkinburg (I prepared to inform fact-for-fact Gus Schneider) had come from Holstein, where he had been Henric Jacobson Falconbre in a native heath across the Danish frontier. Having established a home down the Mullica, this cave that was dug like a rabbit hole with no resemblance at all to log cabins pictured in real estate advertisements sent back to European prospects, Henry discovered that a healthy widower sometimes hungers for a resumption of domesticity, and is not long content with mere meat on the table and a prospect that pleases. One morning, having come to a decision on his lonely couch, he left his venison scraps for the birds and beasts, setting off for Swedesborough in search of a new wife. Wasting no time, he wooed and won the lady and was on his way back with his bride-to-be in less than a month.

4

Within a few hours of their return to the Mullica cave, Henry and his Mary, self-wed according to the ceremony of the Friends, were the center of marital festivities attended by relatives outclassed, at least in number, by Indian kings, queens, has-been warriors, and handsome up-and-coming braves. Henry must have arranged everything ahead of time—he had the ceremony under way so quickly once he was home, they say, that the relatives were not only surprised but out of breath. As for the Indians, unquestionably they were owners of salt and sandy acres with more lots to sell.

Henry Falkinburg probably knew what he was about when he persuaded his betrothed not to hold out for a home wedding. If he had married Mary in her own backyard, he would have faced the prospect of a trail of unpaid bills. I think it was John Watson who wrote in his *Annals of Philadelphia* that "the wedding entertainments of olden times were very expensive and harrassing to the wedded." The house of the bride was, before and after the ritual, filled with folk who didn't know when to go home, people who ate like horses. So hungry were the guests on such occasions that troops of them often jammed the house of the bride, with parents of the groom doing their best to cope with the overflow. In those days the bride's father was not alone in standing treat—the groom was expected to pay at least a share, on his own or with the help of his parents. Henry, all alone in the world, was certainly aware of all the pitfalls when he decided on a wedding journey first and a wedding after.

By announcing that the wedding would be down in Little Egg Harbor, not far from a place called Middle-of-the-Shore, Henry Falkinburg dodged all that business of four-hour dinners, four days of "punch dealt out in profusion," and an endless procession of punch-drunk guests who wanted to play post office. He knew, surely, that of Mary's friends and kinsmen who would follow them down through the wilderness, few could indulge the custom of the day of seeing the groom on the first floor and then paying oral and liquid tribute to the bride one flight up. For Henry, remember, lived one flight down, and underground conveniences were limited. "Even the plain Friends submitted to these things," wrote the Annalist as he noted the necessity of "passing Meeting twice" with an array of twin-

5

bill, double-feature carryings-on. So Henry Jacobs Falkinburg must have chuckled to himself when he married this charming Quaker lady at the river's edge, attended for the most part by Indian real estate clients, who abhorred kissing as vehemently as they wolfed the food that probably repelled the starchier guests.

Once the visitors had wished them well and said good-by, Mr. and Mrs. Falkinburg got down to business—by the time Henry Jacobs Jr. arrived as the first white child born in Little Egg Harbor Township, there was a house with solid mahogany doors, probably wrested from some ship stranded on the shoals. There was a Meeting House, too, where the baby's mother remembered the Sabbath Day to keep it articulately holy, matching eloquence with other equally celebrated lady spokesmen of the Spirit, Ann Gauntt, Ann Willits, and Rhoda Lamb. Soon little Henry's father was joined by the Andrews brothers, Edward and Mordecai, as well as by one Jacob Ong, whose hut goes on being a hat just because people didn't remember their Dutch when they deciphered the name of a forgotten town. Edward Andrews and his violin make a story in themselves, and you shall hear about them later.

However, I was intent upon noting in my pre-Schneider research that Richard Osborn, with Richard and Joseph Willits, came over from Long Island about that time, joining in Little Egg Harbor Ridgways and Pharos who had grown restless, they said, because "Burlington County was becoming crowded." This was in the early 1700's. By 1714 Belangees and Higbees and Dingees were keeping the Falkinburgs and Mathises company. Their descendants, like those of Sam Driver, Peter Cavileer, Yoos Sooy, and Eric Mullica himself, are there today. These details, I concluded, would be enough for the impending barter for facts with Gus Schneider, even if he should prove twice the date-and-happening recorder they said he was, with boatloads of relics to prove the necessity of the Mullica to eventual success at Valley Forge.

"He doesn't write like you do," they told me. "He just digs up things out of the river to prove it's all true."

So I went down to Chestnut Neck. Almost as soon as I arrived, I knew that I had wasted my time gathering inside information on Henry Falkinburg. Gus probably knew whether Henry went to Sunday School and whether he made any money in 1703. I never got around to asking him what he knew about the Falkinburgs. He knew so much about the Chestnut Neck massacre and Patrick Ferguson and a one-eyed, perhaps just shifty-eyed, rascal named Gustav Juliet that I kept my tongue in my cheek and listened. What threw my whole approach out of line from the beginning wasn't Mr. Schneider's vast store of detailed information filched from the river, old archives, and passers-by, but the fact that he knew *me*. I was embarrassed; I had come prepared to trade note for note and here he was, coming down the steps of his perching house, thrusting out a brown, sinewy hand. He called me by name, and his face was instantly familiar. Where on earth had I—? But of course! Historian, indeed! Why, Gus was the man from up at Harry Thurston's, across from Crowleytown.

I put the memories together amid introductions to merry Mrs. Schneider and all the cleverly contrived necessaries of the house on pilings. Built of what appeared to be salvaged lumber, it revealed driftwood planking for a porch, some paint here and there, windows with netting over them, electric lights, and evidence of housekeeping superior to some I've seen in manorial mansions. There stood what had been mistakenly called a "box," leaning sturdily against the gale as would a snug-coated sailor. As soon as I had placed Gus, I knew that he was no native, no kinsman of the Cranmers and Collinses and Sooys I had been told to see. Gus used to live in Berlin, which, as Long-a-Coming, knew no more of the Mullica than the trickle of its headwaters where the first excursionists, the Leni Lenapes, began riding canoes down the Amintonck with the coming of every spring. Gus probably got something contagious out of gazing at the Egg Harbor stagecoach poster in the Berlin Bank, something that sent him bayward. He got to exploring further down all the time, he said. Since then he and his wife have been edging ever nearer the sea. They were right about one thing: Gus Schneider couldn't get closer without falling in.

Gus mends boats. Late in the fall he hauls them up out of the Mullica on the rusted tracks of marine railways when the varied craft of peacetime on the bay come in for the last time. After they are high and dry, Gus keeps watch over them, charging storage until summer's return, climbing over a memorized but uninventoried mis-

7

cellany of chains and jacks and anchors to make repairs between seasons. The channel is deep off Gus's landing, up from the bend at Doctor's Point, almost as deep as it was in 1778 when Patrick Ferguson . . .

"Ever hear of Patrick Ferguson?" Gus asked me, sensing at once what I would be looking for.

"Britisher, wasn't he?" I queried cautiously.

"Sure," he said and then took my breath away. "Captain of His Majesty's Seventieth Regiment. But he wasn't English; he was Scotch. At fifteen he bought a commission as a Cornet—and you know well enough that ain't a horn. You bought commissions then like you buy political jobs now. Later on he served in Flanders, and later still he bought himself another commission as captain in the Seventieth Foot. That was in time," Gus said, "to give Patrick a part in putting down an insurrection in the Island of St. Vincent, wherever that is. And listen: He even invented a new rifle! Why, for a long while they called him the best marksman in the whole damn British army!"

I stared at Gus. It was almost as if he had been reading. But he wasn't reading. Nor was he talking like a parrot. "Ferguson," he went on, "was wounded in the battle at Brandywine, too. He wasn't in very good shape after that. Then they got him, finally, down at King's Mountain—probably because he liked wearing fancy shirts. The red one he had on that day was cut through by six or eight slugs. He always went around dressed like a target, they say—and they buried him there on the mountain."

"But what," I inquired quietly, "has Captain Ferguson to do with —well, with the Mullica?"

"Oh, nothing," Gus told me. "Nothing I know of anyhow. But there's some who say it's him that still wanders around the shore here at Chestnut Neck!"

I laughed a little. "His ghost, you mean?" I asked. "Surely you don't put any faith in nonsense like that!"

"Never saw Ferguson," Gus answered, as if a sudden glimpse of the soldier would be credible enough. "Wouldn't know him if I fell over him. He was here in the flesh, they say, but it was a little before my time. But as for that Juliet! Well, that's something else again. They say *he* still rows out there to go fishing in the bay." Gus

8

watched me, lighting a pipe and squinting through the smoke. You could hear the tide lapping on the stones underneath the house. "Funny as hell if he'd come rowin' along here tonight, wouldn't it?"

Gus left the thought in the air as he pointed out that none of the Schneiders had been anywhere in the vicinity of Chestnut Neck when Pat Ferguson was there. "Unless it was some tipsy trooper of the Landgrave Hessians," he chuckled. "But I doubt that."

"Where did you get all this background?" I asked him.

He was pleased. "Fishin'," he told me, smiling. Then he explained, and I knew what they meant when they said: He doesn't write—he just digs the dope out of the river and keeps it till it makes sense. For Gus *is* a fisherman at that, but not the kind that drops nets and baits hooks for cod and kingfish. Gus angles for bits of information, stray pamphlets, and old books, just as he dips down, when the wind and tide co-operate to suit him, to hook up a tankard or marlinspike from the wreck of a mud-filled British galley of war. Now and then Gus persuades a professional diver to help him hunt naval battle secrets.

It was fishing, Gus told me, that "got this whole Chestnut Neck famous." It was fishing, he said, that was at the bottom of the Chestnut Neck massacre itself. But you won't find anything about a fisherman on the tall column that stands up the road from Gus Schneider's house, a memorial with a statue of Washington at the top, evoking criticism because he faces the bay and not the road. You won't find anything about a fisherman, either, on the roadside marked a few feet away or on that memorial tablet, half concealed by holly and cedar out on the Wireless Road, a stone put there on the field of the massacre by the Society of the Cincinnati in 1894. But it was a fisherman, certainly, who braved the mosquitoes and gnats and sunburn of Revolutionary days to get his companions drunk in a little boat well within sight of where Gus Schneider's house now stands, setting the stage for the wholesale blood-letting in one of the Mullica's most celebrated episodes.

"Juliet," I repeated. "Frenchman, wasn't he?"

"Hell!" Gus made a noise in his throat. "You fell for Pat Ferguson's fairy tale like all the rest," he complained. "Even Len Sooy or Tater Cramer could ha' told you better than that. This here fisherman was nobody else but Lieutenant Gustav Juliet of Brigadier General

9

the Count Casimir Pulaski's Legion!" I gagged a little at that and was grateful for the dark. Gus was a bear for names. "Gustav deserted first from one side and then from the other till he got so mixed up hisself he didn't know what side he belonged to. No, he was no Frenchman. Pat Ferguson tried to say he was when he made out his report—*gave* him a name, he did: Bromville. That was, let's see—oh, yes, October 15, 1778. Pat dated the report in Little Egg Harbor."

Mosquitoes were singing at the window, fortunately not in the quantities that compelled owners of houses along the shore to surround their homes with bonfires in 1858. Mrs. Schneider disappeared. Gus obviously wanted to talk and I was content to let him. There was to be no bartering for facts here. An old friendship had removed the barriers. I don't know, actually, how much I contributed either to the conversation or to the tale. All I know is that the story gained new reality, within reach of where the sound of sudden screams was heard as men were bayoneted to death. Blame the screams or "the Captain who has come over to us, a Frenchman named Bromville," as Patrick Ferguson recounted it in his report.

"The fishing trip was got up by this Gustav," Gus went on, "and it was a pip. Juliet took along five men in a boat on October 13, 1778, and got three of them so drunk that he was able to make the others watch while he signaled one of the ships of the British fleet, anchored in the bay out there. All six were taken aboard on orders of Captain Ferguson, who was pretty much interested in all Juliet could tell him of men, arms, and the disposition of Pulaski's troop."

Selling out was bad enough, I said, but that wasn't the worst. Gustav told Ferguson that Pulaski had issued a "no quarter" order if his Legion came into contact with the British.

"And that was a lie, of course," said Gus. "Afterwards they proved it was a lie. But it was all Pat Ferguson needed to raise the hell he did. Juliet was with the Hessians in 1777—that was when he deserted the first time. Because he seemed pretty brazen and more likely because he was a foreigner, they sent him without commission to Pulaski's Legion as a sublieutenant. Lieutenant-Colonel the Baron de Bosen," Gus went on with that amazing talent for remembering titles, "didn't like the man any more than he liked the arrangement.

10

Any soldier who was with one army and then deserted it might do the same thing all over again, he figured. And he was right at that. Just the same, the poor Baron didn't use his head. He gave this Juliet a snub here and a brush-off there so that Gustav plotted to get even. That's why he worked up the fishing trip, war or no war, so as to set the stage for a second sell out. Imagine fishing for porgies out there with battleships all around? Gustav had guts all right!"

When Juliet and his boatload failed to return, the good Baron was relieved. Good riddance, he said. "The poor guy," as Gus Schneider put it, "didn't know he had a bayonet at his belly even then." Gus took time out to explain how the traitor's name was Juliet. There was a letter dated Newport, Rhode Island, he said, on January 11, 1779, telling how the British fleet had come over from Long Island with some Hessians. Among them, it was said, was a Lieutenant Juliet who deserted the Provincials when the island was besieged and who, presumably, skulked back to New York. "Lots of people wonder," said Gus, "what was ever here to bring the British fleet on a chase down the coast just about then. It's hard to tell them, still harder to make them believe."

I knew that well enough. Few along the shore had heard of Stedman, the British military historian, or, if they had heard of him, none admitted knowledge of his writings sufficient to discover how he had stressed the true cause of the expedition. "The predatory advance of Lord Cornwallis' division in New Jersey on the west side of the Hudson River in September, 1778," wrote the expert, "an incident of which advance was the massacre at Old Tappan and the change of position made by General Knyphausen and his Hessian troops on the east side of the river, was part of the general plan to divert the attention of General Washington from the expedition which had been fitted out to make an incursion on the Jersey coast at Little Egg Harbour." Long-winded and pretty dry stuff now, but it is important. Take a pinch more: "This movement of the British forces was certainly a correct military proceeding to successfully create a diversion of the patriot army."

Gus was not impressed by my approximation of all this. "Whenever I think of ships out there," he said, looking out through the screened door toward the sedges of Doctor's Point, "I get to think-

11

ing about submarines and wondering how far they could get up in here. Of course there's nothing for them to come in here after now," he added thoughtfully as if someone had spoken seriously of a new invasion of the deep and tortuous Mullica. "But there was plenty up here then."

And so there was.

## 2

## ROUNDABOUT ISLANDS

*"Ships are but boards, sailors but men;*
*There be land-rats and water-rats,*
*Land-thieves and water-thieves . . ."*
SHAKESPEARE

ALMOST AS SOON AS BRITISH OFFICERS approached the sloping coasts of the Jersies, they were given to understand that Little Egg Harbor and the Mullica were contrived to conceal a "nest of rebel pirates." Natives of the little river towns, British sailors were told, knew their channels and used their ships so well that they struck and slithered to cover like snakes. As a matter of fact, Jersey daredevils did slip out of Great Bay night after night to capture larger and better-armed vessels before their skippers, unfamiliar with treacherous coasts and hit-and-run tactics, understood what was happening. Prize craft were captured, convoyed in, unloaded, and tied up at landings all along the river from Chestnut Neck to The Forks by farmer-sailors who had been working up to the technique for years. On some occasions as many as thirty armed sloops lay in wait for some hapless, richly laden ship which had been signaled off shore.

"The big shots always talk a lot about the 'Venus' and the 'Major Pearson' down here," Gus said one night, some time after that first meeting. "But they were only the straws that broke the camel's back." The "camel" must have been the patience of Sir Henry Clinton, the British commander. Sir Henry had been caught in too many embarrassing situations. Reports were getting back home that big ships were being boarded and commandeered and driven ashore by ridiculously small and incredibly daring mosquito-boats of their day, craft that pounced from behind the Seven Islands at the mouth of the Mullica. Explanations were being demanded as to what the great British fleet was doing about these water bug pirates, who were piling up foodstuffs and fancy clothing with which to feed and regale country folk of the river towns in unheard-of style. Sir Henry made a resolve, knowing that action would serve much better than words.

Now that we knew each other better and now that I knew whom I was going to see, I brought along on this occasion records of those days of daring. Some of them pictured the Mullica Valley as a land teeming with activity, shipbuilding, logging, ship raiding, and the business of making munitions. An advertisement from the columns of the *Pennsylvania Journal and Weekly Advertiser* showed John Cox campaigning for woodland industry even before the Revolution, offering to pay "a number of hearty men, accustomed to woodchopping" two sixths of a cord for all the wood they would chop to keep Batsto's cannon-ball factory "in full and continuous operation." Actually you can raise the curtain on this Chestnut Neck drama in 1777, for by February, 1778, the *New Jersey Gazette* was printing verbatim "the resolutions, orders and regulations of Congress respecting prizes" for the guidance of those for whom "privateering is rather a novel business." If the business was novel for some, it was as casual and familiar as a game of follow-my-leader to the people down the Mullica.

By May of the same year newspapers were carrying accounts of ships set afire off Cape May and of elusive privateers raiding the shipping off Sandy Hook, Long Beach, Little Egg Harbor, and nearly everywhere else. *The Pennsylvania Evening Post* of August 18, 1778, flashed word of new conquests and warned of "a fleet of ships off the coast of New-Jersey, somewhat southwesterly of Little Egg Harbour." *The New York Gazette* of August 31, 1778, in announcing the arrival from Cork of the ship "Sybella" with "Six Sail of Victuallers

13

under her convoy," said that "the above-mentioned ships were attacked off Egg Harbour the day before they arrived by 5 Privateers . . . and would have taken them all, had they not made use of their oars with uncommon dexterity." Oars that taunted the King's best-trained men, even factually reported, did Sir Henry Clinton's temper and reputation no good. Nor did further intelligence, surprisingly in the Tory press: "About a fortnight since was brought into Egg-Harbour a schooner from Jamaica, bound for New York, laden with spirit. Also a schooner from Nantz, taken by a British cruiser, and retaken by an American privateer." Or this: "Friday last Capt. Wedham arrived here from Providence. Last Sunday he was chased by a schooner privateer from Egg Harbour as far to the Eastward as Martha's Vineyard." Mullica masters of mischief obviously chased their quarry to hell and back.

Gus said that a lot of this went on just the same after "the Affair at Little Egg Harbor" and that the British incursion clearly had little effect. "But what really happened down here?" he asked, obviously inviting himself to repeat his version, his own inimitable approximation of the story pieced together from a dozen sources and handed down through generations with all the color that gathered with layers of years. He had, I was confident, sifted out the best, illustrating and punctuating it with ballast stones and pewter from the river bottom. So I let him tell it—actually, I doubt if there was any stopping him.

It was in the last week of September, 1778, that Sir Henry, his dander up, decided to get together a fleet to break up once and for all this privateering along the Jersey coast. He planned to carry his campaign to the limit, going up the Mullica to put out the fires of Batsto and causing whatever havoc he could along the way. For this task he called in the sloops "Zebra," "Vigilant," and "Nautilus" as well as four other armed boats. Away they sailed with Captain Henry Collins in command aboard the "Zebra."

"The way I got it," said Gus, "is that these guys were just like commandos. There were about three hundred men, the Fifth Regiment British Foot, plus a hundred or more rowdies from the Third Battalion of the New Jersey Volunteers. The military was under the command of this Captain Ferguson we were talking about. Washington heard about the expedition and sent Count Pulaski and his Legion down to what now is Tuckerton and what then was just plain Middle-of-the-Shore. Governor Livingston got a hot tip late the night before and called out the Committee of Safety at three o'clock in the morning to take precautionary action. Express riders went down the trails of Burlington County to tell the country folk what was liable to happen—and the boys got busy. Three captured ships, well-armed, and a pilot boat carrying guns were sent out to sea in a hurry before the arrival of the British fleet. All the ships that couldn't get ready in time were sent back here to Chestnut Neck.

"This John Cox who was asking for woodcutters at Batsto was a colonel, you know. He was the fellow who took over the ironworks everybody forgets were at Mount Holly, making something out of what was left even after the Hessians had been there. When news came of what the British obviously were going to try for, Colonel Cox collected every wagon he could find, ignoring the squawks of farmers that they needed all their rolling stock for getting in the crops. He sent all the finished shot he had overland. What wasn't finished he sent back into the swamps, and some of it, they say, was never located afterwards. Maybe back in the spongs it went on down to China."

I had been hearing snatches of that story for a long, long time. I was to hear more of it later from the Kosters and Gus Miller, who said they remembered cannon balls sprawled and covered over by more than a century and a half of natural camouflage back in the Mordecai Swamp.

"The wind was with the men who had built and skippered the privateers," Gus went on. "These carpenters and sawmill owners and salt makers—they were even making Epsom's Salts down here then, you know—these wise old birds who had helped Colonel Elijah Clark and Colonel Richard Westcott build a fort with money from their own pockets until the Legislature saw fit to pay them back sort of had God on their side. Blustery winds like's blowing tonight kept Captain Collins and his ships outside, off Anchor Island and beyond the old inlet. And right there Pat Ferguson steps in."

Mr. Ferguson was a man of action. He knew that every day's delay gave the folk of Little Egg Harbor more time to prepare a reception

15

for the British ships, which any fool would know were not concentrated beyond the Sheep's Head marshes to admire the view. So Ferguson filled up the galleys and armed boats and then set off up the Mullica. Loyalist spies, the Quislings of the Revolution, had informed the leader that Chestnut Neck was the nearest landing where prize ships would be tied up and where, most likely, their cargoes would still be piled high in shingled storehouses. The Captain decided to row in, braving the fire from the mud fort, and make a landing at any cost.

The rest was easy. The galleys opened a protective fire and the Britishers came ashore. The little fort and a battery on higher ground behind it made a show of resistance, but without adequate artillery no more could be accomplished than a show of courage and a negligible delaying action. The militia, outnumbered, was quickly driven from the breastworks and into the woods. The invaders destroyed two prize ships which they found scuttled; then they turned to burning eight other sloops and schooners and periaguas, almost as serviceable as whaleboats for the tricks of privateering. Although it was distinguished as a village, Chestnut Neck consisted of twelve houses, all of which were first plundered and afterward set afire. The wharf and its adjoining warehouses went up in smoke even as the play-war breastworks were blasted from the sandy crest.

"Ferguson wanted to go on up to The Forks and Batsto, but he didn't dare," Gus told me. "He called to his men and went back under the protection of guns aboard the three sloops. He figured the Mullica was too shallow for his galleys and, anyhow, the objective was further than he wanted to go from supplies now that he had made sure of the distance. The river had a lot more twists and turns than he had counted on—he didn't know the short-cut throroughfares like the river boys, and anyhow he couldn't have used them. That made him mad.

"On his way out to the bay he smashed three of the little saltworks up the Bass River and then tied up at Eli Mathis's. The way I get it, that's where he was when some Tory farmer gave him and his outfit a welcome and a big feed. The other way they tell it is that Ferguson's boys enjoyed the handout first and then smashed the salt-

The old house of Nicholas Sooy, built before the Revolution, and once the Hermann City Hotel in Green Bank glassmaking days, is still home to the Kosters, although patriarchal Leon has gone. Below, Aunt Hattie Ford's store was ever the center of community news, mail, and announcements of community events.

Hollis Koster, who spends more days in Philadelphia than he likes to, is an authority on flora of the Mullica area.

Rare moccasin or lady's-slipper. Once picked, it never blooms again.

works, the sawmill, and twelve or so more houses. Eli's house went with all the rest, and the banquet all set out was wasted."

Next day, October 7, Pat Ferguson got back to the inlet and found the "Zebra" and the "Vigilant" fast on a bar, their steersmen unfamiliar with the shoaling of the harbor. Pat yelled himself hoarse and sweated with the rest of the invaders through all that day and half the following night, lightening the ships. On October 8 Count Pulaski and his Legion arrived in Tuckerton—Clamtown or Middle-of-the-Shore as you prefer. Moving down the Island Road, Pulaski used his glasses to watch the fretting mariners beyond Goose Bar Sedge and the Soldiers' Hole, and ordered camp set up on the farm of James Willits.

"Pulaski had made pretty good time as I figure it," Gus observed. "He didn't get the order to move down to Little Egg Harbor till October 5 and that was way up in Trenton. He started off with three companies of light infantry, a detachment of light artillery, a brass fieldpiece that went bumping along at the end of three troops of light horse, plus whatever other volunteers they could pick up along the road. Pulaski took over the Willits farmhouse as a headquarters —you got a good view of the harbor and the British fleet from there. I know 'cause I went down just where it was. Down near the bay, back of the woods that hid them, the light horse and artillery camped with a few men from the infantry. Still further down the Island Road was a picket post with about fifty infantrymen maybe, in charge of this Baron de Bosen I was telling you about, the one who didn't think so much of Juliet, the fisherman. And that's the way things were on October 13 when Gustav and the men in the boat decided to do a little bottle-fishing. . . ."

I laughed with Gus and let him hurry on. The Mullica was gaining new importance, I thought, with every word. "So that's about it," said the man who lives in a house on stilts. "That's the way it was, I think, from the bits I've hooked into. Just around midnight on the fourteenth Captain Ferguson, the dirty louse, with this jackal Juliet at his heels, left the ships of the fleet with between two hundred and three hundred men. They rowed to what was first Monhunk Island and what later was Osborn's. Out there past the radio station it was.

17

They went up to the Osborn farm and demanded that somebody get up and get dressed so as to show them where Pulaski's picket post was. Nobody in the farmhouse volunteered. So out comes a sword, stuck at the back of a mere boy—that was Thomas, the son of Richard Osborn. And they marched poor Tommy off at sword's point to where old De Bosen, for some reason, had been careless about the posting of a sentinel. At a bend in the road they met one sleepy sentry and clubbed his head in before he could holler. Then the patriots, forty of 'em, were butchered right there, even though they tried to put up some kind of a fight in the dark. Some poor beggars came running out half asleep, pulling on their pants."

"The real dirty work, I say," Gus Schneider told me earnestly, as if the conclusion haunted him, "was from that sniveling little rat, Juliet. The Yankees, woke up by the shouts of the British around their houses, came clumping out in confusion. Colonel de Bosen was a big man, not too young, and he got down the farmhouse stairs with a sword working in one hand and a pistol talking in the other. Maybe he would have had a chance; I don't know. But with that Juliet turning Judas all over again he was sunk. Juliet put the finger on him, they say; and, as if he had ordered it, bayonets ran him through. These men had been told, you remember, that Pulaski's order was 'no quarter'—but you told *me* that, didn't you?"

I had told him very little, I assured him.

Little Tommy Osborn, unwilling guide to the men who crossed his father's land, had run away in the salt meadows, frightened by the clatter of arms and screams of the dying men. When it was all over, he reappeared. He told Count Pulaski, when the great soldier had returned from a futile chase after the British barges, all that had happened. In the fury of the moment a goat was needed, and Tommy was it. They said he was a Tory. They called him a Quaker coward. They tied him to a tree and slapped him, threatening him with death of the particularly unpleasant kind that had been meted out in the massacre that night. Then they took him home and with his father, a respected member of Little Egg Harbor Meeting, hurried him off to Trenton jail. Eventually, however, there came an honorable discharge: "Permit the bearers, Richard and Thomas Osborn, to pass to their home at Egg Harbour; they being examined before the

18

judges in Trenton, and not found guilty, are therefore discharged and at liberty. By order of General Pulaski."

"I'm always wishing," said Gus, with a sly look that ought to be a warning to museums, "that I could come across that military pass. It's got some good autographs on it. Guy named LeBruce de Balquoer," he spelled it out for me, "—the aide-de-camp; a William Clayton, who was a justice of the peace; and Hugh Rossel, the jailor. They all signed it, and the Osborns were let out at the end of the month."

I had made a promising beginning. The roundabout islands at the Mullica's mouth, Johnny Sedge, Good Luck Sedge, and Heather Isle, had now become more than mud and grass. And the Pole, the Sloop, and Newman's Thoroughfares, well down from Deep Point and Turtle Island, reclaimed their glory as short cuts to the hideaways of the rebel pirates' nest. Other names had come suddenly to the surface, like the relics Gus had fished for—Osborn and Mathis and Cramer, too. It seemed to me then, as it does still, that I had picked up more history sitting in one place than I had ever found that way before. Moreover, it became clear after that that Gus had given me all he had, and now the well was dry.

One night when I was trying to draw out my friend on the sub·ject of hulks of British ships said to be not very far off the landing outside, on spoons and even tankards that had been retrieved, the man who lived at the brink of forgotten clash and clatter seemed to be listening. Then he roused himself to remember that I had been asking questions—he answered warily, perhaps just absently, that he had picked up the same gossip as I, that pewter mugs salvaged from a scuttled sloop-of-war in Sir Henry's flotilla, probably the flagship "Zebra" which was set afire deliberately when she settled on a bar for the second time, were being used for beer now at a tavern up the road to New York. There was another night when it seemed to me that Gus's collie acted with similar peculiarity, standing stiff-legged at the door, his hair bristling while he hurled low growls through the screen into the dark. Perhaps it was my imagination. Perhaps it was something else.

And there have been times since then when I have made a point of standing out at the end of Gus's landing and even in the middle of Tater Cramer's drawbridge, trying to separate the sounds of traffic, mosquitoes, and birds of the night from the faraway splash of oars. Once or twice I have wondered by turn whether there was the clatter of oarlocks or only the clinking lapping of the Mullica's tide on ballast of forgotten sailing ships. If, when the night is darkest and the quiet of Chestnut Neck is something you can touch, you hear an invisible boatman pushing his lightless craft against the tide, make very sure of this: It is Juliet—Gustav Juliet, once Lieutenant of Brigadier General the Count Casimir Pulaski's Legion. For Gustav, both Gus and I have heard it said, was doomed, when he died long ago, to fish forever in a little boat where he had betrayed his friends.

3

BISHOP'S BREED

*"Stillness, accompanied by sounds so soft,*
*Charms more than silence. Meditation here*
*May think down hours to moments . . ."*
WILLIAM COWPER

IT WAS ONLY NATURAL that I move on to the bridge, armed with names and dates and happenings more folklore than history, because they had come from more listening than reading. For people outside the valley, sources of such information are tucked away and often hard to come by. For Mullica people the best stories are remembered and passed along—collector's items are often used to keep a window open or to plug a hole where a stovepipe used to be. So I moved on to the bridge down the road from Gus Schneider's, with no warning at all that the man in charge there was Horatio.

There are three Mullica bridges—unless you have a hankering to count the crossings where the river's just a stream, at Pleasant Mills or further up at Atsion. One bridge is at Green Bank behind Aunt

20

Hattie Ford's store. There is another below that, just above Hog Island, beside the sheds that suddenly gave up their emptiness when Charlie Leek began fashioning ships of war. Horatio's bridge, however, is surely the biggest, carrying the road to New York across from the flats below New Gretna to what there is of Chestnut Neck. Probably the bridge is the biggest thing on the Neck unless you insist on measuring the monument or a house or two attainable only by lanes from which trespassers are belligerently forbidden. Gus and his wife, Horatio Cramer and his family, and a cluster of tombstones in the sand across the highway are mostly all that remain of the trading post which, until 1778, was the most important village between Cape May and Sandy Hook.

Horatio Cramer's brooding on the river is a part of a Mullica lament for birds gone from along the shore, sprigtail and sea coot and godwit no longer in the Sheepshead Creeks, snipe and marsh tern and shelldrake that knew a lighthouse on Short Beach, teal and petrel and grebe that come no more to the reaches of Great Bay. Some say there are still brant and mallard and broadbill with here and there a redhead and a canvasback, but—and this is part of the elegy—one must know where to look for them or wait until, unexpectedly, one comes upon them in a secret place. Actually it is less complaint than observation, for life has not changed along the Mullica. Scenes have shifted and new actors have come on, perhaps, but life along the river is the same.

When I hear the song that is more concerned with wayward waterfowl than with the changing of old inlets and the submerging of Tucker's Beach, I am always tempted to ask: What on earth has become of the stork? Once Hollis Koster took me along to where he had found an abandoned heronry, but never have I seen a stork where once he must have been, hardworked probably on three shifts. Cramers and Mathises alone must have kept him going, day and night, and the wonder of it is that Lovelands and Allens and Willitses got any attention at all.

Leah Blackman made as much of a success as anybody in tracing the little twigs of Little Egg Harbor's family trees. She found that the number of Cramers she had collected was exceeded only by Mathises—Levis and Hezekiahs and Barzillais of the Cramers required thirteen printed pages while Micajahs, Elihus, and Phoebes of the Mathises filled fifteen. Whether it was on the islands, by the coves, or up from the banks of the Mullica and its tributaries—creeks called Stump, Bear, Nigger, and Becky Lane—Cramers and Mathises must have kept squads of storks within call.

I never could have called on all the Cranmers or Cramers even if I had found them all—it would take a lifetime. Even Mrs. Blackman gave up, somewhere in the 1860's, writing wearily: "I have tried to form a complete genealogical list of the Cranmer family, but I have found it an impossibility. There were at least four original branches of the Cranmers of Ocean and Burlington Counties, whose descendants are so numerous and are so much mixed up by intermarriage that at this late date there is no such thing as untangling the intricate web of their kinship." Back in 1681 a William Cranmer on Staten Island had three sons, Josiah, William, and John, all of whom came to New Jersey. Later on there was "an addition to the first colony of Cranmers who settled in Monmouth, now Ocean, and Burlington Counties." This addition seems to have been Stephen, who with his wife, Sarah, brought certificates to Meeting at Little Egg Harbor. Thus the complications began.

Few Cranmers or Cramers admit knowing much about bishops unless they happen to be prelates of the Methodist brand. Few, however, deny the story that the family in New Jersey stems from Thomas Cranmer, Archbishop of Canterbury, burned at the stake by order of Queen Mary at Smithfield, England, in May, 1556. Some have been persuaded by those who say they "know faces" that they and most of the Cramers resemble the martyred high priest—perhaps they do, with a clerical nose here and a pontifical chin there. I cannot report about this very adequately. Unable to round up all the Cramers or even to discover a man among them committed to life upon the deep—tradition pledges all males of the family to the sea—I have chosen three at random from my own collection: Horatio, keeper of the bridge at Chestnut Neck; Roy, collector of taxes in Washington Township; and that venerable old lady, his mother, "Granny" to the countryside. Granny says she is distinguished by having been "lanched" with a wooden ship at one of the vanished yards in Crowleytown, but neither she nor Horatio at the bridge or

Roy behind the church look much like Milord Thomas as far as I can see.

Mrs. Blackman was able to find an old lady whose mother was a daughter of the first John Cramer, and she declared her mother used to say that Stephen Cranmer "came from the same place as the other Cranmers" but that made him no relation. That kind of riddle, plus the mixed marriages, may account for the alternative spelling, unless it is true that some of the first Cranmers objected to being linked with a martyred archbishop. From the first some spelled it Cranmer, others Cramer, still others Crammer, the way it is generally pronounced. A few, either actually or by printer's type, were Cranmer. The three I have picked out spelled it Cramer, pronounced it Cranmer, and said that was the way.

Conversation with Horatio, given to spreading his legs and standing defiantly against the wind that sweeps up the river, settled on drivers of automobiles, of whom obviously I was another one. In their zeal to get somewhere in a hurry they got nowhere at all and missed all the things Gus had told me plus a lot more, he said. Horatio was leaning out a window of the sentry box housing the bridge machinery when I saw him first, an appraising look in his eye that was primed for whatever craft that might come up the Mullica or whatever curious fellow might drive down along the road. "Them that drive cars," said my first Cramer, "do a lot of bellyaching over bridges—hold up the more important traffic, they say." I began making friends, I think, the moment I suggested that driving an automobile in jerky procession on hot strands of concrete lacked romance, the true romance that comes under canvas or over Diesel. He administered then a full dose of statistics, the kind that found favor with Horatio B. Cramer, keeper of the bridge on what in peacetime is one of New Jersey's most heavily traveled highways, Route Nine.

Just a few miles below is Atlantic City. Three or four times the distance up the other way is New York. Horatio, whose work was the flagging of automobiles in favor of the rights of ships for over twenty-two years, disclosed that on an average summer Sunday he opened the bridge but ten times. "Even on the big Sundays of August," he said, "she gets opened only eighteen to twenty times."

23

Thumbing the pages of his logbook in which the name of every craft passing up and down the river every day of the year was registered long before Pearl Harbor, Horatio figured it out for me. "Most time ever taken out of smooth driving along this here road in any twenty-four hours," he said, "was twenty minutes. I don't care what they say, I don't hold up traffic more'n four minutes ever. And even if I stopped them here, maybe it'd be a good idea. Maybe they'd get some idea about the country they thump their chests over and say is theirs."

I ought not to go on calling him Horatio. To be sure that's his name, but I've always owned a feeling he doesn't like it. Either that or he didn't like my finding it out. A grinning, well-fed man with plenty of muscle and a slight bulge he could lean on the window sill, he confirmed the name guessed by merest chance. Down along the river they call him "Tater"—I never found out why.

"First name?" he repeated my question. "Oh, make it H.B."

"What's the 'H' stand for? Harry, Harold . . . ?"

"Name you'd never guess."

The subconscious linked the bridge, the swirling tide below, and a recent rereading of a story about a man named Hornblower. "Horatio?" The third try spilled out.

"Well I'll be damned!" Horatio exploded. "How'd you guess? Somebody must ha' told you!"

I stuck to my guess. But as Tater talked of days in the Coast Guard on Tucker's Beach and his resignation to enlist in 1917—"the last man ever to git a dis-charge till he served out his time"—I could tell he didn't quite believe me. "Those were days before the inlet broke through between Tucker's Beach and Long Beach Island," he said. Those were days, moreover, when the Coast Guard patrolled the beaches on the first noisy motorcycles, looking for ships on the shoals, not invaders. "The island that's sinking into the water now," he said, "had fifteen permanent residents then. Most of the men had their families with them out there. Served out there before the war, the first war, first with Cap'n Jarv Ryder, then with Cap'n Lew Smith, after that with Cap'n Manus Kelly." Tater was a surfman when the crew of a station consisted of men actually numbered one to eight.

"That was when there was even a lighthouse on the island,"

Horatio Cramer remembered, spitting down into the water, transparent amber over fragments of white shells. The tide surged along the landing by the house. Mrs. Cramer appeared suddenly, efficiently hanging clothes in the brisk wind sweeping in from the bay. She hurried in shyly, the screen-door banging like a rifle-shot. "That was the light," Horatio went on, "that was kep' by Arthur Ryder, the light that was knowed by every skipper everywheres. Pretty she was, too. But she washed down like everything else out there across from one of the fish factories. Even the station was caught and washed out to Europe one night."

Horatio's bridge, within sight of the bend where British ships were stranded as they fled in 1778, and not far inland from where in 1812 patriots sold tickets for roof-top seats for those who wanted to watch sea-raiders in action, replaced an older span in 1919. "Down there," said Tater, "you can see what's left of the old bridge. My place here's built solid on the foundations, you might say. This here's a better bridge; bigger, too. But the little old one had more picture to it."

Old maps, I said, seemed to show the first road up and down the coast cutting through Leeds Point and on across the Mullica somewhere north of the village, perhaps beside what is now Motts' Creek. There might have been a crude ferry, I suggested. Now the road swung inland through Higbeeville and Johnsontown and then out again toward Tuckerton. "Don't figger there was a ferry," Tater drawled. "Might ha' been a crossing. First Cramers crossed where the Quakers did, up at Quaker Bridge, till the percentage on drownings got bad. Later they went over down here at Swimming Over Point."

Quakers of the old Gloucester County that preceded counties like Camden and Atlantic and Ocean, Horatio said, must have been right good swimmers. They'd swim their horses over when they could, but lots of times they'd swim from island to island until they got where they wanted. That kind of going was the usual thing Sunday mornings when they went to Meeting. "Whole wedding parties done it, too, they say," Tater remembered dreamily. "And when the boys wanted to see their girls on the other side, they'd swim for it, too, dryin' out on the way to the courtin'."

From Swimming Over Point devout Friends, dashing swains, and bridal companies alike must have presented a spectacle, to say nothing of a demonstration of courage, as they moved across the salt marshes beyond to Deep Point and the old Oliphant farm. Then they would pick up the Meeting House Road to Tuckerton. "No, there wasn't nothin' you and I might think of as a ferry," said Tater. There was just a road down to the water; and in those days of sink or swim roads were paths that led, and even now can be found leading, from farm to farm, worn by the feet of fathers, sons, and grandsons.

"The mail," Tater was explaining, "went up to Philadelphia on the Tuckerton stage. There must ha' been something to go to Philadelphia for then. The coaches went up by Washington Field, Quaker Bridge, and Atsion—or if the mail was for Trenton, they went by Cedar Bridge and Ong's Hat."

It seems there was a man named Isaac Jenkins, for whom Jenkins Neck is named, who began operation of the Tuckerton stage in 1816. But a public conveyance was running on regular schedule down the coast before that, they told me. Jim Hughes was an earlier driver and may have been the first. But Jenkins made a name for himself by getting through to Philadelphia from Tuckerton, then Middle-of-the-Shore, in time to make a return trip every week. One trip one way was enough for the passengers and sometimes for the horses, too, in this weekly arrangement; the drivers had to take all the bumps in fair weather and foul. Two days were required for the journey each way—it was not until 1828 that a hardy fellow named John Thompson broke all records, and probably a spring or two, cutting the time to a single day.

I was thinking of the Johnsons of Johnsontown, one of whom was aptly named Pulaski, and of the Higbeeville Higbees who came down from Long Island in the late 1600's, when I heard Tater musing on the stage wagons of Cornelius Kelly, probably an ancestor of the old Coast Guard skipper. Cornelius never owned "a second-class horse or carriage" and "was well-calculated to keep his passengers supplied with speeches over which to make merry during the tedious drive through the wilderness."

"Corny had to do something to make 'em forget the ruts and creaks

26

and strains," the bridgekeeper laughed. "Lots of times you came down the day before, not only because the boat for the beaches left early in the morning but because you wanted to put some liniment on the bruises and sore muscles. I'll bet the stage-wagon ride was so terrific that the passengers stood up by choice when it came to the boat trip."

If Cap'n Horner, proprietor of Horner's House out on Long Beach, had a head wind, his passengers made the beach by ten o'clock, Tom Watson wrote in his *Annals*. I recalled the passage: "The price of going in this vessel to sea or elsewhere is twenty-five cents when company is made." Actually, I have never liked the sound of that "to sea or elsewhere." I reminded myself, however, that Horners and Kellys and Hugheses were all very interesting, but I was trying to know the Cranmers of the Mullica. I told Tater boldly that I figured he was related to the John Cranmer who married Mary Andrews, sister of Edith Andrews, bride of Robert Allen, first neighbor of Great John Mathis, earliest white man to settle in that particular neighborhood. It was too complicated, I guess. Either that or I could have told Tater he was kinsman of Columbus and he wouldn't have minded. "Guess you know more about that than I do," he said, taking up a hoe and moving off abruptly toward the little vegetable patch at the other side of the road.

I searched for more Cranmers. I wanted to meet more of the Mullica people who had put more captains aboard ships, according to the record, than had any other family in the land. I wanted to meet at least one Captain Cranmer, an old sea dog "known in every seaport on the Atlantic, also in the West Indies and South America" to say nothing of "the seaports of Europe." "It is said," wrote Mrs. Blackman, "that as soon as a young Cranmer is weaned, he takes a position on the quarterdeck of a staunch schooner, and during the balance of his life makes his home on the sea." I began a systematic examination of records of ships and lists of wrecks along the Jersey beaches, starting with the "Andrew" from Liverpool, "laden with rich and assorted cargo and tossed up on Long Beach in 1820," and ending among varieties of craft like the East Indian "Yum Chi," which in 1870 dumped her hold of teas and silks "near the Philadelphia Boarding House." No notable Cranmer seemed to have

27

figured in the annals of broken brigs and scuttled schooners. There were, perhaps, successful sailors never at home.

Cranmers seemed oddly elusive, too, in descriptions like that of Annalist Watson whose grandfather, when he went to Little Egg Harbor "to trade," found it a place of "great commerce and prosperity" with the "little river filled with masted vessels . . . hundreds of men engaged in the swamps cutting timber . . . sawmills numerous and always in business, cutting cedar and pine boards . . . New York and Philadelphia and the southern and eastern cities receiving their chief supplies of shingles, boards and iron from this place." There was a William Cranmer who in 1712 signed his name as a witness, along with Preserve Brown, to the will of Edward Andrews, with Mrs. Andrews, Thomas "Orsborn," and Jacob "Onge." The same William, presumably, was on hand for similar service in behalf of Jene Bellange in 1719. Thus it is clear that early Cranmers, when they were at home, were quiet-spoken, unimposing good neighbors, attending Meeting with the Osborns, visiting sick Belangees, and claiming such distinction as there was in using a quill to sign their names. For the most part then they have been seamen, rarely at ease for long with husbandmen, fullers, cordwainers, or mantuamakers.

Not far from the banks of the Mullica at Lower Bank was the tax man, Washington Township assessor for almost twenty years. Roy Cramer laughed a long time when he heard how the family was mixing me up. "From the first," he said, "they been an ornery mess. They don't like titles but like good names—why, there at the beginning they had six Josiahs, all up the road within reaching out of each other. They had to make them sound different even if they looked the same—so they made them Old Josiah and Young Josiah, Big Josiah and Little Josiah, Over-the-Creek Josiah and Poplar Neck Josiah."

You never could count the John Cranmers, Roy said. There were John's John and Semor's John, Long John and Short John, Poplar Neck John and Beach John, Over-the-Plains John and Patty's John, Captain John and Bank John, Neddy's John and Bass River John —and so they went on. You had to know your geography when you called them. "Me now," suggested Roy, "I guess I'm Lower Bank

Roy or just Bank Roy." I thought Becky Lane Roy was more picturesque; accurate, too, because the little house where Roy lived with his mother before he married again is just up from Becky's Creek. Roy passed it by. "The William Cranmers," he said, "are all over the place. Same with Thomases. With so many Cranmers you just got to run out of names some time."

Roy was tall and gaunt, a man who knew the woods and who turned his hand to carpenterin' whenever and wherever there was a demand. Once I found him turning the old Crowleytown school into a house. Another time he was up Bulltown way, converting a potato storehouse into a home for Will, Mrs. Will, and Lonzo Nichols; the Nicholses had been burned out a week before with little more than a shirt or a shoe. I remember that occasion particularly well because Will, Roy, and Lonzo, working together in the cold, had already forgotten the fire in plans they were making to go deer hunting next day.

Roy said he was a great walker, and that brought up the tale they tell of a William Cranmer who walked twelve miles in from Barnegat every First Day so that he could hear Ed Andrews preach at Little Egg Harbor Meeting—Ed had converted him. Then there was one of the Josiahs who was a sure enough poet, Roy said, but who never got famous because he recited everything and never wrote anything down. "All I know is what I found in a book somewheres," I was told. "Josiah did extemporay pieces all the time—he did a fancy one about his children, they claim." When I found the book Roy referred to, I discovered that the poem in question was remembered only as being "uncouth." Rhyming of any sort with the names of Josiah's children, Wilkinson, Josiah, Barzilla, Timothy, Clayton, Joseph, Jarvis, and Rachel might make it sound that way, I thought.

One of the many Jacob Cranmers, whose wife was one of the Lovelands, figured in one of the early tragedies of the Mullica. He had been down in the swamps cutting cedar, and his wife had taken his lunch to him around noon. Suddenly they saw a bear. Jacob grabbed his ax and, brandishing it to ward off the beast, walked all the way home backwards, his wife almost too paralyzed to move. "They got home safe all for nothing," Roy put it. "On the doorstep Jake's wife died from fright."

There was a Hannah, daughter of one of the John Cranmers, who married an English sailor named Joseph Burns. Joseph was on a ship that sank, a wreck of which Mr. Burns was the lone survivor on a bit of timber from which he was taken stark naked four days and nights later. "He lived a long while after that around here," Roy told me. "Long enough to get a reputation as a village storyteller. He used to give the kids a thrill. And he always wound up his story with the old saw that a man borned to be hanged ain't going to get drownded. Guess it works both ways: Joseph was drownded, sure enough. He fell off a ship anchored by the Virginia Capes."

I meant to say something about the Belangees in passing, and now the name Loveland has reminded me. Up from Deep Point there is a stream that flows north among the marshes to some bogs back of Tuckerton; now it is Ballinger's Creek but once it was Belangee's, called for Evi or Ive Belangee, a French Huguenot, first owner of the Oliphant farm. The counterpart of the creek on the other side of Bass River is the Loveland Thoroughfare, called for Captain Charles Loveland who came down from Connecticut. Belangees and Lovelands alike joined the Cranmers in marriage, Lovelands remaining along the Mullica where Belangees were becoming legendary even in Mrs. Blackman's day. Now the name of a creek conceals the identity of pioneer Belangees, who were fullers and physicians and growers of pigs and peaches, fruit dried in rude kilns and sold in Philadelphia as the first delicacy of its kind.

Roy began to talk about his mother, my third Cramer and yet no Cramer at all, for she was the daughter of Watson Cale, a sea captain who gave Egg Harbor storks a little extra work by producing a family of ten in a house that faced the Mullica above Green Bank, between Herman and Crowleytown. "You ought to talk to my mother," Roy said. "She's eighty-four and as chipper as ever. Her father was one of the captains on the river here when New Gretna was Bass River and Wading River was Bridgeport. Ships were a-building then, up and down the Mullica."

Cales and Mathises and Cranmers were neighbors in the first villages on the river and, even earlier, up in Burlington. In 1729 when Daniel Smith was still paying debts of Manuel Smith following an inventory of 1720, William Cale received his due with Allens, Newboulds, and Carlisles, cordwainers, fowlers, millers, and all the rest. Some of the old Burlington County wills in which the Cales and Cranmers appeared reveal something half forgotten about the funerals of long ago; expenses for coffins were linked with costs of ceremonial refreshment. Executors for Mary Smith of Mansfield Township "paid William Collum for bread at the funeral" as well as "Preserve Brown for rum and sugar at the funeral of Joanna, the daughter of Mary." In Mullica wills debts incurred on coffins and cakes—"biscakes"—were paid along with bills for obsequial cider.

Granny Cramer, hobbling about with agility in spite of a stroke, proved lively eyed and cordial, with a dry little chuckle for every five or six words. She was Mary, she said, sister of the children of Captain Cale—Daniel, John, Sarah, William, Reuben, Franklin, two Rebeccas, and Carrie. Three of the boys drowned long ago, one in Great Bay, two on a three-master owned by their father. The second Rebecca, Mrs. Cramer explained, took the place of the first "who wasted away and died."

I was almost close to a captain after all. "That trip the boys drowned on," Granny told me, "Father stayed at home. She was the 'Walter Palmer,' a ship that used to carry phosphate rock and railroad ties and general cargo in and out of New York. She went down somewheres. Leastways, she must ha'. She was never heard from again nor were any that was aboard her. As for the girls, when the first Rebecca died and the next child was a girl, she had to be Rebecca to fill the line."

Once there were shipyards at Bass River, at Green Bank, and at Crowleytown. There were glasshouses, too, at Herman, Bulltown, and Crowleytown—Mary Cale Cramer remembered them all. "Three-masted schooners were everywhere," she said. "Down in the bay and up and down the Mullica." The shipyard across the river from Cap'n Abe Nichols's, near Charcoal Point, was Henderson's. "That's where it was," said Granny, "that they caught me on one of the new ships too late. Just as she was cut loose they let out a yell that I was aboard. So I was 'lanched' with a Mullica River ship sure enough!"

31

She could remember, she told me, a shipyard with three two-masters being built at the same time back of Aunt Hattie Ford's store at Green Bank. "Hattie used to be a schoolteacher when Harrisville was still making paper—she didn't tell you that, did she?" Granny added: "Yes, Hattie and I were both teachers when there was a school in Crowleytown—that school Roy's got to fix so's to be a house."

Granny Cramer said that she could remember twenty-one houses in Crowleytown. Now, she said, only one of them was left—Jerry Moore's. I knew Jerry but I had postponed talking to him at length; from what I had heard he would not only confirm that his house was the last of Crowleytown but that it was where Pulaski changed into a new uniform on his way to Chestnut Neck. "Every one of those houses was a comfortable little home," said the old lady, pushing her spectacles up and down her nose. "You wouldn't ask nicer. People was happy and contented and satisfied with the river. There was a glass factory up the road, Wapler's, and another glasshouse at Bulltown, if you wanted to do your own work. There was still another not far from Jerry's."

Granny talked about her schooldays, about a teacher named Miss Alice who taught seven months in the year, the usual term along the Mullica, about pupils who bought their own books. School "took up" at eight o'clock in the morning then, and if you lived a long way off, you started walking at six, an hour that was darkness in winter. There was an hour's "noonin'" and fifteen minutes for play, morning and afternoon. Gracious Mrs. Cramer lived next door to the schoolhouse and didn't like it. "We always wanted to live further away so we could carry our lunches like the others," she said.

Of that big Cale family that lived on the river, Granny Cramer was the lone survivor. When I saw her, she was boasting of eighteen grandchildren, six great-grandchildren, and countless friends who made every holiday, every Sunday, every reunion at the little Methodist church up the road an occasion to call on her. By now there are more grandchildren, probably, more great-grandchildren, certainly, and many more friends. I have been one of them for a long while now. Granny is on our birthday list, our list of names and addresses for Christmas greetings. Later on, when she is no longer holding court and when my visiting will be in the churchyard instead of the snug little house, I shall feel that Granny is still there, smiling beside the church that is opened once a year.

I will look down the road, the Island Road, and then out to the river, from the tangle that once was the sloping sward of an old farm. All the Cramers will gather around to listen with me as she says: "I can remember when there were six cows here on the farm. They had to be led down to the medders along with the cattle of my man's mother and father. We used to wait till the tide was a-runnin' in so's we could swim the cows home. I *know* for I took care of them. I liked milkin' and the boys didn't—they liked bein' on the river and the river ships." She looked at me when she said that. "Guess I'm like you by now," she smiled, fingering her specs. "I love the old river. Maybe I won't ever go away."

# 4

## CURE FOR OLD AGE

*"E'en so, but why the tale reveal*
*Of those whom, year by year unchanged*
*Brief absence joined anew to feel,*
*Astounded, soul from soul estranged?"*
ARTHUR HUGH CLOUGH

ONCE LONG AGO, not far from Crowleytown on the Mullica, the folk who lived in weather-black unpainted houses facing the water looked through windowlights of Jersey glass upon a sight remarkable except to those who had witnessed it before: An old woman making her way across the frozen ground, an ax in her hand.

Perhaps she was shawled, probably she was hatless: Constant Ford wasn't sure. Only the woman's name was remembered when he told the story, with the added recollection that people in Crowley-

33

town were not alarmed by what they saw, however imperfectly, through flawed glass made by their own hands. They reasoned to themselves very likely that Mrs. Littles, the old woman with the ax, felt a cold coming on and now was on her way to find a sure cure.

No "fresh and good assortment of drugs and medicines" for Mrs. Littles. None of your rhubarb, Jesuit bark, electuaries, and elixirs. No Hooper's Pills or Godfrey's Cordial or King's Honey Water, proclaimed though they were in Mrs. Littles's day. Oh, no. Down went the lady to the river, plodding beyond the landing, out on the ice many inches thick in weather that laid jagged cakes and frozen froth even around the margins of salt bays down shore. Some distance out from the bank the old woman seized her ax and cut a hole. Then, removing shoes and stockings, she plunged her feet into the chill but magical Mullica waters surging beneath.

"And she never caught a cold," said Constant Ford. "She was a big, hearty, fleshy woman and she never caught a cold. She said it was foolish of people to get sick if they didn't want to. All they had to do, she said, was to find a cure."

When Constant told the story the only time I have ever heard it, I found it lacking in reality. Writing it now and remembering from far away the river turning at Charcoal Point, the cedars along the shore, and the dregs of an island from which Tom Proctor and his artillery covered the road, the tale has more assurance of reality than Constant Ford himself. I didn't find him beside the river; I took him there because that was where once he had been and where, I think, he belonged. It was like taking a ghost back to its happy haunting grounds. For after that day I saw the old man only once and even then—

I know there was a letter from George Alrich of Williamstown, who said that Constant, his father-in-law, had been born in Bulltown and later had removed to Winslow, where he was first apprentice and then a blower in the glasshouse there. His father before him "was likewise connected with the Jersey glass industry," Mr. Alrich had said, "and for a man of seventy-nine years his memory is exceptionally clear." I know well enough, too, that we went down to Williamstown and that a man who said he was Constant Ford was waiting for us in front of the poolroom, the Williamstown forum. I know

34

that lively dark eyes, set off by wispy white hair, danced with expectation of a new adventure. But even so the man with the smile and amazing animation are part of a dream made of things said and things that happened.

That is because, you see, I saw Constant Ford only once after that. It is almost as if he materialized from river fog and vanished in the haze along the Mullica. To be sure, I could have wrecked the illusion by returning to Williamstown before I did—if indeed it ended then. But something held me back through days and months that piled up after that first night when we took him home. Somebody had suggested "a new and shorter way home" and the ride ended dismally in retracing the rutted road to the more familiar trail at Atsion. By then it was almost dark and raining; and the man who made more of a little hollow in the ground, a shaggy pine tree that had been hewn down, and a weed-grown field with a cellar hole than all the lost riches of the Mullica had grown old before our eyes. A midnight bell had rung somewhere, the spell had been broken, and youth was stripped away.

So, ever since, wondering with the vanished folk of Crowleytown about Mrs. Littles and her Mullica cold cure, I have been concerned about Constant Ford and his cure for age. For several hours that day I saw it work progressively. Then, as we turned about in the rain and mud of a forsaken cranberry bog, missing a causeway by inches—oh, well, none of us is guilty of anything except intruding upon an old man's happiness in his return to youth and scenes of childhood.

Constant talked freely on the way down. His voice was soft and merry and far off, but I remember it carrying through the drone of the Ford. He spoke of being "borned" in Bulltown in 1862, three years after the glass factory was opened there. "My daddy druv those teams that drug timber and charcoal from the woods for old Sam Crowley," he said. "Granddad was still a-livin' then—he was runnin' the old mill with the up-and-down saw. The Mullica was alive with sailin' ships, loaded or waitin' to be loaded with wood that for years kep' New York warm."

He spoke so longingly of active days that it must have been then that he began to become a part of them.

"Coal wagons—coalboxes they used to call them—were hauling charcoal up the road in long lines when I was a girl," Granny Cramer had said, rocking herself beside the potbellied stove and looking out the window of glass that may have come from sand there beside the river. "Men were loggin' out of the woods with oxen. Did you know charcoal's sprung up again at Lower Bank? Colored man was in to get a permit the other day. My boy Roy's firewarden as well as assessor, you know."

"Folks had me down along the river couple of Sundays ago," Constant was saying. "But we just went through. If you got time to wait a little today, there's things I'd like to stop and see. This here's New Brooklyn by the way. But I guess you know. Like at Winslow there was families livin' here, big families that needed Jersey glass for money to get along. They were the people who moved on to the next good sand when factories went down.

"There was a factory at Waterford once, even one at Laurel Springs. Half the folks livin' in them towns would laugh if you told them now. The other half just wouldn't believe. Oh, yes, at Winslow —know that little place they use now as a post office? I lived there. And at Tansboro, they made a good glass there, too. I remember one day at Winslow we didn't feel like workin' much. We just decided all of a piece to take the day off. There was nothin' the bosses could do but shut down. We decided to pay a visit to the Tansboro boys that was workin' at *their* glasshouse as usual. Walked all the way up there and then all the way back. Over ten mile one way, it was. Next mornin' we was back on the job like nothin' happened at all. Bosses knew we had just been cooped up too much."

Constant, I was sure now, had followed with distinguished brevity the trail of glass along the banks of the Mullica, up the river and through the woods. Sam Smallwood, down in Charlestown, West Virginia, wrote me a letter once, saying that Crowleytown glass started up in 1850 but that Green Bank's fires had been burning five, maybe ten years before. New Columbia at Nesco, near Westcoatville, came along a little later, he said. Herman, or Hermann City, didn't get going until 1870 and came down, according to Aunt Mary Wills, "almost as sudden as it went up." Sam said the glass factory

36

at Hammonton was established in 1820 by William Coffin, ambitious descendant of a Nantucket Yankee; but when I mentioned the name and date to Constant, he said merely that he thought it was wrong.

There are some who speak of Herman, Hermann, Herman City, or Hermantown as having had a much longer life. After all it seems improbable that hopes were kindled and dashed in only a year—I determined to find out about that if I could. Alfred Heston wrote in his *Annals* as recently as 1904 that Hermantown, on the north side of the Mullica about ten miles from Egg Harbor City, should inspire a modern Goldsmith. There were sixty houses then, mostly in ruins, he said, built around the glass factory of Joseph Wapler & Company. Putting establishment of the village in 1870, Heston wrote that "the little settlement was at that time and for many years thereafter the abode of contentment and happiness." This would clash, it seems, with Mary Wills's claim, unless it is that days were but as grass long, long ago to Miss Wills. Heston credits the glass factory closing for lack of business—I have always understood that failure was due to lack of a promised railroad branch, a project abandoned so suddenly over the river at Gloucester Furnace that a couple of cars were left stranded when they began tearing up the rails. What a town is worth, or what it can be sold for after such a crack-up, is revealed in the story of how Joe Wharton bought most of it for $1,500.

"Coffin had a mill down there eight years earlier than that," mused Constant, as if he himself had been there. "He was down at Green Bank, too, buying up timber and running another sawmill. It was somewheres around 1819 that a man named Jonathan Haines took a half interest of this fellow Coffin, and these two turned up as partners in Hammonton glass. That was the first try at using Jersey pine for something big since the bog ore furnaces went down. Workmen came this way by the hundreds, and then William Coffin got to be head man. This here used to be a money center. What happened, I don't know. Sand's still good—good if you're careful with it. So's the timber, and there's more of it now than ever. Of course, the forest fires—"

Fires in the Jersey pine country have been deadly and disastrous since Indians fled before them. One was described as early as 1755 in *The Pennsylvania Gazette:*

From Barnegat, Little Egg Harbour, and Country Round about there, we learn that a great Fire happen'd in the Cedar Swamps on the 20th of May last, and burnt with such Violence that in a few days Time it render'd desolate Lands to the Extent of nearly thirty miles, the Trees and ready cut Shingles being intirely burnt to Cinders and most of the Inhabitants reduced thereby to meer Penury and Want.

It is a little ironical that the sweep of fires and hard times have left only a few crumbling kilns and slag piles down the Mullica Valley to remind the more inquisitive traveler that Jersey sand went into more than a neighborhood product, so often despised beside the Sandwich glass that graces museums and collections everywhere: Six hundred tons of it went every year to Sandwich and Cape Cod, out the Maurice River and up the coast, to return in greater glory. There's an analogy there with the Delaware Bay sturgeon roe that went to Russia and came home imported and expensive caviar. Queer exchanges of products and personalities were going on in those times, Coffins and Searses quitting Cape Cod for Long Island and Long Island for the Mullica, moving with the up tide of the river from Green Bank to Winslow and from Waterford to Jackson. The Coffins, I have concluded, go back to William, who in 1814 purchased from William Griffith two tracts of timberland where Mr. Griffiith already had a sawmill going.

Constant Ford was virtually bubbling over with names and memories. Each house we passed had some association for him. There was Wilsey Horn's at the Nesco corner and further down, Henry Holloway's—Henry used to haul for the plant that made paper at Pleasant Mills up by The Forks. Almost before we knew, we came upon the ruin of Crowleytown's landing, and that was where Constant set Mrs. Littles to walking on ice in search of a cure for a cold.

"Right here," he said, "was Cap'n Abe Nichols's." He pointed to an overgrown clearing where the road had been changed, moved over so the cellar hole was all but filled. "Out there was the landing— see the timbers? See how black the earth is all around? Why, for a mile or more around here the earth's as black as this or blacker underneath—with charcoal that fell off the wagons they called charcoal boxes. Cap'n did a thrivin' business. Ran a jug tavern, he did, when he left off sailin'—he sold what it took and takes to all the boatmen who tied up here."

The tide was low. Below Mordecai's Landing were other places, names for which the kindly Kosters soon supplied. This stretch of water, they said, was Ireland Cove; across the way were High Bank and Bass's Place. Opposite the landing was a long narrow strip of an island, tangled grass and choked, twisted pines with cedar stumps jutting out of the amber water. "That island was bigger once," said Constant, now out of the car and jumping about with the excited agility of a youngster. "Lots bigger. Had to be. That's where, from what they always told us, men from the village joined the militia in mounting some fieldpieces. They was lyin' in wait for Ferguson's men who were expected further up the river. Good spot for waitin'."

Granny Cramer had said something about an island there, and I had passed it up. I went back to my notes. Yes, here it was: "Where the road bends along the Mullica at Crowleytown," she said, "there's an excuse for an island. They put a brass cannon there in the Revolution to cover the trail along the river before the business at Chestnut Neck. Maybe the river was bigger then, I don't know. Seems I always heard tell they hanged a Refugee out on that skimpy island." Maybe I missed the passage deliberately, trying to dodge Pat Ferguson. Now Constant Ford had brought him into it all over again.

Pat had wanted to extend his expedition to raiding The Forks, blotting out the munitions plant there. Fieldpieces, brass cannon, Tom Proctor's artillery, or whatever it was on the island or mainland or what you will, covering the river road was wasted preparation. Pat never got that far up. On October 26, 1778, the *New York Gazette* said: "Intelligence being received of a detachment of 600 rebels, consisting of Polaski's Legion, Proctor's Artillery, the Militia and Four Piece of Cannon being posted with an intention to oppose the Operations of his Majesty's Troops," the raid up the Mullica was called off. Maybe the island in Ireland Cove screened one or more of those "Pieces of Cannon." Probably it was the moated fortress referred to in the patriot press: "It is thought they would have gone up to the Forks in order to destroy the vessels there, if they had not discovered that Col. Proctor with his artillery had taken possession of an important post upon the river betwixt them and that place, and on Wednesday evening they departed in great hurry and confusion. . . ." This island, under the weight of such a tradition, seems to have all but vanished under water.

Now and then Constant Ford gave us sharp peering glances, as if there might have been a curtain between us. Probably he was trying to see whether we believed him as he told us all he saw, the blacksmith's shop that once stood up from the bend, the glass factory that was where scrub oak and pine screen a summer bungalow, the stump of a tree out on the mucky isle from which a Refugee may have been hanged, logs that had served the old wharf and "must be lots more than hundreds of years old. There's stone underneath to support 'em, you see," Constant pointed out. "And over across here's where Cap'n Tom Crowley had his house. Guess I was all of five-year old when I first came down this way with my daddy."

From that moment on until we turned about in the mud on the causeway, Constant Ford was, in spirit, five years old again. Years were peeled off and thrown into the thickets of oak and laurel and holly. A door was closed, quietly, on the world and all the nasty things the world was doing. The war was never thought of—not *that* war. Oh, yes, there was talk of Batsto cannon and shot shipped along roads up from the river. But forge garrisons and militias and even Tom Proctor's artillery were part of a war in which, for the greater part, there was an element of sportsmanship, with the Mullica Valley providing a set of scenery. It did not occur to me that day that people down the river were living as close to the edge of a new fight in which all was treachery and that some daring invader, spying out the river and where it still might lead—but no, the present *was* outside the door. It is a door that closes easily among the river people.

"Daddy worked for Sam Crowley some of the time," Constant said, as if the reflection surprised him as much as anyone, or as if the recollection were something he had tried to catch hold of for years. "He druv a coalbox. Boxes were always made to hold a given load, and horseshoes were nailed on the bottoms so four-mule teams could

In days before pleasure boats filled the Mullica River, oyster boats were not unknown in the area. This one was washed far up across the sedges in a storm. Below, Samuel Southard, "Sud," Norcross, companion on many a Mullica journey, who died in 1962.

There are Cranmers and Cramers along the river. "Mel," or Granny Cramer, as the whole countryside knew her, lived at Lower Bank.

"Tater" Cramer tended the big Mullica drawbridge until it was displaced by the Garden State Parkway

hook on and haul out the boards. Then they could drop the load at any point on the landing. There was some buttonwoods at the bend, and a little lane, too, where we used to cut through the swamps to the school. It ought to be—"

My picturing an early morning with little children romping through the dark spongs, laughing their way across the causeways, was cut short by Constant's pause and staring. I looked where he was looking. Trees, gnarled and broken, were still there. The lane was, too, but now it was less than a path, overgrown with oak and pine and swamp poplar. Constant guessed that only deer hunters used it now. Then he brightened and again was a boy. "Why, we *had* to use it!" he exclaimed. "That's the way we had to come. If we hadn't come that way we'd never been to school on time. They had to get us out o' Bulltown and Tylertown right after seven in the morning or we wouldn't ha' made school even by nine!" I thought of many of today's children, grumbling, dragging their feet into buses that stop at their corners not long before nine o'clock.

Constant led us to the school itself, then a small, plain building with a front door and no front steps. Later on Roy Cramer was to bring his tools and make it into a pleasant little house. Now it was my turn to stare, for Mr. Ford had removed his hat and was looking at the schoolhouse as if it were a shrine. He had known it was there, he told me, but before—well, he had been riding by. Standing here was different. He said he wanted to see the mudhole across from the school where the schoolboys and girls used to wade and get whaled for it. "Yep, here it is!" he exclaimed, with the thrill of finding buried treasure, delight rekindling the glow of every line of his face. What he had found was a dry depression in the tall straggly grass, a hollow that to anyone else would have been part of the ditch. There was no mud; there had been no wading there in years, even for the birds. But somehow now the mudhole was glorified as if it were a magic spring, as important to memory as the schoolhouse. "And there was a tall pine tree just outside. We used to shinny up to make faces at the window and drop down on the roof so we could push stones down the chimbley."

The tree was there, prone where it had been felled perhaps a week before. Constant looked at all of us as if one of us had wielded the ax. For a brief interval I saw the seventy-nine years tumbling down all in a heap, and I wanted to whisper a warning, wondering if the old man were going to cry. Then, as before, he laughed. He had played a game called Anthony Over there by the tree with the other boys, he said. It was a game in which you tossed a ball over the schoolhouse roof; those who didn't catch it had to run the "gantlet." There was another game: he called it Four Hand Cat. "Guess you wouldn't know any games like that," he said quietly, as if he were the last on earth remembering.

There was a spring, too, but it lacked magic. It was down a dark path that once led all the way through to the river. This was the source of water for the schoolroom morning and afternoon. "I used to have to chase out the frogs before I filled the bucket," Mr. Ford turned and told us. "Glory!" he broke off. "Look at that!" As we approached, a lone frog reversed the ancient procedure, diving deep into the black repellent hole in one long frenzied leap.

Sud Norcross was along on that trip. "Just goes to show," he chuckled, "how times have changed. Even the frogs do things backwards!"

Mr. Ford mused on a former teacher, a Mr. Jackson they had called General Jackson for spite. "I wasn't no angel then," he said. "None of us was. Once General Jackson caught me by the ear for suthin' and sent me out to cut a stick. He said he was going to whip me. I cut the stick all right, but as I brought it back I cut it again, mostways through, halfway up. With the first wallop, the stick broke, and that made the boys laugh. But I didn't laugh so much when General Jackson sent me right out after another stick."

Hazleton Birdsall, whose family lived up the road, taught Bible in the schoolhouse on Sundays when it didn't rain too hard. Not far from the Birdsall house was another where lived a woman everybody called "Aunt Suse." Aunt Suse was the village midwife and practically the river people's doctor "for more years than countin'." Suse was an able descendant of women along the Mullica in days when "for the most part the healing art was in the hands of certain skillful females who prescribed according to the root and herb system, many of their most valuable prescriptions having been obtained from the Indians." These early medicine women of the Mullica

42

included Elizabeth, the wife of old Samuel Andrews; Ann Gauntt, the Quaker minister, who preached the devil out of sinners on Sundays and doled out enough sour doses to keep him away during the rest of the week; Mary, the wife of Semor Cranmer, who shared Bass River patients with Catherine, wife of Cap'n Will Leake; and Hannah, wife of Isaac Andrews, who took up medicine in a more professional way. Hannah Andrews used to ride a horse "miles away from her residence" when it was impossible to get word to doctors living in Mount Holly, Pemberton, and Tuckerton where, at last, Doctor Jim Belangee might be found.

"Mrs. Littles never bothered with Aunt Suse, did she?" I asked Mr. Ford.

"Guess not," he said, his mind on something else, something that made him seem, half the time, not there at all. "Watson Cale," he was saying, bringing back the name of Granny Cramer's father, "lived across from Aunt Suse. Jobie Johnson's place was across the river. He hauled for herring when they was a-runnin'—oh, Crowleytown was real lively once." But for all the life breathed into Crowleys and Johnsons and Cales that afternoon, I found Edmund Johnson's gristmill a tumbled ruin and Uncle Cale's house a blackened hut, its windows nailed up as tight as those in the school. Constant Ford was a ghost beside us, and I am not sure of all that happened.

We went down to Aunt Hattie Ford's store at Green Bank, I know, and Aunt Hattie, from the dark that gradually revealed shelves and cases, said that Constant was a Ford all right; once she had checked up on the family and people whose funerals had been missed by few. "Store here used to be run by Billy Sooy," Constant told her, as if he had been asked to show a birth certificate. "Light in here used to be candles. Many's the time I had to walk all the way down here from Bulltown, three miles one way by the cut through the swamp, to fetch a half-gallon of coal oil. I worked in the flint glass factory at Herman once—I remember 'cause the wages was fifty cents a day. Steamboat came into Green Bank from New York then; twicet a week she came. Called the 'Eureka,' sure 'nough.''

We went to Jackie Ford's, too, but he was out somewhere that day with his hound-dogs. And we missed Sammy Ford altogether until another day when he wasn't gathering pine cones for seventy cents a thousand or sphagnum moss for whatever was paying. None of them wanted to say if and how they were related to that William Ford who, in 1854, owned with Stephen Colwell "a vast strip of land now comprising Egg Harbor City and the greater part of Galloway and Mullica Townships" from the channels back of Brigantine to the line beyond Westcoatville.

Constant was getting closer to Tylertown and home now, talking all the time, with stepped-up excitement loosing his tongue at both ends. "Daddy Ford moved up the river and on to Winslow when business was fallin' off down here," he said, as bits of the picture were fitted in the scenic puzzle. "He druv a six-mule team that hauled cars in and out of the depot when the Winslow glass fires was started up. Just a 'prentice then, I was. But I was a blower with a risin' fam'ly of m' own when Winslow lay down and died."

Glass men were always moving from place to place. At Williamstown Constant had worked for John Bodine—he pronounced it "Berdine." Then he was at Green's and later on at Ducky Weyman's. When the fires went down here, he moved on to Poughkeepsie and Ellenville and even Brooklyn, finally doubling back to Salem. "Some times you made enough to take the missus and the kids along," he said. "Sometimes they had to stay put and you sent 'em whatever you could. It wasn't much, sometimes, but everybody made out. Wait!"

It was a quiet but urgent order. I slowed down, then pulled the car up short.

"This ought to be Tylertown," said the old man who was no longer old. "Yep, this is it. All the Fords lived here and made a livin' long before they dreamed you up, boy. Tom and George was here. Jim Patten was here. The Millers and the Nicholses."

He was out of the car, hurrying across the field. There was a tangle beyond, the grass long and tawny, and the crippled apple trees recalled an orchard. In the middle, barely discernible, was a cellar hole. We waited, I remember, at a respectful distance, as if he were a chief mourner looking into a grave or someone we had brought to take flowers to a country churchyard. I know now that we were wrong, that out of this hole in the earth with rubble at the bottom Constant Ford saw something beyond us and the years, a house

44

rising again and with it a village, and men and women and children who had lived there, loving life and the river. But the boy, I think, stayed there; only the old man came home, an old man who had shed youth for a last time and was strangely silent in the realization.

Long after that I summoned courage and made sure that Constant Ford was real and still alive. Coming back to Williamstown had not been deliberate. It was as if the car chose to come home that way all by itself. When we came to the corner and a familiar figure, I knew that the old man had not been a ghost in the usual sense. Closing of the poolroom had made Mr. Ford move on to another stand. Frail, more wistful than I had remembered, his face lighting up as if in anticipation of another return to the land of Mrs. Littles and her cold cure, he recognized Sud and then the rest of us.

As if in that strange journey beside the river we had given him the earth, he grasped our hands and held them, saying over and over: "Old friends."

<br>

## 5

## ROADS UNDER WATER

*"Where village statesmen talk'd with looks profound,*
*And news much older than their ale went round"*
OLIVER GOLDSMITH

THIS GALLIVANTING WITH A GHOST had been only an interlude. Actually I was still at the mouth of the river. One day when I was wondering about a lot of things, the house that old maps show far out on the flats back from Deep Point, Constant Ford's "General" Jackson whom I had identified as Marcellus L. Jackson of Hartland, Maine, and Eric Mullica, the river's namesake, I met Len Sooy.

It will be a long while before I forget the last thing Len said that afternoon on the porch of the weather-blackened house his grandfather had built. It will be longer, probably, before I forget

45

Len, leaning back on a settee made by his grandfather's father and shaking his great shaggy head as he told one story after another. What haunts me now, however, is the sight of the old house as I saw it last, closed and silent, with even its doors and windows boarded up.

I had opened up with Marcellus; and Len Sooy thought he remembered him, a man who came down to Hammonton first in the 1860's, doing a little farming, teaching a little more school—later on giving up both for groceries and politics. I then asked Len how old he was, and he shot a big brown hand through a ragged head of gray hair, blown wild all that day by winds that swept down Little Egg Harbor and in across Great Bay, rocking his clamming garvey. "I ain't old," said Len. "You see, we don't get old down thisaway. Don't die, neither. We just dry up and blow with the wind that loves us."

I had been there at the house before, below New Gretna, not far from the bridge at Chestnut Neck. Tater Cramer thought it would be a good idea. "See Len Sooy," said Tater. "He'll talk you blue in the face, but there ain't nothin' around here he don't know. Ask him about Oak Island and Doctor's Point."

But on the first visit I was too early, just as on the last I was too late. Len Sooy, veteran sailor and authority on trails over land and under water, fifth generation descendant of the almost legendary "Great John" Mathis, had not yet come in from the bay. "He's out on the water," Mrs. Sooy said, as if everybody should have known that Len, bronzed by weather of more years than he chose to tell, figured going out in his boat for clams and oysters the daily fulfillment of a sacred trust. It was a right, sure enough, given first to the Indians and transferred by them to New Jersey's first Americans who passed it on, father to son.

Len began with something like that when I finally found him. He reverted at once to some of the things he told the shell fisheries men in Trenton on a day when even those who didn't agree with him tied their tongues down to listen. "After all," he told me earnestly, "a bunch of men like that can't take away what God gave you 'way back in the beginning."

It would have been worth a day of life to have known Len Sooy on the day he budded and bloomed in the State House, dressed in his

Sunday best, confounding the meddlers and muzzyheads, more senator for the moment than any man in the capital. "Out there along the shore," he boomed, "out past the twists of the river and the sedge islands there's proof that the Indians knowed well enough what God gave and what He gave it for. Beds and mounds of shells along the marsh, hummocks where men without much brains have busted 'em down, all show how long and often the Indians was a-fishin' and a-clammin' before us. There was Indian mounds once, too, neat little graveyards out where the dead was buried long before Columbus was thinkin' of makin' his first visit, lots before Mullica came over the sea."

Len shook his head. "Clams is most of what's out there now," he said. "Oysters, of course—but, you know, there was a time when the mouth of this here Mullica was known for the best oysters that ever was. Listen, if all the money that was made from all those beds was counted out, you'd have enough to stop this war. You'd even surprise the smart alecks that think they know lots about the oyster trade."

The words were strangely similar to those I had read: "The gravelling here has been like a mine of gold to the oystermen of Little Egg Harbor. . . ." To be sure, it was far back in 1720 that laws were passed, not only for the preservation of oysters in the Jerseys but setting up an oyster season like that of today. "Whereas," the forbears of Len Sooy had written, "it has been found by daily experience that the oyster beds within this province are wasted and destroyed by strangers and others, at unseasonable times of the year. . . . Be it therefore enacted by the governor, Council and General Assembly of this province that no person or persons whatsoever shall rake or gather up any oysters or shells, from and off any beds within the said province, from the tenth day of May, to the first day of September, yearly. . . ." Pioneer Sooys went even further than that, restricting the uses of canoes, periaguas, flats, scows, rakes, tongs, tackle, and even furniture in irregular inroads upon the trade.

Len said that the records show Richard Willits and Ruddick Townsend were appointed to demand obedience to the oyster law in those first off-shore beds of Burlington County. "Good names,"

Len said. "The Willitses came down to Little Egg Harbor from Long Island almost as soon as anybody. Four brothers. They brought their father Richard along with them. They had a little trouble with their spellin', as I get it, just like the Cranmers and Mathises. Sometimes they wrote it Wyllis, sometimes Willets; depended on who was doin' the writin', I guess. First the family was up in New London, then on Long Island, and then down here. Odd how people kept comin' till they got to Jersey."

There were two strains of Willitses along the river, Len Sooy said, "one bein' no relation to the other at all. There seems," he told me, "to ha' been some argument about that, although the Egg Harbor Willitses was blue-eyed and the others, kinfolk of Timothy Willits, was dark, with eyes coal-black." We had gone afield among the Willitses, but I listened while Len warmed up. He told me about the death of Timothy.

The usual version is, he said, that Timothy was in his barn near Squan, up in what is now Ocean County—he had migrated north from a farmstead on Cedar Run near Manahawkin. Some Continentals came that way in pursuit of Refugees who, they said, had rushed into the barn. When the soldiers entered no one was in sight but Timothy Willits, who for some reason sat silent, breaking flax as if the war were on the other side of the ocean. Timothy refused to answer questions, made as if he did not hear. He just sat. Suddenly one of the soldiers suggested that Timothy himself might be one of the Refugees they had been chasing, and before there could be much consideration of the point, Timothy had been shot.

"How about this Ruddick Townsend?" I prompted in an effort to get away from Willitses. Len was up on Townsends, too. "Most of 'em are further down the coast," he said. "But if you do any sashayin' among those around Great Bay, you'll get somewheres among the Lovelands. Did I tell you Captain Ebenezer Sooy married Catherine Loveland? Well, Jemima Loveland married Captain Daniel Townsend. This here Ruddick was one of the Collectors of Egg Harbor —down at the Custom House. Knew we had our own once, didn't you?"

I told him I did. I didn't tell him that Ruddick was more likely a tax collector or that historians for years have been hoping to find

48

the books of Ebenezer Tucker, sure-enough Collector of the Port, because letters and copies of laws turned up one day bearing presentation signatures and autographs of Alexander Hamilton. Then there was a Sooy, I recalled aloud, whose name was Augustus and who, as master of the sloop "Juno," had recorded business with the Tuckerton port captains. Len smiled appreciatively and began to talk about proud ships that had sailed from Little Egg Harbor to Amsterdam, Bilboa, Antigua, Nantz, and other world ports. That was in the 1790's.

"There was a master among the Lovelands, too," said Len, "and one of the Clarks from the old landing you're going to see. And there was another Port of Great Egg Harbor—but the records, they got burnt up. What were we talkin' about before you sidetracked me? Oh, yes, the law and clammin' on the bay—"

"The law," I told him, "makes everything clear from the first."

"And that's how I put it to them busybodies that day after they started to hand out to us baymen all kinds of rules and fancy regulations," he rumbled angrily, "tellin' us when we could fish and where and what for. Me and hundreds like me has been workin' what the Indians begun, out on the Mullicky, long ago. The Redskins got their rights from God, and we got ourn from them. That gives us a title beyond the laws that's made by polyticians that don't know the difference between a garvey and a blickey." Len, with a wide grin, was watching me. "Know what a garvey is, don't you?" he asked.

"Certainly," I answered. "A garvey's a boat, sort of like a scow, same at both ends. A Barnegat boat—right?"

"Good!" Len rewarded me as I made a mental note to seek out somebody still building garveys. "But what's a blickey?"

He had me there and I told him so. "A blickey," he said, "is a small bucket or pail. It's a Dutch word, a Sooy word, as Dutch as old Yozo Sooy himself."

Len explained how he was one of an army of New Jersey Sooys who go back to old Joos Sooy, the Dutchman they say was a friend of Eric Mullica. Joos settled near Eric's plantation on the river the Indians called Amintonck when Eric was there. He's the same Joos, or Joseph, whose grave is in a lonely field, marked by a ponderous brown stone graven with skull and bones, back of Charlie Leek's

49

boat works at Lower Bank. The burial of Joos was a century or more before others that came when Sooys were more plentiful and began gathering graves, almost clannishly, behind the white church at Green Bank. Joos settled there in 1701, Len said.

On that day, however, Len was calling his progenitor Yozo and, when I frowned at the pronunciation, assured me that he "always got his kinfolk right. Yozo," he said, "died in 1737. A grandson of his was Ebenezer, and Ebenezer was my grandfather. He's the one that married Catherine Loveland, a granddaughter of Sir Charles Loveland, who toted stone for the buildin' of a house down here all the way from Connecticut. I can show you the stones and the cellar hole. Sir Charles, they say in the family, took it into his head to leave his wife and children and go back to England on some errand or other, and that's the last anybody ever heard of *him!*"

From the first I suspected that Len had lived so long with Leah Blackman's book of Mullica family trees, hard as it is for even those with unlimited budgets to find, that he had swallowed whole pages. But I checked later on and found that Len had given me details which Mrs. Blackman, for all her genealogical authority, didn't have. I could find no mention in her record of any Sir Charles. She talked about Lovelands who lived in Connecticut like the Clarks, choosing a Captain Charles to head the line. It may be Captain Charles, whose brig made frequent voyages abroad and who married Mary Gleason of Connecticut, who got mixed up with a title in Len's recollections. But I don't think so.

"Ah, some of the Sooys had grand names," he laughed, reciting some to prove it: Sabrina, Damietta, Lucretia, Jemima. Among the men there were Josiah, Ebenezer, even a Cowperthwaite. Len gestured suddenly toward the old house that never had known paint. "Still stands on what once was the important road to the bay," he said. "Was an old house already when my mother and father, just married, came here to cook their first meal together. That was July 13, 1866." He spat out the date like a phone number.

The house was built on the frame and foundations of an earlier and smaller Sooy farmhouse. Once the farm was a part of the Great John Mathis place. Great John farmed it until 1765 when his son, Eli, took over. In Eli's time the adjoining fields were those of Ebenezer

50

Sooy; and the two farms, the Enoch Adams, the Sears and, perhaps a third, the Jeremiah Mathis place, were all one impressive property. Eli's farm buildings were on land that became the Arthur Cramer farm, and here it was in 1778 that the British burned everything in sight.

"Old Eli built another house right away," said Len, "but he was too quick on the trigger. He oughter lived with one of the boys till the war was over. For when the Refugees saw that house of bright new timbers and shingles they romped right in and grabbed up all Eli's fittin's. Eli might have put up a fight, for he wasn't a Quaker any more—he had turned Methodist with services held in the house that was burned down—but one of them rascals, so the family story goes, was holdin' a gun to his heart."

Eli Mathis gave the Arthur Cramer farm to his son Amasa; Amasa sold it to Caleb, who gave it to his son, who in turn bequeathed it to Arthur. Eli gave the Ebenezer Sooy farm to his son, Asa; another Ebenezer bought it and gave it to his son, Daniel; "and from then on," Len said, "Sooys have kep' it in the family." Just then, as we talked with the smell of sedges blowing in from the flats around the river mouth, two boys came out, brothers who obviously held their grandsire in the awe due a patriarch and oracle. Len's face lighted up.

"See these boys?" he asked by way of introduction. "They're Paul and Stephen Potter, seventh generation descendants of Great Jawn Mathis." All of us, he said with a sweeping gesture that seemed to embrace most of the shore, were on Great John's land. "O' course," he said, as if in apology, "I was away some of the time. But I was borned and raised right here, and here I stayed 'ceptin' when I was on the water."

Len sailed before the mast full twenty-seven years in one of the smelliest businesses that ever was—the fertilizer and oil trade. "From up off Belfast in Maine to grassy little holes down off Mexico we took up menhaden for the fish oil factories," he said. His last trip was in 1917. "That was another wartime," he reflected. "A wartime that was to be the last but weren't. We were supposed to unload for Standard Oil that trip, next morning. Night before I waked up in the wheelhouse to make out the ship was afire. So there wasn't no next morning. We were lyin' to off Long Island. That fire was close

51

enough for me. I got away from the fish factories and blazin' ships all in one trip. But I stayed on the water; all the Sooys stayed on the water from old Yozo down. And there was ten of us children, all born in this old house—lot of people,, even not countin' the goers, comers, and stoppers . . ."

"Goers, comers, and stoppers," I was left to infer, included neighbors and friends and even transients who found the welcome so warm in the old Sooy house that they stayed days, weeks, even months longer than they intended to.

I was wondering, then, about another Sooy I had heard about, another Joseph, captain of the "Prosperity," a privateer schooner— twenty tons, six carriage guns, twelve men. Letters of marque were granted Joseph on May 3, 1779. What I have wondered most about Joseph, however, is this: Was he the Sooy whose allegiance was seemingly doubted in 1775 and about whom John Cox at Batsto wrote a somewhat nasty letter to the Governor's secretary in 1777? If so, then all seems to have ended well if, indeed, he was on the winning side by 1779. Joseph seems to have been in hot water from the beginning.

It was in October, 1775, that several items appeared in the newspapers, made up of odd bits and observations supplied by the gossips of the times, concerning a ship that had run ashore on Brigantine Beach near Egg Harbor. The first account said merely that "the transport ship Capt. Hastings, of London, bound from Boston to New York, with seventeen seamen, a Capt. Duncan Campble, a Lieut. Sims, a recruiting sergeant and fifteen or twenty raggamuffin fellows that ran from New York and listed, who acted as marines on board" rode up on the shoals. "The seamen and marines were secured soon after coming on shore and were conducted to this city. [Philadelphia] where the seamen are set at liberty but the marines are properly secured." It was supposed that the officers of the ship had planned to land in New York "to list what men they could, by large promises of confiscated land, get them aboard and then transport them to Boston." Foundering in Cranberry Inlet, the ship disgorged several cannon, sixty muskets, and a half barrel of powder before she was deserted.

So far the name of Joseph Sooy does not appear at all. It does turn up, however, in the account that follows, purporting to be a deposition taken from Joseph, "of Little Egg Harbor," duly placed under oath on October 23, 1775. Under the impressive seal of the County of Burlington Joseph is recorded to have said that, as he was going up the Mullica, then the Little Egg Harbor, to engage a craft to bring him some firewood, he perceived a vessel on shore on Brigantine Beach. He immediately went down, he said, went aboard, and asked men of the ship where they were from. He said he was told by a person he since understood to be a Cap'n Campbell that the ship was from Newcastle-on-Tine, had very little lading in except ballast, and had been en route to New York. They admitted carelessness in sounding, said Joseph, and blandly explained away the great number of persons aboard as settlers on their way to America. As none of those present "had any regimentals on," Mr. Sooy swore he had no suspicion that any were officers or soldiers.

Captain Campbell claimed to be part owner of the disabled ship, Joseph said, and wanted most of all to get on to New York, asking help in ships and hands to claim whatever might be salvaged from the wreck. The Captain seems to have written a letter to a Captain Grant, a missive Joseph admitted signing, asking Grant to bring his sloop so that passengers and their possessions might continue on their way. Then those aboard played him dirty, Joseph said. They changed their mind about waiting for Captain Grant or even the safe dispatch of the letter, making off with Joseph Sooy's boat "without his knowledge, privity or consent." Although it all sounded rather fishy, Joseph swore that he received no "bribe, hire, or reward whatsoever from any person or persons to convey away the said Campbell."

Joseph was in a fix. That would seem even more obvious from the account which appeared three days later in the New York Journal. "A gentleman just arrived from the Jerseys" had it from "a young man of character who lives about twenty-five miles from the sea-side" and the editor got it from him. "A Captain, Lieutenant and Sargeant," it read, "came on shore on the beach and offered a large sum in half Johanneses to a man there to put them aboard a man-of-war, which they apprehended to be not far distant, but were refused." The refusal is important, for although the story was twice or thrice told before it got into print, it included details missed before: Sailors who came ashore at Brigantine to tell a story of having been pressed into service, men who revealed how gunpowder and arms had been dumped into the sea when the ship was beached. For anything additional, the only item I have found so far is a letter in the *New Jersey Archives* saying that Captain Campbell had enlisted and carried into Boston sixty men prior to the wreck and was expecting a commission as a reward for breaking the record on the trip that went wrong at the mouth of the Mullica.

Much is left out of the story. I have no intention of guessing at the truth about Joseph, inasmuch as Len thought it of no great importance. It may be that there was something wrong with Joseph's eyes, Len said. "Maybe the men who beached the ship didn't look like soldiers at all," he suggested. "Maybe they looked like peaceable passengers and not ornery devils that ran away in the woods up the river. Maybe no bribe was even offered." That it was refused is what all the Sooys remember, even though John Cox, writing to Charles Pettit, once secretary of William Franklin, New Jersey's Tory governor, said:

"As the bearer waits I have only time to inform you that few days ago a Brig appeared off Little Egg Harbour Inlet and decoyed off Joseph Sowey and two or three of his boys and that yesterday afternoon a Brig of 16, a sloop of 12, a schooner of 8 and a pilot boat of six guns were piloted over the bar and now are at the Fox Burrows and in possession of a Brig in which I was concerned just ready for sea and a very fine vessel belonging to Wilmington and I take it for granted they will continue there as there are several vessels hourly expected from sea, of which I dare say Sowey has informed them. . . . I shall go down to Chestnut Neck tomorrow with a number of men in order to raise a small fortification of 8 or 10 guns to prevent them if possible from penetrating the country."

Clearly Mr. Cox was none too sure of Joseph Sooy, and that is what I said to Len when I gave him this outline of the records.

"That may be," Len admitted with a grin, unperturbed. "But I think you got our Joe wrong, just like Johnny Cox." You'd have thought I was the sheriff, come to nab Joseph on suspicion. "Johnny was jittery. Look up some letters from Batsto, some more I mean, and you'll find out that Johnny was havin' a terrible time with the howitzers he was makin' up there." There was a strange feeling at the back of my neck: Len Sooy was talking as if he himself had been there when it happened. "Jersey iron was all right," he explained, "but they were spreading it too thin—half of what Johnny Cox was turnin' out was blowin' up in provin'. Suppose Joseph *was* decoyed off like he said. Suppose he *did* tell the Britishers what was expected. Suppose he *did* bring in those ships over the bar. What would you ha' done in his shoes, clapped aboard a British sloop-o'-war with a gun at your head and another probably at your gizzard? Why, you'd likely ha' done what Johnny Cox knowed he'd ha' done and what he figgered Joseph would do, hopin' all the while that Johnny and the Clarks and the Wescotts and all the rest of 'em would get that little fort done in time!"

Len's explanation was good enough for me. I had asked none. Never once had there been a suggestion of family honor impugned or that Joseph Sooy, namesake of Joos the Dutchman, had played both ends against the middle. Len knew most of the details by heart and had done some wondering, I knew. In the end it was Joseph who confounded them all, redeeming himself surely in the estimation of John Cox, friend of the Washingtons. For to Joseph Potts, marshal of the Admiralty Court in New Jersey, was committed the sales of prize ships taken by Captain Sooy's privateering schooner, "Prosperity," operating with all legality in 1779.

Len told other stories, tales of the Loveland Thoroughfare, that creek of brackish water that cuts through the black mud and marshes among the muskrat houses to the Wading River, of the Bass River that once was Rock and not a new name for Burlington County's Bridgeport, of the house that Great John Mathis built on Daniel Mathis's island in 1713, of Frenches and Bakers and Leeks who once spelled it Leak without a smile. Of these one or two must be retold. Mention of Leeds Point brought one to light.

"Leeds Point?" Len repeated. "Know it well. That's where old Ebenezer Sooy lived. Let me tell you something about the Ebenezer that was lost in the Gold Rush. He tore down his Leeds Point house, lock, stock, and barrel, and loaded it on a schooner called the 'Mark Leeds.' Then off he sailed to Californy with seventeen other prospectors from the neighborhood as crazy as he. Nobody in the family ever heard of him again. Nary a letter—not even a message by some of the ones that drifted back. You know, it's funny but they

55

say he got right worked up because his mother was late with some socks she was a-makin' special for him.

"She was to meet him in Philadelphy—but Philadelphy was a long jaunt in them days. If you didn't make the stage, you had to take to the boggy roads in a carriage. Anyhow, remember that Ma Sooy had to shear the sheep and card the wool before she started knittin' on the socks. Eb oughta figgered on that but he didn't. When his Ma got to where the 'Mark Leeds' was supposed to be, she was two days late. Eb and his prospectors had sailed away. Story we was always told was that he died some place, plenty rich—so I guess he had plenty socks by that time to stow his money away in."

There is a legend like that among many families along the Mullica. The Leeks of Lower Bank will tell you a story that follows the same pattern with the locale of the denouement in "Floridy" instead. "Once they came after us," Len said, "askin' us to produce Eb's signature, just his name signed to anything we had around. And you know, as well as we know'd him, we didn't have a line of his writin' around anywhere. He'd been a tradin', we heard, between Frisco and Hawaii and had made a pile. Rich as Croesus was the way they put it. But that's all the good it did *us*. The money went to a man in Salem up in Mass'chusetts, kinfolk of a partner, maybe."

That the Sooy house down the clay road to the landing was blackened by everything the elements had to offer from 1866 on as to one end of it and from 1780 on as to the other, was a proud boast to Len. "Same nails, same siding, and never a drop of paint," he chuckled that day. "Fellers was in here about a year ago wantin' me to put on some of these here new asbestos shingles. I chased 'em out. Nobody's disfiggerin' the old place while I'm around." The road, now unimportant, was serving when this was a wealthy country and when there were countless ships in the bay, laden with the best the world could send in exchange for the wood and charcoal of Little Egg Harbor. The road was there, rutted and dusty by turn, when the first commercial travelers occupied every spare room. "This here house know'd 'em all on this same road," Len said, sitting back and looking, squint-eyed, toward the bend. "It went by here, out past the hotel you can't remember, and on up to Tuckerton. There weren't no concrete then, no fancy highway up to New York. A beach was a beach, something to fish and sail from, something to get beach plums beside."

Len began spouting names in a way he himself called "bladderin'" —the Buck Neck Swamp Road, Old Hickory Island, Swimming Over Point, White Frost Cove. Some people wondered, he said, how folks got over the Wading River. "I tell 'em," he said. "They waded. Same as how they got over from Swimming Over Point. They swum. Some day we'll take a look-see together and find that corduroy road that leads right down to the medders where they either swum for it or cut wood to build floats to get them over. Up there across from the Wading River church you can find the road that led over to the house here if you fool around a while lookin' for it. Heard a feller tell once of a bridge that was lower down than Tater Cramer's —but I say that's crazy-like. Too much water down there. Folks swum far enough as it was, first over Mott's Creek and then across to White Frost Cove. Swum first, they did, and thought about it after, dryin' out. There's still a one-horse walkway, logs laid close together through the marsh."

Len wandered back to trips home down the old Fall River Line, to glycerin soap made from mossbunkers, of the fish factories beyond Turtle Island and the old inlet and up at Mystic, Connecticut, to voyages begun in March and ended in December. "Yep," he said, "Sooys has been here a long time, leasin' land and water for cultivatin' clams and oysters since the Indians, bein' good-behaved Americans since them that was here before was gatherin' up what they wanted, roastin' it out, stringin' it up, and haulin' it away. This land, you can say, is ours." He added, as if his expression was the final punctuation: "That's the kind of puddin' that I eat!"

I looked at him then and again later, when he came downstairs with a flag of thirteen stars, family heritage like the house, the road, the old settee. I marveled at the strength of his arms, muscles that rippled through the gray shirt, open at the neck. Life danced from twinkling eyes, matching the vigor that remained to run out the anchor of a big garvey and work the clam tongs every day. I was looking, I thought suddenly, at old Yoos, ancestor of all the Sooys and friend of Sam Driver, Pedro Cavileer, and Eric whose name is the river's. Now his age was unimportant. "I ain't old," he had said. "And anyhow, we don't die down here."

Five weeks after that someone called me to say that Len hadn't been out on the bay all week. Something must be wrong, they said. I could not answer. As soon as I could I hurried down to New Gretna to make inquiry.

I turned from the concrete and drove up the clay road. The weather-black house was surrounded by cars. A funeral service was concluding. I parked a respectful distance away and hurried back, hat in hand, as pallbearers, one of them Tater Cramer, carried the long coffin from the porch. I thought quickly of the road from Swimming Over Point we would never hunt together. Len Sooy, it comes to me, remembering the first things he said, must have dried up suddenly, as quickly must have blown away.

## 6

## LEEDS OF LEEDS

*"Till kindred rivers, from the summit gray,*
*To distant seas their course in beauty bend,*
*And, like the lives of human millions, blend*
*Disparted waves in one immensity!"*
EBENEZER ELLIOTT

I HAD PLANNED, as much as ever I could plan, to go to Clark's Landing on one side of the river, or Lower Bank on the other. I remember reflecting pleasantly over the prospect of prospecting for graves of two of the more romantic Clarks, opposite the two Hog Islands, or determining how it was that Swedish Eric had given his name to end the confusion between Little Egg Harbor, the river, Little Egg Harbor, the bay, and Egg Harbor City, which has neither harbor nor river at its door. For it was Eric Mullica, settling in what is now Lower Bank about fifteen miles from the bay in 1645, who gave clearer identity to the stream that still carries his name with the tides from salt coves of Great Bay to little creeks at Crowfoot. In 1723 when Eric's life had attained a full century, he died not in Burlington but in Gloucester County where stalwart sons had taken him and where, though his grave is unknown, Mullica Hill marks him well.

If these traditions hold as much water as the Mullica's smallest tributary, there was thereafter a succession of post-mortem honors. Not only the river but a township and the village where Eric became less than dust were soon contesting as namesakes. Seemingly the Indian name, Amintonck, had no chance; either it was lost in the rise and fall of colorful years along the river or, as is probable, someone banished it from maps as too difficult to pronounce. There are people who say that what is left of Amintonck has been retained in the name of Hammonton, even though it is a matter of record that the earlier variation, Hammondton, recalled John Hammond Coffin, an early glassmaker, from among other men from Maine, Norths, Ulmers, and Smiths. As for Mullica, it seems to have been a name to baffle many of the earliest spellers, who wrote it Muliicus in 1778, Mollicas in a survey of 1726, and Mullicus in the writings of John Barber and Henry Howe.

I was wallowing, almost, in miscellaneous facts that morning. Eric Mullica, I discovered, was the first plantation owner within twenty-five miles of what was to be Atlantic City. Before him in the neighborhood a Dutch navigator called David Pieterzen DeVries had sailed up the river for at least a look around. Another early bird, Robert Evelin, had exclaimed over wild geese, swans, ducks, and gulls he had claimed to see in 1648, after which he had written tall stories equal to many I was to hear up the river. Earlier still in 1524 old Verrazano was exploring the American coast, and while he was about it he made a landfall at the mouth of the Mullica, writing about Indians who, years after, became identified as Mullicas with all the rest. Pigeons, he said in his journal, darkened the sky; that was the best he could do to vie with Evelin, who said he looked upon wild turkeys, many of which weighed all of forty-six pounds. Verrazano, who was reluctant to go home, played with the wind all

59

that summer, seeing something of the Shrewsbury River, catching fish off Cape May, watching the Indians make wampum on Anchoring Island; sailing away he wrote poetically about a land of "many lakes and ponds of living water." It was as touching a farewell, I was thinking, as must have been the one that Eric Mullica himself bestowed when, as a very old man, he sold his farm to Joseph Pearce and went to Mullica Hill. Then the letter came, just as I was about to toss a coin to decide which side of the river would claim me for the day.

And now, unless I tell you more about the Leeds, the Leeds of Leeds, England, Leeds who were early in Shrewsbury, Monmouth County, and in Northampton, Burlington County, where for a little while at least they made the Crosswicks Creek the Leeds River, there will be more than a letter—there may be dreadful repercussions, indeed, from Mrs. Bowen.

Mrs. Bowen is a teacher—and more, much more. Kin of the Leeds and living in Leeds Point, south of Great Bay and Muddy Creek and the meandering Mullica where once a man could hardly turn without bumping a Leeds or two, she bridles when a wanderer speaks lightly of her people or listens, all unaware, to those who, she says, should never speak at all. When her letter came I took the map and located the Leeds Point Road, considering nearby Smithville that once was a part of the Point but couldn't keep a post office because there was a Smithville already in Burlington County. I remembered the tumble-down ruin of what once had been a hotel, a stop once familiar to stagecoaches rumbling up from the shore. Gearhart Crate had been with me that day we pulled up at an old house, half hidden by shrubs grown wild, crying out with legends of important days and people on the brink of forgetfulness—whatever Mrs. Bowen may say of what transpired, I came away with what I thought was the best of its story.

There was something about the Leeds of Leeds and the almanacs they wrote long before Poor Richard. There was something more of the half-buried times of Oyster Creek, Swamp Creek, Wigwam Creek, Duck Creek. There was a lot more about Jesse Mathis, seventy-one then, who came in from a cedar-plumed field, rake on his shoulder, to see what was wanted. Jesse, kinsman of Great John, talked about the old house, Leedses, Mathises, and of dour-faced Dan Sooy, the man who lived there with him, and more that was and had been Leeds Point. There was not as much as I would have liked in that earlier account, but Jesse said he was one of the last and that no one else, unless he had an ax to grind, would do much authentic talking.

That was a long time before. Suddenly the letter came, a second letter, in reply to one I had tried to forget. Signed by Mrs. Bowen, Carrie J. Bowen, the first note was brief but supercharged with scolding. Leeds Point, Mrs. Bowen had contended, had been dealt with without respect; what was more, some of the Leeds—and the lady proudly boasted that she was one of them—had been tossed about most unfeelingly. Mrs. Bowen said we had talked with impossible people, that everything was wrong, unsympathetic, misconstrued. Letters like that haven't been many, but when they come I know how to deal with them. I explain that most people write me in quite the opposite vein and ask me to help them find their grandmothers or towns where lost ancestors charmed their fellows; I say that it may be that I am sensitive, too, and that I have never knowingly hurt anyone. I told Mrs. Bowen that I remembered Jesse Mathis at the old house half-concealed in the tangle and that he had told me he wanted everything the way it was because that was the way his mother had left it. I had never implied, I pointed out further, concluding the matter as I believed, that Jesse's mother wasn't a delightful old lady, neat as a pin, with an immaculate house surrounded by a colorful garden. I made it clear that I would not run from Carrie J. Bowen and that if I needed to be set right, as she claimed, the process could begin as soon as she chose.

I had forgotten the challenge and its acceptance until the second letter came that morning when I had no intention at all of dawdling further among the Leeds—or even down the road where they have a magical electric screen door that fries flies as they seek an entrance. "To me your reply is rather amusing," said Mrs. Bowen, as if I had responded but yesterday. "I do want to thank you for your expression, 'Where an old man and his sainted mother are concerned . . .' If you had written of my grandmother in this manner, in all probability you would never have known that I existed."

61

There was a barb or two there, of course, and I saw that I had the choice of writing another letter or going down to see Mrs. Bowen. I put my plans aside and determined on—well, it wasn't bearding the lion, was it? Armed with all the facts I could find about the Leeds, some of which I was sure would not be countenanced by Mrs. Bowen then or ever, I hurried down to the Point.

I knew, now, about Titan Leeds, sheriff of Burlington County in 1729: Titan gave damaging evidence at the "tryal" of one Anne Eastworthy, brought into court in a chair to accuse an Irishman, James Burnside, of forcing his attentions upon her, a charge which she was in the habit of bringing against many men according to the evidence. I found the will of Daniel Leeds, dated 1765 at Great Egg Harbor, Gloucester County, witnessed by Hannah and Vincent Leeds of Northampton, Burlington County, a testament filed beside that of a Mullica contemporary, Mordecai Andrews, whose thoughtfulness for his daughters provided each of them with beds. I read the caveat filed by William Leeds against one Daniel in 1688, when Middletown William opposed a grant to Springfield Daniel of acres along Whale Pond Brook. Daniel, I learned further, was a business man on all occasions, for in the will of Benjamin Peck, dated 1772, an accounting was attached by Richard Wescott under which Daniel got seven shillings six "for coming to The Forks" of the Mullica "at the request of the deceased" and sharing, with five other men, two pounds ten "for bringing the corpse from the inlet."

The will of Nehemiah Leeds, bearing date of 1773, left to his daughters, Deborah, Elizabeth, Jemimah, and Hannah "the use of the West End of the house at Great Egg Harbour four years if they remain unmarried." An earlier Daniel, it seemed, had been accused of strange "interlineations" and alterations of surveys, being later prosecuted for "contempts and misdemeanours" in his office as "Surveyor Generall of the Western Division of this Province." Abraham Leeds was associated with one Thomas Elton, I found among the archives, in the sale of a plantation and dwelling a mile from "the landing on Ancocas Creek in 1772," while Leedses with such names as Thomas, William, Daniel, Thomas Jr., and Ann were linked in warrants for land from the East Jersey Proprietors at "Leeds or Smithville" as early as 1676. It became plain, as I thought back on my notes while riding along, that Mathises had been associated with Leedses as witnesses, bondsmen, or in the marriage bed from earliest references to Little Egg Harbor and the Mullica. In 1778 even a race horse named Leeds was making a creditable showing.

I planned my speech for Mrs. Bowen. I would tell her that searching out and recording unwritten history had no point unless one was reasonably accurate. What I was after, I would be sure to point out, was legends, folklore, the stuff that would die with those who said they remembered. At no time, I would tell her, had I said that everything I had written was absolutely factual. Historians who insist on chronicles of dates and discoveries and bare-branched family trees nearly always miss the point. Patting my notebook of data on the family, from Mary whose husband was advertising the theft of doubloons in 1726 to early and continuing innkeepers and hotelmen of Atlantic City, I felt I was well armed for the adventure.

On arrival I discovered that my correspondent with the acid pen was not "Miss" at all, as I had been thinking of her and as I had replied to her after the first letter. I found that out when I located the house she had described, hardly more than a stone's throw from where Jesse Mathis had insisted that nobody else in the neighborhood who knew anything would be likely to talk. The lady's husband, Oscar, was in the garden; it was he, who, somewhat warily I thought, took me into the house. To Mrs. Bowen I repeated some of the things I had worked out—the rest stuck in my throat. Mrs. Bowen began to talk, and soon I was in possession of Leeds Point lore which none of the others had provided. Perhaps when people really "get mad" they become informative in the cooling off process. Perhaps Jesse Mathis who, they say, is dead now, never "got mad" in his life.

Mrs. Bowen didn't begin with Leeds or even Mathises. She said first that too little mention had been made of Robert W. Scott, the inventor who lived at Leeds Point years ago. Mr. Scott was thirty years ahead of his time, Mrs. Bowen told me. An early disciple of Bertrand Russell, he was a believer in companionate marriage, she said, although he always went through the marriage ceremony in his marital progression. "Fancy a Bertrand Russell follower away back here at the Point!" laughed Mrs. Bowen. "And another thing," she added subsiding, "he always looked after the various Mrs. Scotts even as he went on from one marriage and divorce to another." That, she thought, was rather nice.

This Robert Scott had a variety of interests along other than romantic lines, it seems. He experimented with long-range rifles and perfected one that discharged a bullet that flew with surprising accuracy three or four miles, out across Great Bay toward the Seven Islands and the Shooting Thoroughfare, they say. He turned out one weapon, Mrs. Bowen told me, that discharged a bullet in which there were two slugs.

"We can remember when the Scott mansion was down the road behind the old Leeds house, can't we, Oscar?" the lady jogged her husband's memory for collaboration.

Mr. Bowen nodded, preferring to listen. I sat on a couch, writing.

"Mr. Scott had a proving ground across the way, over from the mansion," said the lady.

I was hearing nothing as yet about the Leeds, but I listened spellbound.

This man Scott, whose father had been twice a millionaire and who had died poor, was a millionaire in his own right when, after experiments that were transplanted to Leeds Point about 1905, he died among memories of firearms, new methods for propagating oysters, revolutionary knitting machines, and full living. He had lots of ditches dug, Oscar Bowen spoke up, on the theory that idle water benefits shellfish and a lot of calculations come from the way the tides work. "He was always doing something down in the hummocks," said Oscar.

What Scott accomplished with oysters I have no idea, but I soon found from the sizable hole left behind after fire destroyed the mansion that it must have been the biggest house Leeds Point ever saw. "Cost $37,000 to build in those days," Mr. Bowen confided, "and that was a lot of money then. Carpenters got two dollars a day. Man named Stout over in Atlantic City was the architect. Tom Strickland was boss carpenter. Why, even the barn cost $7,000!"

In almost every case these early pioneers with money boasted one of the first noisy, dangerous automobiles in days when you could count the number of cars the country over in a few minutes. Robert

Scott seems to have had one of the first along the shore, a two-cylinder affair that hurled up a cloud of dust every time it went down the road. "Funny thing," Mrs. Bowen told me suddenly, "it used to get as far as the bridge every time but there's where it would stop. Nothing on earth would induce it to venture beyond." Perhaps, if I had been thinking about the Jersey Devil then, I would have suggested an explanation. "Mr. Scott used to walk the rest of the way to Oyster Creek and then, when it was time to come back, he'd push the car around and start it without any difficulty for the trip up the hill home."

Scott's money came principally from the invention of a knitting machine, Mrs. Bowen said, apparatus that turned out seamless underwear for the first time. The firm name, she told me, was Scott & Williams. "Scott, who started as a poor boy," she explained, "was the one who supplied most of the brains. Williams had the money."

All this was very interesting, I said, but what about the Leeds of Leeds Point. Mrs. Bowen smiled as if to humor me, and then explained quickly where the Scotts came in. The Mrs. Scott of Leeds Point was a daughter of Job Mathis, and of course Mathises and Leedses were pillars of the town.

My hostess began with Daniel who became Surveyor General of West Jersey. Born in 1652 in Leeds, England, he died in 1720, having "taken up" land later called Leeds Point as "the largest land along the New Jersey coast." There had been Leeds of Leeds in New Jersey before, said Mrs. Bowen. Thomas had come to Shrewsbury in 1676, sharing with his wife the title to a tract of land in East Jersey; however, the country didn't agree with Mrs. Thomas and she died in less than two years. Thomas married a second time, as most people expected to in those days when an ailing helpmeet was laid away; the bride on this occasion was Margaret Collier "of Marcus Hook upon ye river Delaware." This Friends' ceremony was the first in the books of "God's people at Burlington." Thomas died at Shrewsbury and was buried in the Meeting House yard beside Mrs. Leeds No. 1; not long after that Mrs. Leeds No. 2 left for the livelier scene of Philadelphia. By the first marriage there were three sons, William, Daniel, and Thomas; William made barrels and lived in Middletown, although he later bought a tract from

Daniel "on the coast near Absecombe Creek" in 1705. Three years later he acquired more land there from Thomas Budd of Philadelphia, who had it direct from the Crown.

Daniel, the speculating surveyor, followed his father from Leeds; and in company with Thomas Revell and his family came ashore at Burlington from the "Shield," first sailing ship to get up the Delaware that far. Daniel's first wife was Ann Stacy, daughter of Robert, the Burlington tanner. With Ann's death following the birth of a daughter in 1681, Daniel was wedded to a lovely girl, Mrs. Bowen said as if she remembered, Dorothy Young—this was a respectful two years after. At this time Daniel's house was at Jackson, not to be confused with the glassmaking village of later years, but a corner in the road above Burlington. But Daniel was much too active a man to stay there: A member of the Assembly in 1682, a member of the notorious Lord Cornbury's Council in 1703, Daniel became one of the Councillors of New Jersey in 1704 and was reappointed in 1706. Meanwhile he had gone down to the sea on the Gloucester County side of the Mullica—there was no Atlantic County then—making surveys, confirmed as grants and giving names to all those little creeks and coves in 1698.

Lower Island, then Further Island, which some say is what Atlantic City was built on and others declare is now Brigantine, was a part of a sale in which a surveyor well looked after his own interests, for Leeds Point, unless it has sunk down in more than memory, is still the highest coastal land between the Atlantic Highlands and the Virginia Capes. There it was that Daniel took his ever-increasing family and began writing his Book of Wisdom and his almanacs, one of which, for 1687, is the earliest imprint of William Bradford.

This was, Mrs. Bowen assured me, by no means aimless climbing among the many-branched boughs of the Leeds family tree. Even if I had known before that those almanacs were priceless, that Daniel kept on writing them from 1687 to 1716, and that two of his sons, Felix and Titan, carried on the work after that, Mrs. Bowen said that many might have overlooked such details in the funny things Jesse Mathis had said. There were more children, so that Leedses began calling overworked storks from duties in behalf of Cranmers and Sooys; Daniel became the father in the order mentioned of Japheth

66

Constant Ford, for whom forgotten Bulltown was home, went back to tramp across the old fields in search of bits of glass, old bricks, and cellarholes, seeking traces of his youth. Below, Len Sooy showed an old flag to two of his grandsons shortly before the "wind that loved him blew him away."

Will and 'Lonzo Nichols, descendants of Mullica pioneers, lived not far from Bulltown and Charcoal Point, or Landing. When their house burned down, they hurried their rebuilding because deer season was opening. Below, the author picks his way through the Mordecai Swamp.

the First, Mary who became Mrs. Sommers, Philo, Bethanah, Ann, a second Daniel, and Titan. Daniel was obviously a titan in his own right.

Now that I have gone back among Leedses before there was a Leeds Point, I must let it go at that. For the Leedses born at the Point were many, and their number was and is only equal to their fame, Mrs. Bowen has told me time and again. To write further about them by name, without discrimination, would be to sink hopelessly among Higbees, Osborns, Steelmans, Smiths, Somerses, Conovers, Ingersolls, and scores of other families who provided healthy and attractive wives. "The first Leeds," said Mrs. Bowen, "were Friends. The records of Haddonfield Quarterly Meeting list the home of Japheth with two others where the first meetings were held in the Gloucester County, which in those days went all the way from the Delaware River to the Atlantic Ocean."

I wanted to ask Mrs. Bowen what Mrs. Leeds it was who spoiled the good times of early travelers on their way to the beaches by forbidding dancing, but I thought better of it. It was one of those later on no doubt. One diarist has written somewhere very sarcastically about festivities interrupted because they might disturb the neighbors, the nearest of these being guests in a nearby hostelry who themselves were dancing. Later I looked it up and found the lady to be a Mrs. Andrew Leeds, hostess at a boarding house not on the mainland at all. And the diarist was upset, anyhow, by the trip over on "a dirty little craft, the 'Henry Clay'" and the sight of a mother providing her three children with "their regular morning bitters."

Mrs. Bowen had suspected inattention. She repeated: "All the way from the Delaware to the sea. The Japheth Leeds house was at the Point, Joseph Scull's was at Somers Point, and Peter White's was at Absecon, and these three men took turns in providing place and provisions for devotional exercises." I thought Mrs. Bowen might be quoting, so, on hearing the name of Joseph Scull, I took a hand in it myself, pulling from my pocket the *Account of the Life and Travels in the Work of the Ministry of John Fothergill*. I had picked up this little book, printed originally in London and reprinted in 1754 by James Chattin in Church Alley, Philadelphia, for a spare dollar. In the 1720's Mr. Fothergill had written, as I read:

'That evening we went to J. Sykes's, intending to set forward from thence toward Egg Harbour. We took our Journey thro' the Desarts to Little-Egg Harbour, and came to Gervas Farrar's, and on the 4th were at a Meeting there, and had a pretty good Time in the Extending of the Love of Truth to the poor People thereaway. The 5th we travelled Part by Land, and thro' dismal Marshes, and Part by Water in Canoes to Great-Egg Harbour, and on the 6th had a Meeting among some poor dark People that came thither; yet the Lord was pleased to draw near, and comforted divers of us sweetly. The 7th we had a Meeting at one John Skull's, where a considerable Number of different Professors came in, and we had a pretty good Time among them. . . .'

"There, you see?" I paused, thumbing the pages. "Now, wait a minute, that's not all. This Fothergill fellow was a traveler without equal, considering all the swimming and bumping and bruising that went with it in those days. He was always going 'over the river into the Jerseys.' Yes," I said, finding the place, "here's another account of his preaching down here. He had come over from Germantown and had been down at Woodbury-Creek, Pilesgrove, and Salem, as well as Alloway-Creek and Greenwich, he says. Then—

'. . . the Day following had a large Meeting, and an open, precious Time, in the Love and Power of the Gospel, at Great-Egg Harbour, as also another pretty large Meeting higher up on the Shore, at Robert Smith's the Day following. That Night we passed over a dangerous Marsh and River to Little-Egg Harbour, where on the 15th we had a Meeting with Friends thereaway, to our true Comfort. . . .'"

"To be sure," said Mrs. Bowen, pleased. "In 1740 the meeting which had been held at Japhet Leeds' was removed to Robert Smith's. And anyhow, the two villages, Leeds Point and Smithville, were together known as Leeds until about 1844, they say."

It was a Jeremiah Leeds, who stood six feet in his stockings and weighed two hundred and fifty pounds, who was first resident of what today is the World's Playground, as his descendants call it. Jeremiah built a log cabin where the old Reading station stood at Atlantic and Baltic Avenues. Land sold for forty cents an acre then, which was a big profit over the eleven or twelve cents the Leedses had paid in the beginning. Of course, forty cents per acre carried with it rights to hunt, fish, and make salt unless the Indians, probably those "poor, dark people" Mr. Fothergill wrote about, came back and insisted on exercising rights originally theirs. Jeremiah, when

68

he was sixty-two, married Millicent Steelman Ingersoll, then twenty-four, proving he could do more than build cabins and brush fences to form sand dunes and make fresh-water ponds for wild fowl which he allowed none but relatives to shoot: Jeremiah had four more children.

It was of Jeremiah that Mrs. Bowen spoke when she told an old story that has been handed down by all the Leeds and Mathises through the better part of two centuries. Long looked upon as a patriarch, Jeremiah found great delight in his last years in embellishing a tale told by his father from the time just ahead of the Revolution, when some British soldiers were sent ashore from a ship that anchored in Great Bay for some foraging. Two barges full of soldiers and sailors hunting fresh meat were beached near Leeds Point. The captain ordered Jeremiah's father to drive his cattle up from the pasture lands so that the best might be chosen. Two fat steers were picked, knocked on the head, quartered, and loaded away. "All right, that's all," said the Captain, waving a farewell.

"Wasn't your father angry?" they used to ask Jeremiah.

"Guess not," Jeremiah used to answer. "Guess he thought he was lucky losing so little."

"How did *you* feel about it?" those who gathered around him asked.

"To tell the truth," answered Jeremiah, "I didn't feel about it quite that way. Those steers, you see, happened to belong to me and my brother. Worth five or six dollars a head in money nowadays. Maybe that's what sent me off to the war!"

Just when I was certain that adventures of the Leeds had come to an end, Mrs. Bowen threw in one more revelation, topping references to the Point as the home of skippers of seagoing sailing ships, the hiding place of boxwood imported from England, and Paisley shawls carried from as far away. After she had made it clear that the house at the corner was not the original Leeds headquarters and that the Daniel Leeds house must have been closer to the water, Mrs. Bowen added, dangling a kind of baited hook:

"They didn't tell you about the castor oil factory, did they?"

"No," I answered contritely. "No, I'm sure they didn't." Nor had they told us that Mr. Bowen, son of Cap'n Jonathan Steelman Bowen, once master of the "Everett Webster," four-master out of Bath, Maine, was born across the road from Jesse's, or that Japheth had built the house where we had listened to Jesse, or that the old Presbyterian Church, built with its back to the road, was so contrived by Felix Leeds, who said that nor'easters would beat in the front door if they turned it around. He said nobody would come to church when it rained. "No," I repeated. "Where was the castor oil factory?"

If Carrie Bowen had said it was on a barge and that it was towed from town to town along the Mullica, I would have believed her. The truth was almost as incredible. The factory stood directly across the road from the old Leeds house of Jesse Mathis, the one with a foundation made of ballast stones. It was owned and operated by a third Japheth Leeds.

# 7

## LEEKS IN LOWER BANK

*"I'll walk where my own nature would be guiding:*
*It vexes me to choose another guide . . ."*
EMILY BRONTË

I CANNOT TELL, now, about the first journey to Lower Bank. Going back has made the first, second, fifth, and all the other lingerings part of a picture, fused with all the color of happenings and happy returns. Lower Bank has become, for me, more than a place, more than a village at a bend of the Mullica below the bridge. It is more, too, than the location Eric Mullica chose for his plantation, much more than the counterpart of Green Bank, which was in the beginning less verdant Upper Bank. Lower Bank has become a tapestry of things and people, the bridge next up from Tater Cramer's, the field where Bill Bailey can always find chips and bits of pottery of Indian days, Mrs. Allen's old store and post office. Fred Noyes, who called himself The Mayor and who came there to die but chose to live; Will Kemble, who made and lost lots of money in big cities and now plays Santa Claus, thinks and likes to be alone; the Cavileers, who let other people wonder and worry about their ancestry; Cliff Terry, who grows trees for New Jersey and hopes to see them tall upon the state's arid and mysterious Plains; and Charlie Leek—all these are interwoven in the pattern.

I think it was Charlie I talked to first, but I am not sure. "Leek," Charlie said, smiling, "is a very bad name to build boats by. But somehow it's had to stand us for a good long time, back to somewheres about 1712 or 1715 anyway. You see," he went on, his enthusiasm spilling his words in bunches, "with us Leeks it's been either ships or the Gospel. You had to take up one or the other. There was never nothin' else." Charlie was wrong there: I remembered the story of John Leek, the self-made eunuch of Cohansie, but I decided to say nothing about him until better acquaintance. For this was my first meeting with Charles Platt Leek, ruddy-faced, jovial, as active a shipwright at sixty-five as you'll find, or as the Navy had discovered for a later emergency.

There is an old map of Lower Bank in the days of Randolph Township, showing two roads or streets to which the village still lays claim, on which are located the houses and their owners. Maps like that were made for the old atlases, large subscription volumes which gave their compilers some return before publication, the much safer course in the writing of books. Three of the houses are marked as belonging to Cavileers, six to Johnsons, three to Weeks, two to Cales. A few of the names seem to have disappeared as owners of the houses, along with the old sawmill and mill pond across from the old Methodist church they open once a year and so many of the men who were designated as captains on every property chart. Actually, the old names are still there if the houses have not burned down; husbands and kinfolk have taken them in charge.

When I first saw him down beside his boat works by the bridge, Charlie pulled down his cap on one side, tried in vain to light the stump of a cigar, and adjusted the black patch over his left eye, an adornment that sometimes makes him look like a good-natured pirate. "They say I just missed bein' a minister," he said, and for a moment I thought I heard something that sounded like contempt

71

in his tone. Whatever his feeling, it was not directed at circumstances that gave him escape from a Methodist circuit. It was more likely aimed at peacetime building of "pleasure boats" where proud schooners were once cradled on the ways. "I build boats," he finished it up, "when boats is wanted."

Perhaps, when you go down to Green Bank, you will take the road that turns toward the Mullica almost directly across from Charlie Weber's farm, a gravel stretch past Captain Carlisle's old house, the old church, and the graveyard beside it. If you miss that, there is the other way in, marked by a fading sign that says more about Charlie's boat works than Lower Bank, pointing down a winding way through the woods. Either road will bring you up sharp among picturesque houses, some of great age, a newer steepled church, and a store that's filled with ghosts who must remember the proprietor who, on seeing a newcomer one night, reached up and presented him with the can of worms he had left on a shelf ten years before. What they said about Lower Bank in 1844 could be said with equal accuracy now:

"Lower Bank, 6 miles below Batsto, on the Little Egg Harbor River, has a Methodist Church and about 30 dwellings." Once you've come to the bridge, very like the one at Green Bank, you have your choice of going over the river and on to Egg Harbor City, the village that deserted a river for a railroad, to the clearing that was old Gloucester Furnace, or to the sandholes and decaying timbers of Clark's Landing further down. Or you can keep on along the Lower Bank side of the Mullica, close to the gray and amber water of the river, although the pathway eventually peters out. Charlie Leek builds his ships beside the bridge for a very good reason: Every now and then Charlie has to drop his tools and hurry out to man the capstan to open the bridge, the signal being either a shrill whistle or a raucous horn.

Roy Cramer, and not Charlie Leek, is the one who will reveal that Eric Mullica's cabin stood about where Charlie's boat shop is. Eric probably admired the view from there like everybody else, watching the river as it hurries seaward by Hog Island or landward by the screening marsh reeds along the Island Road. Charlie will go as far as to mention a walk through the long grass in the field behind the

72

big boat shed over in the direction of Joe Ware's sawmill, for at the end of it will be the lonely tombstone of Joos Sooy, ancestor of all the Down Shore Sooys. Even in wartime Charlie has carried on a tradition within sight of where earlier Leeks and VanSants and Adamses built seagoing craft from trees hewn in the Mullica Valley's cedar swamps. Charlie won't talk tradition or even his work; he much prefers to tilt his cap or pull it down, chewing his cigar and spitting out brown fragments as he lets his boats speak for themselves. What he will say is that this is where sturdy pioneers, people worth their salt, lived before there was an Atlantic City. Charlie doesn't like Atlantic City. Sometimes, acceding to family pressure, he has started there and then; within sight and smell of it, he has turned about and returned home.

"There's a smell of the Mullica," he told me once, "that ain't like any other smell on earth." That's supposed to be a compliment. Just in case you fail to accept it as such, Charlie usually adds, "Once you get the smell of the Mullica up your nose, all other smells are stinks." But while Charlie is explaining olfactory properties of the air along the river, he will admit in between that there were shipyards at Lower Bank and Green Bank, competing in earlier days with yards at Tuckerton, Port Republic, and Mays Landing. Now in the neighborhood only Lower Bank carries on.

"All the big timber was used up," Charlie told me. The words of John Watson came to me then: ". . . The river there used to be filled with masted vessels. It was a place rich in money. Hundreds of men were engaged in the swamps, cutting cedar. Sawmills were numerous and always in business, cutting cedar and pine boards. Many shipyards were there. Vessels were built and loaded out to the West Indies . . ." Suddenly I heard Charlie raising his voice for he knew I wasn't listening. "Generations in the shipbuilding trade," he was saying. "When people hear that, they say there must be money in it. I tell them there is. The money's all in it. Nobody ever took the money out."

Charlie spat. "I always say," he sputtered on, "that in this business there's two kind of mechanics—some is and some ain't. Leeks? There's a million of 'em. They're all divided up. Mixed with the VanSants mostly. The VanSants was always boatbuilders." I told him

73

about my old map and how the name appeared to indicate that one of the VanSants was a preacher—in Lower Bank, too. "Some of 'em slipped," Charlie answered, unperturbed. "Anyhow, preachin' doesn't take all week. Most VanSants had time and money to build big ships, but they had a hell of a time scraping money together to buy boards for their coffins. Stanley VanSant, over to Gardner's Basin, he's cousin o' mine. Then there's Oscar and John. And Sam at Port Republic. Forty years ago Sam VanSant was making more sailing ships than anybody else around here."

I told Charlie about the time I was over in Port Republic and a couple of youngsters brought a capstan bar with the name, "Venus," still discernible, out of a barn. "They had to chase the chickens off it," I said. "Why, that's part of one of the prize ships that started all the trouble at Chestnut Neck."

"Is it still over there?" Charlie wanted to know.

"I don't know," I told him. "Last time I went to see it, they dragged out an old cannon instead." I recalled asking Donny Smallwood, after I had bought the usual dozen eggs to prime the conversation, "Why didn't you tell me that capstan bar from the 'Venus' was still in town?"

"What's a capstan bar?" Donny had scoffed. "Listen, this here town is full of them things. What you want is a cannon, a real Revolutionary cannon. How about it?"

"All right," I had assented, thinking to see a cannon mounted by some Legion post in the park around the Meeting House cemetery. "Where is it?"

Donny said it used to be in Sam French's barn.

"Used to be?" I repeated.

"Sure," he answered. "Maybe they moved it. That's where it *was*. Some WPA men dug it up in the creek out there when they finished spoiling the landscape with that dredge of theirn. Right off Sam's place, it was. So Sam put it in the barn."

It was one of the Cavileers, Gilbert, who helped Sam's boy, Richard, move a couple of boxes, ease over a basket in which a pet skunk reposed, and bring to view a splendid specimen of a cannon. This, for all they knew, tumbled from the deck of one of the hundreds of privateers or their prizes that transferred their lair up Nacote

74

Creek with the burning of Chestnut Neck. "For all anybody knows," I told Charlie Leek, "it may be one of the very guns that Elijah Clark and Richard Wescott mounted behind the sand parapet of the fort. I hope those guns that John Cox said he was mounting down there were better than his howitzers."

Charlie surprised me with his response. "So do I," he said. "Not much good, were they? Out of twelve in the first load three busted in proving. Out of the next dozen five more blowed up. Hell of a workman! Probably blamed Jersey iron!"

I could only nod. As far as I knew—I made certain later on—these details were revealed solely in a letter written by Mr. Cox at Batsto in 1776. Having said what he wanted to, Charlie put his information on the episode back where he'd found it, just as they had put the cannon back in the barn at Port Republic, first replacing the boxes, the basket, and the skunk. Charlie picked up remarkably as if I had never interrupted him.

"All the timber for ships was taken off," he repeated. "Some went for charcoal, some was tied up for cordwood, some was sailed away as dunnage. Good timber for ships came from further and further away. Just the same a few of the Leeks has always kept at it. They made some of the finest coastal schooners that ever was. I have to laugh when people come down here askin' what on earth folks do for a living in Washington Township. Why, I tell them, here's where people were when there was nothin' at Atlantic City. O' course, in those days what was planned to be Egg Harbor City was over here by the Mullica. Go into those woods over there and you'll find the stakes—all along the river there was laid out in streets and lots. Then something changed all that: The railroad went the other way. Somebody suggested that as long as tracks was being laid to pick up timber and glass and iron, maybe they'd like to get washed off in the ocean. The ocean hadn't been figgered on for bathing before."

Charlie recalled the running of the first "narrow-gauge" to Atlantic City. "There was a spur that came right down to the river over there, a place we call Dutch Dock," he said. Some of the rails, long abandoned in the woods and fields, were later to become along with parts of an abandoned bridge the marine railways of Charlie's boatworks. "A steamer from New York used to come up the Mullica on

75

regular schedule," said Charlie, when I asked him about that, "bring down coal and groceries and go out with cordwood, charcoal, and dunnage. Dunnage? That was wood about two feet six inches long. You see, everything was shipped in barrels in those days. Ships had to have dunnage to keep barrels from rolling—cedar, pine, oak, everything went. I'd like to have a penny for every foot of dunnage those near-sighted lunkheads took out of this here valley!"

Ordinarily Charlie Leek doesn't talk about this business of boat-building. Just the same ships made by Leeks go back a century and a half, at least. As far as Charlie's own contribution is concerned, he merely points to a gallery of pictures on his office wall. Those Charlie designed and built are labeled like milestones through the 1890's, the 1900's, and the years since then. Some day, I suppose, there will be added a gallery of what was added in wartime. Even so, I have a feeling that Charlie's thoughts will dwell on earlier years when, after his ships were "lanched," Charlie continued to follow them as if they were members of the family. "I know most of them that's alive and them that's dead," Charlie said quietly one afternoon, as if each vessel had an individual personality easily distinguished.

The first of many days made memorable by Charlie's chatter found three of his sound but somehow despised "pleasure boats" under way in one shed. One was a huge craft, eighty-one feet long and seventeen feet wide, but that was across the road. Alternately Charlie referred to her as his rowboat or the "Queen Mary." Size made little impression on Mr. Leek; a pleasure boat was a pleasure boat, a comedown from the tall ships of former days. One of the smaller boats launched the spring after I saw her was completed for the president of Rider College, a man who liked fishing and who kept her busy chasing tuna off Brielle until war came. The "Queen Mary," which Charlie said could be sailed anywhere, was in pre-Pearl Harbor days drawing bids from South American nations whose agents wanted to enlist her double planking of mahogany, from the keel up, in the service of war. Eventually a navy somewhere south of the equator signed her up, they say. The point, I think, is that in spite of the homespun atmosphere and the rough appearance of those weatherbeaten sheds, plus the droll wholesomeness that is Charles Platt Leek, last of the Mullica shipbuilders, here were craft of con-

76

trasting refinement, expert craftsmanship, and wartime power. Somehow the Leeks who were shipwrights rather than preachers made Charlie heir to their cumulative skill.

"Once there were menhaden fishermen at the end of the bay," said Charlie, with another pull at his cap and a fingering of that patch across his left eye. He showed me, one day I took the old map to Lower Bank, where Smith's Fish Factory had been, opposite Turtle Island. and where years ago two more such establishments had operated near the entrance of Big Sheepshead Creek. "Lots of those fish factories," he said, "were owned and operated like chain-stores by Joe Wharton, who visited them in a boat he named for himself, playing up and down the river here. In those days there was activity all week, and the only time you had off from running that bridge up and down was Saturday night till Monday morning. Now it's the other way around."

Once, Charlie said, with his own kind of cackle, Lower Bank had seven saloons. "Taverns, you historical birds call them," he added. "Now," he observed, "there ain't one." Where they went, nobody knows, any more than they know what happened to the four houses that once were where the boat works is now. "Never been absolutely sure," said Charlie, "that Eric Mullica's cabin was here—or that he had a cabin for that matter. Roy Cramer tells the story about the cabin and says he's got tax maps to prove it, but none of us Leeks has got around to checking on those maps." Musingly, Charlie began to paint a colorful picture of barges going by, loaded down with salt hay for the paper mills up the Mullica and Wading Rivers. One was at Harrisville where there are deer and prickly pear and crumbling walls. The other was at Pleasant Mills where the wheels haven't turned for years. "More than forty scow loads a week used to go through here," Charlie told me then. "The paper? Oh, it was nothing extra. Old-fashioned, kinda brown. But it was good enough for what it was used for."

I asked him one day about the village called Leektown, a place on the map between Lower Bank and New Gretna, the town that was quite content to be Bass River until some newcomer got notions of making it a marriage mill about 1850. Charlie spat again. "You see," he said, "there were two bunches of Leeks, those that's here and the others that's no relation." Charlie himself was born on the river at Lower Bank and then was away for a while in Atlantic City "before it growed up." Then he was a grocer's clerk in Riverton. "Sort of like Mullica, I was," Charlie confided. "Riverton, they said, was in Cinnaminson Township, and that was first of all a Swedish place, like around Swedesboro and Mullica Hill. Guess I had a look at them all, like Eric, before I decided that the Mullica was best."

Charlie's father, William, worked in the paper mill at Harrisville. "First Leek around here," he told me one day as if he had been looking it up, "was buried in Leektown. John, the name was. An Englishman and a surveyor. Made out scrumptiously, they say." I could tell that Charlie had been reading Leah Blackman. Captain John Leek was an Englishman, she had written, settling at Bass River in pioneer times. "It is said that he fared sumptuously every day," was the quotation. "During a considerable portion of his life he lived at Bridgeport, now Wading River, where he died and is buried in the graveyard at that place, formerly called the Leak burying ground . . ."

"And so it should have been," said Charlie, when I repeated the passage. "It was John who left the ground for the cemetery and the church as well. That's the cemetery I told you was full of Leeks."

"But how are you spelling it?" I asked him. "In those days they spelled it *Leak* and were not ashamed." I watched Charlie tip up his cap and nudge the shade over an eye that was injured in the service of one of the first life-saving stations along the coast. "When did you Leeks make the change?"

"Boy," said Charlie with a snap, "the Leeks wasn't ashamed then, and they ain't ashamed now. They liked variety, that's all. Some didn't mind being Leaks, some did. So, if you can make anything out of all those stones, they changed back and forth a lot of the time, whenever it suited their fancy. Go down and look for yourself!"

I told him I already had, pulling from my pocket some notes I had copied on John Leek's will dated May 5, 1777, in which he gave his wife, Phebe, a third of the "movable" estate and "the income of my lands, only the cedar swamps excepted." The rest was to be sold, the legacies to be distributed among John, the Captain's son, Phebe

78

Mathis and Mary Sooy, his daughters. This was a will that referred to Turkle Creek, spelling it the way many people along the Mullica pronounce it even now. "Captain John," Charlie added to my information, "had a sister Phoebe, who was a Mathis and Cranmer by turn. First she was Mrs. Job Mathis, but she outlived Job and married Caleb Cranmer. John himself married Martha Rose."

"Oh, yes," I said, remembering the name, and with it Mrs. Stephen Girard, whose beauty was ever a plague to her husband, coming up the Mullica Valley as the wife of a peddler. Martha was supposed to be the beauty of the Mullica. The records linking +he lady with the Leeks say, "Martha, daughter of Samuel Rose, was claimed to have been a very beautiful woman." Later, in comment on the Roses who were established at Parkertown long before the Revolution, Martha was "said to have been as beautiful as a rose." But no fragile flower was Martha: She had seven or maybe eight children according to the best family Bibles. Hardy annual like her father, Martha is credited with being the progenitor of "a large number of people of Bass River" so that, as Charlie once pointed out, truly enough, where "the old cemetery wasn't full of Leeks it was probably a bed of Roses."

As for the rest of the Leeks, or Leaks, many are notable merely for those rockbound names of long ago, Kesiah, Rosana, Achsah, Hezekiah, and even a Hepsibah or two. Thus they competed well enough with the Mullica's mainstays, Adamses, Lovelands, Cavileers, Mathises, Cranmers, and VanSants. Charlie's story of lost family treasure, companion piece to the tale of Len Sooy, came to him one day as he talked of other things, shavings, the rain, and the man who was due to make another payment on the "Queen Mary" provided, of course, that his tenants had paid their rent on time. "The main street of one of the big cities in Floridy," Charlie said, "is Flagler Street. Well, this Flagler married my grandfather's sister. I'm not so sure of the exact relationship but that will do. She was a Leek, anyhow. Well, it seems the poor gal went a little off abovestairs and Flagler set aside two or three million dollars so's she'd be taken care of. And she lived on and on.

"Finally when she died they started looking for her kinfolk. There was a lot of money, and they were trying to give it away. They went

79

everywhere, it seems, looking up Leeks, even looking us over and measuring chins and noses, making remarks about those who looked like Leeks and those who didn't. Two of the family 'way out west must have looked most like a Leek, for that's the ones who got the money, forty thousand a year apiece, they said, as long as they behaved themselves. As for us Leeks in Lower Bank—oh, well, probably we got more'n they have, at that. We got the Mullica, we have."

Charlie Leek's house, up the road a piece from the boat works, is over a century old, part of the old Zek'l Cavileer estate, facing the river. Zek'l owned ground all the way up, Charlie says, every inch. "They still got it, mostly," he complains sometimes. "They hold on to it, too, though lots of people have tried their darndest to get some. It ain't that they got no use for the money. They're just particular. They say the Mullica country ain't going to be spoiled by comers-in as long as they got a say." Another version is that the Cavileer holdings are "kind of messed up in the family," as one old man explained it to me later on, "and nobody wants to get together long enough to straighten it all out."

Charlie has a story about a railroad that was to come over from Tuckerton and never did. "They was going to connect it," he told me, "with the Tuckerton Railroad, that line they finally sold for junk. Agents went up and down the river here, trying to sell the stock. But they didn't do much business. Most folks was like Cap'n Gus Johnson down below here. They offered him a lot of shares. He offered them three loads of salt hay to pay for 'em. The deal was off, and that was as far as they got with him. They didn't get that far with a lot of other people."

Whenever I go to Lower Bank and see Charlie Leek long enough to talk to, I try to get up courage enough to say something about that kinsman of his, deeper down in Jersey, who is hidden away in the archives except to snoopers like me. For the religion that Charlie says he side-stepped in his choice of shipbuilding seems to have affected a Cumberland County Leek in a most individual fashion. It is *The Pennsylvania Gazette* of October 28, 1742, which must serve as authority for the following:

About two weeks ago one John Leek, of Cohansie in West-New-Jersey, after twelve Months's Deliberation, made himself an Eunuch (as it is said) for the

80

Kingdom of Heaven's Sake, having made such a construction upon Mat. XIX. 12. He is now under Dr. Johnson's hands and in a fair way of doing well.

The Gospel passage? Look it up yourself.

## 8

## OVER TURTLE CREEK

*". . . Before Decay's effacing fingers*
*Have swept away the lines where beauty lingers."*
LORD BYRON

ONE SULTRY DAY I went across the fields behind the boat works at Lower Bank, because someone had rung my telephone to say a giddy wanderer had defaced the town's oldest tombstone. I wondered who could have been guilty of such a prank, or sacrilege, when few but the Lower Bankers knew the stone was there. The inscription which had been scarcely readable before, I was told, now proclaimed details which up to then had been by no means certain. I wondered, as I hastened away, how it was that I had become a keeper of Mullica propriety, a title which obviously could not be assumed by either absentee folklorist or accepted invader for very long. Actually, when I arrived, there was small cause for alarm. No one had added nasty pictures to the graven skull and lines beneath —although I do agree that the one who illuminated the letters at the head of old Yoos Sooy could have selected a much more suitable medium than aluminum paint. However, gaily emblazoned in wavering silver, the inscription, more than two centuries old, now reads:

Here lyes interr'd
the body of Yoos
Sooy who departed
this life the 28th Sep
tember Anno D$^o$
1737—52 years
81

It would have been nice, I think, if while the unknown illuminator was at it, he had found room for additional facts, disclosing how Captain Yoos Sooy of Amsterdam had come to New Amsterdam in the employ of the Dutch West India Trading Company, and how in 1696 he was a close friend and confidante of Eric Mullica, the Swedish explorer. How appropriate it would have been, too, to make it plain, even in the uncertain silver, that Captain Sooy was the spouse of Sarah Vandehoven, granddaughter of the great Dutch general, Cornelius Vandehoven, whom he had married in New York at the old Dutch church, St. Mark's-in-the-Bouerie. There would have been no room on the Captain's headstone, however, for any of that; and even if there had been, I feel sure that the man with silver paint to spare would have spilled it and spoiled everything before completing the job. It is left to tradition to go on from there, remembering that Captain Sooy was accompanied up the Mullica by Pedro or Peter Cavileer and Samuel Driver, all friends of Eric Palsson Mullica who, although Lower Bank is well equipped with three graveyards, has no stone at all to mark the place of his last sleeping. For a long time, I thought, as I looked down at the silver name of Sooy, Lower Bank's living had been outnumbered by its dead.

There was a movement behind me. I looked up to see a man who appeared to have dressed in a hurry. His mouth was stubble-fringed and belligerent. On his head was a tattery hunting hat, pulled down at the angle usually distinguished by Charlie Leek's cap. "Looking for something?" asked the stranger, giving a lift to his pants, one leg of which had been tucked into a thick woolen sock. I hesitated, wondering, as I have wondered many times since, if this was the artist who had touched up Yoos Sooy's stone. "Interested in history?" the newcomer persisted as if he were issuing a challenge.

"Sort of," I told him.

"Reporter for the papers?" There was a world of contempt in the question.

"I write some," I admitted. "They told me about this tombstone."

"Great old boy, Captain Yozo," said my friend, missing a bug with a splash of saliva. "That marker over there, now, is one of the Cavileers. Lots of them are still here. Good ones are all dead, they say, but I think different. Took to variations of spelling their name,

82

as you'll see if you do much looking around. Sometimes they took a fancy to making it E-A-R at the end. None of 'em I know of ever made it Cavalier the way you'd expect it to be."

"Fellow told me once," I said, "that the Cavileers in the beginning didn't tell anybody their real name. They said they had been cavaliers. People addressed them as 'Mister Cavalier' for a long while as a kind of reproval. They liked that as well as anything else, and so they picked it up, spelling it their own way."

"Who told you *that?*" The words had a guttural snap that was hardly pleasant.

"Hollis Koster," I replied.

"You know Hollis?"

"Sure."

"You're not aiming to write about things at Lower Bank, are you?" inquired the man, quickly supplying the answer. " 'Cause if you are, you're wasting your time, that's certain. All this has been written up—in the papers, in books, too. All put down long ago by a lad named Beck. You're just a little late."

"There's a lot more down here that nobody knows about," I suggested meekly.

My friend said he doubted it. "Ever read Beck's stuff?" he demanded, indicating that a negative would have been fatal.

"Yes," I told him, with marked disinterest. "Yes, I've read it."

"How'd it strike you?"

"Hardly at all," I replied, making as dour a face as I could muster. "It's all right, of course, but nothing extra."

The man was plainly angry. "I'll take you up on that," he declared with another tug at his belt and a better-aimed stream directed into the long grass. Clearly, he would have fought about it. "Beck's stuff is all right. Little lop-sided here and there where the old liars have taken him in—but outside of that, Mister, it's my kind of reading, see? You can't do as good, I'll say that to you right here and now. You can't do half as good no matter who you be! Come to think of it, who the hell are you?"

I told him. He stared, spat, lost his gum, not tobacco, and then burst into uproarious laughter that doubled him up. At last, sitting atop Yoos Sooy's tombstone, his guffaws subsided and we shook hands. That is how I met the man who told the world he was the Mayor of Lower Bank. "In Lower Bank," he said, "they got no mayor and so they don't mind me being *it*. When I get outside and tell them who I am, they want to know where the hell is Lower Bank."

Fred Noyes, the Mayor, went down to Lower Bank to die. "A year, they gave me," he said that first day. "Maybe it won't be a year, they said. Go find a nice quiet place along a little river somewhere, and you'll go off as nice as can be. So my wife and I decided on Lower Bank on the Mullica as a place where you could spend the last year having a pretty good time. You know, that was over ten years ago, and I'm better now than ever I was."

Fred took me up the road to the little brown bungalow he thought would be nice for the funeral. It isn't quite like the other houses in town, obviously isn't old or historic or anything like that. But it's snug in winter and virtually covered over with flowers in summer— Mrs. Noyes had seen to that. The Mayor's wife was the kind of particular housekeeper who kept everything shipshape all the time but made no headway at all with things like Fred's sloppy clothes. "Don't look like the country club set, do we?" birdlike Mrs. Noyes asked me that afternoon. "Well, that's what we were! Always going to something, always entertaining or being entertained. If anybody had told me then that we'd come down to a place like Lower Bank and love every minute of it, I'd have told them they were being very silly. Now —well, we just couldn't go back to that other life again."

Fred Noyes at the land end of a fishing pole trying for perch, or down in Charlie Leek's boatyard talking things over, was far removed from the Fred Noyes who for forty-five years was designer, superintendent, and super-salesman in the textile world, consulted by established companies from Maine to Pennsylvania. Gay-eyed, spry, and completely overcome by a passion for old clothes, the Mayor at seventy-five was one of a handful of outsiders who have gone down to the Mullica to make it their one last river to cross. From 1886 to 1906, he told me, he designed textiles and was one of the highest paid men in the business.

"Of course," he explained, "the most I got was between thirty and forty dollars a week, but money was a lot different then. I was never a money-chaser. As long as we had enough for needs with a spare hundred or two in the bank, I didn't bother." Perhaps, I thought, that was why Fred Noyes had become a part of life along the river with such comparative ease. "I used to work for Hoyle, Harrison & Kaye. Jack Hoyle said to me one day, after I told him I was going to knock off and take a canoe trip up in Maine, that this was no way to live. 'Why don't you stick to your work and we'll give you an interest in the business?' he asked me. I told him I already had an interest in a canoe so I went on the trip. All the members of the firm are dead—they died rich, to be sure. But it's lots better to live poor." And that, perhaps, is what the Mayor did, till just the other day.

The Mayor was born in Melrose, Massachusetts, and so, he told me, he got to know all about New England. "But the Mullica," he explained, "has something even the rivers up in Maine don't have. Can't tell you just what it is—but it's here and it ain't there." A young textile artist, Noyes got his start through association with Abbott Graves and went on to study at the Lowell School of Design in Boston. On graduating, he and three other students went to work in the Sanford Mills at Sanford, Maine. "We had to paint out designs full size in those days," he told me, spilling names which undoubtedly were important to the industry of their era. "We got fifty dollars a month the first year. Board and washing was fifteen dollars a month. I managed to save twenty-five dollars and sent it every month to a bank in Boston. But what the hell, you don't want to hear about me. You want to hear about Lower Bank."

One Sunday we walked as we talked and arrived, somehow, in the graveyard behind the old church down Granny Cramer's road. Sunday was just like any other day there unless there was a funeral. "This is where they were going to put me, I guess," said the Mayor, "when they found out this was where we picked. I was a dead pigeon, they said. A little town like this was supposed to be the cushion for me to fall on. Well, it's a nice enough cushion, but I don't figure on using it just yet. By the way, if you got any bugologist friends, tell them about this graveyard. It's a wonderful place for tiger-beetles."

It was a wonderful place for Mullica-famous names and unusual epitaphs, too. The old church, rebuilt in 1842, goes back to 1780, more than fifty years before Mr. Finley's map, which fails to locate any Lower Bank at all, was made. There are two other old maps, made abroad in 1777 and 1778; but these, I found, fail to show anything in the neighborhood in addition to Leeds', Crips', Pettit's, and Willis's, all tavern stops. Perhaps Lower Bank was on the Bargaintown Circuit, formed in 1828. If that is true, you can have your own good time picking a likely name for an earlier Lower Bank from among the layovers on journeys that must have taxed the zeal and stamina of the most robust traveling preachers: Zion, English's, West's, Absecon, Wrangleboro, Leeds', Simkins', Pine Coaling, Gloucester Furnace, Wescoat's, Pleasant Mills, Green Bank, Glass Works, Dutch Mills, Weymouth, and Mays Landing. Of more than half of them, now, there are only names.

In 1938 the VanSants held a reunion in Port Republic, the Mayor said, when a memorial tablet was unveiled in St. Paul's Church. The Reverend S. Monroe VanSant, descendant of another pioneer of privateering days, presented some reminiscences that regained much of the lost importance of this famous port of entry. "Lots of VanSants are buried here," my friend explained. "The earliest New Jersey Van-Sant, descendant of one of the purchasers of Manhattan, was John, another shipbuilder who was turning out strong and seaworthy craft as quickly as letters of marque could be obtained for them. John's shipyard was at The Forks during wartime, but after the Revolution he continued working at New Gretna, then Bass River. When John retired, he and his wife, Rebecca, went to live with their son, Nicholas, at Wrangleboro, on the other side of the Mullica. They're all buried down in the cemetery on Nacote Creek, Smith's or Blackman's, they call it. Think I was right in the family, wouldn't you?" the Mayor laughed.

I felt that all this was leading somewhere. I soon came to know Fred Noyes well enough to realize that he rarely told a story without a point. Suddenly he told me that it was Nicholas VanSant who had closed up all the taverns in Lower Bank, the seven saloons Charlie Leek had told me about.

The disclosure checked with later facts. Nicholas, having learned his trade in his father's shipyard, later established his own in Wrangleboro, or Port Republic, actually a part of the property of the church where the 1939 reunion was held. Nicholas was more than ship-wright and patriot; he was a local preacher, too, having been or-dained a deacon by Bishop Elijah Hedding in 1831. "Grandfather was called on as a local preacher nearly every Sunday," said the pastor who addressed the dedication ceremonies. "That meant driv-ing many miles to the preaching point, frequently a house or a school. He was a strong advocate of temperance reform—when he moved to Lower Bank six or seven licensed hotels were in full op-eration; just before his death in 1879, when he was over ninety, there was but one in the whole territory. And he had achieved a similar record in Port Republic!"

Later, when I was talking to Donny Smallwood, I wondered what he would have said if he could have faced the Reverend Nicholas VanSant. Nicholas was a pensioner of the War of 1812, Mayor Noyes said, even as we faced his headstone with the epitaph they urged me to see when I called at the parsonage in Port Republic. The in-scription was impressive, saying first that Nicholas was a Methodist seventy-three years, "a local preacher almost sixty years, honest in his dealings, uncompromising with sin, firm and fearless in the ad-vocacy of temperance, earnest and unswerving as a Christian." Equally resounding, I thought, was the claim made for Mercy Davis VanSant, wife of Nicholas, the woman who thought nothing of walking from Pleasant Mills to Port Republic, at the very least fifteen miles each way, just to go to church: "In prayer she devoutly and eloquently talked with God and in the class her expression was given with a positiveness and joyous glow which frequently cul-minated in shouting the praise of God." Perhaps even more significant is the simple speech attributed to one of four preacher sons who said, with his hand on the coffin of old Nicholas, his father: "I would rather have the legacy which my father has left me in his Godly life and Christian example than if he had placed in my hands thousands of silver and gold . . ."

"Now here's a funny one," said the Mayor, still leading the way. "Sounds as if somebody stopped taking a bath." I read the lines on Christiana Taylor's stone, a long homespun poem concluding:

No more, no more on thee I'll gaze,
No more can soothe thy brow or bathe.

"Much too personal for so public a place," I answered. So we moved on among the graves in the camp ground of Lower Bank's best known citizens, pioneers of the Mullica, Cranmers, Mathises, Sooys, Cales, VanZants, and Cavileers.

I wanted more information about the Cavileers, but Mayor Noyes for some reason always put me off. I knew well enough that he went fishing with "Ruby" Cavileer and that some of his tallest tales came from Charlie, who was a member of the little group that stole off in the evening to "chew the fat" in a half-hidden gunner's cabin up toward Turkle Creek. Just the same Fred always changed the subject just when I became most expectant. "Find out for yourself," he said finally. "Or shall we call in some really competent snooper?"

That is why Bill Augustine, the photographer, exercising some power he acquired in those years of commuting from a cabin on the shore of Atsion Lake, organized the first, and quite possibly the last, reunion of the Cavileers. Three brothers were ready, and we picked them up as we drove down to Lower Bank where we met Charlie, who was seventy then, beside the Mullica, beside the weedy shallows where Charlie Weber used to tether his salt hay barge. From appearances it might have been concluded that Charlie and George and Raymond and Sam had been in the habit of seeing each other frequently, that they had gone to church together the day before. Actually years had passed, they told me afterwards, since all four had met together, although the miles between were few and the gasoline famine was not, up to then, too severe.

I began with what I had heard about Eric Mullica, the Swede; Yoos Sooy, the Dutchman; Sam Driver, the English surveyor; and Pedro, or Peter, Cavileer. I wasn't certain about Pedro, I said, and Charlie told me quickly enough that the Cavileers weren't certain either. Not far from Yoos Sooy's headstone, he added, a Cavileer was buried, but that wasn't either Pedro or Peter. As for the story that had got around that the Cavileers were Spanish, that was as might be.

Charlie said he had lived all his life, every day of it, at Lower Bank. Raymond, who was sixty-five that day of the reunion, lived at

Atsion. Sam, who was sixty-one, lived at Atsion, too, and George, eight years younger, came along from a little tavern he and his wife operated beside their blueberry patch farther down the Hammonton Road. Oh, yes, certainly there were other Cavileers. There was Bill, they said, then seventy-three and living in Hammonton, about three miles away. Sarah lived down in Bridgeton and Grover Cleveland, well, he had gone out to Denver and had never come back. Joe had died in Atsion four years before.

"But once," said Charlie, volunteering the first of the facts that were offered without resort to tweezers, "there was lots more than that." He pulled a blackened, evil-smelling pipe from his mouth. "Us Cavileers had Rube and Will and John and Zeke and Jess and Jim and Cale and Benny and Walter," he enumerated them thoughtfully as if picturing all the boys one by one, "right here in Lower Bank. And I can't remember the rest."

Father of the four who met to pool reminiscences was William, a fisherman. Charlie didn't put it that way. Using the vernacular of the Mullica towns, he said, "Daddy went by the water." Husband of Mary, one day he came home and said he was tired of fishing. Next day he became a batch maker in the glass factory up the road.

"But what of Peter Cavileer?" I persisted. "Some people say he was a Spanish grandee."

There was a silence which seemed to say that if I was going to call the earliest Cavileer names, I ought to do it in English. "Some people are wrong," Raymond retorted. "Always heard tell the Cavileers was English from the beginning." Charlie added that it was John Cavileer who now kept Captain Sooy company behind the boat works and that John didn't sound much like Peter. But Charlie now had the itch to go fishing, once the occupation of his progenitor had brought up the subject. "I ketched more perch this spring," he said, "than ever I knowed. And I can remember the time when Walter and Ruby and me took fifty-four hundred pound of perch in one haul out of this here Mullica. That's fishin'," he concluded, coaxing his pipe back into action.

Charlie Cavileer boasted suddenly, as if to compliment some magic of the river, that he had never been sick a day of his life. "Had all the bones of my body broke at one time or another," he admitted.

"Sometimes I doctored and sometimes I didn't. When my ribs got out of joint, I'd push 'em back in again. Guess I never got nothin' except the measles." Apparently measles didn't count as anything serious.

Charlie had been a fisherman far beyond the reaches of the Mullica. "Fished in my prime," he said, "on a trawler, from the Kennebec in Maine all the way down. So did Len Sooy and John McAnney—better look up John McAnney some day 'cause he was in the first life-serving stations, too. Len's dead now. Hope he got all the fishin' he wanted." There was no levity in the remark. It was the fond hope of an old friend.

It was Charlie Cavileer who remembered a day when Bear Creek, across the Mullica, got its name. Opposite Stump Creek and Becky Lane Creek, it was another tributary without distinction until the Cavileers went picking berries and Rod Koster supplied its location on my topographical map. "We were all over there a-picking," said Charlie, "when I suddenly caught on to the fact that the picker on the other side of the bush I was working on wasn't my father but a bear. You know, I didn't yell to the others. That would have spoiled everything. I just went home and got my gun. When I got back, the bear was still there, still picking berries like the rest. I shot him and we named the creek."

Charlie told another story that would indicate that early trade as well as life was more casual. His father, William, went down to Richmond one winter on business, he said. When he got there, he decided to go trapping instead. "The mate on the ship decided to go trapping, too. They were supposed to bring home a load of pig iron but they gave the load to another captain, ship and all. They kept on trapping and sold their pelts in Baltimore, so Daddy used to tell us," Charlie remembered with a grin. "Daddy didn't have much to show for the winter when he got back home and the mate had less—he' drank his all up on the way. As for the skipper who was supposed to bring back the iron, nobody ever heard of him again. Him and the load must have been lost off the Capes."

All four Cavileers said they remembered when fifteen or twenty big sailing ships were daily at anchor off Lower Bank. There were ships, they recalled, named "Hazel Dell" and "Ella Robbins" and

"Joseph L. Mott." Uncle John Cavileer owned one ship, Raymond another. "Pop owned a fleet of sloops, loading and hauling wood to New York." Charlie, who said he had never gone to school because he was big and expected to work from the beginning, chuckled as he said his "bag of bones" once weighed a full hundred and eighty. "That was when I was young," he added. "Never weighed it since. Ate too many fish. Turned me to bones."

The Cavileers, like most Mullica families, can piece together an industrial history all their own, for all the casual living of the river towns. Charlie, the fisherman, is still an outdoors man, a guide for many notables, among whom are Walter E. Edge, New Jersey's governor. Charlie told me once he used to barge salt hay and that he was the last of the bargers, next to Charlie Weber. "Used to work in the fish factory, too," he said, "when Joe Wharton ran the one on Crab Island. There was the 'Alert' and the 'Wharton' and the 'Owl' —God, what smelly boats they were! But they made the owners a pot of money!"

Raymond fished, hired out as a laborer, worked in the bay. Once he engaged in sturgeon fishing off Lewes, Delaware, when Delaware Bay sturgeon was being shipped abroad to come back high-priced and much-publicized Russian caviar. Sam was the sawmill man, for a long time at the old mill on Sandy Ridge; later he turned his hand to glass, venturing as far away as Bridgeton and Williamstown, capitalizing on the experience he had gained in the little glasshouses along the Mullica. George, ever interested in cranberry meadows, has been a section foreman, brakeman, conductor, and hostler, working on railroads and railroad spurs that sometimes picture the world as going backwards—they have been abandoned everywhere. George and Sam and Raymond got together for quite a spell without meaning to when the first World War was over— they took jobs scrapping shells down at the Amatol loading station. After that, from all that I could gather, the reunion that Bill Augustine accomplished was perhaps the first on such a scale, apart from funeral suppers. It will be the last, I think, for Charlie will have fish to catch, George will have blueberries to worry over, and Sam and Raymond will have things to do.

Last time I went by George Cavileer's on the long Bordentown-

91

Hammonton Road, I paused long enough to ask him how the family was. George knew about Sam and Raymond; you can walk to where they live if you like walking that much. But George hadn't seen Charlie since that day they gathered by the river. Lower Bank's quite a distance. Takes best part of an hour to get down there from George's.

9

## CAPTAIN'S HOUSE

*"I've often wished that I had clear,*
*For life, six hundred pounds a year,*
*A handsome house to lodge a friend,*
*A river at my garden's end . . ."*
JONATHAN SWIFT

IT IS HIGH TIME that we were pushing on beyond Lower Bank, for a little while at least, now that Leeks and Cavileers and even gruff Mayor Noyes have been so extraordinarily cordial. But before we pay our first visit to Green Bank, I would suggest a pause at an old Lower Bank house which, it seems to me, might be missed by the Mullica traveler who insists on hurrying by. The house I have in mind is plainly marked on the old Atlas map with the name of Allen, even though it serves best to recall Captain John Carlisle.

The Allen house has quiet lines and simplicity that is almost severe. There is the implication that, here and there through the years, the whims of many relatives have taken their toll as if the ancient farmstead were an old gentleman whose white mane is shaggy because of many inexpert snippings. Before it stands a giant sycamore, a survivor of four that were planted there by Cap'n John himself. Inside is concentrated all the dignity of a town that today's Lower Bank knows precious little about. For there was a time when the Cap'n's way called forth a description in Mrs. Blackman's "Bible" singling him out as "one of the jolly sea captains of the olden days."

92

When Cap'n John was at the house, he could look down across his plantation to enjoy an unobstructed view of the river, wide and sweeping. Now you must take for granted that the Mullica is there, because trees and weeds and bushes have grown up to make an effective screen.

It was chance mention of Cap'n Carlisle that one day brought a letter from Mrs. Franklin Adams Gray of New Gretna, inquiring if I had heard that the Captain's house was still in good order and that her aunt, Mrs. Ellen Scott, was living there. I was informed that the lady was alone but not lonely among a collection of old deeds and other papers bearing the sailorman's round and rolling hand. There were some account books, too, said Mrs. Gray, in which I might be interested. I had already marked the house as one kept "in order" and contriving a welcome, possibly, despite the fact that windows, having lost their little panes at some time or other, would surely welcome them back. Soon, because of Mrs. Gray's kindness, Ellen Scott was making the welcome real.

I had looked up as much as I could find about the Cap'n before I came. There had been a number of Carlisles down the valley, I discovered, but beyond their names and whom they had married, there was little information about them. There was something about one of Cap'n Carlisle's children—there was a boy, Richard, and a girl, Elizabeth—that took my eye almost at once, but I have never been able to elaborate upon it. "Richard Risley Carlisle," it was pointed out, "is Prof. Risley of theatrical fame. He was born and spent the early part of his life in Bass River. It is said that from his earliest youth it was manifest that nature had formed him for a play actor."

I was soon to learn that the Cap'n was a man who followed the fashion of his day, combining ordinary bookkeeping with a diary of homespun happenings. Ellen Scott, instead of tossing out an apparently meaningless book of figures, lists of debts long ago incurred and long since paid, paused in time to discover family history buried among "pitch kittles," seed corn, and good salt hay. But before I came to that, I proved myself something of a listener as Mrs. Scott, white-haired, small, and smiling, regaled me with all the family ghosts, the long line of Allens who had called the house their home. These were Bass River Allens, descendants of Robert who came from Shrewsbury to Little Egg Harbor in 1716, and of Robert's son, Peter, who died deep in the woods in a lonely cabin on one of his hunting expeditions. Joseph, Peter's son, became a justice of the peace in Bass River, married two wives, successively of course, and had two sets of children, five in one set, ten in the other—there were two Williams, two Marys, two Sarahs.

Mrs. Scott informed me that she was one of the two daughters of Charles and Achsah Allen—there had been an Achsah since the first family of Allens—sharing with her sister, Esther Matilda Willits, the heritage of the house built by Cap'n Carlisle in 1821. That was about the time that the Cap'n had begun to piece together a plantation against the day when he would retire from the sea. The Cap'n's wife was an Achsah Allen, too, said Ellen Scott; she was the great granddaughter of the original Robert. So the Carlisle farm was filled out, starting with less than fifteen acres sold to John and Achsah by Robert Horner, and ending with the inclusion of cedar swamps and upland of Isaiah Johnson and Robert Leeds until there was almost a full hundred. Unfortunately, I concluded, the sea was kinder than the land to Cap'n Carlisle, for he died a scant seven years from the day of his retirement.

From the Cap'n the house went to the children, Richard and Elizabeth. Elizabeth and her husband, a physician named Asa Egbert, had no thought of coming to live in Lower Bank and so sold their share to Achsah, who resold it to Benjamin Edwards and his wife, Lucy Ann. Benjamin, I am sure, was a kinsman of the original Edwards down shore, one James, a veteran of Braddock's defeat, who carried a musket ball in his leg from that encounter on through the Revolution. Of James it was said that when he was dying he murmured happily: "I am soon to be with Jesus where I will meet my old friend, General Washington." His daughter asked him if he believed that warriors like Mr. Washington went to heaven. "Oh, yes," James Edwards is quoted as replying, "Mr. Washington is the bright star in the regions of glory."

"But what of this Richard, the Cap'n's son, the one they say was a play actor?" I asked Mrs. Scott.

94

"He was known as Dick at home and Professor Risley when he went on the stage," the lady replied. That was all.

"Sounds sort of like a magician," I suggested, hoping to gain something more. "More" concerned the old house, how the Edwardses transferred title to Sammy Sooy in 1848, and how in 1852 Captain Jesse Bodine Allen took possession. Having gone this far with me, you may as well look over Ellen Scott's shoulder and know the rest—Hannah Weeks, wife of Joseph Allen, became the owner in 1873, giving a deed to her youngest son, Charles. And Charles was Mrs. Scott's father.

Although these transactions sound as smooth as the chronicle itself, painstakingly inscribed in the book of accounts, there were a few complications for all that. Cap'n Carlisle had sold an acre here and there, it seems, before he died, so that Ben Edwards, Isaiah Hall, and Cap'n Gus Johnson took over edges of his farm. Now, because of a mix-up somewhere, Mrs. Scott told me with some annoyance, New Jersey says the property includes six more acres than anybody knew they had. "And of course," said Mrs. Scott sharply, "they tax us accordingly."

It is nothing new, this uncertainty about property lines down the Mullica. Sometimes a line makes a difference, usually it doesn't. Hundreds of people have fared well enough side by side for hundreds of years, without knowing exactly where one farm ended and the next began. Little Egg Harbor is the focal point of an argument that continued for a couple of centuries over the exact line of East and West Jersey, George Keith surveying the first in 1687 and John Lawrence setting up another in 1743. I have examined the Lawrence Journal and Proprietors' pamphlets without gaining any certain idea as to who is right and where the actual line may be. I was going to suggest that perhaps some of the Allen land was left behind in East Jersey at the lower end of the triangle, but I knew that would only confuse the issue even more and was, at best, mere provocation.

The early method of transferring title to a piece of land was accompanied by much ceremony and in the presence of several witnesses. The owner or his agent handed a clod of earth from the land being conveyed to the purchaser and accompanied it with a map or description of the land. This was called "livery of seisin," and the documentary evidence to be preserved was in the form of a deed, or at one time a lease and a release to escape certain technical legal objections. There were no recording laws, and purchasers depended for their security upon the responsibility of the vendor and the warranty of his deed. The title depended mainly on possession. There was no way in which the buyer could know of outstanding title, prior defect, or encumbrance—any of those things that the title men talk so glibly about in these days. Recognized title to New Jersey land originally was vested in the British Crown by conquest, having been taken from the Swedes in West Jersey and the Dutch in East Jersey. Down the Mullica family names would indicate that originally Dutchmen and Swedes faced each other across lines and boundaries and rivers where their descendants gaze upon each other today.

Mrs. Scott opened the ancient ledger. The name of John Carlisle was written at the top of opposite pages, one of debits, the other of credits. A scow had been hired four days at the rate of seventy-five cents a day for a total of three dollars. Twenty-five cents had been paid a man who "fetched up some goods from my vessel." Fifty cents was charged for the use of a "pitch kittle," and the same amount had been given "the cook," probably from Cap'n Carlisle's ship, for a day's work. Thirty-eight pound of corn meal was bought for three cents per pound. Four pound of pork cost forty cents. This, according to the date at the top of the page, was in 1818.

John Townsend brought Captain Carlisle a half bushel of corn from the mill for thirty cents. Joseph Allen sold the Cap'n some hay at fifty cents per ton. Andrew Scott unloaded eight tons of good salt hay at the Cap'n's landing and charged twenty-eight dollars— that was in 1824. In 1825 the price of salt hay was even lower, for Andrew came up the river with twelve tons at three dollars per ton. One entry in the book showed considerable restraint in merely noting the purchase of oyster tongs to replace "those borrowed and never returned."

I saw, runnning a finger down the page, items which serve as an index to industry in days when ships from the West Indies and further away were unloading at Lower Bank's dooryards. I said as much, earnestly. There was much more than that, Mrs. Scott told

harlie Weber, last of the
lt hay men to use a
arge, transported horses
nd other gear to an island
t the mouth of the Mul-
ca.

Bringing hay, horses, and equipment back to shore required skill.

Photograph of the old Allen house of Lower Bank superimposed on a ledger page of John Carlisle, who lived there. Below, the brothers Cavileer—George, Charlie, Raymond, and Sam—were assembled for an impromptu reunion on the Mullica by the author.

me. She pointed to these entries, written in the bold hand of her great grandfather:

July 14, 1832: My wife tuck a rattle-snake that was measured and was six feet long.

Nov. 1, 1832: Joseph Kindler built a chimney in my house at the mill which I paid him two dollars in cash for. Then he repaired my oven for which I paid him fifty cents.

July 23, 1833: Hugh Johnson was drowned and found opposite Clark's Landing. And was buried the 26.

Sept. 23, 1835: Sariah Addams departed this life at one o'clock and was interred at the mill graveyard the 24 at 4 o'clock.

"The mill graveyard," I repeated. "Where was that?"

"That's the cemetery up this road behind the old Methodist church," Mrs. Scott said. "The mill was up there before there was a church, so the graveyard must have been associated with the mill in those days. There's been no mill for years."

Thus the diary proceeded, inscribing notations of life and death, combining funerals with the planting of potatoes, reflecting on hay cutting and disastrous frosts amid thoughts of new arrivals, ships, and crowing newcomers in Lower Bank. Just what the lady did when she "tuck" that snake Mrs. Scott couldn't say, but she felt that life was much better when chimneys could be bought for two dollars. "But even I can remember," she added, "when the only coal we could get down here came in by boat."

As for Bodines in the family, mentioned in the ancient ledger, Ellen Scott said she had traced them back to Jean, born in France and already a Staten Island emigree in 1686. The Wright-Andrews-Allen line goes back, she will inform you proudly, to Thomas Wright of Lexham in Norfolk, England, born in 1422, died in 1529. I said that she had quite a family tree. "And that tree out in the front yard," she replied as if reminded, "was planted by the Captain himself when everybody in Lower Bank was building or sailing ships."

Somehow, you will discover, the ghosts of shipbuilders and seafaring men return to the old Allen house as Mrs. Scott talks—and gracious ghosts they are, content to have the house in which they lived in hands so capable now. Sensing them all, with the old ledger yet in my hands, I told Mrs. Scott I would like to live on the Mullica, perhaps in Lower Bank. But good houses, I added, stay in the families of the river people a long while.

"You could buy this," she told me suddenly.

I was unable to answer very quickly. It was above all a sincere compliment. She was smiling, uncertainly now, wondering if I might ask about a price. "What," I inquired, "about all the ghosts? Cap'n John would want no stranger here, doing all sorts of silly things with his house, that's certain. And what of all the Allens—and those Edwardses and Sooys?"

Was there relief, now, in her voice? Was she glad that I had not responded as quixotically as her unexpected show of sentiment would have allowed? "They like you, too," she told me, smiling bravely.

"Perhaps," I told her, probably changing her opinion of writers forever more, "I could afford something like what Cap'n Carlisle paid for the chimney and that good salt hay. And that," I laughed, "would not be enough."

"No," she agreed. "No, it wouldn't." Then both of us laughed together.

I had meant to ask, while at the Allen house, why there was no mention of whiskey or brandy or any intoxicant in Captain Carlisle's account book. I had wanted to ask the question before, after perusing a number of journals kept by Mullica people. At first I was afraid I might end the talk I was enjoying with Mrs. Scott—you never know where the freedom of a man of the sea and the abstinence of his kinsmen begin and end, sometimes. So I took the matter up with my friend, Nat Ewan, Nathaniel R. Ewan to be exact. We were soon talking about the rise and fall of "Jersey Lightning"; and applejack, highly impregnated with raw volatile matter and placed in well made, heart-oak barrels to accumulate its proverbial aroma and mulish kick, may be emblematic of the whole subject.

"Liquor wasn't unusual enough to account for in most cases," said Nat, who somehow manages to run two historical societies, one in Burlington and the other in Camden County. "In the early days applejack was made without any thought of governmental regulation or taxable value. Why, it was commonly sold in every grocery store as an ordinary article of family trade. For many decades, you know, 'two bits a quart' was standard around here."

"My word," I said. "When did they start making something of it?"

"Not until the Civil War—and even then the rate of ninety cents per proof gallon continued until about 1894. That," said Nat, "was when a new rate of $1.10 went into effect. Of course taxes have gone up until levies of four and six dollars a gallon are imposed. So under such excessive taxes the consumption of apple whiskey has decreased and a serious reversal of the onetime popularity of this potent beverage is before us."

I looked at Nat, knowing that he was a total abstinence man, as was his father, who operated a once-celebrated distillery at Ewanville, before him. Once, in the old days long before his ascendancy to historical erudition, he had been Aunt Hattie Ford's vinegar salesman, knowing the Mullica towns as I could never see them for myself.

"Probably the Captain," Mr. Ewan told me, "went down to the store or direct to the distillery—unless, of course, he was an ardent temperance man before he left off sailing his ship. It is difficult for this generation to visualize the great number of distilleries which once flourished in fruit-growing counties like Hunterdon, Burlington, Monmouth, Gloucester, and even Salem. For that matter, the Captain may have had equipment for making what he needed on his own plantation."

I said that we must not suppose any such thing. However, he pointed out, most of the early farms made their own "likker" every year, putting it away in five-gallon demijohns or ten- and fifteen-gallon "kags" as an annual contribution to convivial family atmosphere. In Burlington County, he went on, there were no less than twenty-five registered stills at the time of the Civil War. "That," he said, "is when moonshiners began operating in the county."

"The comparatively short seasonable use of the stills," he told me later on, "was confined to fall operation, when the necessary fermentation of fresh-pressed apple juice would proceed under favorable temperature conditions. Equipment was extremely crude, you know.

99

Outside the professionally made copper 'head' and boiler with a lead or copper 'worm,' the whiskey was processed entirely by home-made paraphernalia."

With few exceptions the water supply for cooling and condensing the alcoholic vapors originated in a flowing spring, and the law of gravitation necessitated the placing of distilling apparatus below the spring level. In consequence these operations were invariably housed in temporary shacks whose dirt floors were in a perpetual state of muddy confusion, highly unsanitary. Only the more pretentious distilleries boasted power equipment whereby water was pumped into overhead storage tanks that allowed the work to proceed in the shelter of conventional aboveground buildings.

I listened to Nat Ewan expound his subject at length, knowing that I was hearing all about it from an eyewitness, one who had seen "Jersey Lightning" in its earliest years and stages. "The process of distilling began, of course," he explained, "with the natural fermentation of fresh cider, generally stored in hogsheads holding about two hundred gallons each. These containers were filled to the three-quarter mark so as to allow proper surface exposure of the liquid to oxidation from the air. The apples from which the cider was pressed were never selected, as I think you know, for any special degree of soundess or cleanliness."

"I once saw them making cider on an old straw press," I told him. "Half-rotted apples were all over the place. And worms—"

"Worms," said Nat, smiling, "possibly added to the flavor. Not being an expert on the tastiness of certain items of the insect kingdom, I cannot say. But is a worm an insect—oh, well, it doesn't matter. The point is that the fermentation was a chemical conversion of the sugar content into alcohol—and here the skill of the old-time distillers was put to a test in determining when maximum development was complete and this unsavory liquid was ready for 'stilling.' Unless the process was properly handled, you know, further exposure to the air would convert the weak alcohol into acetic acid or commercial vinegar. The fermented cider was transferred to a copper boiler and from the heat of a large wood fire thoroughly boiled. The odoriferous vapor or steam was confined within the many coils of a 'worm'—this one was metal!—over which a stream of cold water constantly flowed.

This condensed or liquified the volatile liquor, and the embryo 'Jersey Lightning' emerged in the raw."

While the process is not now quite so simplified, the making of whiskey has not changed materially in centuries. I said as much. "How much cider makes how much 'Jersey Lightning'?" I asked.

"Ten gallons of apple whiskey should come from about one hundred gallons of cider," Mr. Ewan said. "Although you must remember that alcoholic strength varied in relation to the kind and condition of the apples as well as the skill in processing. This strength was soon accurately and officially tested by government men on their periodic visits of inspection; and figures were marked on the whiskey barrels, showing the actual or wine gallon and the taxable or proof gallons, determined by adding the excess degree of alcohol over the standard one hundred degree or 'proof' whiskey."

"Too much for me," I told him. "How about other drinks? I've seen rum mentioned in old wills accounting for funeral expenses but that's about all."

Oh, there was grape brandy and raisin brandy and apricot brandy and blackberry cordial and as many more, Mr. Ewan assured me. He had heard, he said, that some of them were pretty good—but it was all hearsay. "Making the winter's supply of liquors was commonplace, you see," he concluded his lesson. "You wouldn't expect a man to write down how much he had or how much he had made, would you? Probably they handed a demijohn or two across back fences along the Mullica in trade for some smoked herring or a sack of potatoes just like anything else. Oh, by the way," he said suddenly, "are you a teetotaler?"

"Well, you might say," I fumbled my reply. The question was like, "Do you swear?" or "Do you believe in voting a straight Republican ticket?" "I would say," I told him truthfully, "that I mostly am." I put from my mind the day when I had sped the soldier on his way at Lower Bank with a warming toast, and the time down at Buckshutem when I had gulped some weird concoction for the sake of a legend that would have been spoiled otherwise.

"Then," said Mr. Ewan, the sworn disciple of abstinence, "I have something for you." He unveiled a small bottle of peach brandy, dated 1891 and marked one hundred and sixteen proof. "I found

101

some of my father's making that I didn't know I had until the other day," he said. "I have been dividing it up among some friends—who would understand." He removed the cork and sniffed. Then he held it under my nose. "Wonderful, isn't it?" he asked me.

I agreed that it was. It still is. I have not progressed beyond an occasional sniff from that day till this. Some day there will be an occasion when I shall remember Nathaniel R. Ewan and Cap'n John Carlisle with mingled emotions and a healthy swallow. If I survive, I will in all probability go quickly down the Mullica and buy a house before I have recovered.

## 10

## MEADOW MUSK

*"Happy the man, whose wish and care*
*A few paternal acres bound,*
*Content to breath his native air*
*In his own ground . . ."*
ALEXANDER POPE

THERE CAN BE LITTLE DOUBT that Charlie Weber is the last of the Down Jersey hay bargemen, surviving anachronism of an industry that goes back to a time when men along the bays made salt from sea water. Moreover, there is small reason to suppose that when Charlie's barge, loaded down to the water with eleven tons of salt hay, two horses, and mowing machinery, comes up the Mullica River for the last time anybody will ever tow it down again. For Charlie's sons, Ed and Charlie, Jr., who help him most with the meadow harvest, have said that they are not interested in running the business that has been their father's for well over half a century.

"I just bring up my clammin' garvey from the bay because Pop doesn't have many ways to make a dollar any more," Charlie, Jr., told me once as he manipulated the bow rudder of his craft, using ropes as if they were reins guiding a horse. "I like clammin' better, much better."

"Besides," Ed had pointed out before that, "we got to look after Pop. I come up from workin' at Joe Ware's sawmill." Joe is Ed's brother-in-law. "We go out on the medders with Pop because he won't stop. Doctor told him he had to cut it out. But he keeps goin', even when he's sick. Says when he stops, he'll die."

Charlie Weber, who has worked hard all his life, works on as hard as he can now, for like most Down Jersey people—and most rural folk, everywhere, I guess—his work is his life, just as he says. Charlie Weber is seventy-five, heavy, and not as sure-footed as he was. But he's strong enough to bring back stories of his prodigious endurance up and down the rivers of Little Egg Harbor. Take one look at him and you will know at once why the mosquito armies that lay siege to the salt marshes gave him up long ago as a prospect. Like old Clarence Woodmansee, the circuit-rider of Barnegat who laughed at my battle with the pests, he rolls them off his sun-armored arms as if he were rolling down his sleeves.

First sight of Charlie's barge coming up the river makes you wonder what it is. Chances are you would never see it going down empty, for that voyage down the Mullica around the bend and up the Wading River is made very early in the morning, long before the first streak of dawn. At first you would see only what would appear to be a heaped-up, squarish stack of hay, surrounded by water and moving steadily nearer. Not until much later would you make out the garvey and hear the drone of the six-cylinder Dodge engine Charlie, Jr., installed years ago.

I saw it like that on a golden afternoon in September. To me the Mullica was no stranger, even then, although it will never cease to be a river of surprises. I had been up its cedar waters as far as they were now navigable, musing, with Joe Robinson, to the whine of Joe's outboard motor, on the river's forgotten fame, Verrazano's landfall of 1524, Indians making shell money and stringing clams and oysters, Sir Henry Clinton's bad-tempered expedition to smoke out the raiders at Chestnut Neck. Returning to Lower Bank to return Charlie Leek's rowboat, we saw that stack of hay downstream.

"What on earth is that?" I remember asking.

103

"That? Oh, that's Charlie Weber," Joe told me. "Or rather, that's his hay barge."

Charlie Leek already had informed Joe that Charlie Weber was the last Mullica hay barger doing the job that way. Came further exclamations of amazement as the garvey went by, followed by the curious craft that seemed to have a tiny shack at one end, almost concealed by hay except for the crooked stovepipe that twisted out skyward. A man in the garvey, after responding to a friendly hail, hauled high a horn on which he sounded a raucous blast, like that of a big man with a bad cold. That was a signal to suggest to Charlie Leek that he call it a day and hurry out to man the windlass that lifts the bridge.

"All this," I said, "has been spoken of as if it were over long ago, something buried deep in the past." I had seen a few similar barges, of course, carrying possibly a ton or two in their "hay day" but rotting now at the water's edge at Clark's Landing. I had heard that a few salt-hay men still ferried across from there to Hog Island in the middle of the Mullica, where mosquito control projects had as yet prescribed no newfangled ditches. But this was something else and seeing was believing. Charlie Weber and his barge were real.

Charles W. Weber is not the man to be surprised by questions, by interest in his business or the curious way in which he conducts it. He is a little amused, perhaps, when you tell him he works too hard for what he gets or when you repeat what Horatio (Tater) Cramer confided in an off-moment, that "Charlie Weber did the work of three men every day until a little while ago." Salt hay of the quality Charlie grows and mows and rakes and loads, and then unloads and loads all over again for stowing away in his barns, was bringing fourteen dollars a ton that day I talked to him the first time. "Maybe it'll bring more in the spring," was all he said.

At seventy-five Charlie was heavy-set, sun-weathered, usually with several days of beard bristling from a chin stained by the trickle of tobacco juice. "This farm," he said proudly, "is all mine. Nobody owns a nail in anything that's mine. This end of the house is the oldest—the rest was added on. This end's a hundred and fifty years old at least, oldest on the whole damn road." As old, I was sure, as that old tavern which had stood opposite until it burned in a strange fire that nobody would talk about for a long while.

The Weber farm is nondescript, sturdy but unpainted as most of the Down Jersey farms are. There is one big barn and a number of smaller structures, some of them cabins and stables off barges Charlie has used through the years he has worked with the Mullica. Weeds do their best to choke the fields, the corn out back and potatoes on the land that is now Weber property across from the farmhouse. "But usually it's this way," says Charlie, when you let him read your mind. "I don't want rain because of the hay and I want it bad because of the corn and 'taters."

The farm was there when Charlie's father, a grain merchant from Germany, "impoverished by the wars," came to this country with Charlie's mother and two little children. They settled at Weekstown, about four miles from Lower Bank on the other side of the river. "My father wanted this farm when he came to this country," Charlie remembers, "but they were asking too much money. I got it instead." When Charlie told me that it was with a finality and pride of accomplishment which indicated the fulfillment of a sacred trust.

Otto, Lucy, and Emily Weber lived, then, "at the old place the other side of Weekstown." Otto, the oldest, was a baby, Charlie told me, when he and his sister, Mary, came all the way from Berlin in a sailing ship. "The others were born down here—Emily, Lucy, Charles—that's me!—Edward, and Harry." He remembered them, as most Mullica families are remembered, in the order of their appearance in the world. "Five of us are still living. Eddie's in the oyster business. Otto'll be eighty this fall—he thinks he's going to live to be a hundred!"

When Charlie told me that all the Webers had gone to school in Weekstown, I asked him what he knew of the old schoolhouse in Egg Harbor, the only one of which there is any appreciable record. But he could add little to the tale that when Weekstown was Weeksville, the schoolmaster was old Samuel Radcliffe who, during the Revolution, had served with the British army. Samuel, when the war was over, settled down to teaching boys and girls their arithmetic, how to shoot, and what to believe about General Washington, who would have been defeated if Mr. Radcliffe had chosen to throw in his full weight. The famous old man, who went to school with a fowling piece, walking from a log cabin he had built himself, disappeared one day when, like my old Latin *magister*, he told his class he had decided to move on. For a while, it is said, he was a farmer in Ohio; after that he became a fur trader further west. To this old tradition Charlie Weber listened respectfully and then suggested a glass of wine.

Wine, of course, has saturated the Weekstown side of the Mullica for many a year. In a letter from the West New Jersey Society of London to its agent, Jeremiah Basse, under the appropriate date of December 24, 1692, it is disclosed that the Society was concerning itself with providing casks which would be shipped to the Jerseys empty if there was prospect of their returning full "of rome and brandy." The Webers undoubtedly arrived in America when the plan to develop Egg Harbor from both ends, the railroad and the river, was still in favor. Excursions from New York were still being run by steamer; and a commercial city, no mere capital of wine making, was the dream of promoters who proclaimed direct waterways to both New York and Philadelphia. Not until later did rails win out over water, so that even General George B. McClellan, campaigning as a candidate for New Jersey's governor in 1877, made sport of the mythical anchorage Egg Harbor City still implies as real.

When the first train rolled down the track of the Camden & Atlantic Railroad in July, 1854, a number of prominent Germans from Philadelphia were among the guests of the directors. Two physicians, William and Henry Schmoele, with P. M. Wolsiffer and others, began, upon their return from the journey through pine forests and cedar swamps, to talk up a great German settlement in the barrens. These were great days for the Know-Nothing movement, and Germans all over the country, yearning for homes among their countrymen, began to write letters to members of their families in the homeland. Out of the old Gloucester Furnace property was formed the Gloucester Land and Town Association; and although the success of the furnace, established in 1813, was by 1855 almost legendary, a settlement which had once produced twenty-five tons of iron a week—stoves, lampposts and castings made to order—was easy to revive on paper. The projectors bought thirty-three thousand acres from Stephen Colwell and eight thousand more from William Ford, and by 1856 they were telling the world of a new refuge from want and oppression. It is certain that the Webers were among "the sturdy Germans" who came "from East and West, North and South, to find but a wilderness."

It was not a wilderness for long. The Gloucester Town and Land Association had its new paradise laid out in streets, from the railroad to the river, and began at once the erection of impressive buildings. Work was in abundance for the newcomers, and according to the recollections of pioneers not long dead it seemed that industrious Germans would realize great riches in a few years. "In addition to the scheme of building a city," wrote Alfred M. Heston in his *Annals*, "a farming district was planned and the association had its agents in every city in the Union. From out of this wilderness a village soon arose and new settlers came fast. Within five years Egg Harbor City had bright prospects—it was then the largest town in Atlantic County." However, in the rise of the present active municipality, the dream of extending the city limits to the Mullica never came true. Today, far down the road that leads to the river, there are clearings, little vineyards, and the charred stakes of building lots—these give evidence of a colony that intended, long ago, to produce a harbor to match its name.

I accepted Charlie Weber's heady wine. We sipped an unspoken toast to the wine makers of Egg Harbor who persisted, even as piano factories and knife-handle plants gave up, in making their trade the one that has kept the railroad-preferring city world famous.

Charlie Weber started going after salt hay fifty-five years ago. By the second season, he told me, he was harvesting five hundred tons. Then I knew why Charlie persisted in using a barge and old-fashioned wagons. "It was about then," he said, "that automobiles came and ruined everything for always. I can remember when the first farm truck appeared. That was 'way up in Vincentown. I went up to see it. Up to then there were all kinds of barges in the hay business, row-barges, barges with sails, barges that had to be towed like mine. But all the barges have gone now, all except mine, and

107

most of the hay business has gone with them as far as the medders down here are concerned. Nowadays help, if you can get it, costs as much as the hay. All people know about work is ten or fifteen dollars a day."

A practical man, Charlie figures it is much cheaper working with horses. "Lots of farmers talk big about tractors," he once pointed out, chuckling half to himself. "But tractors don't make 'em no manure. I used to have six or eight horses working on the hay all the time. Six was the average, maybe. Two teams a-runnin', two on the mowing machine. Now there's only Prince and Kate."

Two fine horses they are, too. They know the routine as well as Charlie. But they don't remember the days when he loaded his hay on his own sailing ship, when he used row-barges to get down to the "medders" that can't be reached, even now, on foot, tires, or tractor wheels. Of all the meadow land Charlie Weber once mowed for hay, only fifty or sixty acres are left. "There's plenty of good salt hay if only I could get it," he complains mildly. "But they tell me I'm sick, and I got to do all my own mowing and raking and loading on the barge—with the boys helping out.

"I used to mow hundreds of acres. Once on the medders there'd be places with a mile long to mow. It took a good pair of horses to make a round in forty-five minutes. I used to cut from the mouth of the river to Goose Creek Cove—they wasn't always my own medders, you know. I rented some of them. They used to be bid off at auction sales. Many of the renters never paid. But I paid—and sometimes I got them all."

When it is time to go down the Mullica, Charlie Weber's barge is made ready. At one end the stable, two stalls under cover, is cleaned out and given fresh hay. At the other end a cabin, in which there are two bunks, a coal stove, a rude table with boxes for chairs, is equipped and provisioned—for Charlie and the horses stay down on the marshes even when the boys go home. Wagons, like skeletons on wheels, the mower, and the rake go down to the meadows early in the year; pitchforks and all the rest can be carried on the deck of the barge where the hay goes on the voyages up the river.

Sometimes the hay is unloaded below the Lower Bank bridge, just off-shore from the Adams family graveyard, so that Charlie Leek doesn't have to lift the span any more than is necessary. When the barge is anchored for the night and the horses pull the hay home and stay there, operations end at the mouth of Becky Lane Creek, above the bridge. There was a shipyard there once, and deeper water. Now there are reeds and mud and shallows, and the hay barge and all that's on board are safe enough. The mingled smell of hay and horses lingers when the barge is in the cove.

When the barge is anchored above the Lower Bank bridge, one of the boys paddles out from shore in a duckboat, sometimes using an old plank for an oar. The anchors are hauled up and the garvey, coaxed into action, tows the barge to a point below the span where it is usually easier to take the horses aboard. There Prince and Kate, driven down the dusty road past the old church and its cemetery, are unhitched from a light wagon by Charlie himself. The barge is edged to the muddy bottom, stable-end first. The stable door becomes a gangplank, lowered by a block and fall. Two rude rails are attached, and without much urging the horses trot inside. The trip down the river is begun.

The horses are led on the meadows in a similar way with little lost motion. Then they are dressed up for their work by Charlie while the boys swing the barge around so that its deck, unless the tide is high, is even with the black mucky bank of the Mullica's tributary, Wading River. Sacking, with holes for their eyes and ears, goes over the heads of Prince and Kate so that they look like property of the Ku Klux Klan. Then the horses don aprons of burlap and special shoes.

"If they don't have them," Charlie told me one day I went down to the meadows with him, "they'd sink down to their ears out here unless you watched 'em every minute. I've known times when all we could see was their ears, just about, sticking out from some tricky salt pond. You got to watch them all the way."

The sacking and burlap is obviously for protection from flies and mosquitoes. But folk down Jersey are touchy on the subject of mosquitoes, even after all these years. Even as singing hordes swarm from reeds and marsh grass, they will say, as Charlie did: "Mosquitoes bothering you? There's no mosquitoes—except sometimes at night. At night there's some." More than some, surely, when Charlie

109

is keeping a lonely vigil there on the meadows, a home-made door of netting clamped against the opening, a feeble glow of a lantern lighting his cabin.

Prince and Kate are harnessed to the mower, the rake, or the wagon of slats and pegs as the case may be, and the next chapter of the operation begins. Salt hay mowed and raked this Saturday mostly will be loaded on the barge the Saturday after. In the loading process Charlie and the boys ride to the haycocks and the boys walk back. Wearing boots, removed when the hay is transferred from the wagon to the barge, they hike a good twenty miles a day, even when they take short cuts closed to the horses.

Time was, according to Charlie, Jr., when the barge could carry fourteen or fifteen tons of hay home. "But that," he told me, "was when she was new." The barge, built in Port Republic's last ship-building days, was "better than forty feet long and good for plenty of work yet."

Not a moment of precious daylight is lost; but it is usually after the noon hour when Charlie suggests first that the horses, blowing hard from the routine, should be fed, and then that it must be time for dinner. A sandwich or two, a tomato, a swig of water from one of several jugs hidden in a hay pile—and perhaps a chaw of tobacco and a drag at a black and battered pipe—bring a pause in the day's occupation for the Webers, father and sons. Then it's back to work, for the barge must be loaded and tooting for the Lower Bank bridge at sundown.

This taking of salt hay from the marshes along the Mullica and the Bass and the Wading Rivers that wander down to the sea is an old, old story. Hay was hauled by boat as long ago as 1679, according to available written accounts, for it was then that Jasper Dunkers, looking for Henry Jacobs Falkinburg who as often was Hendrik Jacobs and Jacob Hendricks because the Dutch and Swedes often overlooked surnames, wrote this into his Journal:

Before arriving at the village we stopped at the house of one Jacob Hendricks, from Holstein, living on this side, but he was not at home. We therefore rode on in search of lodgings for it had been dark all of an hour or more, but proceeding a little farther, we met this Jacob Hendricks in a canoe with hay. . . .

Of course, this was written of travel along the Delaware and not the Mullica River. The village mentioned by Mr. Dunkers was Burlington, and I wish I knew more definitely where the Falkinburg house of those days, "made according to the Swedish mode," was. The dwelling was "as they usually built their houses here, which are blockhouses, being nothing else than entire trees, split through the middle or squared out of the rough and placed in the form of a square upon each other, as high as they wish to have the house, thus made without a naile or spike." Falkinburg did not yield that little fort until later in life when, with a new wife from Swedesboro, he went down to Little Egg Harbor. The point here is that salt hay and black grass were transported by boat, even in those days.

The Wading River, beside which Charlie Weber has mowed and barged his hay in later years, empties into the Mullica below Swan Bay. It is the second river in size in the whole Mullica Valley. Rated third is the Bass, which once they called the Rock because the first settlers who built homes on its banks found its waters filled with rock fish, or, if you prefer, bass. Principal creek in the neighborhood is the Tuckerton, or as the Indians named it, the Pohatcong, although the changing scene and ownership of passing decades have made it Andrews' Mill Creek, Jacob Andrews' Creek, and even Shourds' Mill Creek. With Osborn's Creek that flows through the marshes into Little Egg Harbor Bay, Belangee's Creek that recalls old Evi Belangee who had a fulling mill at its head, and Job's Creek of Job Mathis's time, the flatlands along the winding Mullica have known salt hay and salt hay men for generations. To them Charlie Weber and his backwoods barge are but understudies in a change of cast and properties.

Salt hay was cut and dried and stored away from earliest times in the Jersies. Grown without control or care, it has ever resisted frost and still shows no sign of winter kill. During dry summers growth is profuse, and year after year roots of the grass supply and hold humus, enriching soil which would otherwise revert to barren sand. Salt marsh hay lands in New Jersey today run to almost three hundred thousand acres.

What's salt hay good for? The answer, it seems to me, is always

111

surprising. Long-stemmed *spartina patens* is ever in demand by makers of silverware, glass, clay, pottery, and bananas, for packing. The long-stemmed variety goes to cattle men and contractors for feed, mulching, and road construction. Black grass, called *juncus gerardi,* is an in-between, neither salt nor upland hay, and always finds a market for fodder.

Salt hay goes in quantity, by truck and boat, to the makers of iron pipes using the old pit-cast method: Wound around the spindles, hay and mud permit easy extraction of the cores. Salt hay from New Jersey, a utility in peace and war, goes usually by bales ranging in weight from one hundred and six to one hundred and fifty-six pounds, to feed mules in Western Pennsylvania, to help nurserymen in New England, to aid shippers in New York, and to complete the routine of pipe manufacturers everywhere. Once salt hay was made into a kind of newsprint, used for a time by a Philadelphia daily whose publisher established his own production center, but the process was later abandoned.

"Ain't concerned much with what they do with my hay," Charlie Weber told me, as I discoursed briefly with forced erudition. "I used to even haul it, once. Hauled a lot of it all the way to towns up and down the White Horse Pike when they were putting down the concrete for people who ride automobiles to the seashore. But I don't even bale it now. I cut it, rake it, and barge it home. Them that wants it usually know where it is and come down and get it here between Green Bank and Lower Bank."

And so, late in the afternoon, Charlie Weber's hay comes around the bend, just as it did that afternoon I saw it for the first time. The horses are unloaded where the light wagon was left, and Charlie drives up the road, the world ever a place that is far away. "You Webers have done enough work today for a whole battalion," I said to Charlie, Jr., and Ed, one day after the barge had been towed upstream and anchored. They looked at each other, laughing at me. They knew their father. "Why, Pop's gone home for the other wagon," Ed told me. "Says he's going to get two loads off'n the barge before he quits."

That is the way it will be for Charlie Weber, who has worked hard all his life, who works as hard as ever now to spite the doctor. That is

112

the way it will be until the last of the salt hay bargemen Down Jersey brings his barge and his horses up the Mullica River for the last time. After that, the past, which stands out of the present like a sore thumb, will be engulfed. Another anachronism of the valley will disappear.

## 11

## GREEN BANK

*"And, when the stream*
*Which overflowed the soul was passed away,*
*A consciousness remained that it had left,*
*Deposited upon the silent shore*
*Of memory, images and precious thoughts*
*That shall not die, and cannot be destroyed."*
WILLIAM WORDSWORTH

AND NOW WE HAVE COME TO GREEN BANK, the Upper Bank which was closer to Lower Bank for those to whom the Mullica was the accepted road. By the river the way between is little more than a mile. By road the shortest distance is almost three, even when you turn at Charlie Weber's farm and go on by the old church and Captain Carlisle's. Although the diarist, Laura Larrabee McConaghy, has called the villages intertwined, each has its own affairs and keeps for the most part strictly to them.

An ample illustration, surely, is the notion at Lower Bank that Sam Driver, the surveyor from England who was Eric Mullica's friend, lies somewhere in an unknown grave. Actually Samuel lies buried in the oldest grave at Green Bank, outside the lovely little church beyond the oldest house, originally Mr. Driver's own. Tradition says that Sam established the burial plot, directing his interment there before he died in 1748 when he was seventy-five. The land for a church, however, was the gift of Nicholas Sooy, probably

113

the brother of Jemima, whose death in 1782 is recorded on the second oldest stone. The Green Bank Road along the river ends at the church and churchyard, which is symbolical. Beyond, the bluffs give way to woods and lowlands.

Mrs. McConaghy, who set out to jot down notes about Sooys, Millers, Birdsalls, Johnsons, Weeks, Wobbars, Crowleys, Maxwells, VanSants, Clarks, and other families who from earliest times, through generation after generation, lived and died in Green Bank, has said that the south unit of Zeke Forman's house, just up from the church, was built by Sam Driver himself. Later the house went to the second Nicholas Sooy, then to Ephraim, grandson of Nicholas. It was Ephraim Cline Sooy, Jr., they say, who improved the burial plot and church and farmhouse; and it is Ephraim's granddaughter, Elizabeth Sooy Forman, who maintains it today. Mrs. Forman persuaded her husband, if he needed persuasion, to make what had been their summer retreat their permanent home several years ago, deserting Atlantic City for this refuge on the river.

In the oldest room of the spacious and dignified old mansion, facing the Mullica for more than two centuries, there is a portrait, in its proper place over the hearth, of Lucy Ann Haywood Sooy. Lucy died young, at twenty-six; her husband had expired two years before, "leaving," as has been said, "her little family to be cared for by her dear ones." Ephraim, who was but a baby when his parents died, felt their lingering presence throughout his life, I'm sure, adding a sunken garden outside the old house in their memory, and listening for their voices as he sat in a wide chair, fashioned from an oaken stump and looking out upon the water. This was Mr. Ephraim's Chair, covered over with the ivy he had planted, long years after his death until in 1932 it was smashed apart by an unknown vandal.

Ephraim Sooy sat there, quietly, on many days in the last year of his life. He wanted to die in Green Bank and to be buried with the dozens of descendants of old Yoos Sooy who long ago took over the majority of graves in the churchyard next door. But he died in Kansas and was buried there instead. On his last visit to Green Bank in 1926 he was observed pacing up and down the high bank of the river of his forefathers; next morning he rose very early, went to the churchyard where the parents he never knew were interred, and

114

then sat in the rustic chair. That was in the autumn. By the early summer of the following year he was dead and far away.

Across the sandy road, adjoining the tract that New Jersey has converted into a State park, is "the old storehouse" mentioned in the last will and testament of Nicholas Sooy II. Looking much like an old boathouse now, it was bequeathed importantly then as part of the great Sooy estate to William, son of Nicholas, along with the loading wharf which was once the scene of commercial activity and which, now, is recalled imaginatively in a series of jagged river pilings. The store remained in William's possession and under his management until he decided that there was a better site down at the corner beside the new bridge. Billy Sooy's store is still in operation at the corner where, with Aunt Hattie Ford presiding, it became the hub of much of Green Bank's living. Linger there long enough and the whole world of the Mullica will come in.

What, because of comparative size, was called "the little cottage" for many years, may have been the lodge of the keeper of the estate. It was acquired by the New Jersey Department of Conservation and Development in 1931 and, remodeled, became the headquarters of the manager of the Green Bank State Forest, Clifford Terry, and his wife, who directs a station of the Burlington County Library there. Cliff Terry, who presides over the nurture of three million of the state's charges, trees, likes to talk most about the reforestation of the New Jersey plains.

Tree planting in Green Bank goes back to Sam Driver. Since then the Sooys have added their share, showing a preference for walnuts along the river road, where the bank mounts higher and higher toward the old Manor House. But there was nothing on so large a scale until Cliff Terry came along to set up the state's all-year-round business. At the tender age of three, New Jersey trees go journeying, as many as four hundred thousand leaving seedling days in Green Bank behind in a single year. It is something to see the long lines of lattice-covered beds, with three thousand baby white pines in a single bed. The state forest, Cliff Terry will usually point out, sells to individuals who have at least ten acres in which to plant them. That, he says, eliminates the criticism that would come if the nursery otherwise competed with private enterprise. White pine

115

transplants, three years old, were selling at seven dollars a thousand last time I was there; pitch pine seedlings, two years old, were being distributed at four dollars for the same number. Norway spruces, shortleaf pines, and loblollies also grow up under the doctor's care in Green Bank.

Many members of the Mullica's best-known families have found work at the nursery from time to time. One of the Sooys, Raymond, was weeding in the plantation's three hundred and seventy covered and uncovered beds one afternoon when I stopped by. Another worker was Arthur Holloway, whose people go back to the papermaking days of Pleasant Mills up at The Forks. Still another was Leon Koster, who lives in Nicholas Sooy's pre-Revolutionary house at Herman, the dwelling that was greatly enlarged to become a hotel when glass was being made virtually at its side door.

Another old house at Green Bank is the William Sooy homestead. William was the second son of Nicholas II, mentioned by name in his father's will of 1850 when family possessions were being distributed among five sons, Samuel, William, Josephus, Ephraim, and Nicholas III. William had three children, Watson, Joel, and Annie, a family that made room for the children of his younger brother, Lydia and Ephraim, Jr. William was a successful merchant, according to the records, which add, "a vast landed estate was his." When the little church needed rebuilding, it was William who took charge of operations in 1871, according to a letter in the possession of Will Johnson, the miller. When William Sooy died, Watson took over the house, at which point Laura McConaghy adds a curious note in her commentaries: "Had information been more accurate about William, and somewhat more generous of this estimable man, a fuller narrative might have been given of a citizen of Green Bank who, it may be said, was one of the chief factors in the community's life." I have asked questions here and there as to what the lady could have meant, and the answers have been for the most part evasive. Signs plainly marked "No Trespassing" have been posted, and I have been forced to conclusions which may be wrong. Billy Sooy, I gather, was more than a local politico, more than one of the men of Green Bank with a substantial house facing the river; in deeper water than the Mullica afforded, he was involved with

116

an associate in public office and chose to accept exposure as the penalty for lack of awareness.

As a merchant Billy began his career as a business man in the old storehouse up the church road. There it was the ships from New York and Philadelphia used to tie up at the wharf, the "Eureka" under Captain Charles Loveland of Tuckerton being among best-recalled visitors. That was where, too, the stages up from Tuckerton used to make their first stop, changing horses because the sand of the winding trail had tired them out. Sebastian Crowley, tavern keeper of Green Bank and father of Mrs. J. C. Clark, Mrs. Thomas Sooy, and Jesse Crowley, all natives of the village, owned the stage line for a long time and naturally delighted in playing host to whatever travelers came his way. How long Billy operated at the old stand, as they say, is uncertain and matters little anyway; with his removal to "Four Corners," down by the bridge, his home became a center of old-time jollity.

Young people were usually there in the evening. There were songs and instrumental music every night. There was what Mrs. Mc-Conaghy has described as "other wholesome fun, rehearsals, exhibitions, and parties." From Watson Sooy's ownership Billy's house went to the late Jesse Ford, whose widow, Aunt Hattie, died last fall. Aunt Hattie was a schoolteacher at Harrisville, which had made munitions for George Washington and which later made paper from black grass. Now, in a clearing marked by crippled apple trees, a few forgotten lilac bushes, and the ruins of the factory there is nothing but the name.

The diarist calls the Watson Sooy house at the corner, opposite the store, one "of mid-American design" with a hall running from front to back and with large, airy, high-ceiling rooms on either side. Watson had few equals as a lover of the river and his home town unless it was his father. To that statement is added the declaration that "both Watson and his wife sang," as if to indicate their warbling among the benefactions. Mrs. Sooy donated the furnishings of the pulpit of the little church, consisting of four walnut chairs with cane seats, a communion table with a marble slab, and other appointments. Mrs. Kate Sooy added a pulpit Bible, and Mrs. Emma Voss of Egg Harbor City presented a pulpit desk. To all this the

117

Watson Sooys added a sizable endowment. To which, I must report, I added a dollar, all the money I happened to have with me, one day when Mrs. Weaver, in the act of cleaning the church for Sunday services, told me of the carpet fund in a delightful but pointed way.

Watson Sooy at length sold the house to Mr. and Mrs. Birdsall Crowley, and the Sooys moved to Billy's old house. "Bert," as they call him up and down the Mullica, is the son of Captain James and Augusta Wobbar Crowley, so you can see that though titles change infrequently, they disclose greater transition than the river family names.

On another of the corners, at the turn, is the old tavern which, when I visited the store, was vacant. Once in a while one of the Koster boys would paint up the sign which announced that it was for sale but, from what Aunt Hattie told me, it was a kind of empty gesture which had gone on through ten or fifteen years. The days of Sebastian Crowley's fourhorse stage that paused at Green Bank and then pushed on to Blue Anchor were soon to pass, with only Jesse Crowley, Sebastian's son, to remember them with all the color of one who had been born at the inn. Later the tavern ended its functions as a hotel, and the Morris Fords went there to live, succeeded by the Jesse Fords. Jesse, who was a member of the township's board of education, died in 1934.

As for Aunt Hattie's store, it was built by Billy Sooy, who added a new wharf that was called Upper Dock even as the landing at the old establishment down the river was given contrast as Lower Dock. Billy, the first proprietor, changed his sign once, to read Sooy & Clark, and the third alteration, superimposing the name of Jesse Ford, stayed that way for a long while. Mr. Ford was the postmaster, setting up a cage and some boxes in a corner among the assorted groceries; his widow presided over the village mail after his death. They have told me of a time when the Odd Fellows Lodge met in the room over the old store, but the members long ago started meeting over in Egg Harbor City.

The first warden of the portions of the old Sooy estate taken over by the state for a reservation was William Woolston, a contemporary of days when great ships were playing up and down the Mullica, coming up with many impressive imports on the tide, going down with cargoes of charcoal, lime, wood, riven lumber, and glass. The eldest son of Peter and Jane Messick Woolston, William was born in Green Bank in 1859, a friend of Captain Joseph Bush Maxwell, who sailed out the Mullica for more than fifty years and then climaxed his career as master of a Navy transport in World War I.

Captain Woolston was a product of what might have been distinguished as Sailorman's Row, the houses facing the river above and below the bridge built following passage of an Act of 1855. Captain Woolston's father was born in Green Bank, the descendant of pioneers who were there in the early 1700's; when he went to sea, as most Green Bankers did, one port of call was Chincoteague, Virginia, and that was where he met the captain's mother. Young William helped his father locate and prepare ship's timbers, long before he himself sailed to sea, first on the schooner "Hazel Dell," whose captain was Watson Cale of Lower Bank. In 1886 William married Janey Broom, the daughter of William and Catherine Broom, whose Green Bank house once stood where I was soon to meet the Birdsalls. The Woolstons were away for a time at Herman, and later in Mount Holly; but they returned to Green Bank with two young sons, where William engaged in the employ of Will Johnson, who was then operating both a grist and a sawmill, "in the interest," as they say it on the scene, "of the community."

Later Captain Woolston was associated with William and Watson Sooy and then, when Eph Sooy purchased the old Nicholas Sooy farm, he became custodian for Eph, who was in Kansas City, spending much of his time, they say, counting the days until he could come home. When Ephraim Sooy died in the West, the Captain continued his services for Zeke Forman. He became the first warden of the Green Bank State Forest when the bulk of the farm was sold to New Jersey and only the farmhouse and a few adjoining acres were excepted from the sale. They speak in Green Bank of the Captain's "conversion" at nineteen by the powerful preachment of the Reverend J. Swain Garrison; later he was to become caretaker of the church, a trustee, counsellor, and collector of funds, and finally, a local preacher. Captain Woolston died in 1939 at "the old homestead," the second oldest house in town.

The bridge at Green Bank was the first built over the navigable Mullica, and in its first days of operation such traffic as there was for Weekstown and Sailor Boy, now Elwood, came in-shore from Tuckerton, by way of Bass River, New Gretna, and Bridgeport, now Wading River. Its establishment was by a curious agreement which called upon "the inhabitants of Green Bank and Weeksville" to "enter into bond to construct the causeway connecting bridge with the mainland. The bridge," it was further provided, "must have a swing of at least thirty-five feet for convenient passage of all vessels navigating the river." The last of the stages saw no reason to alter their routes, continuing their rolling way along the river to Crowleytown, Batsto, and Pleasant Mills.

This, then, is the surface picture of Green Bank, with a little of the background filled in. This is an enlargement of the outline supplied by the pages of notes put together, from time to time, by Laura McConaghy. Mrs. McConaghy was working against time and failing health in full knowledge of more than "sloping bluff banks forever green in the tangle of jasmine, honeysuckle, roses, wild grapes, holly, cedar, and laurel." There was more, she was clearly aware, than kinships or even companionships, more than old houses proud of their lineage of ownership, more beyond anything that could be revealed in cautious answers to the casually put questions of the outsider. It is obvious that our diarist would not have been content for long to report merely that Richard Bull, recalled in the names of Bulltown and Bull's Creek, was surveyor for the Province of West Jersey in 1705 and Eric Mullica's old friend, or to know that Will Johnson's father was the grandson of "the great land baron and colonizer, Nicholas, the grandson of Captain Yoos Sooy." Her notebooks cry out that she wanted to know more, over and above what the epitaphs in the little churchyard serve to index. And then, in the midst of it, she herself became an inscription on a stone.

Let us go on from there, talking with such river notables as "Chink" Simpkins, the village Lazarus; Joe Ware, whose life has been spent in sawing his way across New Jersey; "Snapper" Cobb, for whom big days are marked by turtles and herring in the tide; Jack and Sammy Ford, Bill Birdsall, Jack Updike, Will Johnson, and the others. Some, with half the world, the world that concerns them or that they care

120

anything about, came to Aunt Hattie's store, where, due to atmosphere made up of groceries and candy, seed packets and cigars, iceless soft drinks, dust and disorder, as well as the kindly ministrations of Aunt Hattie in my behalf, I was accepted as harmless. Others were where they said they would be found and where, I discovered, word had been passed along that this was no mere business of prying and spying. But it was, as Mrs. McConaghy must have found, a contradictory procedure, on the one hand a race against time and dying, and on the other a circumspect procedure and wary vigil. Against the antiquity and color and neighborliness that is Sam Driver's ageless refuge of Green Bank, called "Ta-Ko-Kan" by the Indians there before him, let us go to meet them.

## 12

## ONE CORPSE TO ANOTHER

*"I kept him for his humor's sake,*
*For he would oft beguile*
*My heart of thoughts that made it ache*
*And force me to a smile."*
WILLIAM COWPER

FROM THE BEGINNING CHINK SIMPKINS AND I were on, or in, common ground. This may have been because, when I first went to see him, considerations pleasantly ghoulish had converged on Lieutenant-Colonel Patrick Ferguson and what, when the rest had gone, might be found in that hillside grave on King's Mountain. On the other hand it well may have been traced to the crazily illogical system of thinking that could link Mrs. Littles and her habit of plunging bare legs into ice water with the quaint custom of old debtor's widows parading abroad in their underwear, of which we must hear more anon. Most likely, ours was a peculiar kinship beyond all that, bred of the recurrent memory that once, long ago, for the purposes of the play, I myself had been to all appearances a corpse, whereas Chink, they told me, had been dead two years.

I have always looked upon the late Mr. Ferguson as a lad worthy of further study. When Gus Schneider told me something of his exploits at Chestnut Neck, I was constrained to follow the fortunes of that boastful soldier of the Crown further. I can now blame this lapse on Gus's declaration that he fell because, like a certain Nazi notable, he liked "dressing up like a target." But Fergusiana is lacking beyond the facts provided by the late William S. Stryker, Adjutant General of New Jersey, in a pamphlet now hard to find, that after taking a ball in his right arm at Brandywine and a bayonet through his left at McPherson's Plantation, the owner of a scarlet shirt was easy shooting. As for Mrs. Littles, there have been times when I have become a little skeptical. Asking myself if there might not be some explanation for that matutinal icy bath other than a personally devised and practiced cure for a cold, I came upon the following, dated 1734:

> A widow, of Philadelphia, was married in her shift, without any other apparel upon her, from a supposition prevalent then, that such a procedure would secure her husband in the law, from being sued for any debts of his predecessor. . . .

Peter Kalm, the Swedish traveler, has added details which would indicate that the "supposition" was still more prevalent in 1748, for he confirms this fact as common when the woman's husband died in debt. "He tells of a woman going from her former home," John Watson has recorded, "to the house of her intended husband, in her shift only; and he meets her by the way and clothes her, before witnesses, saying, 'he has lent them.'" Which must have been, surely, something of a diverting ceremony in which, even in the earliest of days, husbands-to-be saw more of their betrothed beforehand than was commonly supposed. I am convinced that this forgotten pageantry of pre-Revolutionary days had nothing to do with what Mrs. Littles practiced in Mullica moderation unless, of course, there was practical proof that two cold feet are better, any day, than a cold in the head. As for Chink Simpkins, he was clammy cold all over and virtually committed to the cold, cold ground.

122

I saw Chink first in the warming sun of a false spring afternoon when, as he swung his ax violently down into the remnants of a pig-pen set aside for firewood, there was nothing at all to show that he had truly died. But just a few nights before, at Aunt Hattie's Green Bank store, they had said without smiling that Chink—William H. Simpkins—had been given up one night as "sure enough dead." He was the intended and fully expected victim of pneumonia, they added, the doctor having gone home, very late, telling members of the family and friends who filled the never painted and lamplit house that he had done everything he could. There was no hope at all. Somebody was to call the doctor in the morning to fill out the papers. Beyond that, the funeral arrangements.

No sooner had the doctor departed than Chink began to talk. His people, who had discussed, already, as he told me later, the date for the services and the best suit in which he was to be laid out, told him to lie still. Shuddering sympathetically with every pitiful gasp as the old man struggled for breath, they reminded him dutifully of what the doctor had said. "To hell with the doctor!" Chink managed to wheeze at them—and kept on talking.

Chink then made motions that they were to sit him up; and when they wouldn't, he struggled to a crouch without their help, babbling words, words, words, and then, in between, telling them profanely that he knew well enough what he was doing. Obviously he did, even on the later confirmation of the doctor who had expected a summons with papers for the undertaker. By talking, the physician said, Chink had maintained a continuity of consciousness which, clearly beyond his own strength, defeated the Dark Angel to demand and get more than an even four score years. There may have been something in that. Medicine, so prone to dismiss as impotent anything beyond its own assumed omniscience, usually turns up with plausible alibis for predictions that have gone awry.

It has never occurred to me that Chink took all the credit for his resurrection. Something, he has always implied, told him what to do —"something inside" that he didn't understand much about. Even churchgoing, where Chink is concerned, has been indulged more for the pranks that could be played than for any spiritual benefit. There was one occasion when he told an evangelist visiting Green Bank that he himself was surely saved but that the man beside him was doomed to perdition. Actually, the man beside him was his best friend. "Something inside" was the key, I think, for God himself must have directed the drama enacted that night in the house with all its tiny rooms aglow, as is sometimes the custom along the river when the weary traveler is to be lighted on his lonesome way. However great the desire of Chink Sinkins (they don't say Simpkins along the Mullica) may have been for the fun with which life supplied him, the Almighty's reluctance to yield the fun of watching his antics on earth must have been greater.

Chink was eighty when he came back from the dead. When I saw him first he was eighty-two. "Eighty years alive and two dead," he summed it up for me. "Sort of uneven. Ain't sure which is best yet, bein' dead or alive. You ought to try being dead some time."

I told him I had. It was long ago in a play we had written, a mystery play demanding not only a corpse, but a corpse willing to lie in state in a coffin borrowed from an obliging undertaker. When the magnum opus was being written, we mistakenly expected that there would be considerable competition for the title role. When rehearsals were arranged, no one could be found who wanted to go to such extremes. Things might happen to anybody who went that far, making believe. In the end I had to take the part myself, and the many lines I had to learn were proof that I had no such original intention. All this I explained to Chink on the spur of the moment at our very first meeting. It was the reminiscence of one corpse to another. Bill Augustine, who had come down to take pictures, moved off because, he said afterwards, he thought I was making it up. Sud Norcross puttered around the barn to see if Chink had any pigs left. As for Chink Simpkins, he listened more intently than I had expected.

"You got along further than I did," he said. "They got you in a box. Right up to the funeral. I stopped 'em before they got that far. But then," he added, with a kind of apologetic triumph, "*I* was almost a corpse for real. You was only play-acting. . . ."

Chink is a wispy little man with a grizzled face that is always different when he has it shaved. He has sinewy though skimpy arms that have contributed, I soon found out, whole chapters to the an-

124

The house of "Chink" Simp- kins still stands on an old road that cuts around Green Bank.

Bill Birdsall, son of Haze (Hazleton), treasured the plan of old Harrisville, where Aunt Hattie Ford once taught school.

Some graves behind the Green Bank Methodist Church are green all year because of oblong blankets of pulverized green glass.

The late Fred Noyes, "Mayor" of Lower Bank, showed us the 1737 tombstone of Yoos (Joos) Sooy, early settler and a friend of Eric Mullica.

nals of the Mullica Valley, cutting wood, cording it, and loading it aboard the schooners that used to sail the little rivers. "Used to cut wood for fifty cents a cord," he told me, "and that was mighty good money. You could get lots of what you needed for fifty cents. Fifty cents for cutting timber was more'n fifty cents for working in Gus Foss's bogs up to Bulltown 'cause there you got paid in shinplasters and you had to buy what you wanted in Gus's cranberry store."

Little of that will make sense to the newcomer in Mullica towns. What Chink was trying to tell me was that fifty cents paid for chopping wood was coin of the realm, while fifty cents paid for work in the cranberry bogs was strictly local currency, odd bills of paper money honored only at the store owned and operated by the boss of that particular plantation. Shinplasters were stowed away in the boots and socks of bog workmen and were spent, in a more modern form, in the operation of Uncle Will Kemble's Circular Equation. Just then I considered the whole business highly impractical, even socialistic, with all the horrific implications I once attached to the term. Chink had other views.

"It was nice having both kinds of money," he said. "With one kind you could get suthin' more to drink. When you spent all that, there was always shinplasters left for the things you really had to get."

But Mr. Simpkins, as the countryside knows, has odd ideas of money. "I have plenty of money," he has often declared at the store, quickly adding, "but the trouble is, it's all small money."

Chink told me one day that he had worked all the bogs and swamps along the river so long, gathering huckleberries and cranberries in all the lowlands, that he knew every inch of land for miles around, from Rabbit Island and Cold Spring down to Nigger Creek. He put it in a way that made me realize, more and more, that getting to know the land has been a part of the reward for all these people. And when the land palled a little Chink went on the water for a spell. "You see," he said, turning in the sun so that the wen on his forehead became an egglike lump that was never sensibly explained, "I'm sort of left over. I was part of them days when timber was goin' out of here, out of Green Bank and Crowleytown and further up, keepin' New York warm of a winter. I sort of got chucked up

125

and stuck here like driftwood on the bank. When the wood was all cut, I took to berries. Why, guess I was takin' huckleberries and cranberries into Egg Harbor for nigh on to twenty years. . . ."

Although Chink always managed to have a little farm, what he raised best very often was what Charlie Weber called "rooster corn." Not only did Charlie call it that, but Chink quoted him pleasureably whenever he spoke of his scraggly crops. "I've farmed since I was big enough," he said one night, "and my plow horses have been as good as the best." "How good was that?" I wanted to know. The answer was always unsatisfactory. "Could ha' been better. Could ha' been worse."

Much of the peculiar kind of rustic humor attributed to Chink Simpkins has had to do with horses. One story has traveled up and down the Mullica more than any horse Chink ever owned has crossed a field. A dressy stranger once stopped his car at the edge of a patch where Mr. Simpkins was plowing one day. "Say there," said the newcomer, who by way of preparation had passed the time of day, "tell me this: Why does your horse keep his head down all the time he's plowing?" It was a new variation of the old saw: Why does a chicken cross the road. If the stranger expected confusion, he got no reward. Chink paused, thoughtfully scratching his bristling chin. "That's easy," he drawled at length. "Most folks want to know that, as a matter of fact. You'd never guess why, mister. The poor old cuss lost something while we was plowin' this here field last year, and I just can't keep him from lookin' for it whenever we get out here!" Clucking, Chink shook the lines and away they went, the horse's head as low as ever.

Chink tells that story all over again at the store whenever conversation lags. To it he often adds the recollection of another horse that kicked him, so that for a while he was lame. "Me, not the horse," he will say. Neighbors told him to get rid of the varmint. Mr. Simpkins demurred. Horses were hard enough to come by, he said, no matter what their disposition. "Crazy fool probably meant no harm anyway. I was just a-pattin' him, and he figgered maybe it would be nice to pat me back." On still another occasion Chink was chided for striking out a decidedly crooked furrow. "Well," he is remembered to have answered, frowning, "a blacksnake would break his

126

back crawlin' down it, that's true. But what's the difference? You can plant more in a crooked row!"

They have always quoted Chink as author of the argument that the outside row of a field of corn or beans or potatoes, doomed to struggle in the sand, never amounts to much. "Next year," Chink ever makes known his decision, "I'm going to plow up all the outside rows and quit." It always takes longer, he told me once without a smile, "to plant that there last row, no matter what's your crop." So, he confided, he had devised a system: To plant the last row first.

"Had a neighbor once," he told me with a grin, "whose horse up and died and he wondered why. I told him why. They was tryin' to teach the old *skellington* how to live without eatin', and just about the time they had learnt him how, he ups and fools 'em." Concerning the sudden death of one of his own horses, Chink finishes his story sadly. "Funny," he says, "he never done that before."

There was a time when Chink lived on the old Captain Watson Cale place. Before that, he said, he had worked aboard the Captain's boat. However, they sold the old house over his head and "they got to chasin' me around so much," he told me, "that I actually up and bought myself a place down here at Green Bank—and this is it. Ain't no showplace. Ain't as near the river as I'd like—although some nights maybe I'd fall in if I was nearer up. Been here ever since I bought, more'n fifty years, I guess, although I ain't never learned to tell time. Done my share of farming, timber-gettin', and all that's decent but next to nothin'—with some good fishing, too. Herring's in the river now; that's what made me think of that. Cobby," (Alanson Cobb, the Snapper Man, whom I was soon to meet) "he says him and me has caught us thousands of herring in this old river. Some we sold, some we give away, some we used for compost."

There, in its own green nutshell, is the spirit of life along the Mullica: "Some we sold, some we give away, some we used for compost." Chink, who was there when the river was full of ships, going out with charcoal and coming in with "fancy goods" and anthracite from New York, boiled it down. When there were no more herring to be caught, he "coaled" with Abe Brooms and Steelman Mick.

When he felt in need of the tonic of the sea, he signed up with Captain Cale, Captain Hen Taylor, and later still with Captain Bill Stafford Leek. "Good work and comfortable living," I said one day, half aloud, as if I might be quoting somebody. "Comfortable living," Chink repeated, as if he liked the feel of the words on his tongue. "Yes, that's it, boy. Outside of here, they don't know what it is. They got a idea it's wrong to work for just enough."

One night after that I asked him how long it took those ships loaded with cordwood to get to New York. "We'd sail down the river at sundown," he said, "and with a good wind, we'd be ready to unload in New York next morning."

"Didn't you ever get off in New York?" I inquired.

"No," said Chink.

"Why?"

"Gettin' off'n a boat from down here don't do you no good. Makes you want to be *somebody*. Me, I didn't want to be nobody and I was always it. You stay aboard and you don't get notions. All hands from down here felt the same way. They was scared, maybe. Scared of bringin' home idears and just *things*. Things would mess everything up. We had what was wanted down here. We still got it, I guess."

Chink once shipped as cook aboard a ship whose master was Captain Otto Wobbar, perhaps the very craft whose ribs stick out of the river mud at low tide off the old landing back of the Koster house that was Nicholas Sooy's. Often, in those days, when Mullica ships were loading in the afternoon, the boys would too frequently imbibe the contents of bottles concealed in boots or the long grass along the river. Then, no matter how they felt, they would have to be up and out next morning to catch up with their work. Sometimes they fooled the skipper. On other occasions—

"We wasn't foolin' anybody," Chink said. "But we wasn't havin' nobody check up on us, neither, makin' sure we was on the job, what time we quit. People nowadays don't trust their own shadows, even. Guess you know that, don't you? We was supposed to get the boats loaded. If we got too drunk to finish up before sundown, we was up before it was light next morning. We got the work done just as the skippers knew we would. They didn't come around to snoop."

"Did I ever tell you about Colored Jim Weeks? He used to coal up at the old Sullivan place." To "coal" in New Jersey is to make charcoal. "You wouldn't ha' known about Jim. Or John Sullivan, either. John was a schoolteacher down here, allus went around in a overcoat, carrying an umberelle even when it was hot as blazes. We used to ask John what the hell a umberelle was for on a pretty day. He told us any damn fool could carry a umberelle in the rain, but it tuck a wise man to carry one when the sun was a-shining. Big man, John. Seat of his pants most allus dusted the ground, the way he walked. Walked plenty, too, when he was teachin' at Port Republic and over that way. Bag Bottom, we always called him.

"There was old Doc Curry, too. Anybody tell you about him? Pity, you never knowed him. *He* could ha' told you the stories. Used to be a doctor in the wars of '61. Came down afterwards to tell us what we was sick of and how to ketch more. He used to go clumpin' along the road beside the river in his gum boots. Carried medicines in a knapsack he kept from the war. He'd walk to anywhere and have a go at curin' anything for a dollar. Went all the way to Jenkins Neck 'cause a woman was sick there, one time. When he came away—he always made a hell of a lot of noise—he kep' sayin' in time with the steps he tuck, 'Don't know whether she'll live or die! Don't know whether she'll live or die!' Then he saw me in the road ahead of him and he bellered out like a bull, 'And don't give a damn!' "

There was one old doctor, Chink told me, who treated patients along the Mullica when he was far from sober. After nocturnal visits which meant homeward journeys punctuated by frequent clashes with trees and questionable dignity recovered from among roadside brambles, the physician would hurry out to the home of the patient very early next morning. "Joe," he would shout, if that happened to be the name of the husband for whose wife he had prescribed. "Bring out that medicine I left here last night!" Whereupon the concoction would be procured and exhibited. "Well," the old medico would usually exclaim, in relief, without admitting either mistake or confirmation of the earlier diagnosis, "didn't do her no harm yet, did it? All right, then. What you bellyachin' about?" No one, unless it was the patient, had bellyached.

129

There is little about Chink that resembles a Chinaman. His nose is flattened out a little and his eyes are sometimes squinty. I sought explanation for the nickname, time and again, in vain. "Guinea George called me that first, I think," he said one afternoon, coming as close to an explanation as he ever did. "Called me Uncle Chink from the start. Everybody just sort of tuck it up." Whoever Guinea George was, Chink got even with him one night.

"One time Billy Wilson dressed up fancy in woman's clothes," he said. "We was all standin' around when Billy came by, jerkin' out his hips like a sure-enough woman. 'There's a nice woman for you,' one of us says to Guinea George. 'Why don't you go for her?' So George did, followin' Billy into the woods. A few minutes later there was a hell of a racket, and Billy comes runnin' out, holding up his skirts and goin' like a rabbit. When he was gone, George comes out, too. 'What happened?' we asked him. What do you think the ornery old cuss said? 'She was a angel,' he says. 'She must ha' been a angel 'cause she flowed away!' "

There was a time when a ship loaded with cognac was tied up at the Kosters' landing at Herman. Benny Ford was the skipper, and a generous man was he. Captain Benny, it seems, poured out good-sized drinks for all hands. Soon all hands were lying in the weeds, oblivious to the passage of the day, the mosquitoes, or the fact that the incoming tide partially submerged a lot of them. Chink did not disclose where he had been after the careless hospitality had accomplished its results. "That cognac was sure strong," he told me, proving he was there. "But it wasn't nothin' compared to what we got a holt of when the Good Ship Frances was wrecked. Why, once you let that stuff trickle down, it was full two minutes before you got your breath. The liquor off the Frances was strychnine, that's what it was." He pronounced it "strike-nine" for the better climax of the anecdote. "It was only strike-nine," he said, "but it was powerful enough to kill ten."

There is a ceremonial expression of gratitude down the Mullica, accompanying every drink of Jersey Lightning. "Godamighty," you are supposed to say. "Him's hard but him's good!"

Chink Simpkins, the corpse of Green Bank, has breathed new life into these companion corpses of his, Captain Cale, Bag Bottom

130

Sullivan, Old Doc Curry, Guinea George, and all the others from whom I have chosen these for the record. Now and then he digs up another, with a lack of awareness of any other world that would imply that Green Bankers know of nowhere else, have never heard that another war has been going on. One evening at the store I said as much. Chink himself denied the assumption. "No," he said, "they know. It's just that the war is a long ways off. It don't belong here."

Chink's boy, Andrew, was in the army; I mentally kicked myself for not remembering. A letter had come from Rodney Koster, off in camp, one day. "I am really sorry that Andrew Simpkins has to go," Rod told me. "I wish I had been home long enough to explain to the draft board. His going will leave old Chink practically alone—and, of course, you couldn't get Chink to go anywhere else with a block and tackle. . . ."

Some time later a stranger came along the road to Chink Simpkins' little house. Leaning on the palings of the fence out front, Chink was watching some ants holding a parade. "How do I get to Green Bank?" asked the stranger, strange because he was in uniform. "You won't want to go there," Chink answered, without looking up. "But how do I go? Can't you tell me?" demanded the soldier. "Depends on who you are," replied the old man, looking up for the first time. The newcomer was Andrew Simpkins, home on leave, afterward killed in France. "Well," said Chink, opening the gate, "seeing that it's *you* . . ."

## 13

## PILLAR OF SOCIETY

*"But slighted as it is, and by the great*
*Abandoned, and, which still more I regret,*
*Infected with the manners and the modes*
*It knew not once, the country wins me still."*
WILLIAM COWPER

I HAVE DECIDED that Hazleton Birdsall is my favorite Mullica carpenter. I would like to tell him some time that while I respect all men who can build things with saws and hammers and pieces of wood, I salute him as a prince among craftsmen. It annoys me that I have no means of telling Hazleton Birdsall anything, not for a while, anyway. Haze, you see, was laid away long years ago in a country coffin, probably made of cherry wood, possibly like the coffins Haze measured and fashioned for his neighbors. For all I know, Hazleton Birdsall may be sleeping in one of his own boxes—he always had a few on hand.

I was sure I had heard of Haze before; but it wasn't until I had met Bill Birdsall, Haze's boy who was seventy-seven at the time, that I remembered where. Constant Ford named him when he recalled the man who took over the day school on Sundays and taught the Bible. Constant didn't say much about Haze's being a carpenter during the week—or any of the other things. But carpenter is mainly what he was, all his life, like his father before him. Aaron passed the trade on to Haze, and Haze passed it on to Bill, down at Green Bank. When I think of Haze now, I think of Bill, roly-poly, with very black and beetling brows in contrast to sparse gray hair—and Haze probably wasn't like that at all. And now that Bill is gone, too, perhaps he'll pass on the things I wanted to say to Haze.

Laugh, if you want to, at Jersey houses of pine and cedar, weatherblack and never painted, still standing where the forest fires have left them. And smile, if you have a mind to, in your conclusion that

132

your house, your comforts, your luxuries in a more grown-up town, are preferable and even superior. But don't run away with the idea that these houses were jerry-built, that they're not snug and warm on a winter's night or that the men who built them, called house carpenters, were anything less than the boasting experts of today. Jersey houses stand as sturdily now as ever they did. That is why Hazleton Birdsall is my favorite—one reason with which to begin, at least. Haze built those houses.

Until a while ago, if you disbelieved, you could have gone down to Bill's. Bill Birdsall, who carpentered all his life, would have told you. Bill's father, Haze, was both carpenter and shipwright. Grandfather Aaron taught Haze the business and Haze taught Bill, in days when building houses along the Mullica was a fine art to be passed on down the line like a family crest or a love of horseradish or a watch wound with a key. Houses built by Haze are scattered, but a lot of them are on the Bull Tract at Bulltown, put up when Haze was pretty busy running the sawmill as well as running the wheelwright and blacksmith shop. Bill built that little house of his, too, according to the family tradition, even though he had to tear down what remained of the house next door to do it. There he lived, when I talked with him, beside the river generations of Birdsalls loved. Mrs. Birdsall, daughter of a sea captain from up Nova Scotia way, knows that devotion as she lives on, now, just across the river road.

In summer Mrs. Birdsall goes back to the old cottage where there's a portrait in oils on the wall. It's a picture of Mrs. B.'s father. You can see it from the road along the river when you pass at night; and Mrs. Birdsall, who was Mary Curry of Hortonville, King's County, Nova Scotia, sometimes sits beneath it. Mary Birdsall used to read to Bill there, for Bill's eyes were ailing toward the last. Sometimes the portrait seems almost as big as the house. That, perhaps, was what attracted a wayfarer, somewhat elegant, but nonetheless of the bargaining race, late one night. Mrs. Birdsall told me about it one day I was down, loaning a book or two about the St. Lawrence and the Gaspé. "He asked me if I wanted to sell my father," she said. "It was just a picture of him after all, he told me. A picture was only a picture, but he liked this one particularly—who it was didn't make any difference. He could overlook that, he said; it would look well over his own fireplace which, of course, was bigger. But I wanted Father to stay on with us—and so he stayed."

Bill Birdsall looked back through all the days of his own "carpenterin'"—he had lived for a while in Northfield—to the years when Sam Crowley owned nearly everything in Bulltown. One night I was talking to a Sunday School class; and afterward a man came forward to tell me, as if the revelation made us blood brothers, that this same Haze Birdsall built the house he used to spend the summer in, down near Atlantic City. Sam Crowley was proprietor of a dozen cedar swamps; he sold lumber, did a lot of coalin', and one day, damming off Bull Creek, he built a sawmill at one end of the pond and a glass factory at the other. Then he worked with Haze Birdsall in the "raising" of a big house, fit for the biggest man in the valley. Sam was big because he had a lot of money and was in the way of making a lot more in cordwood, glass, cedar poles, siding, and all the rest. But Hazleton Birdsall was bigger, maybe, because when affairs of life gave him rest, affairs of death and the hereafter found him work, sometimes in the middle of the night.

Uncle Bill told me how it was. "Father might be up on the roof, putting on shingles or fitting a crossbeam, when there'd come a shout and he'd climb down. Nobody wanted lumber or a job of work done or anything like that: They'd be bringing the news, you see, that somebody was dead. If anybody died, they'd have to let Father know; he had the only hearse down this way. But that wasn't the only reason. He had the 'icebox' up in the barn, too. You couldn't keep corpses the way you can now, you know, with embalming and all. You had to put them in a kind of special 'icebox'—little bigger than a coffin, it was, but about the same shape. Like boxes they keep bass fiddles in, maybe. Dad first had to go home and get the 'icebox' down and then dust it out. After that, somebody'd go to where some of last winter's ice was stored away. If the last winter was mild, there wasn't no ice and the funeral just had to be right away. And when the weather was warm—well, they just had to be quick about the funeral even so."

This "icebox," like another public utility Bill Birdsall called "the cooling board," was a community affair, like an ambulance or

134

crutches handed out by the nursing society. This board was also kept in Bill Birdsall's roomy barn, ready for business. "Father always kept a supply of cherry boards stacked up," Bill told me. "Never could tell when he'd have to use 'em in a hurry; he just naturally expected to make the coffins. Folks'd just come down the road and tell Daddy somebody was dead and, man or woman, he'd know what to do. Those boards was milled out of the big wild cherry trees we used to have around here, and Father'd stack 'em up beside the patterns he had for coffins of all different sizes."

In Hazleton Birdsall's routine, building houses for the living had to wait upon the more urgent building of houses for the dead. Haze whispered the news and nobody questioned his walking off the job. Somebody got the ice, maybe, while Haze himself went to the house of the bereaved to measure the corpse. And at this point I've always found myself wondering about Haze and his ministrations and what used to be quaintly called the scruples of sex.

Tom Watson, in the 1830's, was making strange sounds in his *Annals* over the "transfer of midwifery from the hands of grandames to professional men." This, he said, showed the powerful ascendancy of custom. "The same ladies are still living," he wrote, "who once, in all cases short of the extremities of death, would have resisted the approach of the man-midwife. Now the gentlemen of the profession, always men of influence and character, are known in every street and public hall." I am not saying that Haze Birdsall exercised, in addition to his other talents, one of midwife. I am merely reflecting on the point that with feelings of modest women of the times what they were, even where physicians were concerned, it is remarkable that Haze's offices were so obviously taken for granted. Haze, as one of the earliest undertakers in the Jersies, was counted on to consider sex impersonally and so was given, at the last, a share among the secrets of God.

Even when Haze had measured his corpses and then had fashioned and unloaded his coffins, his work was not yet done. "Father would be expected, of course, to have his hearse shining and ready so as to drive it at the head of the procession to the cemetery," Bill told me. "And then, being the Sunday School teacher, he'd leave off driving to be a pallbearer and at the end, as the earth was spilled down, he'd say the prayers of whatever services there would be. You couldn't always get a preacher. By the time you let one know and by the time he found ways of getting where they wanted him, the funeral was likely over."

Now that I think of it, it was in another Birdsall house, down in Waretown, that they told me a story like that years ago. They were listing people who had been married without benefit of clergy and without any pretense of ceremony. Weddings were understandings down country, sometimes with rings that were pieces of wire. Formal pronouncements had to wait for the arrival of a parson on his long circuit. Sometimes he was so laggard that children attended the weddings of their parents. Hazleton Birdsall talked at funerals, that was all. And he was, as Bill informed me, "a very religious man."

Grandfather Aaron Birdsall died young and his children, as Bill put it on a later day, "were put out" to other families. "Daddy himself was 'put out' to an old house near the school where Curtis Wilson lived," he remembered. "Fourteen, he was, at the time. From then on, till he was married, the Wilson house was his home. Meantime he had been going around with Joe Wilson, Curtis's boy, working at the trade his father had started him at when he was less than twelve—building houses for people. That was a good long job, once. You had to know your business. You had to know wood, where to get it, how to handle it, how to make anything. Everything was made by hand, even the hardware."

Just as Hazleton Birdsall worked with Joe Wilson, Bill worked with his father, Haze.

"It was a system you don't hear much about any more," Bill said. He shook his head a little sadly, I thought. "Father took me around on his jobs and worked for just a little less a day so as to get me in on the work. The master mechanic was always slowed up by the apprentice, people said, and the mechanic accepted it. You couldn't expect the boss carpenter to earn top wages if he was teaching a youngster what to do."

Bill's brother, Jim, was a glass blower. But he had learned his trade as a shipwright as well. He worked at the VanSant yard in Green Bank when ships were building there, down behind Aunt Hattie's store. "Big schooners and lots *of* 'em," said Uncle Bill. They built schooners down behind Bill Birdsall's house, for that matter, launching them skillfully so that they shot off up the river. You can still see the deep ridge in the channel.

Another brother, Joseph, "did just about everything that came to hand." There were also Robert, Albert, Hance, Abraham, and John. "John never growed up. Died when he was eight. There was a couple of girls, too, but I can't tell you just where they came in," said Bill. Throughout the whole family the woodworking trade has been the theme of its industry. It began when William Birdsall (they spelled it Burdsall, once, and even Birdsell) came to New Jersey from Long Island in 1713. William, Bill's namesake ancestor, went back to Long Island but his son, Stephen, settled in Barnegat in 1719. The second Stephen married Deliverance Willits in 1738 and became the first "elder" of the Barnegat Friends Meeting, established in 1767 when Monmouth County included what now is Ocean.

The Stephen Birdsall who made a will in 1763 owned a sawmill. The Jacob who lived deep down in Waterford Township in 1731 was also a house carpenter. The Birdsalls, who knew the first Hazletons in the valley and made the last name a first, were carpenters at Cedar Run and Manahawkin and in the neighborhood familiarly described as "Little Egg Harbor." "And so, with the rest, I was a carpenter, too," said Bill. "Sort of came natural, I guess."

One day Bill and I got to talking about the thoroughness of the wood workers who built those old New Jersey houses. I had remembered a barn that had fallen down not long before. All the timbers had been numbered, in the usual way, by carpenters I suggested must be long in their graves. "Not numbered," Bill corrected me, mild in his reproof. "Married is what you mean. All the timbers was married with Roman numerals on ceils as well as studs. Workmen who know anything about their trade still do that."

Bill Birdsall continued working, making his rounds with his box of tools until he surprised a few patrons in the act of frowning and shaking their heads. "I took the hint," he told me, with a disconcertingly humorless chuckle. "They thought I was getting too old. The laugh was on them. I *wasn't* old. I did lots of work after that —cut fire lanes through the woods, tore down that house next door and built this. And, anyhow, I can always say I did a pretty good last day's work. Down at Pleasantville, it was. They were building a new post office. One day's pay, then, was twenty dollars."

Haze Birdsall left his name on something besides a tombstone. He left it, as well, on old regional maps they'll draw for you on invitation, on paper or in the sand at Herman. There is a place called Haze's Crossway, which Bill said was no crossway at all but "a causeway, sure enough. It started out by being Ampley's," he explained. "Ampley was Ampley Hyson, who built it as a way through the swamp when he was hauling charcoal for Sam Crowley. Later on, Father and the family got to using it when we lived over that way. People began calling it Hazleton's Causeway, then Hazle's, and finally Haze's. We make more of first names than last down here. It's less confusing. And, anyhow, people know each other better without the trimmings.

"On the maps you'll find another place called 'the D.S. Road.' That's the road that used to lead to Dennis Sooy's place. And take Asa's Causeway—that was named for Asa Cranmer. McGraw's, all by itself in the woods, always a puddle when the weather's wet for a spell—it was a puddle sure enough when Old Man McGraw, with a little too much aboard, fell down on his face and drownded there in two inches of water. And then there's another place called Noah's Ark—I hadn't thought of that for a month of Sundays. Noah was Noah Sooy and the ark was his house. Leastways we always called it an ark. You see, Noah and his wife broke up, and Noah went back to live in the woods there, all by himself."

I was thinking, the other day, of a funeral or two at which Hazleton Birdsall, having built an appropriate coffin and prepared the hearse, could have added extras of pomp and prayer. Of course, in order to put Haze at either of them, I had to scramble time and space because one would be the burial, at Clark's Landing, of Ruth Clark, wife of Thomas, and the other, over at Tuckerton, would be the disposal of all that was mortal of Edward Andrews. Only by some weird magic of crazy thinking could you get Haze to be at either place, except geographically, but even so—

Watch the hearse which, only a few days ago, was gathering dust in Haze Birdsall's barn, watch it as it passes down the hall of trees leading to the Mullica River. See the mourners, bowed by solemn thought and the need for picking their way over the corduroy road so painstakingly built through the lowlands outside Clark's Landing, down and across from Lower Bank. Here, in 1718, was a village of forty dwellings. Here was a trading house, a log church, and a little navy of trim, river-made ships. Now, as the funeral nears its destination, the whole population of the Landing, nearly three hundred, moves in silence and sorrow for this, you remember, is an illustrious corpse. Sud Norcross and I were the only mourners the day we set out to find the graveyard, the lone intruders of a year, maybe. A deer leaped through the thickets. Crows, sent skyward from their sanctuary, clamored over our approach. Ships and houses and the little church were but sticks and bits of metal to be kicked up in sand among the weather-twisted holly trees.

Now the huddled friends of the deceased make their way across the half-submerged logs of the roadway we found. This is the road that led beyond plantations crowning the rise, a highway once necessary to the business of life, now become the heirloom of death, with one-way traffic culminating in no traffic at all. These are the people who, forty years after the Revolution, were confessing against their will that the Landing had begun to lose heart as well as homes. Colonel Elijah Clark, who helped with the building of the Fort at Chestnut Neck—he isn't among them: The Colonel has been buried already in a ceremony befitting a representative of Gloucester County, a member of the Provincial Congress, and an active associate of the privateering firm of Vanuxem & Clark. Young Tom Clark and Sally, the girl he brought home from Saybrook, Connecticut, with a technique imparted by his father, are here. Their Uncle David, who has five sons and a daughter, allows them to help him to the hill where the grave has been dug deep—it seems to David Clark that he has come to an unusual number of funerals lately. He has lingered on in the old homestead of the Clarks, watching neighbors move elsewhere, refusing to die in the damps of the swamps and marshes that were thought to have struck him down long ago.

Hazleton Birdsall climbs from his perch and then looks solemn as he lends an expert hand to the carrying of the coffin. Nice piece of work, he thinks, his hand caressing one of the handles he turned so well. (When Ruth Clark was buried beside the man who sent his eldest son to complete his courtship, there were no heaps of pine needles, no tangled trees and vines, no mould under scrub oak thickets. More than two headstones were in evidence for grave markers had not yet begun to submerge. Sud and I found only two. With difficulty we discerned the graven names, feeling them out with our fingers. One was Thomas Clark, the other Ruth. The dates were missing from the heavy brownstone slabs, pressed now into concrete flat upon the ground, this "permanence" financed by Clarks far away.)

Not knowing the lady at all, Haze Birdsall is well equipped, in the manner of many preachers of today, who are in what they call their best form, at funerals, to say the "appropriate" words at the grave. They are called appropriate, presumably, because everybody in the company has heard them before, about somebody else. Haze won't go wrong. He has garnered some family history on the way from relatives who won't listen now, but instead will remember that it is raw and cold and that a lot of these people will be coming back to the house for supper. I am listening, however, and I hope you will:

"The servant of the Lord whom we honor here today was Ruth, the faithful relict of Thomas Clark. Tom, as we all know, was married twice . . . most of us has to be content with one wife only. First Mrs. Clark was Hannah. This was Ruth. First Mrs. Clark, Hannah, had four sons, Thomas, David, Samuel, and Elijah. David's here, I see—a little deef, I know, so he can't hear what I'm saying. Samuel ought to be here—he's a preacher and was sent for but couldn't get away. Hannah died a long time ago—1735, I think it was. After the mourning, Tom put his oldest boy to horse and told him to lead the mare up to New Haven. Young Tom was nineteen then. Errand was important just the same: Tom was to bring back this old friend of his father's, this Ruth whom we lay to rest beside Old Tom today, to be the new mother of all the Clarks. . . ."

Let me interrupt Haze Birdsall long enough to say that I always have hoped Tom Clark had the grace to write Ruth at least one parchment letter. Sud Norcross expressed the same hope once but added that he didn't believe Tom had. Men were more forthright then. There was a proposition, and it was take it or leave it all the

140

time. Ruth took it, that's the main consideration here. Perhaps she assented to the proposal without either blushes or delay. Maybe, to imply gracefully that it was all too sudden, she asked time for considering. From the leeway young Tom had, I think she must have delayed a little. Haze is continuing:

"That was a happy errand for young Tom Clark, far removed from the kind of journey that brings us here today. Tom did a lot more than tell Ruth what Clark's Landing and the Mullica and all the people Down Shore were like. Yes, a lot more. He told a few things in his own right to Sally. That was left as unfinished business until two years later when young Tom made the long journey all over again, led horse and all. And he came back home with Sally for his wife. They are here today, my friends, and I know Tom's thinking hard about all of it as we ask God to take His servant, Ruth, the second mother of the Clarks, to his bosom in the sky. . . ."

Unless you can shift eras and geography even more completely around, you can't hear them telling Haze Birdsall, of Bulltown and Green Bank, to get a coffin ready for Edward Andrews. Haze's hearse was impressive but Tuckerton, where Ed lived, was just a little too far. For that matter, I doubt if the good Quakers at Middle-of-the-Shore would have approved of anything as showy as either Haze's carryall or his Methodist graveside manner. But goodness knows that life, which for Ed began as we know it did, ought to have regained something a little more spectacular in death than a mere waiting on the Spirit in Little Egg Harbor.

As Mrs. Blackman has put it, "Edward Andrews' parents were strict Quakers, and it is probable that they brought him up in the way they thought he should go. But it appears he chose his own course in life, and if ever he had been a member of Friends' Meeting (no doubt but that he had a birthright membership) he must have fallen from grace. After he settled at Egg Harbor, it is recorded that he was of a social and jovial disposition; and having married so young, he had not had time to 'sow his wild oats'; and being the owner of a violin, his habitation on Sunday was the resort of his jovial neighbors, who came to hear him play on the violin and sing 'the merrie songs of old England. . . .'"

Then something happened, and that something, they say, was

141

this: When Ed Andrews was plowing one of his fields, he turned up a skeleton, or at least a skull, probably an Indian's. "This solemn spectacle," it is said, "set him to thinking about Man's present and future state, and such were his reflections that the next Sabbath after the exhumation of the bones—when, as usual, his associates came to his dwelling for the purpose of enjoying the accustomed sport of 'dancing on the green' while Andrews played the violin— great was their astonishment when they saw Ed engaged in reading the Bible. Instead of bringing forth the violin, he read a chapter and then knelt down and prayed aloud for his associates and himself. . . ."

Ed had got religion. "And it was lasting," Haze Birdsall would have added in his own quaint way. "Ed began by going down to the medders and tossing away that violin of his. It floated out on the current toward one of the islands. Ed, they say, got him a boat and rowed out after it, smashing it up so it wouldn't fall into the hands of somebody else later on. From then on Ed was a powerful preacher. At first they wondered if he meant it—for lots of people remembered the Sunday dancing and violin tunes. But Ed had got religion through and through, and soon folks was a-comin' from miles around just to hear the Spirit move him. Will Cranmer, so I've heard, used to come afoot all the way from Barnegat."

I hear Haze saying it that way, because that is the way Bill Birdsall told it to me, and for some reason Haze, to me, has always been like Bill. Bill added, that day he bade me come down for some more some day when there would be more time and fewer mosquitoes, that deep down Ed Andrews probably wished every now and then that he hadn't smashed that fiddle. "He'd have liked a tune or two, I'll wager," said Bill. "There isn't nothing wrong with a violin—through the week, anyhow. No, there isn't," Bill repeated, as if he were expecting opposition. You can see why, I hope, that I put Hazleton Birdsall at Ed's funeral, saying the things that should have been said, because they're sound, but probably weren't said for all that.

Clearly now, fancy has gamboled long enough. Hazleton Birdsall, my favorite Mullica carpenter, must be brought back to earth, the earth in which they laid him at Pleasant Mills when Jimmy McAnney, of all people, delivered himself of quite a sermon. I heard of

142

that in Nesco. For years, Mrs. John Stewart said, Haze and Jimmy had shaken hands after all the funerals, pledging to each other that whichever died first would speak at the other's burial. Mrs. Stewart is Haze's daughter. "It was kind of solemn," she told me. "I used to watch them. And then—Jimmy did the preaching."

I am wondering tonight who it was that they called to do the preaching that Wednesday afternoon in the little white church at Green Bank. I am thinking, too, of the little house Bill Birdsall built where he told me about Haze, and the houses *he* built for the people who held to the river. "Come on down again soon," Bill said. "I'll tell you some more." That was good-by from Bill. There was a piece in the Hammonton paper just the other day. "Mr. William Hazleton Birdsall, 78, a lifelong resident of Green Bank," it said, "died at the Atlantic City Hospital following a four days' illness. . . ."

*14*

## SNAPPERS AND GREENTAILS

*". . . Verily I think*
*Such place to me is sometimes like a dream*
*Or a map of the whole world . . ."*
WILLIAM WORDSWORTH

THE FINDING OF SNAPPER COBB AND JACK FORD were part of a quest for a song, the song of countless verses they say was called "The Ballad of the Mullica." But now, long after the chase, I can report no greater success than rewarded me in the hunt for Haze Birdsall's hearse and the last Green Bank stagecoach; the hearse, still used in Hammonton until ten or more years ago, fell apart, forgotten, in a barn, just as did the old coach in a shed back in the woods toward Stump Creek.

Rod Koster said that he had found a man who knew and sang the ballad. His name, Rod told me, was Jack Ford, and he lived, when he wasn't down by the river or out with his hound dogs, beside the kitchen stove, leaning back in his chair against the wall. "They call it Jack Ford's perch," said Aunt Hattie, at the store, when she found out where we were going. Rod had to tell her, for he helped with the store and post office before they took him off to war. Rod had promised to go along so that Jack might be in a mood for easier talking—and singing maybe, too.

"I want to hear the ballad myself," he told me. "I been hearing tell of it since I was what they call a boyzie down here." Rod said it was one of those songs that wandered, like the river. There were as many verses as the singer might fancy, full of rhythm and homespun words, especially when a man was buying pine liquor for his cronies at the bar. Some of the poetry didn't quite fit and a lot of it was hardly elegant, Rod said, but it was a good song just the same. The Mullica had inspired it.

But John Wesley Ford said he didn't know the ballad.

We went in through the shed and the back kitchen to a room where Jack's daughter, Emma Ford Clevenger, was baking bread at a wood fire. Jack, lean and brown and wrinkled mostly from laughing, spoke quietly but with decision. "Seventy-nine, I am," he said, smoking his pipe beside the stove I had heard about. "But in all my years I ain't never heard tell of such a thing!"

Mrs. Clevenger was inclined to argue him down, but Jack was adamant. "I don't know no ballad," he insisted. "Maybe I did know it once; I don't know. If I did, I fergit it now. I fergit lots of things somehow. Not worth rememberin', most of 'em. Maybe, now, if you was askin' for the Huckleberry Song. . . ."

"What's the Huckleberry Song?" I asked him. "Maybe that's the one."

"No, it ain't," Rod Koster declared decisively. "He'll remember the ballad some of these days, you wait and see. Sometimes Jack answers questions like Chink Sinkins, just to provoke, like. But we'll get the ballad. How do the words of the Huckleberry Song go?"

"Guess I don't know that, either," Jack Ford answered, suddenly shy.

"Oh, you do so," objected Mrs. Clevenger again. "It's been sung

144

many a time in and around this house and you know it. Why, you sing it yourself!"

Jack Ford did not deny that he had a voice. But he said it was just as easy for him to whistle, and he preferred whistling. However, he began to recite the words. At first he mumbled and it was difficult to catch the syllables. When we asked him to repeat, he lost his way and forlornly went back to the beginning. Even so, the first line, which was to prove so significant, eluded us then.

"There was a feller here once takin' down all those songs," Mrs. Clevenger broke in at precisely the wrong time. "He promised us our pictures and everything."

This, I thought mistakenly, was a hint that I should pay my way. I promised to come back, not only with pictures but with a basket or two of apples, the yield of some gnarled old trees up a river where they grow better. If, I added, they could use them. There seemed to be no doubt of that. But the promise was not credited so far as I could see. Be it recorded that it was kept, however.

Jack was frowning and murmuring in a monotone:

> ". . . to the swamps will go,
> Loads of merry pickers, seated all in a row;
> They jumped into the thickets and whistled merrily
> While scooping in the treasures of the huckleberry tree!"

I took that down carefully. Then, after a pause, Jack Ford added what is surely a chorus, making the "ed" of the "scrubbed" a syllable of its own as it would have been in Elizabethan times. Jack went on:

> "The short scrubbed oak and the tall standing pine—
> But the dark green cedar is a fav'rite of mine;
> Of all the forest beauties of South Jer-*sey*
> None is to compare with the huckleberry tree!"

With that Jack subsided momentarily. I tried once again to get the first line as it must go, but I postponed further effort until later on. Rod was asking Jack if he could sing the song. Jack Ford chuckled and shook his head as a shaggy spotted dog and an ink-black cat began a parade around the floor. "Tell you what, Rod," said Jack, as if he were soberly offering a proposition. "Some time

145

you 'n' me'll go out in a boat. If'n we get fur enough out in the river, I'll sing it for you then."

Before he began slowly to remember his days aboard the boats that used to supply fish to the glue and fertilizer factories owned and operated by Joe Wharton down in Delaware, up in Rhode Island, and along the New Jersey coast, Jack Ford sat there, leaning back, sucking at his pipe. He was thinking of the river, he said afterward. Hard times could come, good times could go, but there was always the river, he told us, across the road and through the thickets beyond.

Seeking to bring the dreamer back home, I rummaged in my bag for notes on an old clipping. Rod had said that Jack Ford would at least talk about days of mossbunkers and sturgeon, and so I brought along a transcript of an advertisement from *The Pennsylvania Gazette* of 1768. I read it aloud:

> The subscriber, having for many years made it her business to cure sturgeon in North America, which has been esteemed preferable to any manufactured by other persons, and obtained the first premium of Fifty pounds sterling from the Society of Arts and Commerce in London; takes this method of acquainting the public that she intends, as soon as possible, to leave this part of the world, but is desirous and willing to instruct a sober person or family in the whole art, secret and mystery of manufacturing sturgeon in the several branches of making isinglass, pickling, cavear, glue and oil; the subscriber has lately fallen upon a method of doing the isinglass equal to any whatever. Whoever has a mind to treat with the subscriber may apply to her at Mr. Elijah Bond's fishery near Trenton, where is every thing convenient for carrying on the business, and plenty of fish throughout the whole year furnished by Mr. Bond's fish pond.

The subscriber, I pointed out, was a Mrs. Broadfield, who had added in a footnote that the sturgeon manufactory was carried on by Mr. Bond under her own care and inspection. The lady boasted of her "knowledge and experience in that branch of the business" and that "any person may be supplied, either for shipping or home consumption, at fifteen shillings for a three-gallon kegg, or twelve shillings and six pence by the quantity, and in proportion for larger keggs, warranted good. . . ."

How did one manufacture sturgeon, anyhow? Was that not, in all fairness, the prerogative of God? What was known in the valley of the Mullica, I asked, of this isinglass, glue, and oil that came from mashing up fish which, in self-respect, had fled the waters of the Delaware Bay and River long ago? Jack Ford at last stirred his recollections and insisted on starting at the beginning.

As John Wesley Ford, he was born at Lower Bank in 1862 in a little weather-black house of swamp-made shingles that carried on the tradition of being one of the oldest post offices in the United States. John's life as a working man, he said, began when he was five. "Work?" he chuckled. "I worked hard. When I was five I was out in the woods, choppin' wood with my Daddy. Even then I could chop a quarter of a cord a day." He snorted at the memory. "Some days I'd make ten cents!"

It was no tall story, Jack insisted. Nor was there exaggeration in the claim that he had been down there along the Mullica so long that he was among the survivors of those who had carried brick for the tall chimney that was once a part of the glassworks at Herman. Now the chimney is gone, and the kilns are to be found only by careful hunting among the rank growth of trees and thickets. It was not until after "spells of coalin' and woodchoppin'" in Bulltown, Tylertown, and Herman City that Jack Ford followed the ebb of the Mullica one day and got a job in a fish factory.

"That one was Cap'n Cyrus Smith's," he said. He stroked his ragged mustache with the stem of his pipe. "That was where the Tuckerton wireless is now. There was another factory they called Sooy's out on Crab Island. Jim Otis was the foreman for 'em there, and after he quit, one of the Mathises took charge. I don't know which one—there was a million of 'em."

Although fish factories still operated in peacetime, their processes and products are different from those that gave work to Mullica River people. At least that is what Jack Ford maintained. "People knew they made oil and glue," he said, "just as they knew they made caviar from sturgeon roe out of Delaware Bay—but they just caught the fish and didn't pay much attention after that. The fish they caught was mossbunkers, and the stuff they made was mostly oil and fertilizer."

Mossbunkers? I was properly chastised for feigning ignorance. "Most people know mossbunkers as menhaden," Jack said. "Minnies to you, maybe. We've called 'em mossybunkers, greentails, and
147

Sam Days, too." Some say the name is that of a man who was in the business; others have told me Sam Day is the modern variation that began with *samedi,* but the significance has been lost. "Sometimes," said Jack, "we just called 'em bony-fish and mud-shad, but greentails was always the fav'rite. Maybe they got a name like that because they always left a slick behind 'em in the water."

Jack caught them as a member of crews on fishing steamers out of Little Egg Harbor, craft that worked independently, competing with the ships owned by Joe Wharton's factories. In those days Wharton was a name as famous off shore as on, was much more than a name given vast acres first acquired for a New Jersey watershed. In the old days Joe Wharton owned fish factories at Lewes, Delaware, Tiverton, Rhode Island, and a place called Promised Land, Jack informed us, as well as at the mouth of the Mullica. Steamers loaded up and brought fish to the factories for whatever factory men would pay. "We could bring in about a million in a load," estimated the fisherman.

It sounded a messy, slippery business. Jack said it was. You had to be beyond "mindin'" smells. "But it was a job," he explained, "and most of us liked to keep workin'."

The kitchen filled with the pleasant aroma of baking bread. Jack tapped out his pipe in the wood box and filled it again from a battered tin. A vine, drying in the November chill, scratched at the windowpane, half hidden by the plants growing on the sill inside. Across the road, a hound bugled mournfully.

"I was thinkin' of the boats," said Jack Ford. "I was thinkin' of their skippers and their names. There was the 'Joe Wharton' and the 'Alert.' There was a third they called the 'Achsah.' They was trim ships. A few was sail-geared but not many." When berrying fell off and all the wood that was needed was chopped and sold, men of the Mullica drifted down to the shore and signed aboard fish steamers. The wages were never much, nor was the food; but there was a living in the business if the greentails were running and nobody worried any more about the morrow than they do down there today. "We did get tired, now and then, of those everlastin' potato stews," said Jack. "I remember one cookie we had named Bill Dils-

148

worth. When he came lookin' for a job, the skipper asked him if'n he could cook. Sure, he said. That's where the skipper made a mistake.

"So did I—you see, I was the mate on that trip. Ben was just sittin' around and I told him to cook us up somethin'. 'What'll I cook?' he asked me, as if he might be askin' how to cook it at the same time. 'How about a potato stew?' he asked me, as I looked at him wonderin' like. I said all right. Do you know, that was all he knew how to make? We had twenty-one potato stews that week!

"Johnny Allen, after we got rid of the greentails we had, couldn't wait for the steamer to bring us in. Maybe he had come down to meet it and had left a little boat somewhere, I don't know. I do know that he got out in the middle of Bass River and yelled at cookie things you wouldn't hear in Sunday School. And the cookie, Ben, who made such nice potato stews, came right back at him."

Remembering that Leon Koster, Rod's father, also had worked at the fish factories, Jack Ford recalled one Friday night when, as was the custom, a boat went out from New Gretna to bring the men at the factories home. The turning of greentails into glue or oil was never a pleasant business; and even when you got home, after three or four baths and a swim in the cedar waters of the Mullica, you smelled to high Heaven. Few boats had come to the plant on the marshes, Jack told us, and the men were ready to get away home as soon as they could. Then, just as they were about to leave, the first of several fishing steamers appeared on the horizon.

"If a boat blew its whistle once," said Jack, "that meant it had a fair load. Two toots of the whistle meant a load that was better'n half. Three toots meant it was loaded to the gun'les. The first ship blowed three times. So did the second. So did the third. We looked at 'Tede' Allen who was there to take us off. The boss said if we left him in a fix with all those fish, he'd see to it that we never stepped on Crab Island again. Most of us never stepped. We left him."

Skipper and mate of independent boats went aloft, usually, Jack said, when the steamer was "safe outside." From the mastheads they could sight schools of menhaden, usually by the slick, and call down to the men to put off in small boats. "Aloft, we could tell if the fish

149

was workin' up or down the beach. Sometimes the water'd look red where you sighted 'em. The dories'd put off with the nets, two net setters to a boat—they'd circle the fish that way. Sometimes you'd drift a mile or more before you'd be ready to bale 'em in."

No one fish factory was patronized. It depended, Jack said, on where you caught the greentails. Fishing steamers ran between Long Island Sound and Cape Hatteras. Sometimes they would put in at the factory in Tiverton. "And sometimes we'd go in to the factory at Promised Land or in Little Egg Harbor or down to Lewes-town. There'd be maybe six and eight gallons of oil to a thousand fish. But some fish wouldn't make more'n between four or five.

"Got to tell you the story of Cap'n Enoch Smith, out of Port Republic, he was. Cap'n 'Ene' put out o' New York one time with nothin' in the larder, because he expected to be up the Mullica by sundown. Or maybe he didn't feel like eatin' maybe, 'cause it was so hot. Anyways, he started out, and it wasn't long before they were in the middle of a nor'east gale. Well, you can imagine that they was pretty hungry by the time night came. They was hungrier still when they fought the gale through two more days. Finally 'Ene' Smith says to the cookie, 'Say, Cookie, can't you find us a little suthin' to eat?' Cookie says there's nothin' aboard but he'd have a look. Only thing he could find was an old pair of gum boots. They was in good shape, them boots, havin' been sweated in all summer. He took 'em, cookie did, and made a pot o' soup!

"Well, Cap'n 'Ene' and the men didn't like it much but they had to have somethin'—but maybe it wasn't much account. For when Enoch Smith and the crew comed in, they was so skinny that they took holt o' the skin over their breastbones, pulled it up and blowed their noses on it!"

John Wesley Ford put his head back against the wall and laughed. The spotted dog, having heard the story in one form or another through several years, cocked his head and looked up, with apparent disapproval. Suddenly Jack began to sing, a low cautious singsong that began without warning. At last I had the words:

"Soon the sheet-topped wagons to the swamps will go,
  Loads of merry pickers, seated all in a row;

Mullica River specialties include Mrs. John "Bull" Miller's green tomato pie, Mrs. Charles Kell's cranberry potpie, and Aunt Mattie's clam pie.

Kate Albor, as she was often seen, crocheting beside her Atsion window.

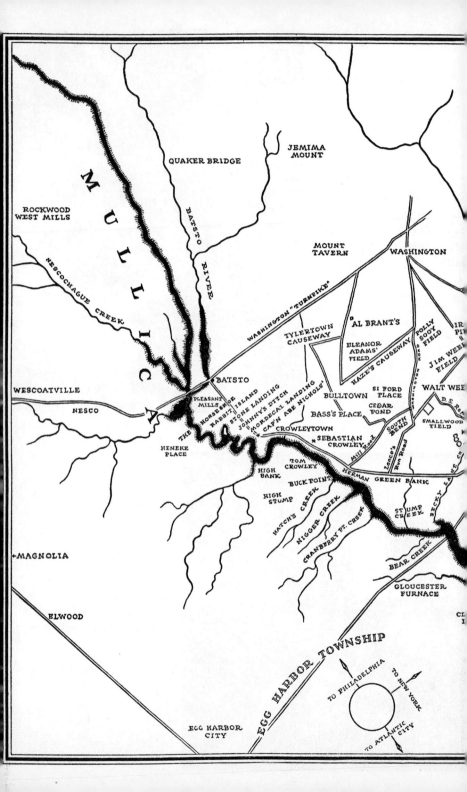

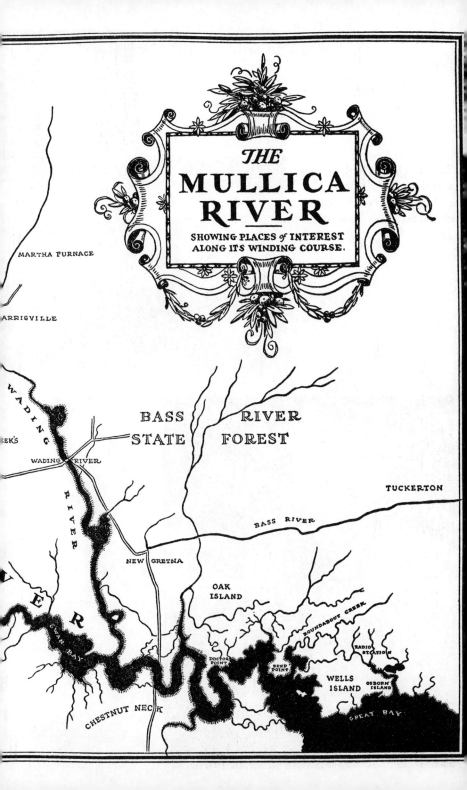

Tilden (Till) Estlow, descendant of the forgemaster of Martha Furnace and one of the last Estlows at Wells Mills.

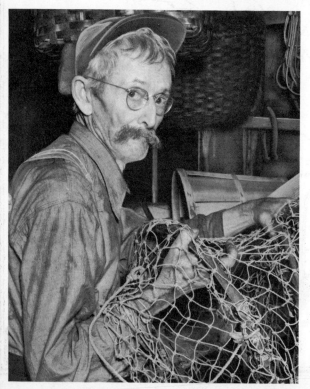

Snapper Cobb, who fare well "fyking" "turkles" i Mullica waters.

They jumped into the thickets and whistled merrily
While scooping in the treasures of the huckleberry tree. . . ."

Sheet-topped wagons? What were they? We had missed the ballad
and had failed to catch much of a tune. Actually, it wasn't until I
talked to Rod Koster's uncle, Lance Cobb, that I found new significance in all this talk of oil and greentails and wagons bound for
the swamps. A vehicle quite as important as Conestoga's own had
been buried for years in a Jerseyism as original as those that have
died with the forges and glass factories that produced them. As for
Jack Ford, he was silent again and tilted back beside the stove in
the place they called his "perch."

Alanson Cobb, lean, agile, and hawk-eyed at seventy-six, looked
up from the barrow in which he was piling the wood he had chopped.
"Hello," I said. "Mr. Cobb?"
"Yup," he answered, and went on piling wood.
"Got any snappers?" I asked him, seeking some solid ground for
conversation. If he had assured me that he had a supply, I don't know
what I should have done except give them to Augie. Bill Augustine
eats muskrat and snapper and 'possum with great relish. I can't even
eat a rabbit.
"Nup," Mr. Cobb replied, and I was safe. This time he didn't look
up.
More wood went atop the stack in the barrow, and the barrow was
moved to where it could be unloaded. There was nothing to do but
wait or follow or else go home. I looked at the never painted boards
of Lance Cobb's house. There had been movement at the window,
a face, I thought. That was Mrs. Cobb, probably, wondering about
an intruder with silly questions. The face did not appear again, and
I have never met Mrs. Cobb.
Cobby was a small, spare man with a droopy mustache. He wore
a hunting cap that day, and whenever I saw him, with ear-tabs
slung back and ready for dull days when the wood he was piling
would be indoors and burning or piled up as a windbreak. I plunged
into my story, telling him how I had been talking to many of his
friends down along the river and that for some time I had expected

151

to see him at the store. A man who saved words and stowed them out of sight like other men's postage stamps, he said nothing at all. In desperation I asked, finally:

"You've always been here beside the river, haven't you?"

"Nup," he said, pausing in his work for the first time. He straightened up and I seized the barrow to push it back to the shed for him. "No?" I echoed his reply. "Nup," he said again. Then, rewarding my assistance, he added: "Borned down to Green Bank almost and not far from Whitetown, they called it once. Mother was one of the Whites, Emmaline White."

Those were days when, if you were a principal citizen with a house that imposed itself upon a group of four or five jerry-built cabins, or if you had a larger family or a more substantial larder to be shared during the winter, the huddle of homes became a town and took your name. Whites, I remembered, were early in Monmouth County, not too far away: Samuel, a carpenter, made a will indicating that he had come down from "Road Island" and that he or whoever it was who wrote out the testament could not spell much better in other particulars: He described his boat as a "slowp" and a slave as "a molata girrell." But that was back in 1683. There were other Whites in Shrewsbury and Freehold about the same time.

The Whites of Burlington City, in the 1750's, were well-to-do, Mary White devising to her heirs, among whom was a sister who had become one of the Leedses, considerable cash, bonds, books, gold rings, and old silver. By 1760, many Whites were in Salem and Cumberland Counties, and still another coterie had settled around Perth Amboy. By the time of the Revolution Whites were almost everywhere with Philip of the Huddy case, Quaker George of the Shrewsbury slaughter, and others edging down the coast to set up in the hotel business with the Leeds family. I hurried over all this for Lance Cobb's benefit, but he was not impressed.

"Yup," said Cobby. I gained nothing at all from my sometimes pitiful excursions into ancestry. Uncle Lance didn't even ask me how I knew his wife's maiden name.

Snapper season was over, Cobby told me, when he had warmed up some time later. I had half expected him to say "turkle" for turtle but he didn't. There is a Turtle Creek not far from where Cobby lives,

152

as you know by now, but no matter what they tell you, the odd spelling was once more general and goes a long way back. John Leek, making a will in the 1770's, mentioned "the cedar swamp I bought of Joshua and Samuel Bellanger, at the head of *Turkle* Creek, on the east side." But Lance pronounced it turtle when he said he had put away his fykes till spring's return and that the sign labeled "Snappers" had been taken down from the tree out front, as I should have noticed. I had, of course.

The Mullica, which year in and year out had brought Lance a living like most river people, would go on flowing and ebbing as usual, but Cobby would not be likely to expect the unusual from it in wintertime. It was a reference to farming that started Lance talking in something more than monosyllables. "Guess your farming's over for now," I told him.

"Farmin'?" He chuckled. "My farmin' never did 'mount to much." He gazed away over a tangled field that stretched from the back of his house to the bank of the river. He could have said, more truthfully, that farming on the land that was his would never add up to any great shakes unless he completely transformed the soil. But that would be a kind of complaining, and Cobby was not the complaining kind. That summer Lance Cobb had raised some corn, some potatoes, some sweet potatoes, some turnips. These had been carefully harvested, he showed me, having been wheeled in the barrow to the small building with the deep cellar. With the forethought and agility of a squirrel, Lance had made many trips across his land, scrambling up and down the ladder with the liveliness of a much younger man. Once, before we went back to the woodpile, he pointed to the turnips. "Nice lot of *winter radishes*," he said.

It was raining a little. Somehow I got him to the shed and edged him back to the subject of snappers. Hanging in the shed were old Jersey baskets, all kinds of homemade and hand-forged implements, and fykes that would need repairs before further use. Fykes? It was a new word to me for a while. The dictionary calls it merely "a kind of fish trap." But they tell me it goes back to Elizabethan times like the "ed" of the "scrubbed oak" in the Huckleberry Song. Lance Cobb's fykes were nets arranged on a series of hoops, set out in season in the Mullica, for snappers that go for mossbunker bait.

"When do you go after snappers?" I asked.

"Now and then," he told me with continuing evasiveness.

"How many have you hauled out of the Mullica through the years?"

"A mess or two," he answered, chuckling. There was that term "mess" again, a word that could mean anything from three to thirty-three, according to the needs of the moment. Cobby admitted finally that he had been fyking snappers for more than thirty years.

And herring? "Oh, my," murmured Cobby. "Mess of herring, too. Quite a mess."

"And just what," I countered boldly, "is a mess of herring?"

"Can be a couple," Lance explained, saving his words as usual. "Can be as much as you got ordered. Can be as much as you want to eat."

I finally pried it out of Cobby that Mullica rivermen usually went after herring with half-pound gill nets, that herring show in the river around March, maybe, but that you don't go after them until April. You see, the first run of herring's the small bucks, and the spawn herring will be up the river a few days after. "You'd go after 'em of an afternoon," Cobby said, "and if you picked your day and tide right, you'd get enough to eat and sell."

It used to be that when the herring were in, the Mullica valley was a mecca for innkeepers and all who wanted herring without the bother of catching them. Mullica people were rarely sticklers for market prices and even prices that were adequate. If the fish were in, you caught them, if you had any sense at all, Cobby said. If you wanted herring, you kept what you needed for a meal or two, more if you intended to smoke or pickle them. If you needed money, you asked the amount you needed, surely not much more.

"You would get, maybe, fifty cents a hundred," confided Alanson Cobb. "And people from all around would come down here and buy." And no wonder!

I suggested that perhaps people along the Mullica ate more fish than elsewhere, that nowadays people probably ate less fish than in the times of which Uncle Lance was speaking. He didn't think so. "Fish," he said, "is good for you. They make brains, they say. So down here we eat as much fish as we ever did. It's always good to get a brain—and when you get one, to keep it. Yup, herring was once

154

so thick in this here river that you could almost walk across on 'em. They used to go up as far as they could get beyond Batsto, almost to Atsion in the old days."

Rod got Uncle Lance back on the subject of snappers one day later. Biggest snapper Cobby remembered catching weighed twenty-seven pounds. "Wonder it didn't blow for all three bridges, I always say," he laughed. "But there was one taken at Lower Bank two or three years ago that weighed forty-six. There's a man who used to come up from Northfield and say he'd taken more'n seven hundred pound of snapper out of the Mullica in a year. That's a lot of snapper."

There was no indication that Cobby doubted the story. There wasn't much that Uncle Lance doubted, Rod said, unless he had proof to the contrary. He was sure in his own mind, at any rate, that the forty-six-pounder that made Lower Bank famous for a week had been patrolling the Mullica ever since the British were there, crashing his way out of the fykes of snapper men, year after year. Cobby said that in the old days he used to catch a thousand herring at a draw. "Maybe I'd smoke six or seven hundred of 'em," he said, "and give the rest away. Some couldn't catch 'em as easy as I could. All of us used to give away whatever was wanted by all the folks that wasn't out on the water in time."

I let Cobby go on about where he went to school in Crowleytown, and what Whitetown was like with its three or four houses, and how one of the two glass factories up the road made the first Mason jars, a claim for which there seems to be much rivalry as you will discover. I listened as Uncle Lance confirmed the dates of the old glass-making enterprises as they had been sent to me by Sam Smallwood, far away in West Virginia: Crowleytown, 1850; Green Bank, between 1840 and 1845; New Columbia, now Nesco, 1845; Bulltown, 1859; and Herman, 1870. I was patient as the Snapper Man jumped to the smoke house technique that used cedar cuttings, old chips, everything, with never a thought for hickory. Pickled herring was better than smoked, any day, Cobby was sure.

Then Rod asked about the Huckleberry Song. Lance said at first that he didn't remember it; but as I recited the words from my notes, his eyes sparkled anew, his wrinkled face wreathed in a full grin for the first time. "That's the song," I said. "Soon the sheet-topped wagons to the swamps will go. . . ." There was a pause, calculated. "What," I asked, "were sheet-topped wagons, Mr. Cobb?"

Cobby looked at me as if I had asked him what state this was or whether he could tell me more about the Whites. "Why," he answered after a moment, "everybody knows *that*. Who you been askin' such a question? Jackie Ford? Well, he knows the answer. Everybody knows. Sheet-topped wagons was the most uncomfortable things ever made, with hoops, big hoop-ribs over which the canvas sheet was thrown against sun and weather. And they fastened the sheet down at both ends with drawin' strings."

Rod and I stared at each other. Augie all but fell over. All of us had heard long ago that New Jersey had had its own covered wagon design, but here we were talking to a man who remembered what Jersey Wagons were like, inside and out. I know, now, that there must have been many more who knew. The trouble was, once again, that a vehicle as important as the Conestoga Wagon had been buried alive in a Jerseyism as strange as apple-palsy and blickey. Cobby smiled but he didn't rub it in. He looked off toward the river, across the grave of a little dog, a plot now adorned with foot and headstone.

"The winter might be cold," said the Snapper Man.

## "AS DYING—"

*"What should we talk of dainties, then*
*Of better meat than's fit for men?*
*These are but vain: that's only good*
*Which God hath blessed and sent for food."*
CHRISTOPHER MARLOWE

SOME OF US have thought for a long while that surely there must be something sinister in the fashion of cookbooks which, in the Jersies, have combined the cuisine with the cure. But when I came upon Aunt Hattie Ford, seated beside the counter of her Green Bank store and post office, calmly consuming cold clam pie, I began to understand that there was something decidedly practical in the routine. Life and living, I said, had been recognized as kin of death and dying.

I am not suggesting that there was anything the matter with Aunt Hattie's pie, clammy cold though it was, or that there were any gastronomical reactions where the eating was concerned. I would not for worlds imply that this neighborly gift from down the river road, eaten after countless interruptions had kept it for hours among much more ordinary staples, tried anything more than Aunt Hattie's patience. I do say, however, that Mullica River constitutions able to stomach cold clam pie as a between-meals snack can hardly enlist mine among their number.

However, because of long years of practice through generations, pies of clams and green tomatoes and cranberries have produced, for the people along the river, a digestive functioning exceeded only by the insistent hospitality that accompanies it. Even as there is ever more room for food, there is also welcome and room for more guests, be they unexpected, unexpecting, or reluctant. There is a special kind of liberal entertainment beside the Mullica that feels snubbed by apologies for intrusion, frustrated when the loosening of belts and stays is refused.

Bill Augustine once told me of a Sunday afternoon when he and his wife turned in at Bull Miller's house, far up the river near Indian Mills. They were unaware that it was Bull's birthday and that the family and its friends to the number of perhaps eighteen were about to sit down around a groaning board. Bull was insistent; so was Mrs. Miller. The Augustines were compelled to join in an organized attack upon several roasted ducks, peas, beets, lima beans, mashed potatoes, potato salad, yams, cranberry sauce, coleslaw, boiled cabbage, stewed peaches, cake, bread, butter, and coffee. "And the best part of it," Augie told me afterwards, "was that all the grub was their own."

That was entirely true. The ducks had been killed out back. Mrs. Miller had "put up" the peas, the beets, the lima beans, and cranberries, all from their own fields and bogs; she had put them up every summer since she could remember, just as every woman for miles around had "canned everything in sight" since she had begun to be "grown up." Yams and white potatoes had been stored away. Cabbages had been dug up from where they had been buried. Mrs. Bull had baked the bread and made the cakes and mixed the coleslaw that morning. "And was it all good!" Augie had said, delighting as much in the anticipation and recollection of food as in the actual eating of it.

"Must have taken Mrs. Miller a week," I said sympathetically.

Augie was as indignant as he knew Mrs. Miller would be. "Nothing of the sort," he said. "I asked her. She started all of it only a little while before. You get a lot done when you don't have to run to the store for everything."

I remembered Mrs. Clevenger bustling about, testing her bread down where Jackie Ford was leaning against the wall beside the stove. She didn't bake much, she told me, maybe three hundred pounds a year. She was a little out of breath, rosy over the heat of the stove whose fire she fed with pieces of wood at intervals. "What with the huckleberryin' and cranberryin' and growin' a pig or two for salt pork and putting away our own sauerkraut," said Mrs. Clevenger, "seems to me I've worked harder this summer than ever."

Not long after, I set off in search of the secrets surrounding Mrs. Bull Miller's green tomato pie, Mrs. Kell's cranberry potpie, and Aunt Kate Albor's new-potato stew. It was not until later that I came upon Mrs. Ford with a cold clam pie for company. Days of rationing were to come but, oddly enough, they were chiefly to affect the world outside. Women of the river towns were never greatly upset by the wartime regulations, because routine had provided almost ample supplies of everything. They were the true descendants of people in the valley who "carded and spun wool, hackled and spun flax and tow, and then dyed the yarn they manufactured with the bark of trees and shrubs." These were the kinsmen of women who wove yarn into cloth and then made it into bedding and wearing apparel in houses "possessing at least one pair of wool cards, a spinning, or what they denominated as a woolen wheel, linen or flax wheel, and a hackle for combing the tow from the flax."

It was our old friend, Mrs. Blackman, who wrote with great reverence and the respect she felt in her heart for prudent ancestors that "a young lady who was not proficient in the above named useful accomplishments had a rather meagre chance of obtaining a worthy husband. In those days, young ladies who would have scorned the idea of doing kitchen work for strangers," she said, "went out among their neighbors to card and spin and weave, and then these occupations were considered as honorable as millinery and dressmaking." There were "no newspapers, magazines, or novels to read." Nor were there "pianos or organs on which to play, and even if young women had been blessed with such articles, they would not have had much time to devote to such amusements."

Homespun clothes and healthy appetites satisfied by products the little farms could produce made for better Mullica towns, we hear, where women "were very beautiful or very amiable or perhaps were possessed of both of these admirable qualities."

It is evident [says the account] that they were very fascinating, for when the young men of distant localities visited the daughters of the Quakers of Little Egg Harbor, they resolved on taking them for wives. No doubt those healthy, rosy-cheeked, industrious and animated young maidens looked very pretty, dressed in robes which had been manufactured by their own competent hands, and their faces encircled with bonnets which were entirely destitute of feathers, flowers or knots of ribbon.

Well, maybe that is how it was. Perhaps rosy cheeks and plain dress and hats that had no feathers in them were all that the young men cared about. Perhaps that was all they saw until their "resolution" was properly declared and modestly rewarded. However, it seems to me that the affluence of well-to-do Quaker fathers "in a place of great commerce and prosperity" could plausibly have had something to do with the situation. Too much has been assumed for innocence, I think, in days of crude commodes, in nights when houses were dark and badly warmed, and at places like Swimming Over Point where "fording was not very pleasant especially for people dressed in their meeting-garments" and where pastors paid infrequent calls. You need not take my word for it. The record shows that Yearly Meeting at Tuckerton was ultimately discontinued because of beach parties, and that "young people's minds, being occupied with such pleasures rather than the meetings" caused the Middle-of-the-Shore Quakers to abandon their annual pilgrimage.

I sought more information about river cookery, because I had been wondering what the great grandmothers of women along the Mullica were like and what they were doing when their men were hauling charcoal and making cedar shingles and going after the iron that seeped from the bogs. There was, I have found, a refreshing pause here and there for the men, but seldom was there letup for the women. I knew that, perhaps, from the day Augie took me to see Mrs. Miller and the widows of Atsion Lake, Mrs. Charles Albor and Mrs. Charles Kell. These, too, are women who inspired their men, and fed them well, in days when pioneer industries were still feeding eager mouths and when the fields continued to fill many a winter's larder.

Mrs. Albor, Aunt Kate, sat beside a window of the old house where she and Mrs. Kell keep each other company most of the summer. Dark-skinned, quiet-voiced, with gray, almost white hair arranged in a way that accentuates her dignity, she smiled as she remembered how she was married in 1884 and how she left Batsto for Pleasant Mills, up at The Forks, not long after when her husband went to work in the paper mill. Mr. Albor's people were German, among the early members of the colony boomed by the Gloucester Farm and Town Association. Charlie Albor—and you will find the name on the stones behind the Methodist Church and in the graveyard that was once behind St. Mary's Roman Catholic Church in Pleasant

Mills—was an expert craftsman in the finishing room of the Pleasant Mills plant that turned out manila paper made from salt hay. Mrs. Albor said she remembered rolls of the stuff, finished paper, big tanks of boiling meadow musk, and the four-mule teams that hauled to Sailor Boy or direct to ships anchored in the river.

"Later on, we went down to Wading River," Mrs. Albor said. That was where her brother, George, another Leek, had a sawmill, and where her father, John Leek, drove a team, dragging logs from the forests. "Then Charlie followed his trade just as the glassmen did," said Aunt Kate. "We went to Jersey City Heights and Hoboken and Paterson. But we always came back to along the Mullica; we came back to Elwood just fifty years ago. Charlie took to clerking in his sister's store when the big trades gave out. There's always work down here for them that want it."

What did the women do? They did as their mothers and grand-mothers and great-grandmothers had done before them, Aunt Kate told me. "They cooked and cooked," she said. "They had to work hard all summer, putting up things that were to last all winter. Some had time for picnics in the groves and dances at the country inns. I never did. Many of us never did. We cooked until we were too tired to do anything but rest for another day."

That was how Aunt Kate led the conversation to Mrs. Kell, whose specialty is what the people of the valley call cranberry potpie. Aunt Kate's needles flashed in the sunlight that streamed across Atsion Lake. Through the window I could see the dam and the main road to Hammonton. "You take a good-sized pan," Mrs. Kell said, "putting a layer of cranberries at the bottom. Then you add a little water, molasses, and sugar so as to make a syrup. Next you make a biscuit batter and drop it in—don't make it stiff! Then you have the potpie and you put it in the oven. There's nothing to that," finished the good lady, spreading her hands on her apron. "I been making cranberry potpies for years and years, and nobody's died of 'em yet. You see, menfolk along the river were great for what they called boiled meals, and cranberry potpies sort of topped 'em off. Everything but the potpie was boiled—potatoes, turnips, and ham. And sometimes, there was Dutch stew."

At first I considered that this might be some relation to the Irish

161

variety. I soon learned better. "For Dutch stew," Mrs. Kell disclosed quickly, "you fry some salt pork in the bottom of the pan, browning it. Then you cut up onions and put them in, browning *them,* too. Finally, you add a little water and some fried potatoes."

Then Aunt Kate remembered new-potato stew, made with the first potatoes to come in from the fields. "The pork is 'fried out' first," she said, "and then the onions are put in, with flour gravy added at the last."

There wasn't much talk of or liking for turkey at Christmas or Thanksgiving in those days along the little rivers, Mrs. Albor wanted me to know. "There was more talk of duck or goose or chicken," she said. "And there was always the old reliable fried meal, with fried pork or fried ham for the centerpiece. You always had the pork on hand, ready, put up in pickle. If you wanted other meats, you had to wait for the traveling butcher. Why, we used to make and string sausages with all the rest. Winters were harder then, I think. We used to hang hams and sausages up in the attic, and they'd stay froze up there all winter."

I consulted some home economists and domestic scientists after that. They said they thought cranberry potpie was original, might be regional in lower New Jersey, or even native of the valley. But when I began talking of Mrs. Bull Miller's green tomato pie, they said that it must have come over from Pennsylvania and was probably "Pennsylvania Dutch." I am scarcely an expert in the culinary arts, but even so I disagree. My feeling is that green tomato pie is more likely to be a Mullica native than cranberry potpie, and I have gone through dozens of regional cookery books without anything to contradict that conclusion. Of course, some authorities have been misled by the name. The sound of it gives off an Italian flavor, and taste itself will make surprising denial there.

I talked about green tomato pie for a long while down at Aunt Hattie's store, over at Koster's, even along the shore. Some people said it was not unusual. Some said it was the most delightful surprise they'd ever had. Still others, who made believe to know, declared that I would either like it very much or dislike it with equal vehemence. I went down to Indian Mills to see Mrs. Miller and surprised her, lively in a way that denied her years, painting the kitchen. Green tomato pie? Well, she said, this was hardly the season for it. "Come down a little later," she suggested with customary Miller-Mullica hospitality, "and I'll let you have some." Then she laughed. "Oh, the recipe," she said, pretending to have misunderstood. "Well, that's a different matter. Let me see, now. . . ."

Green tomato pie, according to Mrs. Miller, is all a matter of tomatoes, lemon, and sugar, plus patience. "You cut the tomatoes, of medium size," she explained, smiling, "into little chips. Dice them, perhaps you'd say, skin and all. Then you take a medium-sized pie plate, putting in the first crust. Now you use eleven heaping tablespoonfuls of sugar, adding part of a lemon, including the rind.

"Now that the dough has been rolled, the bottom of the pie-plate —it ought to be a special kind with a lip all around 'cause the pie's sure to be juicy!—you line the pan with what is to be the first crust. Now comes a good layer of tomatoes. Dust them all over with flour and add half the chipped lemon. Then comes the second layer of tomatoes. Next the rest of the chipped lemon is laid down. You can divide the sugar this way: five tablespoonfuls at the bottom, six at the top. Now, at last, the top crust goes on, and you dust it with flour and put it in the oven. Get all that?"

I explained that I was no cook, but I thought I had. This was important, I said, too important to stay buried in Indian Mills. "How can you tell when it's done?" I inquired, hoping I had the tomatoes and lemon and sugar in the right order and that the war would not eliminate the makings of what sounded like a tempting dish. "Well, you look at it," Mrs. Miller told me, her head cocked on one side. "You test it, of course. Once I was old-fashioned and used a broomstraw. Now I use a toothpick. Guess I been making those pies for forty-five years."

The recipe, Mrs. Miller said, came to her from her mother, Salina Doughty, who also lived in Indian Mills. "You see," she said, "any kind of pie was special, with men depending more on vegetables then. There were more pork meals then than now. Farmers raised their own meats. Farming the place was only part of the life—there was likely a job at one of the mills or glasshouses to carry along with it.

"The kill was once a year, whether it was pigs or something else,

163

and it was never later than February or March. Pork and the rest won't take to salt in warmer weather. You see, we always cut up the pork—guess we always will. Bull says there's some little pigs due today. We always put the pork, cut up, in a barrel, using rock or coarse salt. Layer of salt, layer of pork, layer of salt, that's how it goes into the barrel, just the way it always has."

"Side pork," was folded and carefully "laid in." After the meat was packed, a "pickle" was made of salt and water. "It has to be strong enough," Mrs. Miller explained another test, "to hold a good-sized potato afloat. The meat must always be below the liquid, that is, the brine. Some folks add a little sugar or molasses. Hams? We smoked our own this year as per usual. There used to be some kind of a liquid, a brown sugary kind, that we found pretty good. Now there's a smoke-salt we lay over the hams. You treat them so many days for so many hundred pounds. You have to figure it out for yourself."

One day Mrs. Bull Miller led the way to the cellar. Barrels of the larder were lined against the whitewashed wall. "There's nothing to this," said Mrs. Miller, as I stood there, admiring the full shelves of preserved fruit beyond barrels in operation just as they had been for generations of Mullica folk. "All the folks that's worth their salt," said Mrs. Bull, more appropriately than she knew, "fix up a larder like this. Sugar may go short, but there's always plenty of salt."

I have been thinking, since then, of those first "young ladies who would have scorned the idea of doing kitchen work for strangers" unless, of course, they wanted to make an impression with their culinary proficiency on prospective husbands. I have been reading, too, a little book, a Burlington County cookbook brought to me by Miss Charlotte Rogers who, in these days, tries to impress good recipes on young women of the county's public schools. At one end of the fragile, tattery notes you are exposed to treatments of bone spavins, horse blisters, hog cholera. Then you lapse into ways to make cough syrups, shoe-blacking, and liniments. With no warning at all, you come back to a mixture of zinc and glue for cleaning "cornishes" which is mingled in a friendly way with cures for diphtheria, consumption, diarrhea, hacking coughs, and even sinister cancers. Here were some of the potions of sheep sorrel, potash of

164

grapevine, mullen leaves, sarsaparilla root, oil of hemlock, and pine tar that Uncle Till Estlow was soon to tell me about. All of it, effective or not, seemed closer to death than was pleasant.

I confess here to an abhorrence of those newspaper advertisements which so glibly inquire whether you wouldn't like to have your liver bile stirred up or whether, despite a million irregularities which complicate the day's living, you yourself are "regular." I have been astonished to find that the language of the patent medicine man has ever been, to say the very least, frank. Take for instance an advertisement of 1799, when a mysterious Dr. Ryan was purveying his even more magical "sugar plumbs" at the apothecary shop of James Emerson, in Trenton, in this straight-from-the-shoulder manner:

So exceedingly valued by all people who have had them in Great Britain and Ireland, for their transcendant excellency in the destroying of worms of all kinds, both in the bodies of men, women and children, by not only breaking the knots of the duodenum, or gut next the stomach, they (the plumbs) pass through the smallest passages of the body, and purge away those ropy and slimy humours, which are the cause of those pernicious vermin, and the sources of many other disorders; they are one of the best purges in the world for gross-bodied children that are apt to breed worms and have large bellies . . . they wonderfully cleance the bowels of all stiff and clammy humours which stop up the parts, and prevent the juce of food from being conveyed to the liver and made blood, which is often the case with children, and is attended with a hard belly, stinking breath, frequent fevers, rickets, and a decay of strength in the lower parts. . . .

And now, I suppose, I have allowed Mr. Emerson, indubitably Trenton's pride, to take away whatever appetite you may have had for Mrs. Miller's green tomato pie or Mrs. Kell's cranberry delicacy. I am sorry. I felt I must point out this odd, or perhaps very wise, association of cause and cure, how the pages that yield, in the Jersies, ways to make cocoanut steeples, wafer-jumbles, crullers, kisses, gold and molasses cake as well as pone and ginger-bread, also teach memorable lessons in physiology. Thus, apparently, with great practicability, life and living along the Mullica have been recognized as kin of death and dying, cuisine in need of a companion healing.

. . . as dying, and behold we live; as chastened, and not killed; as sorrowful, yet always rejoicing; as poor, yet making many rich; as having nothing, and yet possessing all things. . . .

Thus the Second Epistle to the Corinthians poetically sums up the philosophy of days that are gone, days that are here and days that are to come, for people along the Mullica shores.

## 16

## THE ADVENTURE OF ASERDATEN

*"Without a stone to mark the spot,*
*And say, what Truth might well have said,*
*By all, save one, perchance forgot,*
*Ah, wherefore art thou truly laid?"*
LORD BYRON

NOW I MUST ASK YOUR INDULGENCE, as well as that of another of the innumerable Fords—for here, in the road, is Sammy, himself, come to tell what he knows of that delightful though unprofitable business of gathering sphagnum moss and cones. But Mr. Ford, I am sure, has waited with patience for many things, and so he protests, sincerely enough, that there could be many worse places in which to idle an hour or so than the twisting road between Green Bank and Herman. Besides, there are cones to be sorted and sphagnum to be raked out in the sun and thus, if he wants to be, Sam will be busy.

Until just now I had not expected to take you to Wells Mills or to prove to you, in a journey to the Brookville that was Tattletown, that a village can be lost altogether, vanishing without trace in New Jersey. I had given up telling you anything of elusive Aserdaten or of leading you back to Mr. Estlow's house where, as far as I am concerned, inquiries ended in new delights but very little certainty. But the postman has come, bringing a letter from Lower Bank, a truly wonderful letter enclosing an entry from a page of the letter-diary of Charles Cramer. Although it was long ago, October 16, 1836, to be precise, that Charles went off to a funeral, what he wrote upon his return, after making a tedious journey through the woods and

166

back, makes our quest for Aserdaten's locale and identity part of our valley and the sequence of our narrative as well. Charles wrote: "Godfrey Estlow died on the 14th and was buried today at Barnharts Place." Belatedly I express my debt and yours to Mr. Cramer, for now we can share acquaintance with Uncle Till, great-great-grandson of Godfrey and last of the Estlows on the old mill pond.

To begin it we must go back together to that summer through which we continued to ask of everybody, everywhere, "Ever hear of Aserdaten? Know where it might have been?" Down at Whiting in the post office, down at Chatsworth at Buzby's store, over at Double Trouble, in Toms River, and even further afield I pursued the inquiry, even after a confusion of answers began coming in. Usually the response was vague, uncertain, disconcerting. There were denials that there had been an Aserdaten, although the name continued to appear on some modern maps. Now, as pieces of the puzzle are fitted together, with the help of that most surprising of all artists, Ned Knox, it would seem that once upon a time there was a man named Dayton, either an Isaiah or Israel that the years wore down to Izzy or Asa, and Asa Dayton's Place became, in time, Aserdaten. That, to date, is the best I can do for you.

It began early in August, long after the June laurel was forgotten on the Barrens, after the turkey beard, goat's-rue, and wild indigo had flowered. And it went on as low oaks began to lose their rich and burnished green, when the sassafras assumed brilliant yellow and scarlet and when heath shrubs turned first to yellow, then finally to scarlet-purple. Nor had the end come when the wild asters and goldenrod brought azure and gold, when the red of wintergreen berries spotted the ground pine and when a quest for Webb's Mill and Aserdaten, persisting because the mislaying of a town seemed absurd, uncovered the unexpected at Wells Mills.

Long after the coming of November made itself known in the dead and dying outdoors elsewhere, the pine country and even the plains were still alive in green, with smilax here and there contrasting the warm colors of the brown scrub, the cedars and yellow-green alder. By then Ned Knox, the bicycle artist who peddles his way along the brushy trails and even over the Forked River Mountains, had joined the posse, pursuing his own disturbing theories about a town linked with the coming of deer and the going of little farms once at the edge of the wastelands. Uncle Dick Walton turned up to talk of rolling charcoal "boxes"; and Tilden Estlow, mildly disturbed by a number of things, said next to nothing of that which would have disturbed me most, his eventual departure from the house of his fathers.

Things that upset Uncle Till were inherited, I suppose, and inherent, too, in a sort of special way. Last time I went through Wells Mills, he strung out his little worries like so many beads. He could not understand how anybody as famous as Godfrey Estlow, who had fought in the battle at Trenton and, driven with his fellows to desperation at Valley Forge, had eaten the toe of a dead colored wanderer, left no record among the names of valiant volunteers. He could not understand why some Estlows, peculiar or perverse, insisted on inserting either an "e" or an "i" in the middle of the family name, making it Estelow or Estilow as best suited their fancy. And he couldn't understand why Mrs. Estlow, overwhelmed by loneliness at Wells Mills, was given to talking of "moving to town"—to Waretown, the village nearer the shore. Even well-meaning historians disturbed him with their dismay and shock at discovering how the Wells Mills millwheel, admittedly fashioned at Martha Furnace, was slowly sinking in the silt. Uncle Till usually supplied assurances that he would get around to digging the "rag-wheel" out next day; but as far as I know it's in the sluiceway still, preserved intact, I hope, by submergence in cedar water.

Your maps will show you that the slag heaps of Martha, where, according to tradition in the family, Godfrey Estlow barged iron and where, according to the Martha Journal, he worked in the mill, is up the Oswego, part of the Wading River that does not get through to the Mullica for some little distance. The way to Wells Mills is roundabout, and Uncle Till, you may reasonably say, has had nothing but long thoughts to link him with our valley in many years. Be all that as it may, Charles Cramer, with three deft lines penned beneath reflections on an early frost and an untimely death, brings the Estlows and Aserdaten to our scene. Where, indeed, was the Barnharts Place he mentions in connection with Godfrey's funeral? Was it, by any chance, the stagecoach stop called Eagle where, Uncle

Till says, his grandfather Christopher lies buried? Or was it the burial plot at Ten Mile Hollow where another Christopher Estlow's name can be descried upon a mossy stone? These were questions I stowed into my bag for the day when an answer might emerge.

I began looking for Aserdaten and the meaning of its name in a variety of places. It offended my sense of order that so many people could say it was a name on a map and that was all they knew. Once I went as far as The Alligator and Horicon, two more puzzlers, but home-coming revealed added riddles, less information than ever. I wrote a letter to John Ernst, then clerk of Ocean County, asking specifically for towns that the county still printed on its charts of roads and villages. "I beg to inform you," he responded after a few days, "that Ocean County maps show the places mentioned, but I do not believe that they are sizable villages" Sizable villages indeed! If Aserdaten and Webb's Mill had been as much as cellar holes, I would have found them. I wrote to Fred Bunnell, publicity director for the county, and to John G. Corrigan, in the Title Department of the Ocean County Trust Company. Mr. Corrigan replied with a map, so that when Fred answered I possessed three, all revealing very plainly the name of Aserdaten and nothing more. They were lovely maps that year and Ocean County was rightfully proud of them; but the names of townships, Little Egg Harbor, Eagleswood, Stafford, Lacey, Plumstead, and many more, bordered by clever little pictures showing the birthplace of Universalism at Good Luck, the ancient Court House at Toms River and even the reputed hiding place of Captain Kidd's treasures made little impression on me. I was looking for a town the state had lost, and the map, as artistic as it was, told no story. Aserdaten was still far off.

Mr. Corrigan said that Bamber once had been Lacey, but I knew that was wrong for I had seen the crossing that had been a station on the Tuckerton Railroad. Bamber had been Ferrago, called "Frago" by Uncle Till, a place with a name that denoted its business, coming from *ferrum* when iron was being dug there, years before they reclaimed the iron rails of the railroad for junk. "As far as Webb's Mill and Aserdaten are concerned," wrote Mr. Corrigan, "the name Aserdaten is seldom found in the records, but Webb's Mill is quite a common call." A later letter to the postmaster and grocer at Whit-

169

ing, a Mr. Christopherson, produced nothing at all about Aserdaten but mentioned Whiting's having been Lancewood for a year or so. "I have been waiting to see our oldest resident," said the postmaster. "John Patton was my informant's father, and he was one of the first here. He says that a man named Whiting came down from New England and bought up all the land he could get and then built a hotel. When Mr. Whiting passed out of the picture, his successor was W. L. Lance. Lance tried to efface the name of Whiting in Lancewood without success."

I recall the storekeeper's letter because of its deflating conclusion. "I know of but one book about our locality," it said, "and I have never read that. I cannot remember the author's name, but I think it is the same as yours."

Fred Bunnell had been making his own inquiries about Aserdaten and so delayed his contribution. To most of his questions as to where the town was, there came the same reply: "Well, it's been in there as long as I can remember." "I talked today to John Grover," said Fred. "He is eighty-eight and knows as much about Ocean County and Toms River as any man I know. But the only thing he remembered about Aserdaten is that it was some place west of Fork*ed* River. I asked our Ocean County road supervisor about it, and he was entirely ignorant of it, didn't even know there was such a place." And yet, county officials had persisted through the years in putting the name where it always had been, never pausing to make sure if there was a town or merely the legend of one. Fred admitted that. He concluded that Horicon, so far as he knew, was in the same plight, except that there was some evidence to show, among people who lived at Lakehurst in its Manchester days, that Horicon was merely a Piney spelling of hurricane. So there we were, in the midst of a passion for bewilderment in the changing of town names and the continuation of some of them, however meaningless and mispelled. Correspondence had accomplished little more than a score of expeditions in the field.

That was when something unbelievable happened.

It may be that you believe in mental telepathy. Perhaps, when you know what followed, you will explain it away by saying that I wanted so earnestly to solve my mystery that a kind of yearning reached out across the wild country lying between to touch another yearning almost half way. Who am I to say anything beyond the fact that it was remarkable that just then, as in the case of the note from Lower Bank, there came a letter from a man who was yet a stranger, the first of many fat letters that were to travel up from Toms River to make up a stout folio in my files? The man who signed himself Edward P. Knox at the end of the first five typewritten pages became a delightful friend, Ned Knox, the bicycle artist of the Jersey Pines.

Ned began with flattery, something that rarely gets me, something that a newspaperman learns to regard with infinite suspicion. Ned said that my books on New Jersey had meant a great deal to him, that they might prove an important influence in his life. That was pure nonsense, I knew, but I read on. "I think you may be interested in knowing why," wrote Ned. "Last year I discovered an entry in an old journal of my father's dated August 4, 1869. He was on his way from Bricksburg, then Lakewood, to Point Pleasant, where he was about to purchase a tract of land from Captain John Arnold. 'Lost in the woods near Burnt Bridge' was all he had written. My father became one of the early summer residents in that region; a clergyman, he organized a church there. When I came along later, I spent my boyhood and college vacations at Point Pleasant. Now, please, be patient with me.

"Some years after, I discovered I was gifted in painting and resolved thirty years ago to come down to this region and paint. The fact that it is no mecca for artists in the sense that New England is did not deter me. If I had had any idea at the time of the difficulty of the job I was tackling, I might not have been so eager to rush in. While demands for making a living have interfered and there have been periods when I had to put all thoughts of painting aside, I am still at it. In 1913 I moved to Toms River, which I selected as a good vantage point. In those days I was working along the bays and beaches—all artists frequent the shore to a certain extent, even here. Self-taught, I went on independently. Some of my first small sketches were exhibited in New York. But I was so intent on seizing the character of the country that modernism never held me despite certain modernistic panels I did on a Barnegat theme. . . ."

171

I hurried my reading. What *was* this?

"I look at the sketches I made along the Barnegat shore and meadows twenty years ago," the letter continued, "and realize that the salt haycocks that made them so picturesque have disappeared entirely. I hear that the salt hay industry is not yet extinct further south, but around here the haycocks are gone and unsightly little shacks take their place . . . it was the brushy mainland that drew and appealed to me in those days. I was forever poking into some unknown road that led I knew not where. I was constantly seeking elevations because they are apt to lend to composition. I had spotted the Fork*ed* River Mountains on the map, and about 1920 made three attempts to get there. What I finally saw from the summit of the 'peaks' was a dark and mysterious region to the west. Some day, I said, I am going to go there. I had to go further west than that, out to Indiana. More years intervened. I returned to my painting, finally, after the lapse of time."

Jane Stanley, who ran a tearoom then in Toms River, handed Ned one of my books, he said, and ever since, he went on (and modesty forbids my quoting him on the point), he had been using the For-gotten Towns chapters as guidebooks. Then one day, turning to a map instead, Ned saw the name of Aserdaten. "I did not have a car," he wrote, "but one rainy March afternoon I and a friend started out. What happened on that trip would make this letter too long, but I made one important discovery. A high percentage of those trails, after the winter rains and before the sand has dried out, make for excellent bicycling. The friend who took me that day agreed with me. . . ." And so the career of the bike-riding artist of the Jersey wilderness began anew. As far as I know, Ned has never given a show. His house is fairly lined with his paintings, and I assure you that there is no painter anywhere who has so deftly caught the color and contrast of Down Jersey. Most remarkable is the fact that Ned, at fifty-eight, had to teach himself to ride all over again, in order to reach the Forgotten Towns he wanted to paint.

And sooner than soon, Knoxian letters revealed that the artist's own search for Aserdaten had begun. "I had rather fail," Ned con-fessed, "on a difficult thing than succeed on an easy one. That is why I have stuck through the years, though I confess to my periods of anguish and temptations to go elsewhere and seek easier fields. The old trails get into the blood, or maybe, somewhere, our blood is already there. . . ." Ned Knox is a poet—I found it out long after his letters should have told me; once, at Christmas, he sent along a little book of his splendid verses. The elusiveness of Aserdaten, a village located by maps but nothing else, was a plague for poets, he told me. No matter what the mystical something might be that had caught and held us there in the midlands wilds, we must recognize it together, he said. Determination to find Webb's Mill and Aserdaten, a challenge made up of ground fog, the tang of cedar water, the crackle of dead leaves and treasures of a country known mostly to God, was now renewed and drawing us together. "It is a beautiful land," said Ned, "one of the finest anywhere. Few people dwell in greater safety, few suffer less from real calamities than those who live there. Like men, regions have their sore disappointments and frustrations. Like men, they rise above them. Our particular job, not that we will it to be so, but because we believe it to be truly ours, is to see to it that some contribution is made to this region's own literature, its own history, its own art, without which it cannot rise. . . ."

It was a fine letter. Not until long after did I fully appreciate it. My first step was to write posthaste and ask Ned Knox what he knew about Aserdaten, telling him of sad experiences we had had in trying to find it and, further, in discovering somebody who knew where it actually was and who provided its enigmatic name. Ned came through a few days later with ten more pages.

"About Aserdaten," he said, "I believe I can now send you some information. It may involve one of the strangest stories you have had to tell. It will be about a man, Aserdaten, who seems to have evaporated. You will do well to go easy on seeking information in this neck of the woods from woodjins and native stock. It is possible that you may be running into a vital matter, about which also I believe people are most reluctant to talk. Now this is all theoretical, based on my own observations. But inasmuch as Aserdaten is associated with a certain deer park, you might obtain some information from the Forked River Game Preserve. As to the man himself—"

Even now, Ned and I are not quite sure there was a man. He may

173

have existed; we do not know. For lack of information on a person, I have sought every other possible explanation, toying with every variation of spelling that seems plausible, *aufseher* instead of *aser*, *deuten* instead of *daten*. Once we conveniently coupled *auserdaten*, out of date, and *hauserdenken*, the imagining of a house, which comes natural enough where the village must have been. Finally Ned got around to the botanical prefix, *acer*, used frequently in the vicinity. But none of these theories matched up with Ned's earlier conclusions that Aserdaten was a man and our later deductions that there was a man, surely, with the probable name of Asa Dayton.

We continued our investigations separately for a time, Ned Knox and his friend, Dr. Loveman, peddling their way out of Toms River, even as I took along others caught in the fascination of seeking a lost town with quite as much enthusiasm as if they were hunting Atlantis. Once a charcoal burner said that he knew well where Aserdaten was, that we were far from it, and that anyhow it was "just a lot of grass among the trees." Once there was a memorable Sunday when a crisscross of trails led to half-hidden gunning clubs, whose occupants at the time were none too pleased that we had found the way that far. There was a day when, quite unexpectedly, Ed Hough and I got through to Webb's Mill. "This place is the most fascinating of all to me," wrote Ned Knox when I told him I thought we were getting closer to our objective. "From Webb's Mill radiate old roads to every point of the compass, Whiting, Pasadena, Tuckerton, Toms River, Daniel's Bridge, Brookville, Cedar Bridge. There is a tree with a buckshot-riddled sign that reads 'Bamber Five Miles.' I hope to stick that in a picture if some vandal does not steal it." Actually a vandal accomplished such a mischief. "I would put it in my will to bury me at Webb's Mill," wrote Ned, "if I had not been told that the state owns a sixty-foot right-of-way through there, and it is on the program to some day sabotage all of it with a highway. . . ."

It was the artist's conclusion that the Lacey Road was headed for Mill Road long before the supposed Mr. Aserdaten came to fasten his name to the junction point. "A mile and a half beyond your broken bridge from the Lacey Road, the one leading across the ridge that once held railroad track," he said, "the road swerves close

The whereabouts of many of Ned Knox's paintings and John McAnney's six-bore shotgun are equally uncertain. Ned rode a bicycle with easel attached even into the Forked River Mountains. John had many tales to tell of his incomparable weapon.

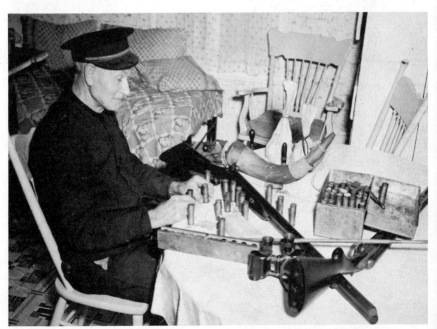

The Bowker family gathering sphagnum moss deep in the pines. Below, Sammy Ford showed a homemade baler, specially designed for sphagnum.

to the swamp; and among the wintergreen berries you will see old tracks leading into the spong over what once was a causeway." I remembered the place; once, on foot, I had walked along the causeway with Doc Crate who was dead when next I came that way. Ned had gone back in the spring, he told me, retracing paths he last trod in 1918, eating his lunch in the same places, nibbling at wintergreen berries that still grew where he remembered them. Butterfly weeds were flaming here and there, sweet flags were coming, and down at the edge of the swampy pools were water lilies on which no human eye had fallen. Ned was sure he had come upon Aserdaten— "big pines, badly blackened; no open spaces. Indian grass in tufts, ground so swampy that one must be on the lookout for snakes." Ned wrote that he was sure he had seen evidence of some sort of a fence or barrier. "Of all the creepy places!" he exclaimed, certain in his mind that this was the town.

One autumnal Sunday after that Alex Garwood and I found Aserdaten, too, or the place Ned Knox had described. Yes, there was the apple tree that Ned had found in bloom. And there were the two cellar holes, yawning pits in the midst of tall Indian grass, cavities in which I dug out bricks and field stones. The clearing reached back under the trees beyond where the houses might have been, trees that had come to maturity since the supposed Mr. Aserdaten had come and gone. But now that we had found the town what, by all that was sacred, was Aserdaten? *Who* was he? Why all the mystery? At best we had but half the story.

Ned, cycling again with his paints and brushes, far more disarming than a mere array of questions such as I possessed, had been told at Double Trouble that there was a man over on the newer Lacey Road who would bed and feed a wandering artist over night, no questions asked. Yes, this man and his wife admitted, they knew of Aserdaten. "Used to be a nice place," they said. "Good land around there, but you couldn't raise anything much. Fast as it growed, the deer came and ate it." "All I could get there," Ned supplemented, "was that Aserdaten was a man who had started a deer park in days long before New Jersey thought of propagating a kind far different from the native species." Next in line was Bert Dorsett. Bert was sixty, the son of Captain John L. Dorsett, of West Point

Pleasant, and owner of a farm and boat shop on Beaver Dam Creek. Bert came right out with assertions that the man at Aserdaten set up a deer park in days when even the red deer had died out in New Jersey.

"The conclusions seem to sum up to this, now," Ned wrote me, "—this man Dayton had an idea, an idea for a deer park. You hear that over and over. There must have been much activity at Lacey in those days at the early part of the century, an echo perhaps of the activity that had been Bamber's before. There are indications of invested fortunes, and that the road in to Lacey Station and on over the track to Aserdaten was humming with life. Was Aserdaten an agent for an early absentee owner? Did someone reason that other pinelands had deer and these pinelands, having none, should be stocked forthwith? It may have happened that way; it may have worked all right. For the people at Lacey and on all the little farms that you can trace along the road to Fork*ed* River, it worked out too well. 'No use to plant—the deer eat up everything!' Can it be that this is something the fathers of these people were saying, perhaps even the grandfathers? Can it be that all the farms were ruined, not by poor soil but by deer that were imported to the deer park of the supposed Aserdaten?

"This is the real plaint among the poorer people—the deer!" wrote the bicycle artist, adding again that it was a touchy subject and that perhaps it would be best to let Aserdaten go unfound. The implications always creeps in that the farmers did something about the man at Aserdaten. Yet there can be no charge unless you have a *corpus delicti.* "So came Aserdaten and so he went," said Ned, "if ever he went at all. Is he the man the farmers had to thank for the loss of all that made them self-sufficient in what now is barren land? Did someone more intelligent than the others see what would happen if the deer multiplied as they were expected to, if they broke down the barriers at Aserdaten and fled to the woods and fields? Did that someone shake his fist in Aserdaten's face? Or did it all happen so quickly that no one really knows just what it was and who was responsible? Who *was* Aserdaten? Whatever became of him?"

Ned Knox gave me the impression that he was content to let sleeping dogs lie, that as far as he was concerned his questions could go without answers. The evidence, I protested, was not all in as yet. He patiently agreed, hurrying off in the gloom of a night when even the lone apple tree of Aserdaten, blooming forlornly in the wilds, seemed like a shrouded ghost.

I kept on. I wrote letters. I went to Ned's house; he came to mine, comparing notes. I kept rattling the skeleton in the closet, contending that if there was a *corpus,* I for one was bent on discovering it. That, really, was how I came upon Dolph Arens again, for the first time in broad daylight, and how we took counsel with old Dick Walton, finally partaking of the friendly hospitality of the Estlows at Wells Mills.

Dick Walton, one of the last Civil War veterans along the coast, answered questions in a way that revealed surprising agility of mind. Aserdaten? Why, of course. He had been there many times. Once, he said, he had delivered a load of salt hay there. Then he switched to recalling the Webbs of Webb's Mill, Joey, Nate, and David. Next he recalled a famous character called Will Hurry for whom, he told us, a station between Whiting and Pasadena had been named. "Pasadena was Wheatlands first, you know," he said. "Will Hurry lived there. Never married. Related to an old Toms River family, he was, the Breckenridges—now scattered and gone." Uncle Dick spoke of Pancake, Tattletown, and Webb's Town, just as if we should know them well. His first child had been born at Wheatlands, he told us, and as if to oblige, his daughter appeared just then. "Can't say as I've even seen the town," she laughed. "Guess now I never will."

"You wouldn't remember Ben and Joe Morey," Dick Walton rambled on, skirting all around the subject in which we were most interested. "I teamed with them for lumber back on the ridges. Pancake—never hear of *that?* That's where the Morey Lot Road started. Tattletown? That was somewhere over Red Oak Grove way. Webb Town was different from Webb's Mill."

All of this was intensely interesting, of course, but it focussed no new light on the immediate objective. As a matter of fact, although we returned to Dick Walton's house on at least two subsequent occasions, we gained nothing more about Aserdaten except that it had been notable enough at one time to boast a resident who could order a quantity of salt hay. Uncle Dick confirmed the fact that the road to Webb's Mill out of Toms River once had been called the "Mule Road," and that there had been a day when all the trails across the plains had been filled with teams hauling salt hay, logs, and coal —charcoal, of course. But beyond this, the best of the riddles went unsolved.

Once we found the grave of Zebulon Collins at Ten Mile Hollow and wondered if he had been the Zeb of Zeb's Bridge, over beyond Keswick. In the same little graveyard, under faded flags and a few clamshells, was buried another of the Cramers, a Civil War veteran himself. A child's grave was marked with some pieces of terra cotta, surrounded by the mounds of Brittons, Bransons, Pattons, Grants, and Hilliards, who surely had known Aserdaten well and had delighted in tall talk at Giberson's Mills before it was Keswick at all. (Even Giberson, you know, is not the name it was: At first it was Gibeson and Guiberson, Gabeson in 1699, Gybertson in 1701, and Giberson only when John Giberson of Revolutionary service came home to set up the mill on Tice VanHorn's Brook.) Then came a Sunday when we used the rumor of wildcats in the Lebanon State Forest as an excuse to approach the site of Aserdaten from what we made believe was a new direction, knowing well enough that there were no more approaches to try.

Instead of taking the obscure left turn where a sign once showed the way to Preacher's Hill and, further on, instead of taking the Mill Road, we swung to the right where, that Sunday with Alex Garwood, the sound of popping guns on the range of the Eureka Gun Club previously deterred us. As soon as we had seen it, in spite of the changes that had come from what we remembered as the Chisler's Club, I knew that we had been there before. Suddenly I realized that if this were so, I had come by Aserdaten years before without knowing. Imagine confessing that you were through a village without any realization of it!

Two men came from the clubhouse as we pulled up. One was tall and tanned and gangling, the other shorter. You must always remember to ask a business-like question when you are confronted like that, in the Jersey wilds. Usually I manage something silly, for all my advice. "Hello," I said that day. "Ever hear of Aserdaten? Was it anywhere near here?" The tall man disclosed a broad grin and

178

then a laugh. "Ha ha," he responded, "I know *you!* You ain't goin'
to fool me with questions like that!" He extended a brown and
horny hand.

"Dolph Arens!" I sang out pleasureably, joining his amusement.
That was when I remembered I had never seen him by daylight. Last
time I talked to him was at Dr. Newberry's in Waretown, when the
mosquitoes defied us all to turn on lights although the house was
well fortified with screens. Dolph poked fun at me for having called
him a woodjin in a book. Just as before, he seemed ageless now, as
if he had wandered out of a hidden lamasery to talk calmly of things
centuries old. "This was the old Chisler's Club," he said. "You been
here before. It was Tilly Collins's before that," he added, as if all of
us should have known Tilly well.

"And who was *she?*"

"Musta been Zeb Collins's wife. She was sister to Tom Sweeney,
wasn't she? Think *so.*" He laughed. "Back here," he said, "they was
all crossed up like scissors grinders!"

This, said Dolph, was the Branson tract. There was Jim Branson,
Huds Branson and Henry Branson, too. "Joe Branson," he explained,
"was the last of 'em here. Webb Field was Webb Town in them days.
And they was still digging clay down at Union Clay Works." Chance
mention of Lacey Station brought Dolph to recall five houses along
the road that led to where the track of the railroad used to be.
"Rutherford Stuyvesant was over there then," he said, "and so was
some Frenchmen who tried growing a vineyard. But it all flunked
up on them."

Dolph tapped some beer from a keg on the porch. Even if you don't
like beer you learn to know better than turn it down in the pine
country when a woodjin is pouring.

"But what about Aserdaten?" It always came back to that.

"There was a deer park there," Dolph said, very quietly. His companion agreed. And then the subject was changed. "I got something
to show you," said Mr. Arens, now the caretaker of the Eureka Club,
rising. First he moved a few feet from the dooryard where an in-
dentation of suitable length hinted at an unmarked grave. "It's a
grave all right," Dolph averred. "They buried 'em right in the yard
in the old days. Who was it? How should I know?"

179

The hint, I have always thought, was that this might have been the resting place of Mr. Aserdaten, or Asa Dayton, buried here after sudden death that paid him in full for loosing wild deer upon the little farms. Dolph was careful to give no clear intimation of anything like that. Instead he led the way through laurel and cinnamonfern to where there was a stone, as large as a crouching man. Into it had been scratched a name and date: "T. G. Black—1858." Who was Black? Dolph said he didn't know that, either. All he knew was that folks always called the little span over which we had come, "Black's Bridge."

Nor was this all. We followed Dolph back to the trail and across to the other side. There, lost in the scrub and baybush was a line of tumbled stones. "It's either a chimney or an Indian mound," Dolph confided casually. "They say there used to be a cabin over here and that this is where the Bransons lived."

More puzzles—but never another syllable about Aserdaten! "But Dolph said something he never did before," I pointed out, when we were climbing Doe Hill. "He said he'd been back here since 1901. In that case, he knows the country—or should—better than any. He *must* know more about Aserdaten."

"Somehow," Ned Knox wrote me after that, "you begin to dread getting at the truth about Aserdaten. It's like a secret that will remain a secret no matter what happens. Maybe it's better that way."

He didn't believe it any more than I. Armed with added information culled from Uncle Dick Walton, Ned and I agreed to go down to see Uncle Tilden Estlow who, I told him, might have a final word. Uncle Dick, faced again with Ned's eternal question, said he never heard tell where the name Aserdaten had come from. "Always figgered it was Indian," he said. "The Bransons had Indian blood. Nothing to be 'shamed of in Indian blood." That was what Dolph Arens had said, adding, "Good as any blood in the country, don't forget."

Willis Estlow got us down to see his Uncle Till, and we found the Estlows gracious hosts, content with nothing less than our coming for Sunday dinner. We talked in the dining room of the house high above the Wells Mills pond that is more than a hundred years old at one end, more than two hundred at the other. Uncle Till began to remember things beside a huge stove whose requirement of a log, now and then, made the only interruption. Mrs. Estlow, ever a mite shy, kept busy in the kitchen.

"Great-great-Grandfather Godfrey and his brother came out from Holland, we always heard tell," said Uncle Till, stretching out his stockinged feet in full comfort. "They set up a mill at Speedwell, the old furnace. Not so long ago some of us went along with Willis to where we found the locks Godfrey Estlow put there for scowing the ore to the forge at Martha. This house was owned first by Sammy Birdsall—the Estlows have been changing it to suit as each family inherited. Father and his six brothers were borned here or at Martha so this and all the land they traveled through is home to me."

I said, with feeling, that the Estlows had made it home to us already.

Uncle Tilden smiled and went on. It was here at Wells Mills that Christopher, his grandfather, built and ran the sawmill. Now rain splashed down the windows and Tilden Estlow looked anxiously down toward the pond where, many years before, he had driven a stake. If the water rose above the top of it, he must hurry down beside the tumbled ruin of the dam and lower the gates. But the top of the stake still showed, and Uncle Till went on talking.

"The wheel," he said, "was built up to Martha. It's down there in the creek bed now. Some day when it's clear I'll show it to you. Some day when I can get around to it, I'll dig it out. History people are always telling me it's a relic and ought to be saved. It's been safe enough down there for years on end. Father invented that wheel. Made every white oak cog himself and called it a rag wheel, a go-back wheel, too, sometimes." I wasn't rude enough to argue that the legend always had been that the go-back wheel was the invention of the proprietor of Webb's Mill. "Come spring, I'll get the wheel up and have a look at it again."

We had to work up to Aserdaten, asking what there was at Daniel's Bridge in earlier years and if Daniel might not have been Daniel Cameron, later Camburn. I pointed out that the Camburns went back to William, the sailor who lived where Captain Jacob Birdsall had a house in Waretown. This, I suggested, could link Sammy Birdsall and perhaps the Green Bank Birdsalls with Daniel Camburn of the bridge down the road. "Don't know nothing about that," said Uncle Till, "but I have heard tell that once there was a young divinity student living down there by the bridge. He stole a lot of lumber, they say, so's to build him a house where he could study to be a preacher."

Zare's Bridge, I suggested, was another oddity. "Zare?" Uncle Tilden laughed. "That's easy. Short for I-zare!"

Uncle Till's broad shoulders and muscular hands betrayed an active life with all the hard work that seems to have been the lot of most of the Estlows from pioneer days. Something of an inventive genius was demonstrated by Christopher and after that, Francis, for neighbors still came around, Uncle Till said, for Christopher's own novel turnip planter. Beats anything you can get by mail, he told us.

"It was Grandfather who brought sawed shingles here first," he went on, barring an interruption. "Before that, shingles was always rived around here. You used a drawknife and a horse. Estlows sawed 'em first at Martha, too. And what's Martha now? Nothing but a slagpile and a lake and a few cellar holes where some of the four hundred people lived when the furnace was going. Good thing Dad brung his go-back wheel with him!"

"But—about Aserdaten . . . "

"Never forget the time I was the champion at sawing shingles. Somebody said that nobody had sawed 'em faster than a thousand an hour. Old Giddy Giberson did that, they said. That was enough for me. I went as fast as I could one day, and I turned out a thousand in less than thirty-five minutes. Johnny Cramer couldn't pack 'em as fast as I sawed."

"Aserdaten," I tried again, "is a funny name."

"Skeekat's Plains is funnier," replied Uncle Till. "Lots of them names nobody mentions now. There was Little Buck Run, Big Buck Run, Hogback, and Fawn Hill. And there was Pancake, too, where the road to Waretown crosses the bed of the Tuckerton Railroad. And Morey Lot—that was where there's always apple trees blooming in May in the middle of the pines. . . ."

"Where," I asked bluntly, "was Aserdaten?"

"Up near Webb Town."

"*What* was Aserdaten?"

182

"There was a deer park there."

"But who was this Aserdaten and what on earth became of him?"

"Guess he was the man who started the deer. I never saw him as I remember. The Bransons looked after the place when I was there. I was a boy when I went gunning with Daddy over that way. We had the dogs with us. Pretty soon they let out a yelp, and we knew they had come on the trail of a deer. Somehow, by the time we got through, the dogs were in the pen at Aserdaten. We had a harry of a time getting 'em out. Good thing the Bransons was away."

"Why wasn't Aserdaten there himself? Where was he when the Bransons were there?"

Uncle Till looked hard at me. "I don't know," he said. "Anyhow, I don't recollect his name *was* Aserdaten."

"What *was* his name?"

"I don't know."

"Was it Dayton? Was he Isaiah Dayton, perhaps?"

"Could ha' been."

"You don't know how long he was there, when he died, or anything."

"No," said Uncle Till quietly, without being particularly convincing.

That was all. There *was* a deer pen at Aserdaten—we had found the timbers of a rotting fence. As for the name and how it came together, I must leave you to your own ingenuity after all. Even Ned Knox, after additional investigation, is not sure there was an Ezra or even Asa Dayton. Even Ned cannot prove what he believes to be the truth, that the owners of little farms that are no more paid the founder of Aserdaten in full for importing the deer that ruined their dreams of happiness.

Uncle Till, full of ideas about Brookville, once Millville, once Headleyville, and even Tattle- or Tattlertown, provoked that he could find no record of Revolutionary ancestry, said nothing more about the town that was and is no more. A chunk of wood went into the stove. "My great-great-grandfather used to say," Tilden Estlow went on, "that he had killed two men in the war. One was with a bay'net at Trenton. The other was with his fist aboard a man-o'-war when a bully stole the rations and looked for a fight. He got it, bare

183

knuckles, although he never knew what hit him." Tilden Estlow smiled and rubbed the knuckles of his own right hand, remembering days when he was a village wrestler, taught by a father who, once confronted in the swamps by a wildcat, killed the animal with a club.

"One night," said Uncle Till, "we was stalkin' deer with spotlights on the Plains. We come on one sudden-like. Somebody shouted he could see his eyes. Most of us could only see one eye, and that made me laugh. But I didn't say anything when one of the boys said he must be a one-eyed deer. We all crept up. Then we let loose together —and found out we was shootin' at old Barnegat Light!"

Thus you have met the redoubtable Tilden Estlow of Wells Mills, son of Francis Robineau who was named for a Hessian soldier who deserted, and grandson of Christopher whose father was the miller at Martha—Godfrey Estlow whose funeral made him part of the lore of the Mullica River. Now we must keep Sammy Ford no longer. I can only report to you, in conclusion, what you already know, that Sunday dinner at Wells Mills was a treat, indeed, and that all of us, due to command performance, ate too much.

*17*

## ROLLING STONES GATHER

*"O for a lodge in some vast wilderness,*
*Some boundless contiguity of shade,*
*Where rumour of depression and deceit,*
*Of unsuccessful or successful war,*
*Might never reach me more."*
WILLIAM COWPER

SAMMY FORD CAME WANDERING UP THE ROAD FROM GREEN BANK. Over his shoulder was a rake, homemade, all wood and fitted together according to the memorized pattern used for years by Mullica people. There's no raking of the leaves that fall along the river, but there's raking of "taters" and a spreading of sphagnum moss to dry whenever the sun is high. Sam had been raking moss.

Day before, he said, he had been gathering and sorting pine cones. Good cones, well-shaped, cones that will color well for wreaths and other decorations in which florists try to improve on God, bring all of two dollars a thousand, Sammy said. It was a statement of fact, nothing in the nature of complaint. Two dollars can go a long way down the river.

Sam told me he had been gathering cones and sphagnum for more than five years on land owned or leased by Vernon Corliss, who has a sign revealing his business, up from Green Bank, nearer Herman, the place that goes on calling itself a city although the city never came to be. The word *sphagnum* is one that confuses the best of moss men, and Vernon is no exception when it comes to spelling it out on the sign. The business itself is more important. "Before down here, I was rakin' moss back of Barnegat and at Simm Place," Sammy went on.

Throughout the hot summer farmers living down near the cedar swamps go out every day with "tater" rakes or home-fashioned grapnels or even "drags" to gather tons of this kind of moss that bears no relationship to rolling stones. The "mossies" may not know how to spell sphagnum, but they know well enough that it must be valuable to somebody and that it is used by floriculturists all over the country, as well as in Canada and Puerto Rico. And they have heard that it has been in great demand for surgery in wartime.

Another Corliss, Clarence, who lives over at Warren Grove, has been harvesting sphagnum more than thirty years. Clarence uses three- and five-tined potato rakes to drag his crop from the beds of cedar swamps up from Barnegat. After the moss is raked out, Sammy explained it to me, it is collected in piles on higher spots of the marsh and then slung on a hummock while some of the moisture drains out. Later still, tied in thirty or thirty-five pound bales, it brings to the "mossies" an average of sixty or seventy cents to the bale, much more to the middleman and something actually worthwhile to the retailer.

Sphagnum, Sammy Ford says, is harder to find now than in the days when people along the little rivers first began harvesting it. Under ideal conditions the moss requires three years to grow to a length suitable for harvesting. Then, the "mossies" say, care must be taken not to rake the swamps too clean. If no seed remains, the crop will disappear. Owners of "estates" as well as careless gatherers have been responsible for cutting down the yield. Invaders of the lowlands often cut off cedars and kill off sphagnum that way; others post the land to protect it from moss gatherers in the belief that they are protecting the cedar bogs. "Now," Sam told me, "we got to lease land to get what we want, lots of times."

It was back in September, 1916, that the front cover of *The London Graphic* carried a query in bold-face: "Are You Collecting Sphagnum Moss?" By November, 1918, the *Scientific American* was carrying a similar appeal for large quantities of moss which was proclaimed to be of great value in World War I surgical dressings. Although cotton prices of World War II indicated from the first that they alone would not be the cause of a shortage such as had been previously experienced, Mullica "mossies" naturally believed that their crop of sphagnum would be shipped as a substitute for cotton absorbents. Sammy said he had heard that.

For it was in the last war, pre-Axis, that Scotland, Ireland, and England went to work collecting bog moss for medical dressings. Some was gathered and shipped from Canada and the Pacific Northwest, but this proved too far from the Atlantic Coast, and transportation costs made the finding of new Eastern sources imperative. With the coming of global war, sources in the East and West were ready to assume an equally important, if not more vital role, for the powers of sphagnum were pictured, meanwhile, as little short of miraculous.

Professor George E. Nichols of the Sheffield Scientific School is authority for the statement that a workman in the peat moors of Northern Germany made the original discovery of the curative values of sphagnum. The laborer, he said, suffered severe wounds of the forearm—that was in the 1870's—and with nothing else available, he wrapped his arm in peat. Ten days later he was able to get surgical aid. So great was the physician's amazement when he found the man's wounds almost healed that he began the first scientific experiments with the moss. Soon similar experiments were under way in many parts of Germany.

In areas of Great Britain, Ireland, and Scotland, as well as these "faraway" lands in New Jersey, this moss always has been used in the home treatment of boils and discharging wounds. Uncle Till Estlow told me a number of stories of how it was rare even to think of calling a doctor unless it looked as if the patient was going to die unless one came. "And even if you thought of the doctor," Sammy Ford said, "thinking wouldn't get him to places in time. You just had to know how to cure up things yourself." By the time of the Napoleonic and Franco-Prussian wars sphagnum was being mildly recommended for use by army surgeons; and when the Russo-Japanese War was under way, Japanese soldiers were given sphagnum dressings and sent on ten-day trips home unattended. Japanese casualties were found to have wounds healing better than those bandaged immediately on the field with cotton.

Shown the way, ironically enough in World War I, by Germans and Japanese, the British War Office at last officially accepted sphagnum dressings in 1915 and, following this official recognition abroad, the American Red Cross began providing moss dressings at the rate of twenty thousand sphagnum pads a month, an extremely small scale compared to the work in other countries.

"Sphagnum," said Professor Nichols in his report, "absorbs liquids three times as fast and will take up greater amounts than absorbent cotton. A pad of the latter will absorb five or six times its weight in water. An average pad of sphagnum will take up sixteen to eighteen times its weight in water—more than three times as much as cotton. Exceptionally good moss will absorb as much as twenty-two times its own weight of water. The moss retains liquids better than cotton so that a dressing need not be changed as often."

Failure to discriminate between species of sphagnum moss—only the old "mossies" know about that, Sam told me,—probably accounted to some extent for the fact that such dressings were less popular with American Army surgeons than with the surgeons of other armies in World War I. Although about twenty-five different kinds of sphagnum are recognized in the United States, only two or three can be used for surgery. To offset the scarcity of cedar swamp sphagnum, some attempts have been made to grow moss on maple beds but this, they tell me, hasn't worked out. The best sphagnum is identified by the experts as *sphagnum papillosum* which, from the sound of it, would seem to have something in common with butter-flies, but of all the invaders of swamps I have seen I can assure you that none have been of the butterfly family. From all I have been able to gather (not moss!) *sphagnum papillosum* has not been dis-covered farther south than New Jersey.

Sphagnum wholesalers say that nurserymen prefer the moss for shipping, because it holds moisture around plant roots longer than most comparable substances. "Sphagnum," said Marshall Reeves, one of the wholesalers, late one afternoon, "is used in the operations of grafting." I am confident the allusion was to the nonpolitical variety. "It is also used in the propagation of such plants as will produce new roots whenever a fistful of bog moss is tied around the stem which, after adventitious roots have appeared, is severed below the ball of moss." I shall have to try that some day, so that I may finally grasp what he was talking about.

Dry moss, neither very good nor very bad, is used for stuffing wreaths and floral pillows so that flowers covering the surface can be more firmly held in place. You have surely come upon graveyards where, long after the flowers have faded and gone, those dreadful-looking frameworks are to be found where relatives and friends deposited their dead and flowers and lamentations, then quickly moved on. It is probable that the moss will vanish only when it is picked up and thrown away.

Diligent inquiry here and there would indicate that in good areas during a wet season, one gatherer, working hard, turns up with as many as eighteen hundred bales in towns along the coast, at Warren Grove, or in Chatsworth where wholesalers have storage space. Sammy Ford would make no estimate of his own harvests, nor would he make extensive comment on aspects of the industry of which I was certain he knew a great deal. "I could guess at what I get," he said, "but you wouldn't want that. Eighteen hundred bale sounds like a lot to me, but I don't stop to count after the money's in. I rake out moss till I get tired or till I want to do something else. Then maybe I take to cones. Or maybe I take to nothin' much at all."

One day I looked into the big storehouse of another of the Estlows —Francis, one of the family who had inserted an "i" in the name— and there I found twelve hundred bales piled up, awaiting a greater demand or a better price. "Mossies" have more than an idea that the wholesaler makes out a lot better than they, especially when prices are below the usual sixty-to-ninety-cent scale and when whatever they bring in is classed arbitrarily as "only fifty-cent moss." But moss gatherers can't wait for prices to rise, as wholesalers will, or for a day when demand will sky the retail figure to two dollars or more.

Sammy says most "mossies" don't stop to figure what will pay them more, sphagnum or cones. "The rakin'," he told me, "depends a little on weather, whether you got a good sun or whether you ain't. There's a lot of work to moss. With pine cones it's just a pickin' of 'em up. And like as not you can count on seventy cents for every thousand pine cones you turn in." I did not tell him what was in my mind, that I did not think I would like to go around picking up a full thousand perfect pine cones for a mere seventy cents.

What launched my rather spotty investigation of this moss business was something that happened long before I met Sammy Ford. I had come upon the most interesting group of "mossies" I had had the good fortune to meet, most of a family, at work down the Jones' Mill Road. I had been looking for gatherers of sphagnum, and Jack Buzby, at the Chatsworth store, called me up one day and suggested that I go along with him by the site of old Jones' Mill. It proved a sunny afternoon, and before it was over I had seen the whole procedure, producer to consumer.

Not far down the road was a clearing. In it were neat little piles of drying moss. In the midst was a typical baler, homemade from odds and ends but entirely serviceable in the job it accomplished. It may be that you have seen this peculiar machine and have wondered what on earth it was. A tall, boxlike affair, made with parts of crates, perhaps with a crank fashioned from an old and rusted pipe that sometimes utilizes a chain to pull the moss tight, puzzled you as much as it bewildered me. Let it puzzle you no more. It was Elmer Lemmon, a short and twisted man with a surprisingly young face, who overcame his infirmities to demonstrate how well the baler worked. He had just turned the moss in the field, he said. Baling it with wire was scheduled for dusk, in the shed, that evening.

Further on, in another clearing bounded by chicken wire which had been taken there for the purpose of keeping moss from blowing away in a sudden wind, Elvin Leek was still spreading sphagnum on the hot white sand of the pine country, using a pitchfork. Elmer Lemmon had said that his clearing was across from Selah Bowker's; and Jack Buzby told me that until I saw Selah, I could not say that I had talked with a true "mossy." And so we came next upon Selah Bowker, his wife, and a coterie of relatives and friends.

Selah was tall and angular and given to monosyllables, even in the answering of questions. Like him, Mrs. Bowker wore rubber boots, into which were stuffed the legs of blue denim pants. Similarly attired was Wayne Lockwood, their son-in-law. All three came marching from the pungent lowlands with the last heaping loads of dripping moss that Selah's truck would hold. I marveled that a truck had penetrated so deeply into the swamps drained by the branches of the Wading River. "Mossin'," Selah told me in one of his few full speeches, "just has to be in the family, or it just don't pay at all."

After that I took notes on all angles of the business of the moss-gatherers. Then, in those journeys down the Mullica, I came upon Sammy Ford.

"In the old days," Sammy said, rounding out the story one night not long ago, "they used to load bales of moss on freight trains of the Jersey Central. But that ain't been done for a good while now. And some of the New York boys has been cuttin' out the wholesalers down here, comin' clear down from Brooklyn when they could get the gas."

"I guess by this time the Red Cross and the Army buy direct," I suggested.

"They don't buy sphagnum at all," Sammy told me, and I wondered, then, if I had told him anything about the moss business he didn't know. For I have checked with Red Cross headquarters, and information men there bear him out. The Red Cross says that no sphagnum pads have been used at all in World War II so far as they are concerned. It is suggested that once again a substitute has been found for the substitute—or, more likely, that there's more cotton, lower-priced, than there was twenty-five years ago.

"I don't think I'd like to do all that work for only seventy cents," I told Sam, thinking of both moss and pine cones.

Sammy Ford looked surprised. "It's nice work," he said. "It's outside. Nobody bothers you much if you go in the right places. The swamps is healthy. And maybe, if you keep quiet and watch, you can see the Jersey Devil."

Sam said it quietly as if there were no hokus-pokus about it. I tried to be as matter-of-fact as he. "I didn't know," I said, "that the Jersey Devil was still around. I didn't know he got back this far."

"Well, he does," Sammy told me. "Sometimes."

## 18

## THE FORUM

*"Wisdom there, and Truth,*
*Not shy as in the world, and to be won*
*By slow solicitation, seize at once*
*The roving thought, and fix it on themselves."*
WILLIAM COWPER

I CONFESS TO NEVER THINKING OF AUNT HATTIE'S STORE at Green Bank without remembering another that is no more than recollection. Will Kemble, I think it was, recalled the old Lower Bank storekeeper who promised to keep a fisherman's can of worms on the shelf behind him. The fisherman, as I told you in passing, returned after ten years had flown. The storekeeper looked up with a mere hello.

"Is that all you have to say to me after ten years?" asked the returned prodigal.

"Didn't guess it was that long," replied the man behind the counter, mildly.

191

"You ought to remember."

"Maybe I do. Yes, of course I do," answered the storekeeper. "You was going fishin' and you gave me some worms to keep while you did an errand or something. Bet the worms is just where I put them for you."

He looked and sure enough the can of worms was still there. They were of no use to the fisherman, however. After ten years even worms are dust.

I have visited that store since Will Kemble told me that story. He described it to me beforehand as a place where many ghosts lingered, Mullica worthies who came there in the evening to inquire for a letter that never came or to talk over the problems of the day. Mrs. Allen, the last postmistress to preside there had died, and the post office was only a house. I was disappointed that no phantom rose to greet me.

Aunt Hattie's store, at the Green Bank corner up from the bridge and across from the old stage-stop hotel, still vacant despite a "for sale" sign that is touched up now and then with dregs of leftover paint, is much different. Although it is also the post office, because of a compartment in a dusty corner devoted to the mails, it is still the village forum. Rodney Koster, the postmaster, long ago went to the wars; but his mother, who took over his work, and her sister, Aunt Hattie, were usually there to preside. With a potbellied stove as a centerpiece and with convenient boxes and barrels and even chairs surrounded by everything from seeds and staples to tobacco and a framed photograph of Green Bank's newest baby, it is perhaps the only country store up and down the river that hasn't been spoiled by notions from outside.

Dick Cornish used to say that if you walked along Federal Street, between Third Street and Broadway in Camden, you could look at people and conclude that you had seen half the world at lunch time. In much the same way, if you linger at Aunt Hattie Ford's long enough, you will be certain to meet most of Green Bank's notables as well as outstanding citizens of Weekstown, Bulltown, New Gretna, Bass River, and houses up nearer The Forks. Most of them walk to the store; if no one's on hand to offer a ride, they walk home. Perhaps, emulating their fathers and grandfathers, they decline riding

192

and walk home anyhow. Gasoline rationing failed to upset many of them. The system was far too complicated to waste time over; and like as not the family car, if there was one, was hitched to a saw or wanted by somebody else or just wouldn't start. Walking long and seemingly lonely miles, by day or dark, has ever been and even now remains the customary way of going to Aunt Hattie's.

It was down at the store where I first met a countless host of Mullica people numbered now among my best friends. I probably followed most of them home, afterward, for more stories or a few more details; but it was usually at the store, in the smiling presence of Aunt Hattie herself, that the last shy uncertainties disappeared. There it was, except for the more specialized perception of the insects, that I was accepted as a native. It took a long while, ten or fifteen years maybe, but now I know of no other satisfaction in accomplishment quite like it. Gratification will be complete, I think, when with Parson Woodmansee's technique, I can run a hand down my bare arm, rolling back a blanket of mosquitoes like moss, smiling at their utter frustration.

It was at the store that I came to know the last miller of Green Bank, Will Johnson, who said he didn't know what the Johnsons would have done for a couple of hundred years if it hadn't been for the Mullica. You'd think that a miller, gazing down the road at what the last big flood did to his mill, would have become gloomy, taciturn. Not Will Johnson, tax collector of Washington Township and township clerk for almost fifty years. "You got to get used to building things up," Will told me, down at Aunt Hattie's. "I guess I've watched a lot of things fall down and get up again down here at Green Bank," he said, "for they've had me in office so long that I go back to when Washington Township really *was* Washington, before they made up a part of it as Randolph, and later on when they got tired of Randolph and made it all Washington again."

Will Johnson was seventy-three when he said that. He was trim, philosophical, and agile in a way that belied his years. He didn't look much like a miller. He was more like the local preacher, I thought, and I found out that in many ways he wasn't far from that. He told me then that he had been treasurer of the little Methodist Church at Green Bank, for which his great-grandfather provided, well over

193

twenty years. Once, from 1914 to 1916, he had even had a fling at outside politics and had served as a Burlington County freeholder. As if I might attach something strange to political affiliations, he added: "You got to have politics just like corn. The more you take care of corn and politics, the better they grow up."

Will's father, Edwin, bought the grist and sawmills that stood across the road, near Herman City, from Nicholas Sooy II. "He ran the gristmill till he died," Will said. "I ran it till it burned down in 1901. The old sawmill washed out in 1903. I built a new one till the flood washed it out in 1939." Even when the gristmill burned down, Will Johnson wasn't beaten. "I set out the old mill pond as a cranberry meadow," he said, as if the task could be accomplished in a day.

For a while he tried modern developments and undertook to run the sawmill by steam. "But I liked water power better," he told me, "and that's why I went back to it. With water, you start it up and that's all there is to it. With water, a flood comes along and it closes down on you before you know, that's true. You can see what happened over by the gates if you want to. Just the same, down here along the river we don't go back on water if it's there."

The turn in the road to Green Bank that for so long was identified by a mill has a mill no longer. However, the miller remains, beside the store he once ran between grinding and sawing, ready in a way that only Mullica people are for whatever it is that lies ahead. "Living only gets complicated when you make it so," Will Johnson assured me. Then quickly he picked up the skein of history.

It was the first Nicholas Sooy, it seems, whose bequest provided for the little church that now has but a handful for its congregation. Nicholas had the first mill, further up the road, living beside the river in Revolutionary times in a house that is the middle section of Leon Koster's today. The pews that serve this remnant of the faithful were cut in Nicholas Sooy's mill with an old-fashioned, up-and-down saw.

Will Johnson's grandmother was Nicholas's daughter, Esther.

"There were five sons and five daughters," Will told me, "and probably they had to make the house bigger right away. To these children Nicholas left his estate—and that covered nearly every-

194

thing down here. That old house that Will Birdsall tore down to build the one he used to live in, that was Esther's share. Will Sooy got the house at the corner and the store that was Aunt Hattie's. There was a big shipyard out back of the store in those days. Josephus Sooy got the land along the river that's the state's now, where Cliff Terry raises trees. Green Bank State Forest, they call it. Ephraim got property below Green Bank, down near the schoolhouse. Sam was a farmer so he got some good land right here in the village. . . ."

The Sooys were and are cornerstones up and down the valley, and the Johnsons share their heritage.

"Grain used to come here to the mill from New Gretna, Mathistown, Clark's Landing, Nesco, Wescottville, and even Egg Harbor City," said Will. "Why, once between this house of mine and the Koster place that was Nicholas Sooy's was one big wheat field all along the river. Look at the forest there now and people, like you maybe, won't believe."

Land holdings along the Mullica used to be called the Samuel Driver Survey, the miller explained, one afternoon at home. That is why many concluded that he built the little church up the road from the store. But it was Nicholas Sooy who provided for that, as his will proves, his mill turning out the timbers that are as solid as they were in the beginning. Until the church was built, there was only the start of a family burying ground, with Sooys rallying around the grave of old Sam Driver.

Will was fourteen, they say, when his father's health failed mysteriously, something odd for a river native. "I started something right away," he told me, "that never was heard of around here. I ran it for forty-eight years—a delivery route. I used to take feed and flour from the mill and then load up with groceries for Lower Bank and Wading River and even Jenkins Neck. That was a lot of territory to cover, over sand roads in summer and through snowdrifts in winter. When there were big snows, I'd have to use three horses, one in the lead to break the path so the two horses back of him could drag the sled through the woods."

Just as it was Sooys who were responsible for Will Johnson's becoming a miller—he had to do something with the mills he inherited, he said—it was a Sooy who "nudged" him, as he put it, into politics.

Will Sooy had been township clerk for years. He began talking of giving it up. "One day he came to me and said he'd retire if I'd run. If I would run with his backing, he said, I couldn't lose. So I ran —and won. That was forty-five years ago this month."

Those were days of spirited town meetings in Green Bank, and Will Johnson said he always thought the Mullica lost something when the meetings came to an end. "Some day they're going to come back," he predicted for the benefit of the store gallery one night. "Maybe they'll come back quicker than the mill. We didn't get around much then but we got on all right. It took even a horse a good while to get anywhere from here, and when you figured it all out you decided it wasn't worthwhile."

One day when a long trip, all the way to Mount Holly, was not only worthwhile but legally necessary, was the day after election. "That was when we had to hitch up the buggy and take in the ballot boxes," Will told me. "First of all, I went along with father, who was freeholder and tax collector before me. Later on I drove in in my own right."

I was down at the store one day, telling Aunt Hattie what Will Johnson had told me, little by little. "He left out one important thing," she told me almost at once. "As close to the Sooys as Will is, because he carried on the mills where they left off, he's even closer to the Birdsalls," she said.

"You mean because Bill Birdsall took Esther Sooy's old house down to build his cottage?" I asked her, looking out of the store window toward where Mrs. Birdsall still lives.

"No," she said, surprising me. "Will's wife should have told you. Her father was Alfred Hance Birdsall, another son of Hazleton Birdsall, the carpenter." The carpenter, I filled it out, who built ships and houses, made coffins, drove the hearse and, being a Sunday School teacher, preached eloquently beside many an open grave.

The mills of Green Bank may be silent, but at Lower Bank a sawmill continues in daily operation. The sawyer is Joe Ware, who rarely visits the store although his house is just around the bend in the road. Mrs. Joe, once a nurse and long a leader in Green Bank's community life, does most of the errands. It took me a long while to associate Mrs. Joe with the woman I first met when she was pitching salt hay with all the skill of a man up at Charlie Weber's. I remembered quickly enough when Aunt Hattie Ford told me Mrs. Joe Ware was one of Charlie's girls.

When Joe was a boy of twelve his father, Frank, had a sawmill at Atco. Joe worked in the mill and liked the routine. He must have for now, close to fifty, he is still in a sawmill all day long, sometimes until it's dark. He's had one job, sawing wood, all his life.

Joe Ware is a big, powerful man who likes work and looks as if he eats heartily. The mill is his, back from the banks of the Mullica, almost within sight of where Charlie Weber and his sons used to tether their hay barge. Like most Jersey sawmills, this one is little more than a shed, a roof to protect the machinery, with the front and one side open to the air that's pungent with the smell of cedar water mingling with the added aroma of cedar sawdust. You can hear the mill quicker than you can see it, for it's back on a winding trail that seems to disappear as effectively as if Joe pulled it up behind him as he left the main road.

Joe's father was a famous man before he turned to the industry that was one of the first on lands adjacent to Mullica cedar swamps. Frank H. Ware was originally a railroad man, pioneer on a pioneer road, the old Camden & Atlantic. His locomotive, of course, was a wood burner and maybe, Joe told me, that turned his mind to wood. Whatever it was, Frank ran his engine up the road one day, announced that it was his last run, and quit to set up a sawmill. He sawed wood between twenty-two and twenty-three years, Joe said.

"We cut all around," he explained, "taking trees off land as we moved along Kettle Run, Oak Knoll, up Maple Branch, beyond Sandy Crossing, and down at Little Mill—wherever the wood was running good, we went after it, daddy and me. Of course, in those days dad was turning out mostly shingles with some siding and laths."

For a while the mill of the Wares was near New Freedom, and that's not in the Mullica Valley at all unless you want to include land drained by the river's headwaters. Later on it was at Penbryn and later still at Iron Mill, below Waterford near Pestletown. So often when you come to look for these names, they've been removed from ordinary maps. Very seldom are they forgotten, however, because the industrial trails that led to them somehow celebrate them

197

forever. Lumber trails wandered in no certain pattern, simply because the miller was looking for the best wood or the easiest way to move his mill.

Moving a mill was a tedious business, Joe Ware said. "You just couldn't pick up your tools and move on. Mills had to be carefully taken apart and as carefully put together again. It was like fitting up a puzzle with numbered pieces. Before that you had to find the best place where good wood would be likely to last a while and make the new site good for a couple of months at least. "I'll bet I could go back the way we came," Joe said, "and pick up the trail by piles of sawdust."

Joe pointed out that even if he made that kind of a trail, you'd have little chance of tracking him down. He sells his sawdust. What's more, he doesn't move around much.

Frank Ware's mill was one of the first that ran by steam. Always moving down toward the coast, it was set up on Hungry Hill, later down on the Pleasant Mills-Elwood Road, and still later over in the Penn Swamp and along Wading River. When his father died, Joe worked with one of the Bozarths, and the name of Bozarth in New Jersey is almost synonymous with sawmills. Bozarthtown, pronounced Boziertown, grew up around one of the earliest sawmills in Burlington County. But the Bozarth mill where Joe worked until he got back on his own was back of New Gretna. Joe bought Bozarth's mill, decided that timber pickings were getting thin at New Gretna, and moved lock, stock, and barrel as his father had taught him, to Lower Bank.

"You wouldn't guess the mill was ever taken apart," Joe told me one night at the store where he was buying, among other things, some chaws of tobacco for Charlie Weber. "It's just the same here as it was over to New Gretna."

Joe Ware's cedar was coming, in those days, from down back of DaCosta. Hauled as logs to Lower Bank, it was quickly sawed into stipulated lengths and then made into blocks. From these were made what Joe and his patrons called "crate shucks"—strips that go into the making of crates for produce. Joe wasn't making the crates or hamper lids, he explained. Bundles of strips were shipped down to Bridgeton. "Seems odd," he admitted then, "to put the best Jersey
198

Watson Lippincott, whose home was a houseboat on the Wading River, built rowboats to order under a weeping willow tree.

Making oyster baskets by hand is a distinctly Down Jersey routine. Clarence Morgan, of Dividing Creek, demonstrated one of the steps.

Jack Updike, of Green Bank, was one of the last of the gifted craftsmen who carved decoys, a jackknife his principal tool. Jay Parker,
of Parkertown, still continues the tradition at eighty-two. Below, Joe
Ware who spent most of his life sawing shingles and other needs,
moving his equipment wherever the swamps yielded the best timber.

cedar into fruit and vegetable crates—but they're doing it. How many? Well, guess we turn out from eighteen to nineteen thousand crate shucks a day when the going's good." The going was unusually good, he said, when Ed Weber, his brother-in-law, came over to help. Ed came when Joe wasn't delivering shucks or when he wasn't helping with the salt hay.

Shucks and shingles usually flew with a speed that was in contrast to words from the lips of Joe Ware—or, for that matter, Ed Weber. They liked working more than talking. Even the darkly protective atmosphere of the store, always an aid to modesty, failed to warm them into any rewarding continuity. I remember reflecting one night that the ratio of questions and answers where Joe and Ed were concerned was about three to one. I said as much to Aunt Hattie, who was immediately on the defensive.

"The boys work hard," she said, as if I didn't know. It was with reluctance, usually, that they cut off the saws to hear what I wanted to know. "They don't waste anything," she went on, to make certain I got the point, "not even words. You know, the outsides of those logs, cedar strips with the bark still on, slabs we call them, get sold for firewood. The longer shucks go to dealers in sphagnum moss who use them for baling. And the waste, curled up shavings the boys call dog-hair, that goes to poultry people and nurseries and kennels. . . ."

One morning down at Aunt Hattie's store a man came in and asked for a jackknife. "Well," he said, smiling, "so it's you!" It was as if we had met many times before. "Joe Ware's wife told me you were in town. Down early today, eh?" Then he went away, fondling his purchase like a boy.

"Talks as if he knows you," said Aunt Hattie, doubtfully. "Does he?"

"If he does," I said, "for the life of me I don't know how. I must be getting some kind of a reputation. Who is he?"

"Jack Updike," replied Mrs. Ford. "His wife said she was going to write you a letter. Wouldn't be surprised if she did. She says that you ought to know about Jack while you're at it around here. Maybe you ought to have followed him out—when he gets a new knife, there's something in the wind."

Not long after that a letter came from Mrs. Updike. She said that Jack was bashful, but just the same I ought to know about his decoys.

199

"Best hand at making decoys along the river," Aunt Hattie had said and obviously Mrs. Jack seconded the motion. Thus it was from Jack —and we now get a card every Christmas signed "the Ducky Updikes"—that I learned all about decoys. Moreover, it was because of him that I bought a fancy book with color plates in order to make sure about more. And, oddly enough, my first lesson began at the store, with talk that belied Jack's appearance and rustic manner.

"The derivation of the term, decoy," said Jack, after introductions had been made, "has a surprising background. Decoys made in the seventeenth century, for instance, were coys or coy ducks, the 'coy' part of it coming from the Dutch, who spelled it k-o-o-i. . . ."

It was at this point that an old man in a battered and stained sailor's cap, a salty old fellow with an elastic imagination whom I know better now, went to the door and spat. Jack Updike shut up like a Barnegat clam. Later, at his little house a stone's throw from the store, he began his lecture over again, with what sounded to me like the same words. Mrs. Updike, who was lingering about and whose letter I kept secret until now, laughed quietly. "That's the way it begins," she said, "but it gets better later on. It starts off with large portions of Britannica!"

There was a Latin word, too, Jack told me, that had something to do with the word decoy. It was *cavea* and it meant "a hollow place." "And that's funny," he said, "because not all decoys are hollow. Some have hollow tops, solid bottoms. It all depends on what you want 'em to do, according to the weather."

Having made decoys since he was fourteen, Jack Updike likes to feel that he's an artist in the business. He knows well enough that he has made a study of it, that he likes carving decoys a lot better than working as a carpenter on wartime Navy craft down at Charlie Leek's. But he always goes out of his way to point out that he is but one of many men whose band saws, spokeshaves, wood gauges and jackknives have turned out countless wooden images of ducks that linger along the Jersey coast from Barnegat down.

"I'm just one," he has told me over and over. "Harry Shores made decoys all year round and shipped 'em all over the country. Cap'n John McAnney, who's a retired Coast Guard man over to New Gretna, he's another of us. Trouble is, people think you just pick up a knife and start whittlin' a duck. Listen, you got to know ducks, really *know* 'em before. . . ."

You have to know a lot of other things, too. No matter how ardent a man's interest in duck hunting, he can't keep a decoy decorator busy all the time, time that must be paid for more adequately by something else. Jack Updike is a painter as well as a carpenter, more painter than carpenter by rights, he says. And when there's nothing to paint, his engineer's ticket comes in handy. He has served as master aboard some of the more elegant yachts which in peacetime plied the waters between Maine and Florida.

"I been aboard the menhaden boats, too," he told me, "and the food-fish boats out of Anglesea after that. My ticket lets me handle ships pushed around by anything from gas to Diesels and fuel oil. I got the idea, this bug on decoys, when I started repairing and painting 'em as a boyzie. And that was all of forty years ago."

Jack Updike knows the turns and shallows of the Mullica River like a book. In fact, he was the first to point out some pilings that jut from the water not far from Weekstown, pilings that show up only when there's been a stiff nor'wester blowing. "Used to be an old man over there at what they called the Files place," he said, "who said that's where a lot of supplies were unloaded for Washington at Valley Forge. Maybe you didn't know it; but even when the Revolution was on, soldiers down here on the river were taking a day off from the war, now and then, to shoot a few ducks. And they used decoys, too.

"Jerseymen from the first took pride in their decoys. They'd study their ducks and make the decoys as natural as they could on the water. Anybody can chop out a block of wood and put a head on. Of course the first decoys were crude—soot and oil were used to color 'em. Now—well, ducks is more eddicated. They just won't come down against something that doesn't look real."

Jack explained that his study of the subject had taken him back to days when Indians used decoys to great advantage. Out in Colorado, he said, they made them of grass, sticking them together and coloring them with clay. "Sometimes," said Jack, "they used live decoys like a lot of hunters did since then till the law put a stop to it. Live decoys used to be anchored where they'd call to the others

—and that wasn't fair. Nowadays you've got to make a honker look just like he is and a quacker the same way." A honker, I found out, is a goose. A quacker's a duck.

Jack Updike goes deep into the swamps for the cedar from which he plans to carve a decoy, and thus the Great Swamp and the Buck Neck Swamp are familiar to him. Jack likes swamps more than is natural, more than is good for him, Mrs. Updike thinks. Excursions through swamp water may have given him those rheumy twinges that so often keep him from painting houses or running boats or even whittling out a decoy. But deep-swamp cedar is what you have to have, Jack assured me.

"The old makers," he said, "got cedar trees that died from great age, trees that were four and five feet around. They got to them when the ground was froze. Gideon and Samuel Lippincott used to work that way and they knew just where to go. Now we got to be content mostly with second growth cedar. You got to have the right kind of wood to work with 'cause decoys come in three pieces, no matter what part is hollow, top, bottom, and head.

"When you get a rig of decoys—sometimes there's a hundred in a rig—they got to be light enough to tote around. They're half the weight when they're hollow. But you must remember something there—hollow birds look the part in quiet weather, but solid birds are best when the weather is rough."

No duck would be convinced, it seems, by a decoy so light that with the first bobble of the tide or a dash of wind across the water it would dance up and down like a jumping jack. The hollow top, solid bottom design is best for all weathers, Jack Updike holds. All this requires knowledge of ducks and actual tests with decoys, he has said time and again. "The trouble with most people," he told me once, "is that they don't reason this out, and so they make a beeline for mail-order stuff. Ask the experts—they'll tell you. Even the heads have to be just right or a live duck'll know the difference and pass over without a second look."

There are still lots of decoys around, Jack says, that recall the master craftsmen who made them. Many are fashioned of white pine and are superbly true to life. Of these, many have been painted and repainted many times. "There's Ridgeway Marter up in Burlington, now—there's a man who knows his decoys. He uses white pine but it's a little hard to get. I go miles to get just the right cedar slabs I want."

I have tried to get Jack to estimate how many decoys he has made through the years, but he always stays on the conservative side. "Maybe a thousand," he said one day when his wife quickly protested and even his little girl, Barbara, told me she knew she had seen at least a million lying around the house in her short memory. "Oh, well," said Jack, "I forget. I used to make more than I do now. But, then, maybe I wasn't so particular as I am now."

Jack has seen, in his looking around for ideas, some brant, goose, and black duck decoys that must be, he figures, between fifty and sixty years old. In his time he has made wooden counterparts of redheads, canvasbacks, bluebills, Greenway teal, male and female sprig, and geese. Now there's no call to make some of these down along the Mullica. "The broadbill and the sprig just don't come in here any more," Jack complains. "Their feed's gone from Swan Bay now— broadbill used to feed on what we call duck clams, about as big as a grain of corn. Since a lot of the cedars were cut and since the duck clams disappeared, the broadbill and some of the others went away. They always say that cedars draw the squalls, and that's when waterfowl come inland."

Black ducks, Jack told me not long ago, are on the increase. "And there were more geese this year than ever before," he declared. "But when you got 'em, they weren't fit to eat, mostly. Don't know where they'd got their last square meal."

It takes seven days to make a dozen decoys, Jack says, from the time you get the rough blocks home. It takes careful carving, expert painting, and a full knowledge of anatomy and plumage. The paint, among other things, can't be reflected from the water or an intelligent duck won't bother coming down. Nonreflective paint requires a special preparation—and that's a secret of "Ducky" Updike.

"There's always something," he once said, "that shows a decoy to have been made by this man or that. Some of the boys have imitated models made by Harry Shores. Others brought notions down from New England. Still others are partial to lines of Joel Salmons of

Parkertown, or John McAnney of New Gretna. Mine? Guess I wouldn't know about that. All I know is, you got to be pretty smart to fool a duck."

One night at Aunt Hattie's store they were talking up tricks of trade. Joe Ware had just crossed the road toward the bridge and Will Johnson went by on his way to the church. Somebody said that Jack Updike's decoys would still recall their maker when Joe's cedar shucks for crates and the last big timber from Will's wrecked saw-mill lost their identity. And that, probably, is very true.

*19*

## NAMES AND BIG GUNS

*"We who with songs beguile your pilgrimage*
  *And swear that Beauty lives though lilies die,*
*We Poets of the proud old lineage*
  *Who sing to find your hearts, we know not why,—*
*What shall we tell you? Tales, marvellous tales*
  *Of ships and stars and isles where good men rest,*
*Where nevermore the rose of sunset pales,*
  *And winds and shadows fall toward the West . . ."*
                                     JAMES ELROY FLECKER

NAMES, BIG NAMES, are inescapable here in the Mullica Valley. They tumble out and pile up like clues, indices to the long-ago and nearer-now. Here, in casual conversation, Jack Updike had spoken of Lippin-cotts and McAnneys. There, in only a word or two, Sammy Ford had taken me back to Leeds Point, for the alias of The Jersey Devil is Leeds's Ghost. And there were always letters, too, to distract atten-tion and obliterate the scent, letters from ladies in search of lost ancestors along the shore, a pamphlet about Shamong Township's "Paisley: The Magic City," and a full variety of mail from people

204

half way across the country, always anxious to help in the quest for forgotten towns and people. However, my journey at the moment was upstream and so, in seeking the meaning lingering in the name Katesputa Pond, I came upon Watson Lippincott, the one-man shipyard.

Watson Lippincott, of Wading River, once Bridgeport, knows little or nothing of the Delaware River as a trade rival of the little rivers all about him. Of equally negligible concern, too, are ships launched with greater frequency as mounts the tempo of the world's demands. For Watson, you see, is his own shipyard. He's designer, manufacturer, salesman, and boss. Not far from where a more obvious series of ways once gave schooners to charcoal and coastal trade, Watson Lippincott builds rowboats on order. Whenever I've been by, he's been busy as a beaver.

Watson must be in his eighties by now. And that is the span of a lifetime spent in the neighborhood of the Sooys and Adamses and Leeks who, with Lovelands and Allens and Cranmers, have maintained that living is more than work and that life is worth much more where the workshop is bounded by sea and sky and your own bit of land. Watson told me he has been down there so long that they changed the name of the place during his lifetime. "Wading River was just a river, as it should be," he said. "Then they said two Bridgeports was mixing them up—they say there's one over on the Delaware somewhere, though I ain't ever seen it and ain't likely to, now. And there's a Bridgeport up in Connecticut, too, I hear tell. It was confusin', I guess. So now this is Wading River, the town."

Living beside Wading River, the river, in a scowboat that's a cabin on a barge, working in the shade of a graceful willow he planted there years ago, Watson Lippincott has been building boats beside the drawbridge abut two of the thirteen years in which the houseboat has been his home. "I ain't been buildin' boats only 'bout couple of years," he told me, long ago at the beginning, "and before that I followed the bay. Part of the time I was clammin' and oysterin' down Great Bay. Part of the time I tried a farm."

"How come you turned to boat building?"

"You have to do somethin'," Watson answered simply. "You work or you starve. If you don't need much, the work don't have to be hard. But you got to find it. And there's always work if that is what you want."

It was the same elementary credo of Mullica men, perhaps the same that had served an army of Lippincotts Watson never knew much about. Lippincotts were early husbands of the Atwoods and wives of the Snows from up Massachusetts way when Joseph Lippincott, a weaver, came from England and the family began wandering down from Freehold to Barnegat and Tuckerton. Watson was born in Green Bank and by degrees worked his way over to the Mullica's tributary. It took a long while, he says, to go the six miles from one river to the other. Now, from where Watson lives and works, he can look across the drawbridge, tended by Sam Merchant, to the ridge topped by brown and white stones of Leeks, Adamses, McKeens, and our old friend from Lower Bank, Captain John Carlisle,—at the beginning, as they say, a cemetery full of Leeks.

"Them that worked in the Green Bank glass factory is buried over there," said Sam. "A good many worked in the shipyard here beside the river."

There are skeleton hulks of sailing ships in the water near the draw, one on the other side and one a stone's throw from Watson's scowboat. Neither of these, Watson informed me authoritatively, was built at Wading River. "That one close by here," he said, "was built down to Atlantic City. A man had an idea of picking up truck from farms along here and running it down shore for good profit. The idea didn't work out, and so the ship went to the dogs. There come a big tide and she washed up from over there to over here where you see she fetched up. Some boys got aboard her after that and set her afire."

As for the other wreck, she was the "Huntress." "She was a sloop-boat, maybe a sixty-footer, probably a freighter," said Watson. "I don't know no more'n that, really. She's been here longer 'n me and pretty much the way you see her now."

Watson Lippincott will say that he gave up clamming because "there was nothing in it" although there are many who will give him an argument on the point. Farming was paying more, at least, when he made the change. "What are they paying now?" I asked. "Three dollars a hundred?"

206

"Three dollars a thousand, more like," Watson replied, as if there were elements of his association with clamming that I would best not know about. "Highest I ever know'd 'em was dollar-twenty a hundred for big chowder clams. That was in the first World War."

As for clam prices in the new war, Watson ignored them along with much that the world was doing. As a matter of fact, he said, he liked to listen to news of the world only occasionally. "I could have a radio," he said. "Maybe there's not much room for much in the cabin, but there's room for a radio. But I don't want to listen to soap ads and ways to use corn plasters and how long your guts is. That's why, when I want the news, I walk up the road and visit for a while. People usually have a radio on and if they don't, they know that's what I come for."

Now and then, he told me one day when I brought him some information on boat prices elsewhere, he heard from a nephew up in Jacksonville, once Slabtown, near the Copany Meeting House. "I go see him sometimes," he said. "Different country up there—nice change. But I always like to come home here."

I told him some things about Copany he didn't know, details which had been sent to me in one of those letters. John K. M. Ewing of Washington, D. C., supported an earlier contention I had made to the effect that Revolutionary fighting near Slabtown eased the victory at Trenton December 26, 1776. Concerning the engagement at Petticoat Bridge, below the Meeting House, Mr. Ewing had written:

"There was fighting at the bridge near Slabtown on December 22, 1776, when a party of militia from South Jersey drove a picket of the Highland Watch back to their supports at Black Horse, now Columbus, and there was fighting at the Copany Meeting House and at Mount Holly December 23, three days before Washington struck at Trenton. VonDonop's brigade of 2000 with adequate artillery fought and won against some 500 militiamen with two three-pounders, drove back an outpost of the militia from the meeting house and then took possession of Mount Holly after more fighting, before the militia retired. It was this fighting by the South Jersey militia that accomplished for Washington the very thing he counted on with Ewing at Trenton Ferry and Cadwalader at Bristol—namely, to make it impossible for Hessian reinforcements to reach Trenton before the American force had gained a victory."

Mr. Ewing said that his authority for the story of the fighting, as well as a probable basis for the legends, was a notation in the journal of his great-grandfather, a volunteer in the militia ranks at the time, substantiated by VonDonop's report. The letter quoted most illuminatingly from the report. What was most interesting was the commentary on the Copany Meeting House legend of the bloody handprints. These, reappearing on the backs of the never painted pews, despite all manner of cleaning and scraping, were not, said Mr. Ewing, as much imagination as many believed.

"It occurs to me," the attorney's letter concluded, "that the incident at Petticoat Bridge could very well have occurred about December 14 or 15, when VonDonop, with headquarters in Bordentown, established an outpost at Black Horse and sent out patrols to search for any militia in the neighborhood, that Copany Meeting House was used as a hospital for those who were wounded in the fighting there on the morning of December 23 and that 'the bloody handmarks' were made by those Hessians or British whom my great-grandfather's journal notes were 'killed on the spot' rather than those militiamen VonDonop reports were either wounded or killed."

Watson Lippincott was not impressed. "The second branch of the Lippincotts was probably mixed up in that," he said. "But it was a long while ago."

I quoted Mr. Ewing in my own defense. "As a collector of homely incidents of local importance," I said, "I found it very interesting. You said you got up to Slabtown now and then, and I've always thought that old meeting house ought to have a plate on it about its service as a hospital. There's as much to show there was something more than a notion behind those bloody smears on the seats as there is to show the Tennant Church was ever a hospital at Monmouth. After all, a plaque has been put up there and all because a fellow who sat atop a tombstone to watch the battle was shot off!"

"People get things wrong," Watson Lippincott said quietly. "Next time I'm up there I'll have a look for those handmarks. Funny as hell if I found 'em wet, wouldn't it?"

Actually, I don't believe Watson would have been at all surprised

208

if he had made such a discovery. Perhaps he has. All I know is that he admits having gone up into the gallery of Copany Meeting at one time or another, and there his discussion of the experience comes to an end. He quickly switches to something else.

"You was asking me if I was married," he changed the subject on one occasion. I had asked him nothing of the kind. "Naow!" he answered the question just the same. "Never been. I always said it's all right for them that gets the right kind of stuff but—!"

The implication always has been that Watson Lippincott was afraid the "right kind of stuff" would make him give up his ideas of living in a scowboat, without a radio, without neighbors closer than half a mile.

Up the road from the Wading River bridge there is a church. Sight of weather-stained and fraying window shades has ever compelled a look inside whenever I have gone by that way. I asked Watson Lippincott about it one day, and he told me the church had "given up" some seven or eight years before. "We could do with a church down here," he said. "But some of the folks got a little out of sorts with some of the rest, and so they closed it up. Church is up at New Gretna now. There was another church once up there where you see the graveyard, but that burned down in one of the forest fires."

The legend is that all of Bridgeport—Wading River—was once owned by Great John Mathis and that he sold it to Captain John Leake, who settled there "at any early date." It is probable, Mrs. Blackman says, that Captain John left the village to one of his sons, who sold it to Robert McKean. Mr. McKean can best be remembered in connection with that Joseph Burns story of the Cranmers—Joseph was the lad who was the sole survivor of shipwreck, the sailor who said if you were born to be drowned nothing could stop you. Joseph *was* drowned, you may remember, when he fell off a ship at anchor up a river in Virginia. Well, Robert McKean—spelled McKeen on many of the Wading River stones—married Margaret Burns, Joseph's daughter, and their children inherited virtually all the town.

Watson Lippincott gets his wood for boats in New Gretna, insisting on red cedar. He mixes his paint in whatever comes handy— last time I was down he was using an old coffeepot. "The reason I get orders for rowboats," he confided just the other night, "is that people who come by have seen me here for over fifteen years. They

209

figure I'm kind of permanent and a good man to order a boat from. I been here as long as the bridge almost, as long as that hotel that ain't a hotel now, some of them thinks. There was always some kind of a shipyard here, and they like the cut of a clammer like me who keeps the business alive at the old stand. They stopped buildin' schooners here when the charcoal trade run out. I'll stop when they stop orderin' and not before."

There is one story about that hotel, only a house where Watson told me Alice Adams was living then, which I am sure you will want to hear before I go on to see Johnny McAnney. The Adamses go back to old Hezekiah Adams, who settled at Bass River, now New Gretna, on a farm that was in the family for generations. It is comforting to find one of the extant Adamses lingering on in the atmosphere of an ancient inn not far from where the Bass River Hotel was operated by Franklin and Isaiah Adams. Both men were strict observers of total abstinence, Isaiah making his personal viewpoint on intoxicants known whether he was at the bar, launching Bridgeport ships, or bartering timber. Isaiah cleared and cultivated one of the most successful of the earliest farms in the neighborhood; and I have often wondered if there is not something somewhere to show where the vast orchards of apples, cherries, and peaches he pioneered were set out.

"I'll ask Alice next time I'm up to the hotel," Watson Lippincott suggested once. "Maybe they got the radio fixed by now."

New Gretna seemed to be legitimate territory for me since it had been Bass River. Inasmuch as Bass River (the river) is a Mullica tributary, that ought to give the right to recall the men who saw it first, New Englanders to whom a sea bass was a rock and who named the stream Rock River. I am inclined to believe that some literal-minded villager years later, pointing out that whatever else the little rivers of the area might have they owned no rocks, made the alteration which, for a time, became the town's own name, too. So, hearing the name McAnney from Jack Updike, after it had come to me first in the story of the man who with Haze Birdsall exchanged that burial sermon pledge with every funeral, I went over to see Johnny.

Sud Norcross and I found him, wearing what was left of a coast-guardman's cap and smiling under a framed honorable discharge

210

from the service of which he was a part for more than twenty years. Jack said he was a decoy man, but I wanted to start him off on something else. I mentioned the Coast Guard. "I was in the service before there was a Coast Guard," he said, "seven years before. That was when there was the old Life Saving Service."

John McAnney—in-shore further the name becomes McAnniney —is one of a loyal army of men, retired from active duty in the Life Saving Service and the Coast Guard, but as familiar as ever with the coastal waters, the shoals, the channels, and the thoroughfares they memorized long ago. "We know 'em," said John, "because we never really left off bein' on the water."

Johnny, pointing out that he was as active as ever he was, boasted that he had never missed a day of any gunning season.

"Guess that brings me to something I want to ask you about," I told him. "I understand you have quite a remarkable gun."

"Who told you that?"

"Jack Updike."

"Oh," said Johnny and then laughed. "Good old Jack. Biggest liar in seventeen states." Since then I have learned that it is a ruse of the tellers of tall tales to so label their rivals in order to indicate that they themselves are paragons of truth. "Gunning ain't what it once was, you know," Mr. McAnney confided. "I used to take that gun when it was legal. Six-bore shotgun. Here it is."

He pulled the oversized weapon down from the wall, not far from the framed discharge certificate. "Made in New York," he went on. "Most people never saw one, say there ain't any such. But here she is —I've had her thirty year, I guess. But I can't use her any more. You can't use an eight-bore either. Why, this here gun took a quarter pound of shot down each barrel!"

Johnny McAnney fondled the weapon, slapped it into position for all its weight, and aimed it out the window. "She might go into action in a hurry if anybody comes up the beach that has no right to," he said. "Otherwise—well, you got to stay mostly law-abidin' even down here. See this powder horn?" He pulled out a big one, empty now. "Came with the gun. Capacity's four pounds of powder. Up in the garret I got thousands of Number Six wads I ain't never used. This here gun took five or six to a load."

211

You see, these old baymen not only know how to handle guns but they have to know how to make up their own ammunition as well. However, it was neither the big gun nor the ammunition (nor, to tell you the truth, the recollection that it was a McAnney who preached at Haze Birdsall's funeral) that brought us to Johnny's door. It was a legend of Johnny's six-bore gun, told up and down the Mullica Valley.

Once, the way they tell it, John fired the weapon in its legal days into a flock of broadbill and brought down sixty-seven, by actual count, with both barrels. I wanted Johnny to tell the story his way. To have told it first would have spoiled it all. So I let Mr. McAnney talk on.

He served, he told me, five years at the South Brigantine Station, eleven in Atlantic City. "Finished up my time," he said, "at Corson's Inlet. Since then—well, here's my muskrat traps. Just brought 'em in. Best season it's been in years."

"How about decoys?" Sud asked. "Jack Updike said you were one of the best."

"Best decoys?" Johnny took him up. "That's good. Yep, guess I was at that. Had quite a demand for 'em once. Fiddle around mostly now. Help the old lady wash."

John McAnney was putting on an act. He's wary in his own way or in the way that some old sea dogs are. Mr. McAnney, born in Wading River when it was Bridgeport, said he remembered Green Bank when Freddy Miner was the blacksmith there and when the fish factories were going "full tilt and full smell" off-shore.

"*Those* were places to work!" Johnny exclaimed, with the proper emphasis. You became hardened to hardship. You got used to the smell. You got accustomed to long hours of loneliness on Crab Island and Little Crab Island. As for Mrs. McAnney, she never got used to any of it, Johnny said.

"We were out on the islands all winter long," she told us, after repeated assurances that all newspapermen did not carry concealed deadly cameras, ready for candid shots of the unwary at inopportune moments. Sud told her frankly that people who acted like that usually *wanted* their picture taken. "There was just us four—John and me and the youngsters. You couldn't go anywhere except in a boat. Sometimes the bay froze up and some men would walk out to us over the ice. I often think: What would we ha' done if one of us got abed, sick?"

"We'd have got over it," Johnny told her. Whatever his ideas may be concerning "good old days" it was clear from the first that Mrs. McAnney was glad those days were over. Those were rigorous times when you just had to be hardy. John worked in the factory that "brought in menhaden and pressed 'em out," and his wife cooked for the factory hands, eighteen to twenty-five of them three times a day. Those were days, moreover, when ships called "sail-rigs" worked for the factories, to be joined later on by a little steamer called the "Osprey," brought from Down East for the routine.

"Later she was rebuilt and called the 'Active,'" Johnny said. "The 'Alert' was lost at sea. It was on a July Fourth, I remember. Some of the other factory ships were the 'C. Charles Harvey,' the 'Jesse Smith,' the 'Mary A. Mott,' and the 'Ella Robbins' of Johnny Cavileer. Later on the 'Ella Robbins' was put to oysterin', and still later on, when Joe Wharton, the mayor of Philadelphia, took over the fish factories, Will Sooy became the boss. Then Jim Otis took charge. When the factory finally burned down, O. J. Delaney was runnin' it." He remembered the names as if he were reading them out of a book. "Joe Wharton thought a lot of Delaney," he said. "Said he was the only man who could 'beat' him under his very eyes. Yep, the factories were going good then. All kinds of oil was comin' up out of fish in those days. Hair oil, linseed oil, soap—and it was good soap, too."

"I always thought," I said, "that linseed oil was made from flax-seed."

"Is that so?" retorted Johnny, unsmiling. "Well, what do you think of that?"

Already he had begun to talk about oysters and the lore of clams. "Oysters," he said, "will drink water wherever you put 'em. Fresh or salt, it makes no difference. Clams is different. There'll be salt juice in 'em wherever they die. There's talk about fresh water clams down to the French place, but I don't put no stock in any of that."

Conversation veered back to the fish factories, to Mark Adams and John Cavileer and George Valiant, who ran one of them, and then to six years when Mrs. McAnney, still camera shy, was cook. Not un-

213

til long after did I discover where Mrs. McAnney got her odd notions about the tactics of newspaper photographers, and then the explanation came from one of them. Bill Augustine, having convinced the lady that no mysterious equipment was hidden in his pocket, elicited an answer to the riddle.

"She says too many Fords have had their pictures taken lately," he told me later. " 'None of them are as awful-looking as their pictures make out,' she told me. You see," he explained, "she's one of them. She was Sophie Ford."

I wanted to ask John his age, but I lacked the nerve. Sud, who was over seventy, asked for me. "How old do I look?" asked Johnny.

"Sixty," I said, "sixty-five at the most." And I was trying to be honest about it.

He smiled, complimented and content. "I'm seventy-seven," he said. "And I'm good for a lot of gunning yet, if it's me that says. Even if the good gunning's gone forever. Listen, there was a day down here when even blue heron was fair game and, boy, they tasted same as chicken. Why listen, we didn't have to be so partic'lar about decoys then, handy with a knife and ticklish with a paint brush the way Jack Updike is. No, sir. Why, in those days we could even use old boots for decoys sometimes. We'd put them on top of stakes in the little creeks, and even the herons never knew the difference."

I held my breath. I could feel the story that I hoped for was imminent.

"Why, I can remember the time when all we had for decoys was the boots we had on," said Johnny. "The air was full of herons, and we wanted to get some of 'em so we lay down in the water and stuck our boots up in the air, holding our guns clear and ready. I was usin' that there six-bore. Down came the herons and we let go. How many do you think we got? Fifty-two of 'em—yes, sir, fifty-two!"

I cannot tell you whether John McAnney varied the tale or whether the telling of it, up and down the Mullica, turned the heron into broadbill and the number into sixty-seven. Nor am I at all certain how the legend grew up around one gun whose double-barreled discharge performed the feat alone with but one, and not several, pairs of boots for makeshift decoys. All I know is that the further from

214

home a story is, the taller it gets and the better it's told—unless, perhaps, kibitzing wives are out of earshot.

## 20

## TOWARD THE PORT

*"Men converge no more to the fire,*
*Men are one with the isolation:*
*The pride of science stands, and the final desolation."*
                                        DOROTHY WELLESLEY

I AM GOING BACK THROUGH GREEN BANK NOW, and I hope you will come with me. We are going shoreward again, perhaps for the last time this way; after one or two excursions down at the river's mouth and up Nacote Creek, we will hurry on to The Forks. Cliff Terry will most likely be at the corner, getting his mail, and Birdsall Crowley will be delivering ice, and Fiddler Ford will be just coming down or just going away, like any other day. They will wonder what takes us so early in the morning across the bridge and down the road on the other side of the river, and ordinarily we would tarry long enough to tell them because their interest is friendly. But there are times when telling spoils the luck, and we mustn't take chances on spoiling it now, with pirates and privateers and even The Jersey Devil just around the corner.

We shall talk together as we ride along, through Weekstown and on to where another road comes over from Lower Bank. Near the junction we must turn, through a land that slopes, almost imperceptibly, down to the river, screened by trees and ragged fields, a land of more places than people. This lower side of the Mullica will seem mostly desolate unless we sharpen our perception and set the stage. That can be done with some of the letters I have brought along,

215

some of which reclaim the pirate scene so as to keep the country, from Cranberry Point down, more than tanglewood trails and stumps and roots going down in the dark. For here there were rascals and honest men, cottages and caves, busy days and languid, starry nights—now the days are languid and only the stars stay as they were. Here then, to begin with, is a letter from Nelson B. Gaskill, Esq., who tells me I have been taken in by Barnegat kinsmen of the wreckers who were not so legendary as I may have believed. Mr. Gaskill, a solicitor and the only man I know who can with authority solve the riddle of Ong's Hat, encloses for our perusal a facsimile of an old newspaper cutting, and says by way of explanation:

Verifying the old adage that where there is smoke there must be some fire, it would seem that we cannot discharge the Jersey longshoremen too readily from the accusation of having more than an unselfish interest in wrecks. I am sending you an advertisement from *The Gazette of the United States* and *Daily Evening Advertiser* for October 22, 1794. It would seem from this certificate that while there is no charge that the longshoremen lured the vessel on the bar, questions of title and ownership of wrecked peoperty were held rather lightly.

Mr. Gaskill recalls then that similar events are not necessarily history, for in his time, he says, there was a vessel wrecked off Little Egg Harbor, the cargo in prohibition days being alcohol in five-gallon cans that disappeared, somehow, "like dew before the morning sun." There was, among many, another ship wrecked during the same period, a vessel carrying Italian wines in casks. "These also evaporated," says our correspondent, "before anybody could come along to claim the ownership of the vessel and the cargo." The casks, Mr. Gaskill asserts, later appeared in many longshore houses, painted green and white to look like kerosene oil barrels. The enclosed photostat, commending the celebrated chief officer of the Port of Little Egg Harbor, reads:

We, the Chief Mate and passengers wrecked on the Bar of Little Egg-Harbour, on the 7th inst. in the ship Sant Francisco di Paulo of Genoa, from Nantz in France, bound to New York, Nicholas Castuline master unfortunately drowned; take the opportunity of publicly acknowledging our gratitude to Ebenezer Tucker, Esq., Surveyor of the Customs of the Port of Little Egg Harbour, for his humane and spirited exertions in our behalf in endeavoring to secure and recover the effects and cloathes of the unfortunate, who were plundered by the unprincipled

Shallopmen and inhabitants on the coast; but we have to regret that when we first grounded, Mr. Tucker was absent at Philadelphia on business, or we have every reason to believe we should have saved property from the wreck to a considerable amount. . . .

This certificate, as Mr. Gaskill labels it, leaves little to the imagination. Mr. Tucker, once he had come home, had made every effort to recover what men with little boats rowed out to steal, with the kind of audacity that snatches pennies from dead men's eyes, even as the surf was burying the Sant Francisco di Paulo deeper and deeper in the sand. However, he did not accomplish much, despite the complimentary tone of the notice, as the appended paragraph would indicate. For if any should doubt the gravity of the charges leveled at those who annexed wearing apparel from those who could not effectively remonstrate, he has only to read the postscript, added after the ancient notice had been duly sworn to and witnessed by the ship's officers:

Any person who has got any of the cargo of said ship, and will deliver it to the officers of the Customs of Philadelphia, New York, or Egg Harbour, shall have a salvage according to law.

Think about that, if you will, as we turn into the clay road that mostly parallels the river. What has Mr. Gaskill said? That the people here and up the coast were one with the mooncussers of Cape Cod? That if they did not actually lure ships upon the shoals with false signals and bewildering lights, they did nothing to help the doomed souls upon them? That here is the real clue to the riches that once celebrated the Port and the country around it? That the privateersman was first cousin to the pirate and that finders were keepers as long as it was made legal? We can wonder a little about all these questions even as we pass through Weekstown where, if we had been earlier, we could have asked Sam Radcliffe his opinions on it all.

Sam was there when the town was Weeksville, presiding over a nondescript class in a log schoolhouse after he had renounced his allegiance to King George, giving up soldiering to teach. Of Mr. Radcliffe it is written that "besides laboring patiently and diligently to improve the minds of the youth, he gathered wild flowers for the girls, shared in the athletic games of the boys and entertained them all with anecdotes of his military career." Sam, who walked to the school with his fowling piece in hand and who kept bachelor's hall in a river cabin filled with the labeled specimens of the naturalist, birds and animals and flowers, would have been the man to tell us much; but he went away long ago. One day without warning, he distributed his collection among his pupils, made a rough but touching farewell speech, and traveled West, first into Ohio and later beyond, where he was rumored to have become an Indian trader.

Just ahead now, a little off the road and on the river, are the ruins of Gloucester Furnace. Here's another place where, if we had come along with notebooks and pencils in time, we could have cleared up some of the details about privateers and pirates in short order. However, it may be that we would have had to run for our lives if our probing had seemed too personal, for Gloucester then was far different from what we could see of it now. Once there was a charcoal blast furnace, a sawmill, and several hundred workmen living in rows of tenant houses in the midst of acres shorn of timber for the making of twenty-five tons of iron every week. Today there is little more than a broken bridge, a scattering of bog ore slag, and a stream that courses through the choked bottom of an empty pond— there, not long ago, you could dig up shot that dropped from a vanished tower.

In days of the tower and the furnace we could have sought out John Richards, manager of the enterprise, who as a boy came down to visit his great-uncle, William, and never went home—he arrived in 1807. Proving his mettle as a storekeeper in store-famous Green Bank, John was first put in charge of the iron works at Weymouth and later at Gloucester where, in addition to increasing the trade in castings made to order, lampposts, the first Philadelphia water pipes not made of wood, and a departure in wood-burning stoves designed in Albany, he succumbed to political persuasions. In 1836 he was elected to the legislature. A Whig, he declared himself against the creation of Atlantic County, soon to be cut from Gloucester and divided from Burlington by the Mullica in spite of his arguments. John Richards would have known about wreckers and privateers even though he might have kept a wary tongue in cheek for reasons of the vote—but there is no use conjecturing further, for John isn't there any more than are the post office and the school that was a church on Sunday. His memory has dimmed almost as completely as the recollection of all those hundreds of the valiant who, like similar hundreds who toiled at Martha, up on the Oswego, became legendary a century ago. John, buried in Pennsylvania, is not among the Richards mounds at Pleasant Mills.

But we must move on down the road, along the very trail John Richards used, climbing into coaches that called at Gloucester Furnace three times a week. We may as well look at our tattered maps as we go, for this was one of the stage roads familiar to Whigs and Tories alike in those days when Little Egg Harbor, the port, was the crossways for wartime traffic between New York, Delaware, and Maryland. Long before the notion of a city with a harbor had been proposed and given up, there was a rutted path, which, even as late as 1850, had been widened to take rickety and rumbling conveyances down from Long-a-Coming through Blue Anchor and Higbee's to Leeds Point. Thus this dusty road was a main street in country that knew "great commerce and activity" where, not far off, "the little river used to be filled with masted vessels" that made the "place rich in money." Men who knew all about wrecks and wreckers must have lived along here everywhere, driving hard bargains and winning favors of women who "wore more imported apparel than in any other country place." This, then, for all its quiet and fields without houses, and houses where the people now are mostly unaware of traditions, was the old Egg Harbor Road by the Little Egg Harbor River, now tired out and worn down and overgrown in its own anonymity.

It was here before the survivors of Chestnut Neck retreated up Nacote Creek to set about the building of a new town with whatever they had salvaged. It was here in 1816 when John Halleck, the Public Friend, came down to the mouth of the Mullica from New York, intent upon making a fortune from the bean that ever has yielded curative oil, good for every ill of man or beast. It was here when our old genius, Ebenezer Tucker, turned without a qualm from fitting out privateers to rescuing survivors and some of their effects from foundered ships. It was here when the two colonels, Elijah Clark

219

and Richard Wescott, were hurriedly turning the Fox Burrows of Chestnut Neck into a rude fortification and, later, when the same soldiers, living variously in leaner days, sold real estate, prize ships, limes, pineapples, turtles, and dress goods snatched from submerging holds. And here the road has remained, in passing phases of great prosperity and utter desolation, from the glories of a busy and colorful past to the dreamy uncertainty of a confused and calamitous present.

These were the men who fled up the river from the sea, for reasons of their own or the lack of reason in the world outside, men who wanted peace, men who knew how to run away so as to fight again. This was where, at times, they had little but their threadbare uniforms to remind them of days of daring and where, in whatever arbitrary course they followed, some were reluctant to believe the war was over. Now it is as if a chunk of years was cut from their lives, as if a slice of living was carved from life along the river. Where are the Weeks of Weekstown, the Clarks of Clark's Landing, the kinsmen of James Clarke who ran the "Royal Charles" between Long Island Sound and Chesapeake Bay? Where are the families whose progenitors saw bear up Bear Creek and swans in Swan Bay and spoke proudly of fathers and grandfathers who were privateers? Perhaps they are among the few who know the river lowlands for their muskrats and salt hay and wild ducks. Perhaps, if you had an ancestor who manned a privateer or presided, pompously, at an Admiralty Court, you would keep quiet about it, too—I don't know. Whatever the cause of silence, the feeling seems to be abroad that when elusive kinsmen of Yankee daredevils take such pains to bury their dead, men who seized armed merchantmen with flats and rowboats were fearless but hardly respectable.

Over and over, let me tell you as we ride along, I have led conversation around to the viewpoint that there was something much more reasonable about privateering than modern warfare of the sea in which underwater scoundrels fire on surface ships, sending cargoes to the bottom and their crews after them. I remember saying in Port Republic, for instance, that there is a lot more sense in taking enemy sailors off to jail and a ship's valuables to the auction block where proceeds revert to those who prove their claims in court, than in wholesale murder for the hell of it. But no one openly agreed, there or anywhere else, that it was at least good business. And that is one reason why we are going back to the only Port hereabouts that has a harbor as well as a name.

I would like to find someone with admitted family ties to Captain Storer, who took two small boats through the British fleet in the Narrows, capturing a sloop of His Majesty's Engineers. I would be delighted if someone would step out and admit distant relationship with Captain William Marriner who, with his lieutenant John Schenck and eleven picked men, rode a mere whaleboat to seize ships by the dozen and prisoners by half-hundred lots, bringing them shackled up this Mullica River of ours. But so far such notables as Captain Jackson and his "Greyhound," Captain Stoeker and his "Susannah," Major Cook, the renowned Adam Huyler, Moses Griffing, William Treen, and even old Rufus Gardner may as well have been orphans from the first. Phoebe Cox, of the Barnegat Coxes, married.an Isaac Jackson; there were early Cooks at Tuckerton and Manahawkin, and Gardners mingled with Ridgeways and Pharos along Tuckerton Creek, but there is next to nothing to link them definitely with masters and owners of privateers of the Revolution and the War of 1812. The trouble is, I think, that the world puts privateers and Admiralty Courts in one bundle, marked piracy or, as the letter of Mr. Gaskill would imply, something even less.

Even John Franklin Jameson, who wrote a fat book about privateering in the Colonial period, failed to keep piracy out of the title. Of course, Mr. Jameson was trying to show that piracy and privateering were two separate things, differing in theory and legal definition. Legally, he pointed out, a privateer was an armed vessel or a skipper commissioned by a belligerent government to commit acts of warfare on vessels of the enemy, even though owners and officers and crew might be carpenters and iron-mongers and fishermen on duller days. Legally, Mr. Jameson says, a pirate was one who committed robbery on the high seas or on land "through descent from the sea" without any authority at all. There is an obvious difference. While a pirate indulges bloodshed and murder if he has to, privateering seeks to remain comparatively polite. In between, somewhere, are the longshoremen of Mr. Gaskill's advertisement, both as

221

to character and time, although it was not until 1856 that abuses had piled so high that privateering, as a legal, logical, and profitable means of attack as was ever devised for war, was abandoned.

Not so quickly discarded was this notion that to have been a privateer was to have been a pirate king. Perhaps, after all, it isn't that our friends up from the shore shun the implication of glamor or feel that such transient glory is contaminating. Maybe they aren't at all afraid, as we believed, of being linked with privateers as they are of being associated with their descendants, these who waited, hawk-like by the sea, to pounce on whatever the shoals might trap for them. Most sensible conclusion of all, it seems to me, is that if Great-grandfather Enoch was famous as a privateersman, his lingering family does not know of it. John Schenck was, to his people, a lad who picked up an old boat that more than likely smelled of fish and sailed it out to sea with the help of his cronies to see what could be picked up in a private parttime war. Gruff Abel Akin may have assumed dignity in the annals of an Admiralty Court although, in between, he was only a country justice of the peace. Silence down the Mullica, in matters such as these, means that heroes, to most of their kin, were and are no great pumpkins.

There is always an exception to such generalizing and so, as we rise and fall on this dusty road which sooner than you know will have us in Port Republic, I must tell you about Georgianna Blake of Pleasantville, who would challenge any such conclusion. I have never met Mrs. Blake. That pleasure has been postponed over and over, first by conflicting schedules of work, later by war and curtailment of gasoline. I do not know if Mrs. Blake is tall or short, stout or slim, charmingly young or as charmingly ageless. From her letters I picture her very much like another old friend, Mother Pennypacker in Haddonfield, who still writes verses and sings old songs and proves, in her eighties, what she has ever preached, that no one can really build a fence between past and present. One thing I have decided about Georgianna Blake—and in that she is like Mother Pen, too—she has a good chin. That plump and well rounded chin was well out, I am sure, when Mrs. Blake first wrote to me of ancestors who fitted out privateers and sailed aboard them.

In contrast to so many, she wrote defiantly of those kinsmen of

222

Aunt Hattie Ford's store at Green Bank still retains the atmosphere
of a forum, with all the neighbors assembling to exchange news
and opinions, even though mail time is no more, with mail coming
through from Egg Harbor. The store is still in the family, but many
changes have been made, inside and out.

Aunt Mary Wills, a berry-picking champion at eighty-five, was born at the Mount Tavern.

John Wesley Ford, know better as "Jackie," remen bered New Jersey's ov covered wagon, the Shee topped Wagon, and tl song to go with it.

hers who, shaking their heads as they looked back on Chestnut Neck, decided to move the whole town, or what they might dig from the ashes, up Nacote Creeek. It was safer up there, they said. You had to watch the tides more, of course, but even so the risks, like the mosquitoes, were no worse. Georgianna said that the British Navy, for all its bursts of bombs and rhetoric, failed to put the slightest crimp in Little Egg Harbor's happy-go-lucky war. I replied, a mail or two later, that her boast of blood from the Down Shore privateers was as an oasis in a desert land. Quickly I was rewarded by further details.

"They decided," wrote Mrs. Blake in her second communique, "to rebuild up Nacot or Nacote Creek near the Mills. By the Mills is meant Clark's Mills or Micajah Smith's Mills, as you probably know." I stared at the name: Micajah was, I remembered, among the privateers listed in half-forgotten Naval records of the Revolution. "Clark's Mills, you see," Mrs. Blake hurried on, "had been established by Thomas Clark, the older brother of Colonel Elijah and David Clark. Three sons of Thomas settled Clark's Landing on the Mullica. Thomas himself built Clark's Mills, and that is Port Republic now. David retained the old homestead even when Elijah, the more practical man, sensed more activity up at The Forks, where prize ships were being unloaded and refitted."

Mrs. Blake reminded me quickly that Thomas Clark built the Clark's Mills Meeting House at the clearing along the creek that became in time Port Republic. This, she said, was in 1762. Both this early church and another, called Clark's Log Meeting House up at The Forks, were preaching stations of John Brainerd, whose hell-fire sermons were understood even by the Indians who said he had mastered their language fairly well. The more I heard about these Clarks, the better I liked them. They ran their mills along the creek, they attended Sunday service in the churches they built, and then, when war came, they became a navy content to be paid in silks and sustenance snatched offshore.

"The first house in Port Republic," wrote Mrs. Blake with an authority that only a great-great-granddaughter of David Clark could exercise, "was one of a row facing the creek. When you remember that it was October and that the Chestnut Neck homes of these

223

people, with all that was in them, had been destroyed by the British when the first heavy frosts were on the ground and when, by day, mists from the swamps mingled with fogs sweeping in from the sea, you respect the courage of long ago more and more. And when you remember that every male between the ages of fourteen and fifty was in the service of his country, you begin to feel, like I do, that we know very little of being brave. You get a new concept of the character of these people along the Mullica and the bay when you realize that everything had to be done, even in the building of a new town, by women, little children, and men who were rheumy, half-fed, and probably bad-tempered."

Who was it I heard grumbling about the manpower draft? Who was it who boasted that women were working for war as they never did before? I have wanted to applaud all over again each time I reread that passage in Georgianna Blake's correspondence. There were considerations here that I for one had little thought of before. I have respected as much as anybody those who built early, sturdy houses, knowing well enough my own batting average with a hammer. But this evidence that something was created out of nothing, that a whole new town rose from fragments collected from among smoking embers and gathered together by tireless women, earnest youngsters, and old men who complained about food, weather, and the way the war was being run, was startling. There was, of course, another side of the picture—Chestnut Neck had no traffic with crochety landlords increasing rentals and decreasing improvements, no need for licenses to go fishing, no call for building permits or union cards or resourcefulness with which to dissuade insurance men. Women were not yet worrying about beauty parlor dates or how they looked in the pants of wartime industry. Children were not whining for ice cream cones. Even for the old men, discarded as too old to fight, life was comparatively simple and complaints, centered on a limited number of targets, were counted on to be varied and on time.

Having run out of letters from Mrs. Blake one Saturday morning, I tried to change the privateering pace by seeking sensible explanation of the "wrangle" behind Wrangleboro. Wrangleboro, I had found, was on many of the old maps before Port Republic, and on about the same spot. I was unable to glean much from printed records or Mrs. Blake or even the very co-operative Methodist minister stationed in Port Republic. After I had listened politely to the old stories about Captain Johnson and his sand fort, Captain Baylin and the Rangers who rode down from The Forks, Jack Fenton who served as a scout with the Continentals, and even Doctor Collins, first resident physician of the area and later a regimental surgeon, I still lacked clues to either "wrangle" or ancestral privateers in any imposing quantity. And just as I was about to conclude that the name implied more than ever was behind it and that the "wrangle" of Wrangleboro was perhaps like the "reckless" of Recklesstown, a quip or family connotation, I looked up from a copy of Heston's *Waggon Jaunts* which ignores the matter altogether, in time to hear a medley of gossip.

Harry P. Grim, the parson, said there might have been wrangling at the village taverns. Wrangles bred tangles and tangles bred at least one fight, described by Pastor Grim with good Methodist restraint as "boisterous behavior in one of the hotels." Services in a church across from one of the bar parlors were disturbed, he said, and that seems to have been the beginning of the end. Soon the local prohibitionists were abroad, and taverns were closed one by one. But Wrangleboro, some say, was "up the road a piece" from the site of Port Republic. The name may have evolved, they often add with Mrs. Bowen in Leeds Point, when the good folk who lived there wrangled most of the time "and maybe are wrangling still." To which sentiments Mr. Grim attached reassuring addenda: Since the Methodists and Presbyterians of Port Republic got along so well together that they united long ago, as an example of good fellowship in an unfriendly world, I could safely conclude that any serious wrangling was over now.

It was on another morning, in the cooling shade of the parsonage porch, that I heard something more of life along the Nacote from papers which the parson had been collecting at a variety of meetings, many of which he frankly promoted for that purpose. His methods of digging up half-buried history, I told him, were much better than mine. But then, I added, I was neither Methodist nor parson. Mr. Grim shook his head, saying, "I live in dread that the church will

225

move me on before I've collected it all—or worse, just when I'm getting at something I've wanted for a long time." However, when last I came that way, I heard from reliable sources that this kindly pulpiteering researcher was as yet mixing family reunions and congregational homecomings with preachment and the cure of souls, obtaining from descendants of pioneers the tales that soon might vanish away.

*21*

## PORT OF THE REPUBLIC

*"When the great markets by the sea shut fast*
*All that calm Sunday that goes on and on:*
*When even lovers find their peace at last,*
*And Earth is but a star, that once had shone."*
JAMES ELROY FLECKER

THIS, THEN, IS PORT REPUBLIC with its tall church and taller spire, with its idle mill-pond and darkly shaded main street, and over there, spoiled by tons of fill, the creek up which crept survivors of Chestnut Neck. There, carefully screened, is the parsonage where sometimes, Mr. Grim told me, he campaigned quite shamelessly for money with which to erect granite boulders, duly inscribed, in pioneer clearings up from the Mullica. This is where the business got its start among the graves of privateers.

"First of the lot," the parson said, "was Micajah Smith. You know Mrs. Blake over in Pleasantville? Well, her daughter, Mida, read a paper about Micajah when we set up a bronze marker where he's buried here. Now the grave is marked as a Revolutionary soldier's ought to be. It's in the yard of the meeting house Micajah built down the road."

This impressive ceremony was in 1935, I found out, when the Gen-

226

eral Lafayette Chapter, D. A. R., officiated at ceremonies in Port Republic.

"Micajah Smith," Parson Grim went on, as if he had been transported suddenly to a pulpit, "was one of the outstanding privateersmen in all of New Jersey." I was certain that much of the same New Jersey could hear plainly as he seemed to quote, "There is little doubt that his repeated coups brought retaliations by the Crown that gave Tucker's Beach and Chestnut Neck their bloody distinction."

Micajah, you should know as we linger beside the bridge, was the son of John Smith and Mary Ireland. He was born in 1741. He was thirty-four years old when the Revolution came. His mills, said Miss Blake in her patriotic paper, had been established in 1774 by Evi Smith, Hugh McCollum, and Richard Wescoat, the same Richard who was to combine the selling of ships and snapping turtles later on. Three years after, in that heart-gnawing winter of 1777–1778, Washington was at Valley Forge, his ragged army starving. New York was under siege and Philadelphia, drab and gay by turns, was likewise lost to the invaders. "Something had to be done and it was," said Mida Blake with considerable directness, although I have always had an idea that much of what happened was indirectly due to the fact that the invaders were revealed as having a pretty good time. That made the Jersey boys mad. Some time I must tell you of the pageant the visiting British put on in Philadelphia in 1778, a fancy-dress affair called the "Meschianza."

Little Egg Harbor was made a port of entry so that much-needed supplies, unloaded at the Neck, could be taken, along with Mullica munitions, on flatboats to The Forks and from there overland by ox teams. Here let me quote Miss Blake, a copy of whose paper has been kept in still another pocket for just this moment: "Thus our community was for a time the very heart of the cause for independence. It was due to the patriotic efforts of our people on the South Jersey shore at Egg Harbor that General Washington's army was supplied with food and ammunition. We can in very truth say that it was our people who made the victory possible."

I want none of your sneering, none of your smiles, eloquently laden with the notion that here was a mere burst of school-girl oratory under a tree. This was no bid for commending nods of a packed

227

gallery of flag-waving relatives and friends, no outcry of youth fed on pap about patriots and pioneers and cardboard ancestors. It was and ever will be the simple truth. Why it has been passed over so easily, I don't know. Mida Blake, daughter of Georgianna, felt the force of Jersey's genesis throbbing from the ground upon which she stood that day, sensed inspiration in the very air she breathed. So she gave to dimming memory new and greater glory.

You may find it easier to comprehend those conditions, thinking of them, scaled down, as conditions we know. There are parallels everywhere—we have grown up but we have not learned. There were spies, then, and fifth columnists—saboteurs, too. There were government men with natural ability and training, paid to track down traitors, hunting witches without charge. There were people who thought that George Washington was God Almighty, and there were other people who said that any one of a dozen generals would do a better job. There were people who thought that winning the war was less important than getting back in power. And there were people who said that Congressmen and printers of newspapers and leaders of business were the real enemies of freedom.

Workmen at The Forks and elsewhere were exempted from military service by a legislature meeting in Haddonfield, seeking to keep defense industries going, while ragged soldiers, far from home, threatened their superiors and deserted to their neglected farms because draft-dodging braggarts with only brawn to commend them got big money. Government contracts were honored and filled in spite of blockade, red tape, and priorities that cut in on material and transportation. Men were switched from making ovens and skillets and sugar-mill gudgeons to cannon, cannon shot, and camp kettles. Shipwrights, colliers, nailers, and laborers wanted more than the promised "best wages," spent their money as quickly as it was paid them, and said this working for victory was so much eyewash. Admittedly terms were different, as different as the names of Port Republic and Gravelly Landing, Moss Mill and Morse's Mill, Naked and Nacote Creek. Spies were Refugees or Pine Robbers; fifth columnists were Tories, official and unofficial members of the Associated Loyalists; mosquito boat pilots were privateers. Even so, the Mullica Valley was a cross section of a nation at war, even as it is today an index in miniature to all the country.

More than that: Here, up a half-forgotten river and back from a shoaling bay were the people who built a new town when the old was destroyed, dug bog ore for munitions and the cylinder of John Fitch's steamboat, goaded every burden animal incapable of bearing a militiaman into hauling whatever vehicles were left with food and arms to where a nation's liberty, like many of those who fought for it, missed death by seconds and inches in the cold. Here, up the same river, are their kinsmen, neighbors as in the beginning, mindful that what they have inherited and what they want most is a life that is more than immolation.

Mrs. Blake has told me since then that as far as she can discover —and she has made an extensive study of the subject, let me tell you!—New Jersey, for some reason, did not issue letters of marque. These were commissions, and, at the same time, boomerangs, for the first letters of marque came through warrants issued by the Lords of the Admiralty to colonial governors. As far back as 1739 George II had been issuing instructions to captains of privateers or "Commanders of such Merchant Ships and Vessells as may have Letters of Marque or Commissions for Private Men of War against the King of Spain." All the letters of marque Georgianna Blake knew of, she said, were listed in the Pennsylvania *Archives* and were granted to New Jersey captains from Philadelphia. "I think some for New Jersey must have been granted that are not listed in Pennsylvania," she wrote me once, "but so far they have eluded me." So, it must be concluded, for Mr. Gaskill's benefit as well as our own, some of the most skillful privateersmen were at best pirates without portfolio.

As for authentic Egg Harbor privateers, Mrs. Blake has listed several. But Captain Micajah Smith is the only one she knows much about, she warned me. It was Micajah who left his mill early in the war to take command of the sloop, "Sly," equipped with three carriage guns and eight swivels. He put to sea with a crew of twenty, men who knew that although the craft was but twenty tons, she was clever in maneuvering, capable of slipping out of many a close call. With Cap'n Micajah aboard, as certain of the waters and the shoals as a fish, excitement was certain and not long in coming. Records show that six prize vessels were captured before Micajah took the "Venus," a large British merchantman and queen of them all.

"Cap'n Micajah came in with the 'Venus' in August, 1778," Mrs. Blake disclosed in another of her letters, writing as if she, too, had been aboard. "She was probably one of the most valuable prizes taken during the war." Our correspondent at this point dipped into what she called family tradition for details that are not written anywhere. "The Smiths and Clarks have always been told," she wrote, "that the 'Venus' was passing Little Egg Harbor on her way to New York, loaded down with silks and silver plate and plenty more. Like merchant ships of the day, she carried a ferocious-looking cannon on her stern. When the 'Sly' drew up for attack, the 'Venus' naturally prepared to defend herself. But somehow in the firing of the ponderous stern cannon, the mate, who was also the captain's brother, forgot to prime it. The cannon exploded, killing the mate and several of the crew. The Captain struck his colors and quickly surrendered."

There, presumably, the family story stops. Tradition, partisan as ever, seems to have held something back. Mrs. Blake admitted as much when she confided that Frank Stewart, as thorough a historian as ever was in Jersey, once uncovered a court record of a suit brought by David Stevens, skipper of the "Chance," another privateer, for a share of the prize money. "However," Mrs. Blake wrote me, "in what way the 'Chance' was concerned, if at all, I do not know. Neither do I know the result of the court action. There is no family tradition in reference to any of it."

Not with any intention of finding something behind Mrs. Blake's back but with an urge to settle the matter, I kept looking. In Mr. Stewart's own compendium, *Notes On Old Gloucester County*, there is this blunt statement: "The Schooner 'Sly' and the ship 'Chance' commanded by Micajah Smith and David Stevens respectively, captured the ship 'Venus' according to a Gloucester County law suit, 1780." This was two years after Joseph Potts, Marshal, advertised the sale at the house of Colonel Richard Wescott "at the Forks of Little Egg Harbor," of the Privateer Sloop "Chance" which "lately took the ship 'Venus,' per inventory to be seen then, being completely fitted and now ready for a cruize." To which Mr. Stewart added thoughtfully a later scrap of information dated 1782: Major Lardner Clark, son of Colonel Elijah, sold to John M. Taylor for five hundred dollars "the cargo and outfit of the brig 'Chance'" and accepted note in payment. Was this the same "Chance"? A sloop is a one-masted vessel with a fore-and-aft rig. A brig is a square-rigged two-master.

It is at best confusing. Hazarding a guess, always dangerous where family honor is at stake, I would say that Captain Stevens's "Chance" was somehow in at the kill of the "Venus" and that two privateersmen, rather than one, converged on their quarry, causing the strange and somewhat fantastic forgetfulness that exploded the cannon on the afterdeck. Or, if you persist in being less charitable, you can stand by the facts advertised by John Stokes, Marshal, in the *Pennsylvania Packet*:

A very valuable cargo of the ship VENUS (bound from London to New York, lately captured and brought in there by Capt. David Stevens) consisting of fine and coarse broadcloaths, fine and coarse linens, calicoes, chintzes, lawns and cambricks, silks and sattins, silk and thread stockings, mens and womens shoes, a great variety of medicines and books, hard ware, beef, pork, butter, cheese and porter, in short the greatest variety of all kinds of merchandise, too tedious to be inserted. . . .

Here, you see, Captain Stevens alone is the hero. Two months later his name had vanished from the public prints. The same John Stokes, posting a new sale of bargain leftovers at Sam Cooper's ferry on the Delaware—it may have rained on the original bargain day—listed proud fittings of the "Venus" with table cutlery and even Epsom salts:

. . . some small guns, swivels, howitz, 6d and 10d nails, a few pieces of crocus, and thin linen fit for sleeve linings, furniture and other brushes, Epsom salts, saddlers tacks, china, silver, ebony, buck and bone handled knives and forks; men and womens shoes, a number of earrings and necklaces, watch and clock springs, watch crystals, watchmakers tools, and a variety of other articles, being part of the cargo of the Prize Ship VENUS. . . .

It seems to me, now that we have looked through all the letters and notes on ancient records, that I have had to leave the bulk of the Mullica privateers in the graves where first I found them. Except for names like Humphrey Hughes and Nicholas Keen and Henry Thorne and Joshua Baker & Company, the shrouds of anonymity are as tightly as ever wrapped about them and adventures that must have been theirs. Of course, you can say that Micajah Smith was typical of them all. You can say, too, that the taking of the "Venus" was a typical engagement, with a score of Mullica sailors never honored for every skipper whose name went into whatever records there may be. Let me whisper that if the taking of the "Venus" *was* typical, here may be the cause of wrangling that found its way into the earlier name of the town they moved up the creek. Now that we are considering it dispassionately, it sounds as if the whole privateering routine, from fond farewells to climax on the auction block, was largely a matter of making faces. The man with the nastiest face or the ugliest cannon or the most bluff in his makeup, usually came off top dog for his impudence.

Well it was that the "Venus" was stripped of even tacks and watch springs when Mr. Stokes presided over the final sale. Otherwise the event would have centered mostly on goods damaged by fire. For the blackened hulk of the ship whose capture, with that of the "Major Pearson," brought British vengeance to Chestnut Neck, lies somewhere in the Mullica mud off the weed-grown clearing of a village similarly destroyed. A pulley wheel on exhibit in Woodbury and a capstan bar, occasionally brought out into the light in a house in Port Republic, are all that remain above water. My relics are more personal: Added days at the Port, a sheaf of letters from Georgianna Blake, and a bit of special information that must add something, I think, to my peculiar store.

"What on earth," I asked almost everywhere, "are pieces of crocus?"

At length, from the most unexpected of sources came the answer. "Don't you know? Why, they're crumbling oxides of iron, calcined to a powder, sometimes used for polishing." Donny Smallwood told me that. And now, lest you conclude that the bones of places and people are so much crocus, too, here at the Port, I'm taking you to Donny himself. For Donny's the man who says he's been living, these last few years, for the first time. If someone had only told him how it would be, he says, he would have come to Port Republic long, long ago.

In the end it was Donny Smallwood who told me to find out about religion and the Andrews family. But that was after he said his real name was Frank and that he hadn't thought of coming to the Port until Judge French wanted a new house and asked him to build it. I told Donny that I hadn't planned to come down to the Port either, at least not that day in June. I had started out for Clark's Landing, because Frank Stewart told me if I had missed the cemetery I had never been there at all. But there I was, as we are now, in Port Republic, thinking that going down the Mullica is a lot like having heaven for your destination. You feel instinctively that you will come to the gates some day, but meanwhile there are interesting places and people on the way there.

Sud Norcross was with me then—Samuel Southard Norcross, descendant of innkeepers and stagecoach drivers, incredibly agile at seventy-five and as salty and sententious a companion as one could ask. Sud's memory for names and faces and the countless odd corners where recollection catalogued them will ever be its own miracle to me. Never once have I gone anywhere with Sud, my guardian guide, that he could not, after a moment's reflection, scratch at the edge of his baldish pate and say: "What did you call this place? Oh. Why say, I've heard my father tell about the hotel they used to have down here. Quite a place. One night they had a big jollification, and the haymow in the barn was more popular with the young folks than anything in the bar or on the dance floor. Or was it Uncle 'Ri' who took the day off from reg'lar business and druv his stage down just for the ride? Well, anyhow, seems to me I got an old aunt somewheres up one o' these here streets. Wonder if she's a-livin' now? Let's go see!"

We would always go see. Soon, with Sud buying some eggs and asking for all the folks, unrecorded legend would begin to flow. At first that afternoon in Port Republic loomed as an exception. Sud had shaken his head. All the people he had known at the Port had gone to glory, he said. As for Clark's Landing, that was sure to be a washout. Nobody had been living where that was for generations. "Cemetery? Maybe was, once. But you been down there. I was with you and we didn't see any graveyard!"

So we started for Clark's Landing and arrived in Port Republic. However accidental was the return to the churned banks of the

Nacote, quests for Mullica Clarks could well begin just there. Not only are there dozens of Clarks among the Higbees, Cakes, Blakes, Burnetts, and Blackmans of the old village in the remembrance of a few still living, but it was here that Tom Clark built his meeting house before preaching and privateering were progressing hand in hand. And that, of course, was long before Donny Smallwood, looking up from the caulking of a rowboat, proved his peevish humor transient. Donny was annoyed at the way they had changed Nacote Creek, upset about the way the chickens weren't laying and where the corn was coming from to feed them, out of sorts about an habitual something people call their religion. And, as he talked, Donny looked beyond us at the church behind the house that was his, a church with a steeple like those in Quebec.

Donny began, as I approached, by saying: "If that old buck you went by here with is named Norcross, tell him to get the hell out of that graveyard and come back here off his high horse." Then his face creased with smiles under a cloth hat once white. The Port was no exception after all. This time the routine had worked in reverse. Sud had discovered no old friend in town. Instead, an old friend with an equally prodigious memory had reached across the years to rediscover him. Sooner than soon Sud was a newspaper circulation manager again, and Donny was selling his papers on corners in Camden.

"I was a master mechanic up there after that," Donny said. "Then the Judge asked me to come down and build him a house. The country kind of got me, like it gets most everybody. I been here ever since, raisin' hell and chickens. 'Course, Smallwoods belong down here as much as them that's planted in that graveyard up the road. There used to be another Smallwood on the other side of the creek, they tell me. Never took time to look him up till it was too late. Wish he was here now, to tell you the truth. It would sort of balance the community."

I told Mr. Smallwood we had come down to see the graveyard at Clark's Landing. "It ain't much of a place," he told me thoughtfully. "Ain't worth all the stickers you got to go through to get there. Ain't been a funeral there in fifty year, that's how popular it is. Stick

around here for a while—we got much better graveyards." And so
they have. Micajah Smith himself is in one of them, under date of
1807—Micajah in his will provided for "a new Methodist Church"
and deeded to his son-in-law, Nehemiah Blackman, husband of his
daughter Sarah, the Wrangle Borough Mills, with three quarters of
an acre reserved for "the Meeting House and burying ground." I
told Donny that Mrs. Blake said there was at least one relic of that
meeting house still in the family—a tin sconce once one of several
that had reflected candlelight at evening devotions.

That was when Donny sprang one of his usual surprises by saying
that Frank Stewart, whose mother had been one of the Port Republic Burnetts, descendant of Thomas Burnett who was on Long
Island in 1644, had dug up an old deed dated February 9, 1799. In
it Robert Leeds, Jr., and his wife Dorcas, trustees for the building
of a Methodist church, gave over, for the consideration of twelve
dollars, one and a half acres if a church "should be wanted in the
place of the church already built thereon." Micajah Smith, who was
one of the witnesses, didn't deed his property to the Methodists,
Miss Blake had argued in that fervent address of hers, because no
Methodist society was incorporated there until 1837. Micajah then
was long in his grave outside the meeting house he had planned.
"This churchyard has been known, as far back as any member of
my family can remember," said Georgianna's daughter, "as 'the
old Union Burying Ground,' although the corporate name of the
church has been 'the Methodist Union Chapel at Blackman's Mills.' "

"There was a church operating before the land was deeded to
anybody," Donny said. "Blackman's Mills became the Wrangle Borough Mills, and then when mills got to be a secondary consideration
and people got around to figuring there was some heroes among
them, they smoked up a patriotic name like Port Republic. That's
what the name was in 1847, anyway. By then everybody was talking
about the ships they were building over at the Port. Deeds don't
mean nothing half the time."

I spoke to Donny of the Brainerd preaching places Mrs. Blake had
written about. I said, feeling my way, that Mr. Brainerd's religion
was a special kind, perhaps, something that combined a love of

travel and privation with a spirit to live and let live. "Live and leave live" is the way they say it, mostly down the river. Religion, somehow, is all things to all men.

"Yes," Donny Smallwood agreed, getting up and finding a dry spot to sit on the back of his boat. "Religion *was* different then, just as different as this creek they changed and spoiled by dredging it all over the place in the name of improvement. Those old bucks who drove stages by here, coming up from Leeds when the Port was Gravelly Landing and stopping up there at the Franklyn Inn, they wouldn't know the old place. Neither would them Revolutionary soldiers in the graves you and Sud was a-looking at. Religion in their days was something that let a man do privateering through the week provided he came to church and heard a pious sermon on Sundays. Religion later on turned out to be something that closed up all the gin mills around here—and there was six, mind you!"

It was Daniel Mathis, innkeeper at Chestnut Neck, who went back after the burning to gather up what scraps he could so he could begin building, almost at once, the Franklyn Inn, still proud in its original lines near the Port Republic dam. I don't know how old Daniel was or how he came to be at home with wartime on his hands unless he was one of the old men. Jonas Miller, definitely spoken of as the young fellow who helped Daniel with the building, fell in love with Daniel's daughter and later annexed the inn as well. There must be a special charm about life in an inn, because the four daughters of Jonas made sure their husbands were men trained in the entertainment of travelers like their father—that's the way they would have you think about it down there. But maybe, just maybe, the husbands had something to say about it, being on the lookout for strong, buxom females who would understand and help the business. You were given an extra smile by one of the daughters of Jonas Miller when you stepped from the Philadelphia stage, calling twice each week at Clark's Mills Hotel, Blue Anchor, and Long-a-Coming. Jonas himself was still extending his hotel chain when he built and opened Congress Hall, Cape May's historic hideaway, his four daughters taking their celebrated beauty down the cape to lend an extra sparkle to opening night.

Donny listened to my lore and changed the subject. "To most people," he said, "that name of 'Union' has always been a puzzler around here. It gets you all the more when you start wondering about a place called Wrangleboro, and you come out of it with something that sounds like complete harmony. Ever hear of Mrs. Collins? Anna C.? She wrote a little history of the Methodist churches in Port Republic and Smithville. Said there wasn't much you could say about the 'wrangle' part of it. But she inferred, just the same, that it was because of the taverns that the nickname started. Personally, I don't believe it."

Neither, I said, did I. It was much more reasonable to conclude that the "wrangles" had been legal and that they concerned prolonged claims to prize ships. However, I produced Mrs. Collins's book and here is what she really said:

> The supposition is that it [the name] was suggested by the character of some of the residents who were frequent visitors at the six public houses in the neighborhood. By this time it [Port Republic] was at first designated in the Minutes of the Bargaintown Quarterly Conference. But when the seeds of genuine piety had germinated in this seemingly unpromising soil, it bore blessed fruit and old things passed away and for many years the church was known as Union Chapel, Unionville. . . .

Donny spat, eloquently. "You see!" he exclaimed, as I shut the book borrowed from Pastor Grim. " 'Some of the residents'—I would have been one of them, probably, if I had been down here then. Why, like as not they were already ashamed of their privateering ancestors! And if those oldtimers had been a-living here when these 'seeds of gen-u-wine piety' were being sowed, they'd have turned Tory for a drink!"

I quieted him. I told him there was more to it than that. Mr. Grim had emphasized what Miss Blake had written in that paper of hers. The real union of the name, I explained, was in the merger of Presbyterians and Methodists under Methodist leadership. The Friends had a stronghold at Leeds Point as early as 1740, and Presbyterians were worshipping in Clark's Meeting House about a mile from Port Republic in 1762, a year after John Brainerd recorded a preaching call at Chestnut Neck, I pointed out. But Sud Norcross, who said he was "sometimes Methodist, sometimes Episcopal," declared that the Methodists, closing taverns as they went, had gained the best of the bargain, outlasting all the others. "No wonder they called it the Bargaintown Circuit," he chuckled.

But preaching was precarious business in the first Mullica days. I reminded Sud and Donny of that as I recalled John Fothergill, who wrote in his *Journal* that in 1721, in bitter December weather, he "went to J. Sykes's, intending to set forward from thence toward Egg-Harbour." Next day, when the weather had calmed a little, he "took his journey thro' the Desarts to Little Egg Harbour and came to Gervas Farrar's and on the 4th went to a meeting there and had a pretty good Time in the Extending of the Love of the Truth to the poor People thereaway. . . ." I was thinking, too, of the Reverend Philip Vickers Fithian, licensed to preach by the Philadelphia Presbytery in 1774, who a year later preached at the Clark's Mill Meeting House as well as at Elijah Clark's up at The Forks. "Down the road," I said aloud, "there was a Mr. Fithian who worked pretty hard. The books say he preached two hours for a dollar."

"Too much," Sud said. "A dollar too much if he was out to close taverns."

"That was the Methodists later on," Donny rebuked him. "Anyhow, this fellow Fithian probably got at least a couple of good square meals and a night's lodging out of it. And when the weather was what it was, you can't tell me those fellows didn't take a drink if it was offered to them in a nice way. Sure they worked hard. But they didn't go around bellyaching that chatter in the inn across the street bothered their hymns and hallelujahs. And anyhow, the taverns wasn't open on Sunday mornings. If the complaints were on weekdays, the innkeepers had a perfect right to turn around and say the hymns disturbed their business!"

I was thoughtful then and I am thoughtful now, wondering about the great array of parsons I have known. Which of them would do a job like that for a dollar or an equal amount, translated into terms of today. Were any concerned primarily with the propagation of "the Love of the Truth"? Would any be willing to go, on the promise of nothing more than a certainty that they would advance the Kingdom, the distances on foot required of those pioneering preachers, or thumb rides in coaches bestowing bruises and banning sleep. I doubted it then and I doubt it now. Many I know would be concerned with prepaid convenient travel, the certainty of good contacts for the future, all or even more than the comforts of home. Brave Mr. Fithian wrote glowingly in his *Journal:*

"I rode to The Forks at Little Egg Harbour and put up according to direction at Elijah Clark's, Esq. Mr. Clark is a man of fortune and taste. He appears also to be a man of integrity and piety, an Israelite indeed. And O Religion, thou hast one warm and unfeigned advocate in good and useful Mrs. Clark. I had rather have her spirit with the condition of a starving beggar, than destitute of it to have the wealth of worlds. She has more than the form — she has the spirit of religion. This peaceful, friendly, heavenlike spirit is breathing from her in every sentence. . . ."

"Damn if she didn't make a hit with the preacher!" Sud Norcross observed as I finished reading the passage.

"Elijah kept his eyes open," said Donny, confidently. I watched him walk back to the old houses across the road built by James Bell in 1812. James, Donny had said, was in one of those graves up the road, except when he came back looking for things. "Ghost?" I had inquired. "Something peculiar," said Mr. Smallwood.

"Maybe the Jersey Devil," I suggested.

"Oh, no," Donny had told me, shaking his head. "Jersey Devil don't come over this way. Gets up as far as The Forks now and then," he admitted, unsmilingly, as if the famous phantom might be a traveling butcher or wandering preacher of old, "but most of the time he's in Leeds Point."

And that, for all the charm of Port Republic, is where we are going now.

# 22

# THE JERSEY DEVIL

*"I played a soft and doleful air,*
*I sang an old and moving story—*
*An old rude song that suited well*
*That ruin wild and hoary."*
SAMUEL TAYLOR COLERIDGE

BY NOW IT MAY BE that New Jersey's most celebrated of all unwanted children has come back as he or she or it was supposed to long ago. Perhaps there have been unexplained flutterings of ghostly wings at Leeds Point, unearthy cries at midnight down a Pleasantville chimney, or even a clumsy clutter of cloven footprints, neither human nor animal, in the snow of an Estellville dooryard. For in his old haunts further afield The Jersey Devil has been long overdue.

Since first they were aware, Jersey ears have heard grim whisperings about The Jersey Devil. Newspapers used to carry little stories and sometimes long feature articles concerned with certain inexplicable happenings in queer places, odd noises strangely linked with swamps and salt marshes and Mullica fastnesses, with reputable folk telling and repeating shuddersome anecdotes lacking what old-fashioned mortals call common sense. If a man's hen house happened to be invaded with nothing in the way of a clue left behind except a misshapen hoofprint in the mud, if a group of friends boisterous in some moonlit country house became suddenly transfixed by uncanny howls that descended from the roof peak, if some romantic pair driving along an equally romantic lane was tossed unwarned into a ditch because a horse reared and dashed away—"it must have been The Jersey Devil!"

I had been reading Mr. Fithian again, one day, awaiting Mrs. Bowen's return home at Leeds Point. I had remarked the contrasts made by the preacher between the people of the upper side of the Mullica and those further down the coast. At Great Egg Harbor, he wrote, were "straggling, impertinent, and vociferous swamp men"

240

while closer by the river were "people in this wild and thinly settled country" who, nevertheless, were "extremely nice and difficult to be suited in preaching." The good folk of Port Republic, Clark's Landing, and Leeds Point, he said further, "must have, before they can be entertained, good speaking, good sense, sound divinity, and neatness and cleanliness in the person and dress of the preacher." That wandering parsons were not always as washed as they urged their congregations to be, spiritually as well as physically, was indicated, Mr. Fithian said, "from remarks freely made upon gentlemen who formerly preached here."

Such particular people, so full of common sense, would own no belief in a ghost, be he ever so celebrated, I thought. And yet, when Mrs. Bowen in Leeds Point had all but concluded that highly informative scolding, her attitude was something of a contradiction. So many stories, she said, simply could not be credited by sensible people. Then, at the end, she said casually: "Of course you knew that The Jersey Devil was born here!" Stammering somehow that yes, I knew, I confessed afterwards, when I had recovered from the surprise of it, too far away to make amends, that I didn't know at all.

Once when I was talking to Mrs. Sam Layer in Haddonfield about vanished amusement parks and suspended county fairs, the venerable old lady, then very ill, spoke of a gibbering ghost likely to reappear anywhere in New Jersey when days began again to bring their procession of ordinary events. I said that perhaps the phantom had given up in the face of competition. But then, as I picked up the dead words and the sound of a voice long stilled, I heard Mrs. Layer correct me, saying: "Not The Jersey Devil! Leeds's Devil!"

There it began to fit together, and I launched a quest for all the facts, a quest undertaken at intervals throughout the years by better stalkers than I. Leeds Point, I said at the start, must have had some traffic with Leeds's Devil, and at once I scented danger from dozens of Mrs. Bowens who might be expected to object to whatever an honest ghost hunter might find out. That was why I went back to make sure of what Mrs. Bowen had said. And that, really, was how she came to lead us on—you see, I took a witness with me—to what remained of the house in which, Mrs. Bowen said, "they always say The Jersey Devil was born."

241

Between that time and my previous call, the afternoon on which I was roundly chastised, I had concluded that I knew the house she meant, a perfect ruin of a place, literally rotting apart, a hollow shell probably full of rats and wood ticks, with weeds grown as tall about it as the lilacs in the front yard. Surely, I said, this place must be haunted. Certainly this must be The Devil's birthplace. But it wasn't at all.

Mrs. Bowen came home at length and graciously consented to accompany us down the gravel road, leading off the roadway to Oyster Creek, where I shall always remember my first and last steamed clams, put away to the "bzzzt!" of flies being fried on an electrified screen door. We passed the old house that would have been so appropriate—no, that was merely another of the old Leeds houses, said Mrs. Bowen. The house she wanted to show us, she said, was farther on. The Shourds house, she called it. When we came to a bend, Mrs. Bowen slowed us up with a show of bewilderment. I began to wonder if the shuddersome goblin had taken his hideout away, too, now that we had come to see it.

"That's strange," said Mrs. Bowen. "It used to be somewhere here. I could have sworn that over there, beside those cedars . . ."

"How long has it been," I inquired quietly, "since you were down this far?"

No sarcasm was meant. Just the same, it seemed a little incredible that the Bowen house was scarcely more than five hundred yards away across the fields and that Mrs. Bowen had not come down this road at least once in a while. Something like an economy of motion was involved, I think.

"Guess it's all of fifteen years," Mrs. Bowen confessed, as if there was nothing at all unusual in that. There was nothing of any special interest that the Bowens wanted or wanted to see again. There was nothing of any special interest to Mrs. Bowen, that was evident. Even so, at the moment and now, too, it was and is a little difficult to believe that a house as famous as the birthplace of The Jersey Devil had vanished without the knowledge of neighbors who lived, all the while, just the other side of the screen of trees. But that was exactly what had happened.

From the car we could see nothing that looked remotely like a house, even though we were within a few feet of where it had stood. At last, when Mrs. Bowen had gained her bearings, we plunged into the thickets and there, in the midst of a tangle of weeds and honeysuckle and brambles which had grown up through the years, we came upon fallen timbers and the old bricks of a chimney, tumbling in the rubble of a filling cellar hole.

Mrs. Bowen told the story quite simply as we stood there. There had been a Mrs. Shourds, she said, the mother of a family presumably large. One day she was heard to make a wish, as dreadful a wish as ever was made: She hoped that if she was to be burdened by any more children the next would be a devil. And a devil the next offspring, poor dwarfed misshapen being, proved to be! The creature, Mrs. Bowen said, grew painfully in size until the time came when it could move clumsily about in the house in which it was born and where, from most accounts, it was sheltered mercifully from the curious who came to peep in at the windows.

Just think how you would have acted if the story had come to you that Mrs. Shourds had wished for a devil and had begotten it. Wouldn't you have sidled by of an evening, on one imaginary errand or another, to see what you could see? Well, you probably would not have seen very much, even so. Few saw anything at all, according to all the variations of the story. Presumably those who heard a snatch or two filled in the details of the most incredible part of the tale, as it was told again by Mrs. Bowen there in the ruin of plaster and cedar siding which by now must be dust again.

One evening when the wind was howling outside and when a shivery fog came creeping in from the sea, the twisted being cried out wildly and with a flapping of its long arms, turned suddenly to wings, swooped up the Shourds' chimney and disappeared forever as far as the family was concerned. As far as the rest of New Jersey is concerned, this was and is The Jersey Devil, Leeds's Devil, or the Devil of Leeds Point which in cycles of years that vary in the manifold accounts has continued to haunt the countryside with one technique or another. This, at least, was Mrs. Bowen's sketchy recollection of it.

The story and mention of it in a letter or two began the turning of many invisible wheels. Our friend, Mr. Gaskill, in Washington, replied that it was an old associate, Frank Lee, who had made a life's business of uncovering information on the Leeds Point phantom. "He kept his notes on scraps of paper, however," warned our correspondent, "and they may have disappeared long ago. But if you will look up Mrs. Lee, who I believe lives in Vincentown, you may get something that ought to be preserved."

I wrote a letter to Mrs. Lee. For a long time there was no answer. When a reply came, finally, it was from Mrs. Rhoda Lee Compton, Mrs. Lee's daughter. Mrs. Lee had died, too, and while there were many old books about, Mrs. Compton was certain there had been no notes about the ghost. Not until some time after that did I realize that Frank Lee, to whom Mr. Gaskill had referred me, was Francis Baizley Lee whose books on New Jersey are well known.

I began to think my luck was out, especially when an obituary appeared telling of the death of Fire Warden Bozarth, at Batsto near The Forks, in which it was declared that he "was the last man known to have seen The Jersey Devil." I had met and talked with Mr. Bozarth, but never in any of our conversations did he reveal knowledge of such a distinguished visitor. It was while I had reverted to looking up the family history of the Shourds, descended surely from one Cornelius Shourds, a stockbroker who came all the way from Holland, back in 1684, on the urgent invitation of that pioneer of Pennsylvania, William Penn, that a second letter came from Mrs. Compton saying that her cousin, J. Elfreth Watkins of Philadelphia, had come to visit her. "Oddly enough," she wrote, "he was with my father years ago when they were tracking down those Jersey Devil stories. He says he may be able to find some trace of them in his files."

After some friendly correspondence in which Mr. Watkins said that much of the material in his files had been stolen, he came upon a yellowing clipping of an article he syndicated in 1905, headed boldly "On The Trail Of Leeds' Devil" and subtitled "The Dread Monster of Jersey's Big Forest." "Just back of the white and velvety coastline of New Jersey," Mr. Watkins began, with the full glory of early newspaper writing, "there tapers up from its deep base along Delaware Bay to its apex at Long Branch a green triangle known as 'The Pines.' Its black, innermost heart has suffered a hiatus, a quick transition from twentieth to eighteenth century, plunged into a dark, sylvan mediaeval realm of witches, wizards, conjurers and monsters. . . ."

His scene established, Mr. Watkins proceeded, saying that he did not believe that "anywhere in your mythologies you will find any reference to 'Leeds' Devil' but it was a pilgrimage in search of the lair of this monster (which has kept the 'pine hawkers' in the State in terror since Colonial days) that made me turn my back upon the sea and sent me trudging across the white floor of 'The Pines' and wading through its dismal cedar swamps." I had joined that quest, you see. Now, so must you.

"I was set upon the monster's trail by Mr. Francis B. Lee, of Trenton," wrote Mr. Watkins, then the head of a news and feature syndicate, "an astute historian who has made a careful study of the folklore and dialect of the 'pine hawker.' The story goes that back in mid-Colonial days there lived in Burlington, on the Delaware, a city far beyond the frontier of The Pines, a woman known as 'Mother Leeds.' Witchcraft was then at its height in the Colonies and she was accused as an adept in its black arts. In 1735, according to the tale, Mother Leeds gave birth to a male child whose father, at first unidentified, was later said to have been none other than the foul fiend and prince of darkness, otherwise known as Old Horny and Beelzebub.

"The child was normal at birth but before the termination of the tempestuous night of its arrival it horrified several old crones gathered about the bedside of Mother Leeds by assuming a serpent-like body, cloven hoofs, the head of a horse, the wings of a bat and the forked tail of a dragon. The coloring of the terrible monster turned to a dusky brown and after bepummeling its mother and her chapfallen companions it uttered a series of loud, raucous cries and flew up the chimney. Circling about from village to village, while the tempest still screamed through the trees, the monster stopped on its way to devour several sleeping babes and then made for The Pines."

Pause should be made here, interrupting Mr. Watkins's fascinating narrative to point out, for the benefit of Mrs. Bowen and others, that here is direct quotation from the Sunday supplements of over

245

thirty-five years ago. "Mother Leeds" is no more the creature of my imagination than she was of the man who wrote the article after working with Mr. Lee, the "astute historian." Mrs. Bowen's version, it becomes evident at once, lost much more than names in years of retelling the story.

"During the hundred and forty years that have since elapsed belated travelers crossing that dark sylvan tract have seen and heard the monster. Joseph Bonaparte, ex-King of Spain, who loved to hunt deer in this forest, is said to have encountered it once, while Commodore Decatur, who came to The Pines to test cannon balls made from the native bog ore at the since crumbled foundry at Hanover, is said to have fired one of these projectiles—designed for the Algerian pirates—directly through the monster 'without halting its mad pace.' The pine hawkers, who tell experiences even more terrible, attribute to it such supernatural powers as were assigned to the black witches of English folklore. It turns the milk sour in the pails, lames horses in their stalls, dries up the cows in the clearing pastures, seres the corn in the fields.

"Accompanied, as it usually is, by the howling of dogs and the hooting of owls, there can be no surer forerunner of disaster. Where the barrens line the shore it flits from one desolate grass-grown dune to another and is especially watchful upon those wild heights when coasting schooners, driving their prows into the sand, pound to splinters upon the bars and distribute upon the waves their freight of goods and human lives.

"Upon such occasions Leeds' Devil is seen in the companionship of a beautiful golden-haired woman in white, or yet of some fierce-eyed, cutlass-bearing disembodied spirit of a buccaneer whose galleon, centuries ago, was wrecked upon the shore of Cape May County. Again this monster is said to share its haunts with a headless seaman who, the Barnegat people say, was decapitated by none other than Captain Kidd himself and whose stiffened trunk that pirate king left sentinel over buried, ill-gotten gold.

"At other times Leeds' Devil is seen to hover, like a giant bird of prey, above some silent, star-bespangled pond within the umbrous recess of a cedar swamp. On such occasions its foul breath blasts the lives of hundreds of fishes, found floating next day upon the surface,

typical scene at the edge
f one of the cedar swamps
the Mullica country.

One of the most memorable
characters of the Mullica
was William Fretz Kemble,
who ran a nursery, planted
exotic flowers in odd places
in the woods to bewilder
naturalists, and became
known as the Santa Claus
of Lower Bank.

Across from the old paper plant at Sweetwater, turned into a charming private home, is the Elijah Clark house, setting for the romantic novel, *Kate Aylesford*. An old boat, beached long ago at Clark's Landing, recalls the Landing, and early Clark patriots, privateers, millers, and church-builders.

tainted and unfit for food. Half cantering, half flying through the shadowy vistas of the forest, it drives before it to their coverts deer, rabbits and squirrels. Such," Mr. Watkins at last concluded his colorful story, "is the black record of Leeds' Devil, transposed from the nasal dialect of the Pine Hawkers—and these human denizens of the forest we must not pass by unnoticed. . . ."

Clearly the original legend, pieced together by Mr. Watkins and the late Mr. Lee, has everything: A monster that combines the worst of the animal, bird, and reptile kingdoms, notable witnesses of its frightfulness, the original touch of trying to shoot down a ghost with a cannon—and even a blonde. Beside the narrative in which Mother Leeds, and not Mrs. Shourds, became the mother of the horrific villain of the piece, the more modern derivation is feeble and forlorn. Even so, I had not heard the whole of it.

From Mrs. Blake in Pleasantville came response to a further inquiry. Mrs. Blake wrote me that The Jersey Devil was "positively born" in three places and that Burlington was *not* one of these. In Leeds Point, she said, he was born in a house on the site of the old Shourds house. In Pleasantville, she disclosed further, he was born in a house that stood on the site of a dwelling occupied then by Dr. Rieck at 507 South Main Street. "I presume," she wrote, "that in Estellville the site of his birthplace can be as positively identified."

The story in each instance was the same, Mrs. Blake pointed out —"the unwanted child, the home already filled with numerous offspring from the poor feeble-minded parents. The mother wishes the child may be a devil when born; the child has a cloven foot and hands like claws. He finally claws his mother's breast and flies up the chimney and away into the night with horrible screeches. The same screeches seem to attend his return-visits," said Mrs. Blake, "which, by the way, come every seven years and always portend disaster."

Expressing an opinion that the germ of the legend was traceable to Old World superstitions "brought with the people from Europe," Mrs. Blake confessed that she never had heard "when the Devil developed the vampire wings he is supposed to have." While the monster may have developed from superstitions, there must have been some foundation to the story of his birth, Mrs. Blake told me later. "Possibly a deformed and degenerate child was born into such a home in each of the locations along the shore," she suggested. "The child may have run away, either perishing from cold or dying when attacked by wild beasts. Parents and neighbors imagine all sorts of stories," she added, "and it is probable that every tragic event along the shore was placed to the credit of The Jersey Devil."

Alfred M. Heston, the Atlantic County historian, writing as recently as 1928, recounted the legend, favoring Estellville for the opening scene, declaring the mother of the beast to be a Mrs. Leeds who lived there and not in Leeds Point at all. The baby was normal, he said, and it was soon exchanged, in some baffling manner, for the monstrosity that turned up a few days later. Mr. Heston pictures the creature swooping out the window, not up the chimney, and so loses much of the effect. Details for this departure seeem to have come from one George Gregory, whom Mr. Heston calls "a matter-of-fact gentleman" whose home was in Philadelphia but whose summers were spent in Cape May County. There it was, in Goshen, that Mr. Gregory obtained the facts from a Mrs. McCormack who, inspired by an "appearance" of the Devil in 1909, spoke at length on the subject with all the authority of her eighty-four years. Mr. Heston said that Mr. Gregory had it from Mrs. McCormack who had it from the nurse, probably midwife, who attended the Mrs. Leeds of Estellville, that "every day, for a time, the child-devil returned to the home of Mrs. Leeds and perched on the fence."

Mr. Heston appends still another and singularly flat claim that the mother of the monster was neither a Shourds nor a Leeds but a woman who, having refused food to a gypsy, was consequently cursed, her first-born subsequently performing most of the tricks ascribed to The Jersey Devil, making its debut, as in other variations, in the house at Leeds Point.

The Devil's name could have been Leeds, and it could have been Shourds, too. Daniel Leeds "located land" in Great Egg Harbor in 1694. Samuel Shourds, Sr., came to Little Egg Harbor in 1735. Daniel and his family lived at Leeds Point. The Shourds, almost legion, were scattered all through the Mullica neighborhood within surprisingly few years. It is impossible, however, to speak with any certainty, to conclude that The Jersey Devil gained its aliases from a person or a place, although there may be something more than coincidence

248

in the fact that Sam Shourds moved shoreward from Bristol, Pa., directly across the Delaware from Burlington, reputed home of "Mother Leeds" in 1735, the year of the supposed diabolical visitation.

Writing in 1929, the late Squire Hargrove of Pemberton, whose tall stories have thrust me into many a tight corner, managed to revive The Jersey Devil for a time, giving him birth at Leeds Point but not at any dwelling of the Shourdses—the Squire drops him at the old Leeds homestead, then occupied by Jesse Mathis. The Squire quotes Jesse as saying that people along the Mullica Valley and beyond believed that children born half-witted had been "touched" by Leeds's Devil and that this was the origin of a modern derivation. By 1934, however, the monster had lost so many of his trappings that a man whom police named as Willis Borton, wanted in five states on charges ranging from burglary to murder, glibly called himself "The Jersey Devil," and as such made the headlines.

I think it was Mrs. Blake who told me that people along the shore fully expected the Devil to make a spirited comeback in 1940. If he appeared, the billing must have been on a small rural circuit and none too sensational at that, for I heard nothing of it. What I did hear, only the other day, is that Mrs. Bowen, disowning the family connections and adhering to the name of Shourds instead of Leeds, could have gone all the way and discounted Leeds Point as the Devil's birthplace. Mrs. Underhill, down in Lower Bank, told me he belongs to the Mullica after all.

"Up Cale Cavileer's Lane," she said, "there is an old house. It was formerly owned by Moses Leeds, whose daughter, Jane, married Uncle Jake Johnson. She had so many children that she finally decided not to have any more, but if she did, she said, she hoped he would be a devil. Later a boy was born, and stories are told that after he was born he flew out the window. That is the beginning of the many different stories about Leeds's Devil. All kinds of descriptions were given of him, none as a natural human being. People down here say they have often seen him running along the rail fence between our house and the fields toward Leeds's Lane and the old Leeds house."

As I have said, whether the name be Leeds or Shourds or something else, and whether the cloven hoof or horse's head or writhing serpent's body will again lend chills to the manifestations, the lurking prodigy is long overdue. It may be that as a harbinger of disaster he has perished, long since, from overexertion.

## 23

## SANTA CLAUS OF LOWER BANK

*"Donne, I suppose, was such another*
*Who found no substitute for sense;*
*To seize and clutch and penetrate,*
*Expert beyond experience."*

T. S. ELIOT

ORDINARILY I DO NOT WILLINGLY ADDRESS THE LUNCHEON CLUBS. Usually there is some legitimate excuse to save me from an ordeal in which I find myself wondering if the food is contrived to make the members overlook the speaker or whether, by some chance, the opposite is true. Once I escaped by inches when, fifteen minutes before I was scheduled to appear, Alden Cottrell, a State forester, came to see me and somehow I persuaded him to be my substitute. Next time I was not as lucky.

Somehow I drifted into my usual enthusiasm for Mullicana. I spoke of people for whom ancestral acres by the river was Beulah Land, people who shun the world outside or despair of it, people who get along with just enough, who make what they need and who have achieved a kind of economic order worth investigating. The interest seemed general, the comment kind. Then, afterward, there appeared in the club's little newspaper something so patronizing that before I had considered the wisdom of retort, I had answered the challenge. Conditions I had described, it was said, could not produce greatness nor could these people make lasting contribution to civilization. That was enough to set me going. I responded:

250

"I am considerably in your debt for your commentary on my address before the club. However, your conclusion that these Down Jersey people of mine have made little in the way of new contributions to civilization is hardly based on fact. Through several generations these people, possessing some of the best blood in New Jersey, have made tremendous contributions, chiefly by minding their own business and preserving something we lack, a true community kind of living and a talent for making an economic order work. Their ingenuity is undoubted: When they need balers and rakes for sphagnum moss gathering, they make them; when boats are wanted, they make them—most boat-builders are either working for the Navy in their own yards along the little rivers or they have been brought to Camden shipyards in the emergency; when there is any great need for anything, their own talents fashion it, from a house to a coffin. I don't think you meant to reflect on these people. Actually, one must define civilization. Probably what you meant by civilization to me is decadence. Civilization does not consist of large spoonfuls of profit motive, great demands for legal twists and turns, great thirsts for things we have to immolate ourselves to get. There are almost as many people down country who have left off what I think you mean by civilization to live in a civilization they believe superior as there are natives happily unaware of being super-civilized—at least two are in Who's Who and one has proved, at least to his own satisfaction, that collectivism works and is only beaten by systems that have titles like WPA. Honesty, integrity, making what you have do, lack of suspicion—all these, I believe, are nearer to civilization than the spirit which grips a group of men and makes it sing something about coughing up a dime."

I ought not to have made any reference to the singing. As I was quickly informed, I had missed the real purpose of it. I had missed, as well, the true meaning of civilization and, in addition, I was sadly lacking in any concept of the club's service. I still maintain, however, apart from everything else, that it is something of a spectacle of foolishness when grown men, suddenly spying a late-comer, as suddenly lend their voices to words set to the tune, "She'll Be Coming 'Round the Mountain when She Comes"—

"He'll be coughing up a dime when he comes,
He'll be coughing up a dime when he comes,
He'll be coughing up a dime
'Cause he wasn't here on time,
He'll be coughing up a dime when he comes!"

The club publicist, hurriedly denying any intention of implication that "Mr. Beck's Mullica River dwellers" were inferior to anyone else, expressed the lingering doubt that people who lived in the fashion I had described "would be likely to produce a Beethoven, an Einstein or a Booker T. Washington. We feel," my correspondent replied further, "that the word civilization when applied to human beings means the removal of man from an animal state to that more approaching the ideals expressed in the teachings of Christ." Which was, I think, fairly far off the track. The squelcher proceeded: "We wonder whether the Mullica River dwellers have ever taken the trouble to organize a disinterested charity in which the more favored of them endeavor to benefit some less favored members of their community and if, perhaps, they extend helpful hands to some members of the community which they individually might not personally know."

This wonderment showed clearly that if anyone had been listening to what I said, some had not understood. Community life beside the Mullica is, in most of the little villages, a charitable living. What of the man who catches twice as many herring as he needs because the herring are there suddenly to be caught, and the man next door is not at home? What of the woman who stays in her kitchen over a wood fire twice as long as she would ordinarily because she was remembered by her neighbor with fish or farm products she was not able to get? What of the family that finds clothing and edibles heaped up on its temporary doorstep after a house has burned? What of Santa Claus of Lower Bank, of whom I must tell you more in just a moment? All these, whom I had mentioned in passing, were forgotten or ignored as I was further censured: "The thought with which Mr. Beck seems to close his letter perhaps has some of the criticism given by the highly educated to the Babbitts of this world. It seems to overlook the fact that we, as an organization, are a group

252

of strangers who meet once a week and use song as a spiritual cock-tail, sometimes merely to keep ourselves awake so that we may listen attentively to our guest speaker, sometimes to cement a little more thoroughly the loose ends of friendship that are formed in an organization of our type. Besides these two purposes, perhaps our songs also improve our digestion which is, in itself, a worthy result."

Ah, me! I had missed the sparkle and spiritual lift of the singing altogether. And I had failed to appreciate the dubious benefit of turning strangers into intimates, perhaps because I had proved cal-lous or immune. I could fully understand, however, that singing, no matter what its theme and sound, fills time, makes it pass quickly, proves the singer still alive, and best of all pares down the interval allotted to the speaker. All of it should have ended there, but some-how I felt that I should provide an impressive list of Mullica men, present and past, who would in themselves prove my contentions. I suppose that my list was received and filed in the usual manner. My ardent club defender in reporting that fact, however, continued to maintain that "if the entire world lived this rural life, producing all that it needed to consume in its own back yard, even the admit-tedly competent and able citizens mentioned by Mr. Beck would be a part of the world that would go on and on, and practically nothing would ever happen." I wanted to say that I *had* left my *own* back yard—and look what *had* happened! I was idiotically covetous of the last word. Even so, although I wrote out what I felt should be sent as a suitable finale, better judgment than mine kept it at home:

"It seems to me that when 'intelligentsia'
Would diagnose this Mullica dementia,
There should be greater certainty of scions
Than is betrayed by men who think they're lions!"

I was thinking, during the exchange, of men from down along the river and the shore who, in person or by their works, had left their mark far beyond their refuge. Edward Andrews and all those Quaker preachers, those brothers of his who died far away on travels of their ministry, those women whose text was hope and peace and common sense, Ann Gauntt, Mary Jacobs, Rhoda Lamb. Ebenezer Tucker, congressman and judge; Thomas Page, physician and legislator;

253

Elihu Mathis, Isaiah Adams, Stephen Willits, Joseph Pharo, all re-markable in their political beliefs and in the honesty of purpose be-queathed to their kinsmen. The Ridgeways, famous in Philadelphia commerce; the Giffords, descendants of Lord John, taken at Ban-nockburn; the Parkers, celebrated in many enterprises throughout the world; the Carrs, Motts, Sawyers, the Burtons, Rockhills, and Atwoods, all had their beginnings here. And I was thinking of Charlie Leek and Ned Knox and Donny Smallwood and Tater Cramer, saw-mill men, iron founders, paper men, and men who merely minded their own affairs to best achieve the cause of all. More than think-ing may be required, I know now, for in a weak moment I suggested that the club ought to meet down the Mullica, some day when once again there's peace and gasoline and good digestion. If I am held to the proposal, I shall make a beeline for Lower Bank and Santa Claus.

Santa Claus is William Fretz Kemble, who lives in a very old house set in a garden he calls heaven. To tell his story I must begin in 1898 when as an uncommonly tall graduate of Drew Seminary Will Kemble climbed a mountain at Delaware Water Gap, prepared by fasting to put to God a few pointed questions. God's answers, Will will tell you now, were eminently unburdening and no less clear. Be that as it may, Mr. Kemble, who climbed the heights a bachelor of divinity and descended a metaphysician in the making, on that oc-casion hurled a questionnaire into the heaven of other men for the first and last time. Since then, finding exercise in a dozen less spiritual vocations and producing a book in 1917 which momentarily made him American Industry's first Professor Quiz, Will Kemble has kept his light under a bushel. Only recently was there any threat that he might emerge from self-imposed, rustic obscurity as the apostle of taxless government and, spelled his way, Kolektovist Keeper of Heaven, New Jersey, geographically Lower Bank.

Will Kemble's book made him, briefly, the employer's pal and the worker's bogey man. All that is almost as forgotten now as is Uncle Will himself, even by the family that was taught to consider him its most successful and exemplary member. Mr. Kemble himself says that in the biography of Fanny Kemble the breed was characterized as a species that walks the earth heedless of the whimsies of the throng. Maybe, he says, he is like that. Whatever the case, here on the river at a littered drawing-board and battered typewriter the once-celebrated author of *Choosing Employes By Test* recalls transient glories of this book that drew a fine international press and squeals of delight from no less than Thomas Alva Edison. Will Kemble broods on solving the vibrations of the spectrum, ponders his sixty-letter algebraic multiplication table, and reflects frequently upon the rejected manuscript of *Taxless Government.* Staring thoughtfully through the small-paned window of a house built by his wife's grandfather, watching snow and snowdrops, rain and roses, sun and smilax in their season, he lives among plain folk of the Mullica who know him either as intimate stranger, annual Santa Claus, or founder of something that was formally known as Fellowship Society Number One of Lower Bank and Long Branch. This society was a sociological laboratory in which Mr. Kemble feels he proved the practicability of the Circular Equation, without which, he says, the world is doomed to panic.

Testing his highly individual beliefs with ever changing questionnaires, Uncle Will says the world is done with individualism, that only with the government going into business, as he proposed in *Taxless Government,* which in 1928 shocked so many regretful editors, can there be a permanent postwar solution. Answers to his current questions come not from God but from seventy years of life in which Will Kemble has built up and lost two fortunes of $100,000, designed churches, developed the science of light, created and demonstrated third and fourth dimensional art, landscaped big development and housing projects, climbed high and crashed low as a real estate promoter, applying mathematics to all the riddles of life to become, in his homespun way, the prolific father of provocative, premature ideas.

Mr. Kemble averages, he told me, about one invention a month. "Sometimes I send them off to the government as I think them out and finish them," he said. "I get replies, usually either to the effect that the ideas are useless or that they are being filed away for future consideration. Something will happen to them some day. It's fun to wait and see what that will be." Actually, Uncle Will doesn't wait. He forgets, turning to something else. Later on, somebody will remind him that the idea of a new departure announced by some celebrated auspices was really his. Slowly he will smile and seem to remember. It was that way when his son recalled he had designed prefabricated houses in 1915, only to scrap the drawings because, practical as they obviously were, they were not beautiful. It was that way with his book of business tests, buried effectively by World War I and revived and elaborated on by a whole crop of business professors after victory came. Certainly it was that way with Mr. Kemble's inventions for that first clashing of the nations when he submitted to Washington plans for mobile armored trucks capable of moving large numbers of troops with speed and efficiency—Washington formally acknowledged that one, too. The trouble is, they say, that Will Kemble is always one war ahead.

Mr. Kemble says that belief that wars are fought for democracy, for world freedom, or even for survival is all wrong. This arithmetical anchorite with the quiet voice and trim VanDyke will look down at an adoring black cat and say, with an authority that precludes disputation, "The struggle of the nations is for possession of the Circular Equation." You must agree. There is nothing else. This is the verdict of a man who says he has practiced thinking the way Heifetz has practiced playing the violin. When you have cut away the trimmings and polished the facets well, this Circular Equation will shine out as the way to taxless government, the key to the mystery of a war prolonged by apparently impoverished nations, and the panacea for all the troubles of the universe for all the days to come. "The Circular Equation," Mr. Kemble told me, "is at once one of the simplest and most abstruse things in philosophy, mathematics, and sociology. It has been more or less abstract, and until a thing becomes concrete we cannot get its full usefulness. The first operation in concreteness is to assign a name. When trees ceased to be abstractions for monkeys, for instance, they assigned a name for them and so civilization began."

I will watch my club members closely when Mr. Kemble gives them that verdict on civilization for at this point the visitors, whoever they are, may conclude that all life is an abstraction and that their own minds, obviously, are worse than fuzzy. The casual caller may with deliberation begin to believe that William Fretz Kemble, who deliberately buried himself to think, has been laid away so long that his is another language, requiring an interpreter with supernatural powers. Just then, however, is when the man who has spent much of his lifetime posing pretty questions turns to supplying impressive, if slightly complex, answers. His explanation of the Circular Equation makes sense, but somehow, afterwards, you sound foolish when you repeat it, even word for word. Perhaps, I have thought, a beard and a professorial mien are requisites.

Having made it all sound very simple, Mr. Kemble moves to higher ground. "America," he explains, "got the idea before the first World War that she was the most progressive country on earth. Probably she was. Wars, you see, induce progress. When that one was over, we had our opportunity to lead civilization to peace and great heights but we muffed it. Politics and musicians interfered. We became a nation of jitterbugs. Even business men danced to jitterbug tunes, carried away by jitterbug syncopation at national conventions where the chief aim was to get drunk. But Europe worked on until we dropped into a position rating, among the seven great nations, next to India and China. All this was due to our rejection of the Circular Equation." However, when I last talked with Uncle Will, he had to admit that we have such resiliency that we are well on our way back to second place.

You might think, on listening to this lean giant, that his knowledge of bankers, business men, politicians, and world affairs is something gained from the newspapers. I doubt if he sees a newspaper more than once a week. He listens to the radio but is confused, he says, by battles broadcast by breakfast foods and world planning accomplished through the courtesy of kidney cures. A lot of Uncle Will's conclusions go all the way back to his theological studies and, after that, to what happened when he climbed a mountain to ask God what he really ought to do about the religion of his fathers. Here he was, on the eve of ordination, abhorring what he still calls the hallelujah and hellfire preaching. Mr. Kemble says he was told to go home and make his life a denial of all such nonsense, if it would add to his peace of mind. After that, from a conviction that men have made of God a Being so wonderful that even He could not possibly exist and that men, consequently, are as irrational as their ideas of the Almighty, Uncle Will has preached the Circular Equation as a basis for Collectivism.

Lower Bank may know little or nothing of the Kemble philosophies, kept indoors in Levi Johnson's house when they escape the Kemble mind, but it has heard a lot of Collectivism. Lower Bank may not know that Uncle Will's father was the Reverend Samuel T. Kemble, a Philadelphia preacher who made his Beelzebub glow and his brimstone smell realistically, but it has heard that while Mr. Kemble was away he made and lost a lot of money and then came back convinced that money wasn't much. Lower Bank knows its Lama as the man who loves the country and the people, the man who ran that Fellowship Society, the man who has that nursery up the road. To tell anybody that Uncle Will is a preacher's son, was almost a preacher himself, and now among other things is a mild believer in reincarnation—he is respectful to little fishes in the brook because they may have been Kemble folk—would convey no impression. That would be the personal business of Mr. Kemble, Lower Bank's Santa Claus.

He was no Santa Claus when, at Ocean Grove, he failed as an emotion-rouser and turned instead to cornering the newstand market. There was no spirit of Christmas when he came home and told his father he had just obtained God's release. "I was sorry," he told me, "for I think it broke my father's heart." He was no Santa Claus to either himself or the publishers when, periodically, he dabbled in poetry, writing verses titled variously as "Futility," "Hope," "Realization," and "Divinity." The same can be said of his excursion into the field of detective fiction in which he wrote a thriller with the impossible title of *Pitted Against Anarchists* which, he admits, made very little money. The Midas mind of Santa Claus emerged for the first time, probably, when he gave up designing churches and church windows and began the buying and selling of real estate, specializing in small twenty-room hotels in the Rockaways for a quick turnover. Once he bought a hotel property at Rockaway Beach for $55,-000 with a down payment of only $500, holding his breath until a buyer came to give him the rest and a profit as well. Mr. Kemble was climbing high as a real estate promoter in 1904 when he married

Ada Hope Johnson and made her father his partner in order to raise money to close a number of pending deals.

"We made," he told me, $35,000 in two years. With part of this money I bought fifty acres, half a mile of frontage in North Yonkers and Hastings-on-Hudson, which for a while sold at a tremendous profit. I laid out the Pinecrest section of these towns. I spent my money lavishly," he recalls. "We had a big house and four servants. About then, I guess, I was considered to be worth $100,000. Then came the depression of 1907. You couldn't sell city lots for $100. We had to get Joseph P. Day to auction off our holdings, and we got about $50 for most of the lots. I was broke. The final foreclosure came in 1914."

Then came the idea that blossomed into the book *Choosing Employes By Test*. "I conceived the plan," he says, "that psychological tests could be used for grown people in business—although previous to that time tests had been used almost entirely in schoolwork. I consulted psychologists both at Penn and Columbia. They listened and then looked at me as if I were a bug. They refused, finally, to talk on the subject at all." Uncle Will went ahead anyway and was soon testing employes of the Underwood Typewriter Company and workers of the Baltimore & Ohio Railroad. Executives as well as Harrington Emerson and F. W. Taylor, pioneers of business enineering, thought well of the system devised by this tall man with a beard, then black. That is when Mr. Kemble figured it might help to get Tom Edison's reactions to the tests given at the B. & O.

"I went to see him, and when he saw what had been going on," he recalled the meeting, "he was delighted. Mr. Edison was very deaf and he shouted gleefully, 'Why, that's great! Here we have been guessing all our lives at what men can do, and you can find out, can't you?' Edison was so interested that he developed a set of tests of his own so as to quiz his executive force in the future."

From Edison's offices Uncle Will Kemble went to those of the Diamond Match Company and from there to Eastman Kodak. Having worked out a lot of questions and answers, making notes on reactions in a variety of industrial plants, he now took time out to write his book, as thorough a study of tests and the technique for applying them as ever had been written. Reviewers were kind, both with compliments and space. All leading magazines hailed the new gauge of business acumen. Mr. Kemble showed me the reviews and editorials, now yellowing with age. "It was all so new then," he said that day. "Efficiency tests are part of big business today." He has said he believes he is the man in all the world who made business tests popular. "But," he usually adds, "development of the idea had to wait for the first World War, for employers as usual were anxious to get all the workers they could, with no thought about tests. By the time the war was over some of the other men had put their time to good use and were ready with newer books with a postwar slant."

The Kemble luck was down temporarily. Uncle Will tried to join the Army, was turned down because of age. He joined the Home Guards. Then he went away, prospecting for oil this time, finding a trickle of it down in Louisiana. He leased as much land as he could with what money he had, but forty acres failed to interest experts who talked in terms of thousands. He dropped the oil lease and became a newspaper columnist, working for a syndicate, McClure's. As the dream of oil faded out, another took its place. "I dreamed," he said, "of a beautiful garden seacoast city, and I awoke determined to enlarge my technical knowledge of landscape architecture, which I had periodically studied and used in my real estate developments. I hired out as a laborer at the Bobbink & Atkins nurseries."

Armed with lessons of experience, Mr. Kemble extended the Beaux Arts nurseries, which he had set up on his father-in-law's farm in Lower Bank. "I landed some good designing jobs," he says, "and I finally won a $50,000 assignment in landscaping." That was Marvin Gardens in Atlantic City, designed, laid out, and planted by Uncle Will who had to buy another nursery at Long Branch so as to finish the job. "I had to get the stock somewhere," he'll say, smiling. "And I had just figured it out, a year or so later, that I was worth $100,000 again when another depression came. Patrons of nurseries, people who bought pretty trees and shrubs with which to beautify estates, wanted to sell the shrubs and trees they had to keep something from the smash." Will Kemble lost the nursery at Long Branch, but his wife's inheritance saved the farm and house in Lower Bank.

It was in 1932, when millions were picking up the pieces, that William Fretz Kemble decided to give some of his earlier considerations of the Circular Equation a test. Inviting all unencumbered men willing to work to join him, he founded Fellowship Society Number One. Under an Egg Harbor City dateline, a nearby daily discovered what was going on in the spring of 1934 and announced that "what may not be a Utopia but the collective co-operative living plan inaugurated by a Lower Bank nurseryman and onetime New York architect and author, may prove one of the biggest factors in solving the national unemployment problem." Another news writer said: "At fifty-nine this tall, gray-white-headed sponsor of the movement stands out as the holder and loser of three fortunes estimated between $250,000 and $300,000. The loss of his last fortune, in the neighborhood of $100,000, came at the height of the economic depression and set Kemble to thinking." The writer was wrong there. Thinking had been Uncle Will's outdoor and indoor sport long before the first plunge from riches to rags. However, a typical Kemble sentiment was caught in the quotation, "When the latest depression became serious and I saw my nursery customers dropping off one by one, I reached the conclusion that none of us who saved money in the past for a rainy day had learned anything from past experiences. I decided that since so many were in the same situation, all our ideas of the social structure must be wrong, and there must be some solution by which we would not be continually saving money and losing it again."

You may conclude what you like about Will Kemble's experiment. He says it was a success. After two years of operation in which the "Kolektovist Kolony" traded for pigs and poultry, accepted the government's interest expressed in the loan of six cows and a bull, bartered for fifty ducklings and raised sweet and white potatoes, it barreled sauer kraut and pickles, canned and dried both vegetables and fruit, and filled a silo and storage bins against the approaching winter. The government's interest was eventually fatal, Mr. Kemble says. Along came WPA and CCC work camps, with actual wages instead of spending money and meals—there were several camps within walking distance of Lower Bank. The "laboratory" collapsed and the experiment, as democratic as anything ever tried down the Mullica in its founder's belief, was over. Many people in Lower Bank were glad, for, they will tell you, Fellowship Society brought the wrong kind of people to town. "They didn't want to work," they will say if you press them. "We wouldn't say a thing about Mr. Kemble," they will point out, "except that he's easily fooled. He's too good-hearted."

The last big project was this book *Taxless Government* that nobody will publish. How long it took Uncle Will to work out what he says is the new, truer, and coming democratic system of government, he himself does not know. Obviously, once such chapters as "New Problems for Democracy," "Taxes," "Taxless Financing," "Legislative Functions," and "Business Engineering" are examined, even the layman who is stranger to economic trends becomes aware of two things: One, that many of the ideas worked out here several years ago have been talked about recently and two, that once again Will Kemble, with charts, graphs, and revolutionary ideas, is back on his favorite theme, the successful operation of the Circular Equation. "Everybody got scared when they saw it," Mr. Kemble told me. "They knew that the myth of the present democratic operation had to be maintained at all costs."

"What is true of the individual is true of government," said Uncle Will in concluding his book. "The sins of government are as great as those of the individual. Government indulges in material theft when it lays upon us needless taxes to support a great body of leisurely working people when we have to work so earnestly ourselves. Government sins against us in coercing our wills to act according to standards set by superstition or by impostors who claim to represent God. The old visions of Utopia are simply the conception of a material heaven. We are upon the brink of Utopia without the social organization in government to take care of it or the mental attitude to appreciate it."

I hope my friends of the service club bring along the proper mental attitude that day they go to Lower Bank. I hope they won't resent Will Kemble's conclusions as, he says, many people do. "Probably," he suggests, "they resent what seems to be assumed omnipotence, auguries spoken as if they were mathematical truths. But remember, mathematical truths are beyond contradiction. People accuse me of conceit because I think I am right. Thinking is like any other trade.

A plumber becomes skillful in his line—why should I be damned if I believe myself skillful in mine?"

I will leave the answer to that one for the visitors. I will merely tell them that my philosophic friend, begging gifts of toys and dressing up in a red suit that makes him no more like Santa Claus than Brom Bones, brings Christmas to the Mullica Valley.

## 24

## FAREWELL TO LOWER BANK

*"From this church they led their brides,*
*From this church themselves were led*
*Shoulder high; on these waysides*
*Sat to take their beer and bread.*
*Names are gone—what men they were*
*These their cottages declare."*
                                   EDMUND BLUNDEN

ALTHOUGH HE IS WILL KEMBLE'S NEIGHBOR, in full view of the bower of bloom the Kolektovist has planted, Charles Reginald Underhill is the only man I know who isn't entirely satisfied with living on the river. Although it was at Lower Bank or within reach of it that Joseph Wharton, F. Hopkinson Smith, William Lippincott, and Governor William Newell first proved their greatness, Charles Reginald is not impressed. At seventy, living in a house once known as Johnson's Cottage, he feels his genius is all but buried here, that the address at the bottom of impressive paragraphs describing his career in Who's Who is anticlimax. "I am not like my neighbors," he told me once. "I do not live here entirely as a matter of choice."

The proximity of another man of ideas does not move the genius of Mr. Underhill, even though at one time, back in 1905 or 1906, he worked with Uncle Will Kemble on a solution of the mathematical lines of the spectrum. "We found a formula for the lines in the hydrogen spectrum," Uncle Will told me once, "but we discovered that a European scientist had beaten us to it with a formula which could be resolved into ours." It is likely that Mr. Underhill, who since then has made a name for himself as an electrical engineer, considers Uncle Will a most impractical man. That consideration may be based on age old principles, although the poet-scientist must ever be an enigma to the expert on electromagnets, for Charles Reginald and William Fretz are brothers-in-law. Mrs. Kemble and Mrs. Underhill are daughters of the schoolmaster of Pleasant Mills and Bridgeport, now Wading River.

Mr. Underhill was born in Chappaqua, New York, the son of Joshua Brown and Elizabeth Green, names that should have imposed an interest in colors long before Uncle Will began his manifold experiments. Because of deafness he did not attend college and was largely self-educated, specializing through correspondence and textbooks in mathematics, physics, and engineering. The record in Who's Who traces his career through a maze of important connections beginning in 1892, when he began service of eight years with the inspection department of Western Electric. Thereafter he was chief electrical engineer with the Varley Duplex Magnet Company of Jersey City and Providence; editor and technical writer for a time and then consulting engineer with such firms as Westinghouse, the American Electric Fuse Company, the Acme Wire Company, and the Wappler Electric Company. At one period he was developing surgery and other high frequency apparatus. At another he was making "extensive researches into the action of electro-magnets," the results of which were widely published. He lectured in the nation's leading colleges and universities, and he took time to invent a wireless telegraph printing system as well as other telegraphic and signaling devices. Finally, he seems to have been something of a pioneer in aviation radio, being associated with the Signal Corps in 1917 and going to Langley Field the following year. Nowadays most of his work is writing, and a long list of his works, from a book on the electromagnet to others on solenoids, coils, and electrons, proves his activity. No wonder the appended address, Lower Bank, comes at least as a surprise.

Still as active as ever in the preparation of articles for technical magazines, Mr. Underhill rarely moves about in the Mullica world. The ancient house in which he works, originally a curious structure with a big loft attainable only by a kind of ladder over the kitchen fireplace, is intimately connected with the river life of old; but it is Mrs. Underhill who knows about that. Mr. Underhill remains, for villagers and passers-by, the man who shared their views about Will Kemble's Fellowship, the man who must be famous because of all the mail he gets, and the man who has a couple of cats trained to perform military tricks in uniform. To my suggestion of an interview he replied courteously enough, but he pointed out very plainly that he possessed none of the Lower Bank that I wanted.

It was some time later, when I was calling on Mr. Kemble in the Levi Johnson house down the road, that Mrs. Underhill appeared and thrust a sheaf of typescript into my hands. She had been remembering things, she said, for the benefit of the family. Inasmuch as I was so interested in the Lower Bank that is, I might like to know more about the town that was, she told me. Then, almost before I had adequately expressed my appreciation, she was gone. Examining the notes, I found Mrs. Underhill's memory prodigious, reaching back to restore houses long gone, roads long grown over, and folk of Lower Bank long buried in the yard of the old church that wasn't a church at all at the beginning. It was a school, wrote Ella Underhill, moved to its present location in 1810. Now the village emerges, not only as an important Mullica landing but also a clearing along the river where the oldest Down Shore families were, and in many instances continue to be, concentrated.

Lower Bank, like Egg Harbor City, has done its own moving, although it has gathered at the river during the last century instead of drifting away. Now, where the Lower Bank Road meets the Green Bank-Wading River highway, there was once a crossroads instead of a shaded corner—that tangled trail now plunging through the trees across the way was once the direct route to paper-making Harrisville. "Job Weeks lived about a mile up that road," said Mrs. Underhill. "His children were Job, Sam, Hannah, and Josephus—when I lived down here as a child, I went to school with them. Later on 'Seph' lived there with his daughters, Louie and Flora. Flora married Will Bozarth and lives these days in Williamsburg, Virginia."

The town began, you might say, there at the cross-roads, now a tangle of vines and trees except for the trimming the road men do at the corner. "My grandfather's cranberry bog was there at the crossroads," Mrs. Underhill told me. "How long does it take for a bog to disappear? Well, the bog was planted when Aunt Beckie Leek was a child, and she was eighty-seven in 1942. Not so long, you see. A colored man named Weasy, who lived in a cabin there, he cleared the land and planted the cranberries. There was another man who worked for grandfather at the time—Lower Bank knew him as 'Johnny Come Lately' because he was always late for work. His real name was Johnny Robinson."

The first house in from the crossroads was that of John Johnson and his wife, Margaret, who was another Cramer. It is still in the possession of the family although the name has changed. John was Mrs. Underhill's grandfather's brother. "Coming on down the River Road, as we always called it," said Mrs. Underhill, "the next house was owned by Job Weeks, son of the Job of the woods and brother of Seph. He built it by himself. Job must have been the village cobbler as well as a carpenter when there were no shoes to mend. I remember taking my shoes to his house for mending, and I can still see him as he sat at his bench just inside the door. One of his sons to whom my mother gave music lessons became a notable doctor in Philadelphia, Dr. Harry Weeks."

The next house was standing until the summer of 1940 when it burned to the ground. It was first owned, my chronicler said, by a man named Brooks. Leeks and Cales lived there, and so did Isaac VanSant and his wife, Margaret, when they were first married. "Later," said the record, "Isaac left the house to go into the ministry. Nathaniel VanSant, Uncle Thannie as we always called him, lived nearly opposite with his wife, who was Sarah Cramer. Uncle Thannie built the first house on what Lower Bank always called 'The Island,' and Nicholas Cramer and his wife, Aunt Mel, Roy's mother, went to live in it." I remembered Granny Cramer's story of bringing

266

the cows home from the marshes and discovered that long before she became Granny Cramer to the world at large she was Aunt Mel to the town. "Nick Cramer," Mrs. Underhill went on, "had long white whiskers that glowed, some say, in the dark. After Isaac Van-Sant went away, Uncle Thannie moved into his house—moving wasn't much of a problem then. He sold the place to the Cales later on and moved into a house that most of us remember better as the real Uncle Thannie's."

Uncle Thannie was a deacon in the church and opposed mixing instrumental music and religion. "You can imagine what the singing sounded like," said Mrs. Underhill, "with nothing to give the pitch. Uncle Thannie said that the devil lurked in music and that both organ and melodeon were the devil's own instruments, and so a church was no place for them. When I lived here as a child, my mother used to give lessons on her melodeon to some of the young people. Once she got up an entertainment for the church and pro-posed that the melodeon should be taken inside for the program. She had a hard time persuading Uncle Thannie, but he finally gave in. But there was never an organ for the hymn-singing until many years after."

Then came houses of more Cales, more Leeks, more Cramers. Next was the home of Cap'n Jess Allen, occupied by Cap'n Dan Cale and his family when the Allens moved on. Next to Uncle Thannie's on the other side of the road was the house of Zacheus Johnson, whose wife was the village newspaper. "She made a business of visiting from house to house straight down the road all her life," Mrs. Underhill confided. "The last house she visited always got the most news."

Cap'n Mahlon Johnson built the house where Harold and Hannah Maxwell live now, running the Lower Bank post office. Hannah's father was Cale Cavileer. Cap'n Mahlon was Mrs. Underhill's great-uncle. "His wife, Hannah," she told me, "was always called Hannah Mahlon to distinguish her from my grandmother, who was always called Hannah Levi, even in the most ordinary conversation. Lower Bank always had a lot of Hannahs."

Grandfather Levi Johnson had a cow barn at the corner of the nursery nearest to the house that's now the Underhills'—that was where, as a girl, Mrs. Underhill used to sit on a rail fence and watch

267

Colored Bill at milking time. "I used to try and whistle," she said, "but I never could manage it because I drew in my breath. Uncle Ed Oliver used to give me a penny every time I'd make it sound anything like. And then I'd buy a stick of peppermint candy always kept in a jar in the window of Maggie Allen's store and postoffice. Funny how you remember things like that, isn't it? Uncle Ed was a sea captain from Martha's Vineyard, who made long voyages to distant places. Once he brought back a monkey which grandmother kept for years, chained to the fence outside, cutting up capers for all Lower Bank. Once he stole Father's cuff buttons just as we were getting ready for church, and he wouldn't give them back. He'd sit looking at them and then, when you started after him, he'd put them in his mouth. Father had to get another pair for the service and didn't get the others until much later—he would never say where."

The Beaux Arts Nurseries of Uncle Will Kemble were originally the fields of Levi Johnson's farm. Between the Underhill house and the fields was a lane, called Leeds's Lane because it led back to Moses Leeds' house, later Cale Cavileer's. Grandfather Johnson closed off the lane when he built the cow barn. However, the remains of it continued to carry a name, inasmuch as the name of Leeds was kept alive in Lower Bank by the recurrent appearances of the troubled ghost. The Underhills', known at the beginning as Johnson's Cottage, boasted a stairless attic and two rooms on the lower floor without a hall. "Uncle Harry made some alterations when he bought the cottage from grandfather's sister, Achsah Pharo, who lived there before that," Mrs. Underhill recalled. "After Uncle Harry and Aunt Maria left here, the house was often rented to the preachers appointed to Lower Bank, as well as to other families. Aunt Beckie Leek lived here a short time, too, when Charlie, who is building those Navy ships down the road, was a baby."

There were merry days, said Mrs. Underhill, when the family lived first in Lower Bank, then in Hammonton, then in New York with summers in Ocean Grove, and in the end Lower Bank again. "Father and mother went sometimes to the Adirondacks, and I would stay on down here to look after the younger ones," she told me. "That was when I used to go to all the church festivals that were held in different places—Batsto, Pleasant Mills, Green Bank, Bridgeport, and even Gloucester Landing. Imagine festivals, even houses, in some of those places now! Those were horse-and-buggy days. I usually went with Walter Cavileer, son of Cap'n Johnny. The festivals were always held in cleared places in the woods, but here at Lower Bank they were either on the church lawn or over at Uncle Thannie's. After dark the festivities were lighted up by regular pyres made by four upright posts or the trunks of small trees, with crosspieces of logs, then dirt and sand—on the top wood fires were kept burning. Somebody had to throw up the wood whenever it was needed, for the fires not only gave light but kept away mosquitoes."

Sometimes all the young people would go to such affairs in big hay wagons, stuffed with hay or straw to sit upon. "On such occasions," said Mrs. Underhill, "I played the banjo and often helped to entertain, especially if the festival was at Green Bank near the Sooy home. Watson Sooy, whose wife was Hattie Lane and who was also a brother of my stepmother, brought his organ out on the grass to accompany the music and singing. On the way home we'd all sing as I twanged the banjo. All of that seeems so magical and far-away.

"It was in one of those summers that the young people gave me a surprise birthday party. Lew Adams called it the mules' birthday because my father always reckoned the age of the mules my grandfather owned from the year that I was born. The boys all brought big watermelons with them, and after all the games were over they'd wash the girls' faces with melon rind."

Mrs. Underhill said that once she came upon what she thought was a real ghost story. "A cousin of mine was visiting me one summer when I was looking after the younger sisters and brothers, and we all went to call on the Sooys in Green Bank. The road from the old church to the main road was sandy and very narrow, the carriage wheels brushing against the bushes in many places with an occasional clearing or turnout for passing another team. We left rather late on the return trip, finding it so dark in the narrow road that we had to allow the horse to take his own way. Suddenly he slowed down, and we called out so as to know if we should turn out for somebody coming the other way. There was no answer, and we concluded that a cow had got loose and was in the road. Finally, an opening in the trees gave us just enough light to see something white bobbing up and down just ahead of us. The children were sure it was a ghost, escaped from the cemetery we were passing just then. When we finally reached the wider road, we saw that it was a sulky drawn by a white horse and driven by somebody who, apparently, did not want to be recognized."

Next day Ella Underhill made her own conclusions about that. A mysterious fire had been started in a barn behind a big house at Gloucester Landing on the other side of the river, and some oil-soaked rags were discovered when the flames were extinguished. "We had come upon the firebug on his way home without a doubt," she told me, "but we never found out who he was. He had come across the old bridge and the road that used to cross the lowlands on the Atlantic County side of the Mullica. All the houses and the old hotel at old Gloucester are gone now and so is the bridge over Gloucester Creek. We always drove that way to Egg Harbor when we were children, turning off on the road across the meadows just over the Lower Bank bridge. When the new bridge was built, Gloucester Landing, all that was left of Gloucester Furnace, was cut off from the world."

The newer Lower Bank Methodist Church was built in 1874. "I always understood," said Mrs. Underhill, "that grandfather gave the land for it but Aunt Beckie Leek says she did. However, there is a deed showing that grandfather sold some land to the church for seventy-five dollars, which might mean that some extra land was bought besides that on which the church stands." The cornerstone was laid by Louis Atkinson, a young preacher stationed in town at that time. The Reverend Louis later married Julia Lane, of the old Lane house out on "The Island." Many years later as a widow, Julia became the wife of the Reverend Swayne Garrison, Lower Bank's preacher in 1897. Although they moved about to many Methodist appointments, Swayne and Julia were always coming back to Lower Bank, at least in the summertime, and finally, when the pastor retired, they came to live in the old Lane house. There they died in 1939, Julia, who was 92, preceding her husband, who was 71, by just three months.

The old church that was first a school was established, Mrs. Underhill says, through the efforts of Sam Weeks, Isaac Cramer, and John

The old Richards mansion at Batsto as the author first saw it, long before New Jersey had purchased the Wharton Tract and outlined a plan for the restoration of Batsto village. Recently there has been talk of removing the tower, a Wharton addition. Below, arches of the Weymouth millrace.

Rod Koster, of Green Bank, who served as guide for the author, became postmaster after World War II, now mans the Batsto fire tower.

Bob Stewart, great grand son of the last manager o the Batsto estate.

Cavileer, who persuaded a parson named Deerhart, a saddlebag preacher, to make a stop there on his rounds. Nicholas VanSant, of the shipbuilding preachers' line, was the local preacher there in 1856. "Pleasant Mills Church goes back to Bishop Asbury's time," Mrs. Underhill pointed out, "being built in 1808. My father attended church there when he taught school in Pleasant Mills. He always said he had been converted in the old church here at Lower Bank when he was a young man. He marked his name and date under the bench where he knelt, and I saw it there a short time ago. It was at a revival, he said, and the preacher's name was Boyle. With his conversion my father gave up tobacco and never touched it again."

After the other two founders had died, Sam Weeks brought in a bill for what he said was owed him on the church. When it couldn't be paid on such short notice, Sam locked the church door and took away the Bible. "The church was closed for a time," Mrs. Underhill declared, "and the congregation worshipped in an old store along the river until the money was raised by the Conference for the present church on a new location nearer the heart of the shifting village."

"Was Sam Weeks left holding the bag—or the Bible?" I asked.

"No," it was explained, "he got his money. There must have been some left over from the new church fund. Sam was paid and the congregation went back to the old church for about a year—until the new church was finished. It was dedicated by Uncle Thannie, old Nathaniel VanSant."

Cap'n Jacob Johnson, brother of Grandfather Levi, owned and lived in the house at the other side of the new church. There he had a store and at one time an inn, where horses were changed for the stage route through town. Uncle Jake also sold notions, everything presumably from a needle to an anchor. "I remember that Olive Cale and another girl went in one day, modestly asking for some elastic tape," Mrs. Underhill recalled. "Uncle Jake answered in his gruff way, 'If you mean garter 'lastic, say so!'" When Maggie Allen, Monty's mother, decided to give up the post office one year, Uncle Jake Johnson set it up in a corner of his store. "We got room for everything," he said. He was the storekeeper whose shelves had room, I think, for the can of fishworms left in his care ten years.

The Johnson homestead, where I go to see Will Kemble whenever I can, was built in 1832. There were additions in 1860 and, as Mrs. Underhill told me, when additions to the family demanded more room. "As long as I can remember," she said, "there was always a paling fence around it and a front gate, just as there is today. I can remember grandfather standing at the gate, even after he was blind, looking for all the world as if he could see all that was around him. Even after he had lost his sight, he looked after his mules, feeling around with his cane, which all the animals got used to. Let anyone else approach those mules and they'd kick readily enough. Many a ride we had back of those mules down here, over the sandy roads. When we came down to Lower Bank, we were always met at the station—it would take two hours to make the nine miles here!"

The old Lower Bank School stood nearer the River Road until it was moved back to become the Community House. It was built when Mrs. Underhill's father was nine, Grandfather Levi giving the ground and assisting in the construction because, as he explained it, the sooner it was finished the sooner his children could be educated. "In those days," Mrs. Underhill reminded me, "the teacher was paid according to the number of pupils she had, so much for each student being given when the total was figured out. I can remember some of those teachers, a Mr. McCorey, a Mr. Boswell, and Ben Gratz. Hattie Lane taught us for a time, too, but Watson Sooy soon took her off to live at the Green Bank corner."

Opposite Will Kemble's is the Monty Allen house, now occupied by Jonas and Edna Corson. Cap'n Gus Johnson, Monty's father, owned it once before it boasted a store and temporary possession of Lower Bank's wandering post office. Then, just around the corner, is the Allen house, but you have been there already. "That is where Jesse Allen lived," said our chronicler as she went on to add to our lore. "His father, you know, was Josie Allen, and Josie kept an inn that stood across from Charlie Weber's up on the Green Bank Road. The corner there is a field of corn now, and you'd never guess that there was once a hotel where the stage stopped by." And up the road from the Allen house was still another inn, this one kept in order by Sam Weeks, celebrated from now on for locking of a church and snitching the Bible for debt.

There is no evidence at all of the sawmill that stood back from the road along the stream that is now a trickle but in the old days helped set apart "The Island" where Roy Cramer lives. Beyond the dried-up mill pond are two cabins, one built by Allie Core, which I always find remarkable whenever I see it as I pass by—there, in two tiny rooms, Allie and his wife raised a family of seven children, one of whom was married and another teaching school when last I heard. Actually "The Island" across the way has a name, Mrs. Underhill says. "They always called it Nigger Island," she remembers, "because David Mapes, a colored man, bought it." That must have been a long time ago, even in the ancient history of Lower Bank, for David Mapes was the man who gave ground for the old church, moved to the head of the graveyard in 1810.

Down toward the river there once were several story-and-a-half houses with sloping kitchen rooves. One of these was Cap'n Dan Cale's—Cap'n Dan was one of Aunt Mel Cramer's brothers—and a son, John, owns it now. Next to the school is the homestead of the Cavileers, where Reuben's Reuben lived until one of the second Reuben's sons, Cap'n Jess, turned it into a barn for some fine trotting horses, building a new house with a fancy windmill next door. The new house burned down and Cap'n Jess moved away. This was a signal for Charlie Cavileer and his wife, Nettie, to push history in reverse: They bought the old barn and made it into a dwelling all over again.

Ownership of old houses along River Road to the elbow where it turns to parallel the bank that gave the village its name is a tangle of Adamses, Cramers, Maxwells, Lanes, and more Cavileers. Cap'n Jim Bartlett built the house that's last before the turn and nearest the old landing. Here, beyond where Cliff Terry and others from Mullica towns sat in a shed and spied on airplanes, was one of the busiest points along the river. "Large boats were built there," Mrs. Underhill said, "three- and four-masted schooners, as well as smaller boats and hay scows like the survivor that Charlie Weber ran down to the meadows."

Lower Bank once was home to a little army of seafaring men, many of them masters of their own ships. "Large vessels sailed from the landing and docked there on their return so that the river was covered, most of the time, with craft of every description. Many of them laid up here for the winter after journeys to New York, Philadelphia, the West Indies, and even ports in Europe. Grandfather Johnson," Mrs. Underhill told me, "built his own vessel at the landing."

Jesse Richards, for whom Levi Johnson carried iron ore on his ship from Batsto to New York, got Mrs. Underhill's father a job on one occasion in the City National Bank in Philadelphia. The pay was fifty dollars a month, and he was there ten years. Asked to provide security for his son, Levi Johnson replied, "My word is my security." His word was accepted. Levi Johnson's Mullica boat was called the "Walter Lemuel" after his two eldest boys. In 1856, when the launching had been arranged, Grandmother Johnson's chicken potpie for all hands got cold when John Hall, who had helped build the boat, adopted tactics akin to those of Sam Weeks, holding up the ceremonies until he was paid five hundred dollars. Jesse Richards heard what had happened and hurried down to pay the amount so the ship could be put over without further delay. After many years of operation Grandfather Johnson sold the "Walter Lemuel" and bought the "Walter Palmer," trading through the South and New England. After a steamer cut the craft in two, Levi put his money in cranberry bogs bought from Billy Sooy.

"During the Civil War," Mrs. Underhill recalled, "he tried raising potatoes. People along the river said it couldn't be done. He harvested a thousand bushels and got a dollar apiece. Once he sent my father up the river to an old house near Batsto near which he used to anchor his boat. My father had just unloaded twenty bushels of potatoes for the farmer there without measuring them, when the buyer insisted on measuring to make certain he had not been cheated. Father measured them out, and when he had finished he found he had two bushels left over. The farmer wanted to keep them, of course. My father shook his head. 'You insisted on twenty bushels and there they are,' he said. 'The other two belong to me for having to measure them out and having my word doubted.'"

Down beyond the bridge, the inn once presided over by Granny Brush is forgotten. Forgotten, too, are the legends of buried treasure that persuaded both men and women of Lower Bank to dig in the

274

Adams cemetery. Half-remembered is the story told by Cap'n Dan Cale, for many years the gravedigger there, in which he described the finding of the body of an Indian, "buried sitting up with a shawl around him." I marvel as I look out on the river now, quiet in the sun of afternoon, and think of the Lower Bank that began with houses far out toward the sea and ended at the hidden cross-roads and Fred Miner's house and blacksmith shop, half way to Green Bank.

"Aunt Becky Leek tells a story," Mrs. Underhill concluded her record, from which I have tried to choose lore of general interest, "about the brother of Betsy Lewis, wife of old Reuben Cavileer. He fell off a wagon in front of Josie Allen's inn and was stunned. Companions who picked him up carried him inside and there rubbed the juice of poke berries on his hands and face. Finally, when he felt better, he got up to look at himself in a mirror. When he saw what he thought was blood, he sat down with a bump and said, 'You better send for mother.' "

Charlie Leek thinks the story of Jess Johnson is even better. Jess was a big, strong man, but no mental giant. He often pulled his mother in a wagon to places she wished to visit, even Egg Harbor City. He had shafts designed in such a way that the pulling was easy and he made good time. One day, after years of playing horse, Jess said to his mother, "Mother, look out! I am going to get scairt and run away!" And run he did so that the poor old lady fell out of the wagon and broke her arm.

Charlie says that Jess, who collected clocks from houses up and down the Mullica, lived in a house where clocks were ticking and striking every hour of the day and night. I'd like to find the house. I was going to ask Charlie where it was the other day when, as his house came into sight, I stopped in my tracks. Out of keeping with everything that was ever Lower Bank, Mr. Leek had celebrated his Navy boat building in an arresting way: He had painted the shutters of his house, the old Zeke Cavileer place, a flashy, tropical blue.

25

## THE FORKS

*"While the silver mist upstealeth silently,*
*And the broad, cloud-driven moon in the clear sky*
*Lifts o'er the firs her shining shield*
*And in her tranquil light*
*Sleep falls on forest and field."*

ROBERT BRIDGES

IT IS SURELY IRONICAL that of all the landings up and down the Mullica, The Forks, signally celebrated in every record of the countryside, should have gone so fast asleep, its kings and captains departed for so long. Here at the head of navigation, five or six miles from Elwood, once Sailor Boy, there is a kind of island, formed by the meeting of Batsto River, Nescochague and Mechescatauxen Creeks, and the Atsion or main branch of the Mullica itself. Pleasant Mills, once Sweetwater, is on the island and Batsto, separated by the bridge, is just beyond. In Revolutionary days there were houses and barns and wharves along the shore, and in the river were hundreds of ships, privateers, and their prizes. Now there is an old church, an empty paper mill, some old houses and the mansion of Kate Aylesford. Those who could have told us of the big days are names on stones in the churchyard where the Reverend Simon Lucas, himself a Revolutionary soldier, took the first funerals.

Batsto was the objective, you remember, when the British fleet anchored at the river mouth and, frustrated in its plan to get that far, resorted to the burning of Chestnut Neck and whatever else came handy. An iron furnace had been established at Batsto ten years before independence was declared, and then with the coming of war the output became exclusively cannon, shot, and shell. Israel Pemberton, first owner of the furnace, called the place Whitcomb Manor, the second establishment of its kind in the State. Later it was sold to Charles Read and still later to Colonel John Knox and Thomas

276

Mayberry. Joseph Ball, a wealthy Philadelphia Quaker, was there when peacetime manufacture gave way to wartime munitions, sending the first of the Batsto giants, William Richards, to become the manager in 1784. By this time there was a considerable population at The Forks, the workers deferred from the draft and protected from the Refugees by a small military force. This was the company that joined the militia and Proctor's artillerymen to move down the river when invasion threatened.

Much that was Batsto, apart from the village of the workmen, is as it always was, except for the unnatural quiet. No one goes to the old store for there is nothing to buy. The old Richards manor house, with its thirty-six rooms and a surmounting tower which once served as a forest fire lookout, remains high on a shaded knoll, restored and maintained by Joseph Wharton, who bought the vast estate in 1876, and by his descendants, the Lippincotts of Philadelphia. The store, the manor, and the barns went unscathed on the night of January 23, 1874, when a spark from the chimney of Robert Stewart's house set fire to the dwelling and, before the flames were checked, laid the village in ashes.

As for Pleasant Mills, boasting a lake of its own and another celebrated manor, there were log huts here, they say, in 1718. Here was Clark's Meeting House, not very far from the present church and like it facing the waters of Lake Nescochague. First industry established was a sawmill, supplanted by a cotton factory and succeeded in 1861 by a paper-making plant. At the turn of the century people were still talking of the Pleasant Mills Paper Company as the sole survivor of early industries in Atlantic County, for then it was still flourishing as "one of the leading paper mills of its kind in this country." There was a hum of the wheels across Nesco Pond, as it later became, as a rough kraft paper was made from marsh grass, salt hay, and other materials brought up the Mullica River from the Philippines, India, England, and Germany. Now there is no hum, some of the machinery has been sold for munitions of a newer war and rotting rooves have fallen here and there. Across the road, a trail that follows the river for a time and then swings off into Weekstown, is the mansion of Kate Aylesford, heroine of the early American novel of Charles Peterson. Kate Aylesford is the name of the book and not the girl, who, the story goes, was Honoré Read, daughter of Charles Read, the ironmaster of Batsto.

Such information can be collected by anybody who takes the trouble to search for old books. More scattered in half a hundred journals and as many volumes of archives are references to The Forks which, piled up, reveal Batsto and Sweetwater as places that once had more promise than most New Jersey centers of today. There is no one at The Forks to tell you that here Tom Proctor built and occupied a barracks with men who, with the aid of Pulaski, repelled invasion. There is no one here who knows without considering for a while where Joe Mulliner, leader of the Refugees, lies buried alone. There are none who have lingered, as kinsmen have lingered at Tuckerton and Port Republic and Lower Bank, to inherit on the scene the legends of Batsto cannon-moulders, Sweetwater shipbuilders, owners and operators of privateering ships that made The Forks their haven. Iron and glass and pottery are, with those who made them, slag and chips and ineloquent dust.

Myriad are advertisements such as these, appearing in the newspapers from the earliest 1750's on:

"To be sold or lett for a Term of Years, a Saw Mill, with several Lots of Cedar-Swamp, lying in Little Egg-Harbour, near the Forks, very commodious for Carting, with a constant stream at the dryest times. . . . Bond and good Security will be required by Captain Samuel Bayard, in New-York."

"Four Dollars Reward. Run away from the Subscriber living at Batsto Furnace; A Servant Lad, named Anthony M'Garvey, about 18 or 20 years of age, 5 feet 7 inches high, has short hair, thick, well set fellow. . . . Whoever apprehends said servant so that his master may have him again, shall receive the above reward, and if brought home, reasonable charges paid by William Doughten."

"To be SOLD by private SALE, a COMPLETE saw-mill, with two saws, on a very good stream of water, and about 5000 acres of pine land, and 50 acres of cedar swamp with a good house, four rooms and two fire places on the lower floor, and two rooms on the upper one, with a good kitchen, and a well of good water at the door, and a very convenient barn, and stabling sufficient for 15 horses . . . with two log-houses for sawyers and other outbuildings; situated on the main branch of the Little Egg-Harbour river, two miles from Addison's ironworks and seven from the Forks of Egg-Harbour, where lumber is transported by water at the moderate price of three shillings per thousand. Josiah Foster, Evesham, Burlington County, 1777."

"WILL BE SOLD. The fourth day of June next, at Chestnut Neck, Little Egg Harbour, State of New Jersey, The Brigantine or vessel called the Betsey, with her tackle, apparel, furniture and cargo; consisting of tobacco, salt, coffee, mustard, china and queen's ware, with sundry other articles, lately captured by Thomas Quigley in the boat, Lively. By order of the Admiralty. James M'Comb, Marshal. Princeton, May 28, 1782."

"State of New Jersey, April 22, 1780. TO BE SOLD, at public vendue, at the Forks of Little Egg-Harbour river, on Thursday the 4th of May next, at ten o'clock in the forenoon of the same day, the Sloop Dispatch or Speedwell; together with her tackle, apparel and furniture. Also sundry merchandize taken in the said sloop, captured by Capt. William Treen, in the schooner Rattlesnake. By order of his Honor the Judge of the Admiralty. Za. Rossell, Marshall."

"To be SOLD by PUBLIC VENDUE on Monday the twenty-ninth of this instant, at the house of Mr. Richard Wescott, at the Forks of Little Egg-Harbour River, the Prize BRIG BLACK SNAKE and the Schooner MORNING STAR, with their tackle, and apparel, &c. captured by Captain William Marriner. Zachariah Rossell, Marshall. May 24, 1780."

I have selected these at random. There are hundreds more, similar in text and terms, tucked away in such publications of the day as *The Pennsylvania Journal,* the *New Jersey Journal, The Pennsylvania Gazette* and the *New York Gazette and Weekly Mercury.* In sales of land and mills, in Courts of Admiralty disposition of captured ships and cargoes, and in a variety of traffic involving such picturesque names as "Granville Packet," "Fair American," "Amphitrite," and "Lady Washington," the Mullica and its hideaway Forks are shown to have had an important part in America's struggle to win and move ahead. Important men of trade mingled with colorful military and naval officials. Women of charm and elegance enlivened the progress of the place, going down to the landings as new prizes arrived, taking part in festivities of the paneled rooms of the Richards mansion in honor of new heroes, and snapping up bargains from displays under seizure when occasion offered. For the better part of a century, as Annalist Watson wrote, "The Forks of Egg Harbour was the place of chief prosperity; many shipyards were there; vessels were built and loaded out to the West Indies; New York, Philadelphia and the southern and eastern cities receiving their chief supplies of shingles, boards and iron, from this place."

The trade in iron castings, while fuel remained abundant, was very great, says Mr. Watson. "The numerous workmen, all without dependence on cultivation of the soil, required constant supplies of beef, pork, flour, groceries &c from abroad. Merchants from New York and Philadelphia went there occasionally in such numbers that the inns and boarding houses could not contain them, and they had to be distributed among the private houses. On such occasions they would club and have a general dance, and other like entertainments. . . . Sometimes rich cargoes came ashore on the beach, and were brought up the river for public sale, and brought many traders there to buy. The vessels from New York and New England on trading voyages were numerous. The inlet was formerly the best on the coast; and many vessels destined for Philadelphia in the winter, because of the ice in the Delaware, made into the river and there sold their cargoes to traders from New York and Philadelphia." So reflecting, ignoring the legal and extralegal complications of such activity, Mr. Watson hurried on to Tuckerton, wondering idly about the vanished trade in sassafras sent to Holland, cordwood sent to New York, and vital supplies and munitions sent to fighting men just in time. So you and I may reflect and wonder now, finding Sweetwater, Batsto, and The Forks in dreamless sleep. Only an ageless river, the Mullica, can dream here of what has been.

I have always held to the belief that a careful exploration of the banks of the Mullica, from Green Bank to Pleasant Mills and even on up to Atsion, will some day reveal many unexpected things. After all, the river was the principal means of travel far inland from the sea long before there were any established roads, even when the first trails began developing from old Indian paths. One day when there was gasoline to be had without restrictions, Joe Robinson left off editing news from Europe's underground press, and we went down to Lower Bank where we attached an outboard motor to a rowboat loaned us by Charlie Leek. While several days, perhaps a long, dry summer, might be required for the kind of quest I have in mind, we made something of a rough survey in about six hours, traveling from Charlie's boat works to the bridge at The Forks in Pleasant Mills. Our principal find was the stone buttresses of an ancient bridge that once served a roadway coming up from the shore and making a direct cut into Batsto.

The main channel of the river was plainly marked, and we followed it carefully, especially as we neared the head of navigation that used to be. Even so, we had to lift the motor repeatedly so that the propeller missed the shoaling, and it was clear that a ship of any appreciable draft would fail to get that far. Although the Mullica is wide and deep enough as far as the bends above Crowleytown and perhaps to Ireland Cove, it becomes evident there that man, in his search for fuel, has joined with fires that recurrently have swept the forest, denuding the land so that long ago floods began to find new channels in which to disappear. In Civil War times there was still enough water power on the Batsto and Atsion Rivers, as well as the Jackson and West Mill Creeks, to drive a mill in any month of the year. However, even when dams and canals had been provided, the paper mill at Sweetwater found the going difficult in its last days of operation. While there is more water in this area than many on automobile roads know—there are always recurrent expressions of the belief that the dream of the vast Wharton Estate as a watershed will come true—there are times when, except for the narrow channel, the upper river seems to have no depth at all. Our journey was made on such a day.

Joe, on the balcony of a villa somewhere in Africa when he wrote to me last, said that in between bouts of censoring reports of war correspondents he had found time to steer a boat far into the mysteries of darker rivers. He was wondering, wistfully I think, about the Mullica, remembering that day in Charlie's rowboat when we talked of many things, especially John Watson and his journeys in the 1820's when the promise of The Forks was fading and when the Annalist, seemingly upset by the encroachment of decadence, sought happier scenes down at Tuckerton and Cape May. "Table fare that consisted of fish and such salted meats as the visitors could bring with them" were preferable, Mr. Watson felt, to ghosts of people and ideas. And at Cape May there was always that curious outdoor sport, indulged by the ladies, of poking sticks into the snapping jaws of beheaded sharks.

"Mr. Watson overlooked the fact," Joe said, "that neither the people nor the ideas they hatched out at The Forks were necessarily dead. Take those Clarks, for example. There was a Rebecca who

281

married James Vanuxem—Vanuxem & Clark became a well known firm of shipchandlers in Philadelphia. Her sister, Emeline, became the wife of John Clark Sims, I think it was, and the mother of the line that soon became famous out in early Arkansas. General Enoch Doughty and Judge Joseph Porter were in the family. And you know the story of Nehemiah."

Nehemiah Clark lived at Clark's Landing and took part in the life at The Forks. He had a son, Parker, who fought in the Revolution and wasn't finished with fighting when the war was over. It would have been better if he had been. In those days there were boxing bouts, and the best fistic experts of Burlington County tackled the pride of Atlantic County, across the Mullica, on dull Saturday nights. In one such contest Parker, representing Atlantic, overcame the champion of Burlington, and for some reason the Burlington County men vowed vengeance if they ever caught Parker Clark alone. Next time he went among the rivals without an escort he failed to come home. Long afterwards his body was found in the reeds far down the river.

"You can say as much for lots of others," Joe said. "The Albertsons, descended from Jan Albertson, who came from Stemeyk, Holland; the Bartletts, whose ancestor was Oswald Good Bartlett, a German soldier; the Collinses from Ireland, the Frambeses, the Endicotts, the Lakes, the Penningtons. All of them knew the river well and followed their trades beside it. They were probably part of the rise and fall of The Forks as well. But when The Forks faded out, that didn't mean they gave up. They merely moved on."

Not long after Joe went away, I learned many old names of places that belong to "The Island" and The Forks. Rod Koster, the postmaster of Green Bank who was later shipped to England, came home on leave. The war had interrupted our river excursions. Before he went back to camp, we spent a long evening at Herman at his father's house, begun before the Revolution by Nicholas Sooy. There by lamplight we pored over a topographical map that now hangs before me with the additions we noted that night—Henneke's Place, across the Horseshoe where the river swings around "The Island"; Goodwater Run, the Meadow House, and Rabbit Island; Cold Spring, Johnny's Ditch, and Stone Landing; Ireland Cove, the High Bank, and Mordecai Landing. Down the river further, Rod showed me, was Tom Crowley's, and over on the opposite shore Bass's Place—Bass was Sebastian Crowley. One name was of special interest and still is.

"This Mordecai," I said. "They pronounce it "Mor-de-key" down the river. "Who was he?"

"Don't rightly know," said Rod surprisingly.

"Same Mordecai of the Mordecai Swamp?"

"Could be." Then: "What about it?"

"You must have heard the stories," I told him. "There's supposed to be a pile of cannon balls somewhere in there. Lots of old men say they remember seeing it when they were boys. Seems that when The Forks heard that the British were coming, some of the unfinished ammunition was carted deep into the swamp and hidden there. Either they couldn't find the stuff afterwards or they were too busy with other things to go back and look for it. You've heard about that?"

Rod thought he had but he was not impressed. "We used to have a couple of cannon balls around here somewhere," he said. "Dad brought 'em in from somewhere. Mordecai Swamp, may be."

"We ought to *do* that swamp some day," I suggested. "From one end to the other."

Rod smiled across the table. "After the war," he said.

War, never a stranger along the river, had come again, as much of a nuisance, something to get over, as it always has been. Although they rarely talked about it, Mullica families had been touched by it, just like the Kosters. For a long time the Army, discerning Rod's prowess with firearms due to years in the deer woods, kept him in this country training others. Glendin, his brother, left off being an electrical engineer; and as a first lieutenant went first to Camp Edwards, then to New Orleans, finally to Australia. Another brother, Courtland, who was a radio newscaster, also went into the Army. Only Hollis, older than Rod, lingered by the river and then, when work in one of the State forests fell off, went to work in a shipyard.

It was with Hollis, an expert on ferns and fungi, as gifted a naturalist as the valley has produced, that I ventured into the Mordecai Swamp, intrigued by the mystery of the piled-up cannon balls and also the legend that Hollis had heard, that the hideaway of Joe Mulliner, the executed Refugee, was there. Once with Hollis and later with Bill Bailey, I tramped in mushy circles for what seemed endless miles, to emerge at sundown with but two discoveries: mistletoe, growing in clumps high in some oaks deep in the sunless waste, and ruins of an old saw mill beside a tall mountain of sawdust.

The Kosters won't tell you about themselves. Rod's father, Leon, who works with Cliff Terry raising trees for the state at Green Bank, knows a lot of lore, but you can rarely get him to talk. It was like pulling teeth to get the information I eventually pieced together. It seems that Augustus Ernst Koster, born in Hanover, Germany, in 1840, was the first ancestor they know much about. It was a large family—two brothers were in China as missionaries long before there was any great stir about China missions. When Augustus was fourteen, his mother obtained a release from the Emperor, freeing the boy from compulsory military training so that he might come to America. One brother, Charles, was already here, in business in New York.

"Charles was an artist," Rod wrote me from camp when I insisted on knowing the details. "He did decorations for the Columbian Exposition." Augustus married Augusta Rapp on July 30, 1868. Augusta was the daughter of John H. Rapp, who was in the fuel business. When you spoke of the fuel industry in those days, you meant charcoal and cordwood for New York's fires; and "the need of them," Rod told me, "was what brought the family down on the Mullica." There was a firm of Wing & Rapp, and this was the company that promoted the glass factory at Herman, or Hermann. The broken kilns are in a field adjoining the Koster house; and in the river just off the landing there are two ships that sank, loaded with glass according to the legend, when the venture failed.

"Plans for Hermann," Rodney wrote, "were on a large scale. There was to be a village with its own Lutheran Church. Augustus himself came to Hermann in 1869, supervising the building of some of the houses and conducting the store and hotel. The hotel's our house." Augustus went into politics. A staunch Democrat, he soon annexed every office in Washington Township, tax assessor, tax collector, county committeeman, and all the rest. He died in 1925. The dream of a prosperous glass town died long before, for they speak of the life of Hermann City being but six months long. Aunt Hattie Ford and Rod Koster's mother, who took over the post office when Rod went away, were sisters.

"I'm having a time," I told Aunt Hattie one day, "finding anybody from The Forks who can tell me anything that isn't hearsay. Aunt Kate Albor's husband worked in the paper mill at Pleasant Mills and Mr. Holloway, who works down at the nursery, says his father was in charge of the teams that hauled for the mill. But that's the most of it so far."

"Ella Underhill must have remembered paper being made," Aunt Hattie suggested, "and for that matter, I was teaching school up at Harrisville when they were still making paper up there. But that wasn't so long ago. You want something that goes back before all that, don't you?" I said I did, and for a moment she was thoughtful. Then she inquired: "What about the Stewarts, there to the other side of Pleasant Mills? Ever talk to them?"

"Stewarts?" I repeated. Bill Augustine surprised me then by saying he knew Bob Stewart well. Suddenly the name meant something—odd, how your memory tricks you now and then. It was in 1874, according to my notes, when a spark from the chimney of the house of Robert Stewart, then manager of the Batsto Estate, set fire to the dwelling, the flames spreading through the village and on into the woods. After that, it was said, Batsto never actually had recovered. The village we knew was supposed to be but a shadow of what it had been. Mortgages, according to one record, had accumulated, and Mount Holly Courts had given Robert Stewart a mortgage for $20,000 with others of smaller amounts to interested business men. Then in 1876 at a Master's Sale, on another mortgage of $14,000 which had been running since 1845, Joseph Wharton purchased what is still the big Wharton Estate, at the time a property of about a hundred acres square.

"Surely this can't be the same Robert Stewart," I said. But Aunt Hattie merely laughed. "Why don't you go find out?" she asked and we hurried away.

We found Bob Stewart's house. When Bill made the introduction, I read my notes on the Batsto fire. The estate manager, I pointed out, was one Robert Stewart, and it was a spark from the chimney of his house that crippled Batsto for life.

"That ain't exactly right," Bob told me, making a peculiar correction. "A spark from his chimney started the fire all right but *his* house wasn't burned at all. Wind was the other way. I ought to know 'cause Robert Stewart was my grandfather. I'm the twelfth Robert in the family. My boy, here, is the thirteenth."

Until Aunt Hattie had spoken, I had no intimation that Robert Stewart, woodcutter, carpenter, and glasscutter's son, was kin of Robert, pioneer of The Forks, a man who had known Jesse Richards and who had watched the old man's heartbreak when the Batsto furnaces cooled forever in 1848. Nor had anyone said that John, his brother, living a stone's throw up the road, shared memories of an industrial dynasty of which the family long had been a part. We had passed their houses many times through the years on our way to Green Bank and the river. That is how these people are. Leon Koster kicked up a cannon ball in Mordecai Swamp and merely brought it home. John Stewart inherited the dust-laden account books of the Richards Estate, which many a historian must covet, and here merely put them in the attic, certain that The Forks was where they belonged.

Bob works for the Wharton Estate, just as his grandsire did. John has his own little farm. Both are lean, agile, quiet-voiced. They told me that the Wharton Estate was once one hundred and ten thousand acres but that now, in spite of the signs that seem to post the land everywhere about, it's down to a mere ninety thousand. Grandfather Robert used to tell, they say, how Joe Wharton spent forty thousand dollars on the place after he bought it in, then offered it to New Jersey as a watershed, or maybe it was a deal with Philadelphia. It happened in 1915 at any rate, and it was voted down by a vote of 123,995 to 103,456. Such counties as Atlantic and Burlington were against it, with Essex, Hudson, and Passaic approving.

Robert Patterson Stewart was born in Nesco, or Wescottville, about a mile from where he lives. "Mostly," he told me, "I stayed right here in Batsto although they got me up as far as Seaside Park, once, on a carpenterin' job—I helped build some bulkheads. And I helped build the fish factory that Joe Wharton once ran, out on the medders opposite Crab Island. Might say I been a carpenter, on and off, thirty year or more. Between, I done anything come to hand."

Robert's father was a glass cutter when Batsto had a factory making "winder lights" not far from where the road begins to bend, now an open field near the sawmill that the estate keeps in operation. It was Bob himself who tore down the factory buildings when Batsto was not only in the glass business but also the manufacture of "a great variety of iron pots, kettles, Dutch ovens, and oval fish kettles of different sizes, much lighter, neater, and superior to any imported from Great Britain."

"There was lots of cattle on the estate once," Bob said, "steers, teams of mules and horses, with sales held at the Batsto store that's as solid now as ever was. That store was the center of business at The Forks. People came up here all the way from Egg Harbor to get groceries. Ships was still comin' and goin' in the Mullica and the Batsto river, too." Bob smiled. "Guess you'd never guess," he added shyly, "but I was once hot punkins as a baseball player—yes, sir, something of a champeen pitcher. And don't forget my brother, Andrew—he was in charge at the Weymouth store. Had a trick, Andrew did, of making paper-bags with one hand while he got what the customer wanted with the other. People came miles to see him even if they didn't really need nothing, they say."

"Andy" ran the Weymouth sawmill, too. "Famous, he was," John said. "Had a piece and a picture in the paper when he died."

The account books John permitted me to read one night are indices to life as it was lived at The Forks for more than half a century. Woven among the calculations are notes like those of a diary, recalling terms half-forgotten now. The working time of "ore-raisers" and "colliers" is noted among dates and payments for coal drawings and "firing of the pit." There is one pact recorded in which William Sooy was pledged to "wheel and set the wood in a workmanlike manner" and another dated 1839 in which delivery of sixty-eight windowpanes was promised for two dollars plus a bushel of corn. A page from the entries for December, 1837, shows the month to have been the mildest ever known "in the Jarseys."

John and Josiah Ford, William Burr, John Haney, Thomas and Samuel Cobb are among the Batsto "ore-raisers" listed. "These Cobbs," I asked, "are they any relation to Cobby, the Snapper Man near Herman?"

"Surest thing," said Mrs. John heartily, and then she was off. "Why, Lance Cobb's wife was my Sunday School teacher! 'Course, Cobby wouldn't tell you that! Didn't tell you Reuben Mick's wife down to Batsto was his sister, either, did he? See the name of Charles Peterson there in the book? Lots of receipts, looks like. He was the fellow wrote the book, 'Kate Aylesford, the Maid of Sweetwater'—ever read it? Copies turn up now and then between here and Hammonton. Imagine putting an author down in the book among the moulders and core makers at the forge! Maybe he worked at something else besides books, would you think?"

I assured the lady that such a course was singularly wise. The Stewarts remembered the lines and names of ships that plied the river up to The Forks, but I had heard many of the names further down. All in a jerk Bob remember the sloop, "Sally," and the day he found a cannon ball at Harrisville and how he carried bricks from the dismantled kilns at Herman and the fact that Jersey iron never rusts. John kept his head down, reading and listening. Mrs. John, full of more facts, began bubbling over with family background— Uncle Josephus Sooy who became a state treasurer; Sam Crowley who had, she said, four wives in legal succession; and Birdsall Crowley's "Dutch" grandfather, Otto Wobbar. John Stewart broke in warily, reading aloud the recorded dimensions of a giant hearth built at Batsto in 1836. There was no need for such caution. I had learned my lesson at Leeds Point.

# 26

# HEADWATERS

*"Our friends go with us as we go*
*Down the long path where beauty wends,*
*Where all we love forgathers, so*
*Why should we fear to join our friends?"*
OLIVER ST. JOHN GOGARTY

SO WE COME FROM BULLTOWN UP TO THE HEADWATERS, the end of our journey and the river's end as well.

The end of a journey suggests good-by and good-by implies a special sort of sadness. For me, and perhaps for you, the journey will not end, and so there is no sadness of farewell. I will be always going back, I suppose, even when there are no gasoline, no busses, no friendly offers to meet me at Egg Harbor Station, and no immediate means to bridge the land or water that may come between. For I have only to close my eyes to return, to Chestnut Neck, to Lower Bank, to Gloucester, Batsto, and the Green Bank store. I have but to close my door on sounds and sights and smells of suburbia to call about me those who have been a part of this adventure, Bill Birdsall, Charlie Leek, Chink Simpkins, Roy Cramer, Aunt Hattie, Aunt Kate, Rod, Sud, and countless others. There is a magic in the process I cannot describe.

I am wondering, now that we approach the headwaters, if this is where our travels along the river should have begun. Would it have been better to have sought the Mullica where it rises sluggishly near Crowfoot, following it as it carries its legends seaward in exchange for men? Or would it have been more practical to have traveled with the tides, instead of coming up from Little Egg Harbor, through Swan Bay, and up beyond The Forks and Atsion? I am not sure—but anyway, it is too late now to change. Actually, when I come to think of it, I am never certain of our journey's beginning, its "where" and its "when" . . .

The "where," I believe, was Ong's Hat, which isn't on the Mullica at all. The "when," surely, was every day of fifteen years ago when, they told me, Mr. Ong was either an innkeeper or rustic dancer and not the Mullica traveler I since have discovered him to be. (Remind me to tell you the true story of Mr. Ong, of Middle-of-the-Shore, before we part—without good-by!) Good-bys that should concern us here are not ours to give—they are the farewells that were not heard except by a narrowing circle of friends along the river; I was not there to ask about the tales that went before. This, I know, is the lone regret I have as we come to the end of our wandering for a time: That so many were so near the end of theirs and I was not aware. Thus, in one sense the story of the river must be incomplete, the outline on the canvas left sketchy here and there. Even so, the picture is finished.

In all of us there is something left out, something that our friends find indispensable in themselves, without which they cannot imagine how we survive. Some play bridge and find it a balance wheel; I know nothing of bridge and have no inclination to understand it. Some have a passion for the races, even with the element of gambling eliminated; I once saw a track but never a horse to run upon it, and at the moment I can see no need for combining the two in my experience. Some of my friends, when they have acquired new houses, think I should be interested in how well their possessions suit the rooms and hallways, expecting me, I know, to go into some kind of ecstasies over their talents and tastes; they are upset when I express a preference for sitting and hearing about other matters. There are dozens of things that I do without, and the more I do without them the more I discover how unnecessary they are. So I, too, am incomplete in the same sense as may be this life along the Mullica and the picture I have made of it, except to those who live and love it.

The headwaters, I must tell you quickly now, flow through a land that is lacking in the contrast of color and topography that lies below them. Except where the Mullica's crossing of the Jackson Road is proclaimed by a sign denoting the county line, the river's whereabouts is unobserved and secret. Beyond in one direction is Berlin, a town that yielded a better name in the midst of another argument, striving to be the county seat; historians long have quarreled as to whether a stagecach or a supply of water were long in coming, just as they have differed about another coach stop where horses were changed, Blue Anchor. More pertinent to us is the fact that Atco, in the same neighborhood, took its name from the Atlantic Transportation Company organized by the Richards Estate, that Jackson was Jackson Glassworks in Waterford Township, a factory established in 1827 by the same interests. Those were days when men from down the Mullica, thinking in terms beyond the river's length and power, were by way of becoming railroad-minded.

As fires of the forges went out and new glass kilns replaced the old, men and women who had lived happily in Mullica towns moved far beyond the tide and tributary creeks. Sawmills were dismantled over and over and set up where there was more timber. Settlements sprang up around new glassworks moved to where there was more fuel. Those unwilling to turn to other trades or put their full confidence in God and the river, magnifying a contentment inherited with the belief, somewhat Micawberish, that something would turn up in time up the river or down the road beside it, were swept up and away as if by a tidal wave. Some began new lives at Jackson, at Hammonton, at Winslow, at Tansboro, or at Williamstown. Some went farther on, to New York, Pennsylvania, and Virginia, following the business in which they were most skilled. Those who remained, lived and died, for the most part, amid the ruin of an industrial dream, without the solace of the river if they had fled too far afield. The first railroads, built to bring men and man's expectancy of the expanded river kingdom closer together, hastened the doom of enterprise with a divided allegiance so that the river had the last laugh —if indeed the river has been ungenerous. Railroad backers, listening to prospective patrons and compelled to choose between business and pleasure, chose pleasure—with such business as could be conveniently attended to on the way.

Mullica industrialists who were either by birth or conversion Philadelphia business men were tired of sandy roads. Some were provoked by having to work so hard for so little. Some wanted short cuts, better timber and easier ways to get it, more glass sand and easier ways to reach it. Generally, all of them feared the looming consequences of slow transportation from the river's highest land-

ings to the centers of commerce. Thus it is that even the name of
Hammonton recalls John Hammond Coffin, who had operated a
glassworks at Green Bank and perhaps at Nesco on his way up the
river. Thus Winslow memorializes Edward Winslow Coffin, his
brother, who kept moving inland as if in search of treasure, digging
in the earth that traces its title to Charles II, through Berkeley and
Carteret, Fenwick and Byllinge, Robinson and Bell, and then the
Richardses. William Coffin, father of John and Edward, had come
down from New England and had established industries, but the
wheel of his mill had stopped before his sons brought with them
the renewed interest and vigor of their youth. The Richards clan,
descending from Owen, that broad-shouldered Welshman who was
in this country before 1718, headed up the merchants who began the
railroad campaign, men who saw rails accomplishing what ships and
barges failed to complete, supplanting oxcarts and crude wagons
that connected river landings with the world outside.

It was Thomas Richards who became a glass manufacturer at
Jackson, in Camden County, at a corner of the estate of his father,
William; by 1850 Samuel, William's son, had joined him as a partner.
At the same period Joseph Porter at Waterford was proprietor of
another glass-making establishment, center of a tract of six thousand acres. Over at Winslow Andrew K. Hay and William Coffin's
sons were partners in the operation of more glass kilns, while at
Batsto our old friend, Jesse Richards, seeking to match with faster
transport the lure of better ore in greater quantity nearer the Delaware River landings, saw a railroad as sure salvation for Jersey bog
iron. Stephen Colwell and Dwight Bell, over at Weymouth, shared
similar hope, for their father-in-law had been Samuel Richards, another son of William. Down at Absecon General Enoch Doughty,
taking tar and wood and charcoal from another estate of twenty-
five thousand acres, was invited to join the railroad promoters; and
perhaps, as we see it now, he had more to do with the final outcome
than any of the others. For General Doughty with Doctor Jonathan
Pitney began their own campaign for a road of rails that would go
beyond the glass and iron kilns and furnaces all the way to the seashore and, as it turned out, were the two who drafted the Camden
& Atlantic's charter.

Although Stephen Colwell and Dwight Bell took four hundred shares of stock in the proposed railroad and although Thomas Richards, Joseph Porter, and Andrew Hay acquired six hundred shares between them, a plan for a road to a new resort whose name had just been decided, Atlantic City, took precedence over the original plan to connect Jackson, Waterford, Winslow, Batsto, and Weymouth. Closest to Jackson that the railroad came was Long-a-Coming, now Berlin; closest to Batsto was Hammonton, and that wasn't close at all. A branch of the road that served Atlantic City for twenty-three years, from 1854 to 1877, with a single track, was put down over to Winslow, but many of the original ideas of the original supporters went up in woodsmoke and bickering.

I was wondering one day if all those who had known the story of the railroad's battle with the river were in their graves, as I had been assured they were, when one of my friends sent me an old price list of the Winslow Glass Works. The name of Hay & Company headed the columns of various products and prices, with window, coach, sheet, and double-thick glass for sale, together with "wine, porter, minerals, and all kinds of hollowware" at the premises, No. 94 North Front Street, Philadelphia. There was an interesting engraving at the top of the list, a picture I presumed to be that of Winslow as it was in better days, its chimneys smoking and teams, harnessed to a Jersey wagon, drawn up in the foreground. Armed with the yellowing reproduction, I hurried down to Winslow. On the scene, having made the distinction between Winslow Glassworks and Winslow Junction a mile or so away, I was told that the one to see was Miss Kitty Bernadou, who lived around the spruce-lined curve of a road appropriately named Hay Street.

Some people, I have been told, have no idea why the street is so called, concluding probably that hay was hauled along it years ago. No one could have more quickly dispelled that notion than Miss Kitty, whom I have seen on several occasions near the house in which she lives, a dwelling which, they tell me, was the hostler's in the glorious days of Hay. The property, I believe, is known as the estate of George Cochran, and Mr. Cochran was the son-in-law of Squire Andrew. Miss Kitty herself is Andrew K. Hay's granddaughter and would have given us many precious details of the life of the old town, I know, if she could have been induced to chat. But I was turned away at the door on several visits, and after that letters brought no response.

Next I came upon another Norcross. This lady, to whom I showed my picture of the old town, informed me that it "was a little too fancy like advertisements sometimes be," but she recognized buildings that were there when she arrived some fifty-four years before. I found Mrs. Norcross at the Winslow School where she did some dusting and sweeping after helping the pupils on with their coats. She insisted on talking in her own home, and so I listened in a warm and friendly kitchen. "Norcross," she said of her husband, "was sort of washed up here like all the rest when the glass plant was started. This is where he worked. It was a thriving place once, although you'd never guess, would you? Why, there was music all night long."

When the Hays departed, the Tillyers came, she said. That was in 1884 after John B. Hay and the heirs of Andrew K. withdrew. "First," Mrs. Norcross told me, "there was William Coffin Jr. & Company. Then there was Coffin & Perce. After that came the Hays, and the firm was Coffin & Hay. Squire Andrew, they always said, had been in the glass business with his brother-in-law, Bodine Coffin, down to Hammonton before coming here. Later on Tristram Bowdle joined in, and they made the name Coffin, Hay, & Bowdle." It was in 1850 that Mr. Bowdle retired, and in 1851 Edward Coffin sold out to Squire Andrew, who, with his son—or was it nephew?—became sole owners.

From Mrs. Norcross I went to see Granny Sutts who lived, Mrs. Norcross told me, in a house just like hers down the road. "The houses are pretty much all alike," she said, "because they made the workmen's houses that way. Manus Sutts used to work beside Old Norcross." Mrs. Sutts was eighty-eight when I talked with her first, eighty-nine when I returned a year later to make a birthday call. She sat close by a big stove, warmly clad just the same, even to the wearing of a tam-o'-shanter. She smiled as she talked, said she didn't get around like she used to, complained that the stove was burning a lot of wood, forty dollars worth so far that winter.

"This house?" she repeated. "Ninety year old if it's a day. See these here winders? They're original glass, glass made here to Winslow. And those weatherboards are the first, never been painted."

Manus, she said, had been a "gathering boy" at the glass works. The fire? The fire that burned out the old town forever? She was no more able to set the exact date of that than Mrs. Norcross. "It was in the spring," she said, looking out the window. "We moved all our things out and then we moved them in again. You see, the fire only took the glass works. Only the factory burned down. The houses was left. But the houses wasn't much good without the factory. Yes, the fire, you might say, burned out the heart of Winslow."

A little later on I found two more of the glass town pioneers who had been left behind, Walter Woolford of Riverside and John Sampson, still on the scene at a place they call Hay's Crossing just for old time's sake. It was Granny Sutts who said that John must be somewhere around.

John Sampson looked carefully at my introductory engraving and said: "This ain't like Winslow. This ain't like old Winslow at all." John sat on the back porch of a little house where he lives with his wife about two miles from the glass town site. Winslow, he told me, has always been outside the door, really, for there he has mounted the old Winslow bell that was used to summon the workmen for meals and batches of glass. "Now, this here wagon with the six mules attached," he went on, musing again over the picture, "that's pure imagination. We had wood-wagons, built specially to haul wood that was cut in two-foot lengths, but they wasn't like this. There was a lot of tall pine timber all around here when those wood-wagons was running, but there's none here now to show you what I mean."

John was born in Winslow in 1866. His father worked at the "glass house" before him. "With the woodchoppers and all," he told me, "at least five hundred men was working here in those days. The fire? Sure. I know the date of it well. It was in the spring of 1892. Andrew Hay died in 1882, that's how I know. Squire Andrew was still president of the Camden & Atlantic when he died. Why, say, one of the locomotives on the line was named for him and was used for the funeral. Ever hear of an engine being used for a funeral? Well, this one was. And, somehow, it was both pretty and appropriate. After all, Squire Hay was a part of the railroad, like a big wheel or a camshaft, you might say. I can remember that funeral now. I was a boy over in the bottle factory then, and I climbed up on top of the cars."

John Sampson tapped on the old bell to let me hear the sound of it. "Sounds nice, don't it?" he asked me, as if he had heard the music of a cathedral organ. "More'n one bell they had over to the factory. Rang 'em for meals and for fires—and for gettin' up. You was supposed to eat by five o'clock so the bells was rung at four. And there was a whistle, too. Dan Barnett, the engineer, used to pride himself on blowing that whistle right on the dot. Held his big watch in one hand and the whistle cord in the other, he did. Why, one time he let *me* blow it!"

The trail that had led where now there were neither bells nor whistles from the clean and quiet little houses of Mrs. Norcross and Granny Sutts drew me next to the corner where John Albertson lived. John used to be another Winslow blower, Mr. Sampson said, adding that his friend was a lonely man. "It's been bad for him before," he said, "but it's worse now. His wife died last week. We used to know everybody there was around here, but now there are as few to remember as there are that remember *them*."

But soon, after I had asked about the old log houses at the end of Hay Street down from the store, the two old men were smiling, matching recollections of the workmen whose homes they had been —Billy Beard, Johnny Parks, Jerry Strang, Hank Hoffner, Uncle Charlie Smith, Louis Marks, and Lou McCloskey. There was Jake Roller, the village blacksmith, and Chris, the wheelwright—Winslow grew in stature and reality as they talked. The picture on the old price list was of no use at all. Then I heard John Albertson saying that what people needed was a lot more walking. "If you got to walk to see somebody, that means you *want* to be friendly," he told me. "That's why I say the automobile stopped a lot of folks from being friends."

There was a man named Hex at Winslow, John Albertson said, who was so good he designed his own bottles. "Sort of made 'em up as he went along, they say. I remember because one bottle was the Hex gallon and the other the Hex half-gallon. They was mighty pretty."

John Sampson stopped blowing glass in 1907, but John Albertson went on for a while, following his trade down to Virginia. "I found

# WINSLOW GLASS WORKS, CAMDEN CO., N. J.

This old likeness of the Winslow Glass Works, taken from an early price list, shows a Jersey Wagon or "Sheet-topped Wagon" in the foreground. Uncle Joe Norcross and his wife, below, ran a store on the road between Blue Anchor and Tansboro, not far from the headwaters of the Mullica, a road familiar to the old stages.

The late "Bull" Miller stands beside an old watergate, recalling days of Atsion as a shipping center, days of Indian Mills (where he lived) which now are forgotten.

"Granny" Sutts, widow of a pioneer maker of Jersey glass, made the most of memories of Winslow in a house whose windows were Winslow glass and whose old-fashioned stove called for wood.

out I could make as much money farming," said the man who owned the bell, "and I didn't have to use half as much wind."

When Walter Woolford said that he, too, had learned his trade at Winslow and that he had been a gatherer, I seized the opportunity. "What's a gatherer?" I asked him.

"Well," said Mr. Woolford, a much smaller man than the two Johns from Hay's Crossing, "it's this way. In a glasshouse there are three men in each group on a job. One's the blower, one's the gatherer, and the other's the second-hander or helper."

"But what," I persisted, "does the gatherer do?"

"Why, he *gathers*," said Mr. Woolford, and I had to make the most of that.

Next time Walter Woolford goes down to Winslow—and he goes back every year—he is going to tell John Sampson about the date of the glassworks fire. "I been goin' down to the annual service in the old church," he said, "ever since I come away. That was in 1908. Us old glass boys get together for some yarnin' after the service. You ought to come down some time. You'd get an earful all at once. But when I go down this time I'm going to make John Sampson put down the fire plain in his book. It was Decoration Day in 1892."

Sud Norcross used to get spells in which he thought it would be nice to make sure of all the Norcrosses, where they were buried and what their birth and death dates were. So we went to many of the old cemeteries time and again, because Sud was always losing his notes or telling me, as if he were quite serious, that I had lost them. Once Sud's interest took us down to Tansboro where, after a talk with Mr. and Mrs. Joe Norcross, Mrs. Joe parted Sud from some money for a graveyard fence. I wanted to meet Uncle Joe because he was nearest of kin to the operators of the famous Norcross stage.

Sud's only story about the stage was of the Norcross system for eliminating competition with the line. "They used to tie a couple of cedar trees on the back," Sud said, "and then get just ahead of the rival coach. The trees would stir up the dust all over the horses, drivers, and passengers. After a couple of trips like that the patrons usually decided to take the coach sure to keep in front."

Uncle Joe, who said he would be ninety in May, the month follow- ing, had been setting out onions and admittedly was "a little played out." "Well, Suddy boy," he greeted Sud, then seventy-three, "what brings you to town? Somebody dead I don't know about?"

"We were wondering," Sud told him, "what you could remember of the old stage—you know, the one that Uncle 'Ri' used to drive along the road here to the shore."

"Uncle 'Ri' has give it up," Uncle Joe answered promptly, as if the stage had stopped running the day before. "Yup, you're right, the old stage came right by here up the Tansboro Road." It left Pierson's Ferry at Market Street in Camden at four o'clock in the morning and John Knisell's Ferry a half hour later. That was as much, Uncle Joe said, as he could keep in his head. "The rest," he said, "is on the poster."

There was a family conference and then some rummaging about upstairs. After that Joe and Mrs. Joe reappeared with a yellowing trade announcement of the United States Mail Stage Lines, running daily to Great Egg Harbor. "On Tuesdays, Thursdays and Saturdays," I read, "this line passes through Haddonfield, Long-a-Coming, Tansboro, Blue Anchor, Winslow Glass Works, Weymouth Iron Works, Mays Landing, Bargintown, Somer's Point, Smith's Landing to Absecon." The return trip was explained with equal detail. The proprietors ready to serve the public were listed as Uriah and William Norcross, John C. Briggs, James Stoy, and our old friend from down the river, William Coffin.

"Where'd you get this?" Sud inquired as Uncle Joe snatched it back as if he expected us to run out the door with it.

"In the family," Uncle Joe responded, none too specifically. "There's another one in the Berlin Bank. *That* one came from the Blue Anchor Hotel before the place burned down. I like this one because it tells you where you could buy the tickets—see? Wescott's Hotel in Mays Landing, Hughes's Hotel in Absecon, Briggs's at Weymouth, and down at Coffin & Hay's in Winslow. Guess they're all closed now, from what I hear."

That was where I tried again for an explanation of the meaning of the name, Tansboro. I said there must have been a tannery. Uncle Joe, whose memory must have been failing, said he didn't think so. There was a bottle factory, he said. "It was just the other side of the tracks. I don't know how long ago." Mrs. Joe asserted immediately that she remembered things better in her own sure-fire way. "My oldest boy Lonzo was just a year old when the glass yard bursted up," she told me, "and Lonzo, he's fifty-two now!"

Once, Uncle Joe said, all Tansboro was Norcrosses. Several generations had it all figured out that the family was descended from Norsemen who carried a banner on which there was a Norse cross. Thus the first variation of the name, Norecross, was derived, they said, from Norsecross. Sud said that a Norcross up in Lynn, Massachusetts, had let the family know on one occasion that the clan went back to 1550 at the very least.

Grandpa Job Norcross, it seems, had seven sons. There were Samuel, Uriah, Isaiah, John, William, Job, and Charles. "Samuel, John, William, and Job live within a short distance of their birthplace," wrote Samuel, himself, in 1878, "in Winslow Township, Camden County, a place locally known as Tansboro. Isaiah lives near Kirkwood and Charles at Winslow." According to that, I told Sud, I had probably met Charles's widow.

"What good did it do you?" Sud asked me, and made a face.

Isaiah and Uriah were Uncle Zare and Uncle Ri to Uncle Joe. "My grandfather was a Norcross, too," Mrs. Joe put in. "Seems we was all Norcrossed up together."

I went down to see Uncle Joe several times. He and his wife ran a curious kind of store, a place that looked no more what it was inside than it did outside. And yet, as we talked, children came with money in their hands, asking for loaves of bread and cans of beans, procured from mysterious places after a moment by Mrs. Joe. Uncle Joe was never an easy talker. Yes, he chopped wood when nothing much else offered in the old days. Yup, he had burned charcoal, too. Nine dollars a load it was, hauled up the old Long-a-coming Road. Wagons held three cords, hundred bushel to the load. Price was usually ten cents a bushel. Sometimes, gathering wood, they'd get farther and farther away. Maybe all the way to Pleasant Mills if the weather was good.

"And I used to help him haul that wood," said Mrs. Joe, smiling. "My people didn't like it much, and the doctor said it'd kill me. Looks as if it had tuck a long time to catch up with us, wouldn't you say?"

Then there was John Fowler who, Uncle Joe and his friend the preacher, Mr. Warrington, told me, would know all about the name of Tansboro. What was more, John had been in town since there were coaches going by, they insisted. I looked at the date on Uncle Joe's poster, 1846, and decided that the ones they meant must have been after that.

That was when John Fowler lived in a tiny house over the track of a railroad spur used for sand diggings. There were three rooms, I think. There was a kitchen, built around a pump, and a bedroom kept almost dark because Mrs. Fowler was there, never quite well. John talked in whispers in the small adjoining parlor. "All Tansboro," he said pedantically, as in the classic description of Gaul, "is divided into three parts—Hogshutem, Skin Hill, and Tansboro proper.

"There was a hog-killin', you see," he said quietly, "and a lot of the boys got drunk. So instead of sticking this pig, they shot him instead. They called *that* place Hogshutem. Then they came along, draggin' the carcass to where they decided to skin it, sudden-like. From then on *that* place became Skin Hill. The next move was up to the tanyard where the hide was really 'tended to. *That* was Tansboro—and still is!"

I remember Mr. Fowler wanting his picture taken under a tree across the road. His father planted it, he said, as I helped him up the hill, for even then he was shaky on his feet. "I was just a boy then," he explained, "and I been lovin' this tree like it was in the family for a very long time. There was a place on the railroad they called Florence Station then—ain't far from here. There was still some Indians over there." I suppose I looked at him then, without meaning to. "People don't believe me when I tell them," he said, quietly, "but it's true. Come to think of it, they didn't call it Florence—it was Guineatown then. Guineas was what we always called those Indians."

John Fowler said there ought to be no doubt about a glass plant in Tansboro. Even as he was then, he told me, he could toss a stone across the track to where it had stood. "Why, I used to work in that glasshouse," he went on. "Fact is, I got a bottle here that was blowed over there." He tiptoed into the darkened bedroom and returned to display it proudly. I asked him if it was a liquor bottle. "Well," he answered thoughtfully, "you might call it that. But you got your liquor in jugs in those days. And you started working young. Guess I was fourteen when I started in to the factory.

"Mattie Zimmerman and Leon Mason ran the glass business here. You ought to put Leon down in what you're writin', 'cause he's the man who invented the Mason jar. They'll tell you Mason jars was first made in lots of places, even down to Green Bank and Bulltown, maybe, but it ain't so. This is where Mattie Zimmerman and Leon worked together, and Leon turned 'em out for the first time. And you never saw those stagecoaches, did you? Well, they was something to see even though they wasn't like what you see in the pictures. Usually the baggage was stowed up so high they was topheavy. I ought to know. Guess I'm the only one left to know." He smiled, pausing. "I was the boy," he announced, "who had to water the horses!"

The old man insisted that I take the bottle he had prized. I declined it until I saw that refusal was upsetting him. "Take it, please," he said. "You been nice in listenin' and it's done me good. Besides, I ain't got much time." Now and then I look at the bottle of Jersey glass, blown in Tansboro where they made, according to John Fowler, the first Mason jars. Less than a year from the day he gave it to me he died, sitting in the room where we had talked. Mrs. Fowler had died the day before in the darkened room.

Once Sud Norcross and I went back to Winslow for no special reason. As we looked along Hay Street, it was as if we were at the end of a long hall, with the river on one side. The weather-scarred and ageless houses of the town, the battered store, the long lines of patriarchal trees, all were the same, almost, up and down the valley. Half asleep, perhaps drowsily expectant or merely resigned. Everybody, everything everywhere was waiting. Waiting again for railroads to get through, for coaches to arrive, for herring to start their flipping in the up-tide. Waiting for somebody else to take over the store, or buy the house on the corner, or build a landing where the shipyard used to be. Waiting patiently for people to get over their notions, their thirst for newness and for power, their blindness to beauty in the little things they always had. Waiting for

301

the world outside to find quiet again, peace like there was in Eric Mullica's land where ordinary things had been exciting—and still could be. . . .

I ought to take you, now, to Weymouth and Fountain Gale; to Tylertown and the Nicholses, Will and Lonzo, and then down to Indian Mills and Atsion where Mr. John "Bull" Miller could show us, as few others can, where Salter's Ditch recalls a legal feud. But Fountain may be on the river with his gill nets and the Nicholses, grandsons of the famous Cap'n Abe of Crowleytown, may still be self-conscious about the house they made from a potato shed when fire swept them out into the cold. As for "Bull," he will want to talk and ask Mrs. Miller if there isn't something nice to eat—and, well, it's late as it is. You will undoubtedly fault me in the end by saying that Weymouth's beyond the headwaters and that going to Bulltown and Atsion is but a ruse to turn us back to the banks of the Mullica.

Somewhere along the way I have picked up an odd reputation. I know all the obscure places and people, I am told. A bus company official has just called up to ask how he might best speed a patron to the Penn State Forest—would Munion Field be the nearest stop? It might, I said, but there would be little reason for anyone to stop there as there have been no houses or persons to occupy them in more than sixty years. Not long ago a florist consulted me about the delivery of flowers, sent by a soldier to his mother but misdirected to Woodland, New Jersey. Woodlynne? Emphatically not; that had been tried. Well, then, there was a choice of two Woodland Townships and an abandoned wayside station. In the end the posies arrived in good order and with no appreciable delay. Where is Catawba? Was there a place on Delaware Bay called Caviar? Where on earth was Progress? I am supposed to know all the answers. In some queer way I cannot account for, I sometimes do.

I really wish more inquiries concerned Ong's Hat. If people would only ask questions the way I have had to ask questions, that would give me the chance to tell them that the story I picked up and passed along in another book is wrong, after all. Elaborate traps were laid for me, and I fell into all of them, coming away in the case of Ong's Hat with two lovely legends explaining how the "town," then a clearing and now grown over, got its name. By this time, aided by my

302

faithful Washington correspondent, Nelson Gaskill, I can bravely brand so-called tradition a fairy tale and say that Mr. Ong, an inveterate traveler of the early 1700's, was wont to come up the valley from Little Egg Harbor at least once a year. Half way up he and his family spent the night in a cabin he had built just for that purpose. Being a Dutchman, Mr. Ong called his lean-to a "hoet"—hut to you and me. This, then, was Ong's Hut. There never was a hat—never, of course, unless it was the one through which my informants talked when they told me Jacob Ong was a dancer whose hat was tossed by an irate partner high into a tree. The same headgear must have served equally well when the mapmakers were around, for the "hat" remains official on state and county charts these many years after. Now you know why it is, really, that when I wear a hat it's under protest!

# BIBLIOGRAPHY

*An Account of the Life and Travels in the Work of the Ministry of John Fothergill.* Philadelphia, reprinted and sold by James Chattin in Church-Alley, 1754.

BLACKMAN, LEAH. *History of Little Egg Harbor Township, Burlington County, N.J., from its First Settlement to the Present Time.* Published by Surveyors Association of West New Jersey, 1879.

HALL, JOHN F. *The Daily Union History of Atlantic City and County.* Atlantic City, The Daily Union Printing Company, 1900.

HESTON, ALFRED M. *Absegami: Annals of Eyren Haven and Atlantic City, 1609 to 1904.* Camden, printed for the author by Sinnickson Chew & Sons Company, 1904. 2 vols.

————. *Jersey Waggon Jaunts.* Camden, Atlantic County Historical Society, 1926. 2 vols.

LAWRENCE, JAMES. *A Journal Kept by James Lawrence in Running the Division Line of the Province of New Jersey in 1743.* Photostats of manuscript in the State Museum, Trenton, N.J.

LEE, FRANCIS B. and others, comp. *Jerseyisms of Dialect in Glass and Shingle Industries and General Use.* Trenton, 1893.

*New Jersey Archives.* Newark, N.J. Historical Society, 1880–. First and 2nd series.

*Report of Committee of the Council of Proprietors of West New Jersey in Relation to the Province Line Between East and West New Jersey.* Pamphlet printed in 1887.

STEWART, FRANK H., ed. and comp. *Notes on Old Gloucester County, New Jersey.* Historical Records Published by the New Jersey Society of Pennsylvania, 1917, 1934, and 1937. 3 vols.

STRYKER, WILLIAM S. *The Affair at Egg Harbor, New Jersey, October 15, 1778.* Pamphlet. Trenton, Naar, Day, and Naar, 1894.

WATSON, JOHN F. *Annals of Philadelphia and Pennsylvania in the Olden Time.* Phila., published by the author, 1850. 2 vols.

# INDEX

"Absecombe Creek," 66
Absecon, 67, 86, 292
Adams. Alice, 210; Enoch, 51; Franklin, 210; Hezekiah, 210; Isaiah, 210, 254; Lew, 269; Mark, 213; family, 79, 108, 206, 273
Addams, Sariah, 97
Albertson. Jan, 282; John, 296
Allen. Achsah, 94; Charles, 94, 95; Edith, 27; Capt. Jesse Bodine, 95, 267, 272; Johnny, 149; Josie, 272, 275; Joseph, 94, 95, 96; Maggie, 70, 268, 271; Monty, 272; Peter, 94; Robert, 27, 94; family, 21, 31, 93, 97, 98
"Alligator," the, 169
Alloway-Creek, 68
Akin, Abel, 222
Albor. Charles, 160, 161; Mrs. Charles (Aunt Kate), 158, 160, 161, 162, 285, 289
Alrich, George, 34
Amintonck (Mullica) River, xii, 49, 58
"Ampley's," 138
Anchor Island, 15, 60
Andrews. Edith, 27; Edward, 6, 28, 138, 141, 142, 143, 253; Elizabeth, 43; Hannah, 43; Isaac, 43; Mary, 27; Mordecai, 6, 62; Samuel, 43; family, 97, 233

Ancocas Creek, 62
Andrews Mill Creek, 111
*Annals of Philadelphia,* 5
Arens, Dolph, 177, 179
Arnold, Capt. John, 171
Asa's Causeway, 138
Aserdaten, 166, 167, 169-183
Atkinson. Julia Lane, 270; Rev. Louis, 270
Atco, 197
Atlantic City, ix, 23, 59, 63, 66, 73
Atlantic County, 25, 107
Atsion, 20, 26, 34, 89, 155, 289, 302
Atsion Lake, 88, 160, 161
Atsion River, 281
Atwood family, 206, 254
Augustine, William F., 88, 91, 124, 151, 156, 157, 158, 214, 285

Bailey, Bill, 70, 284
Baker, Joshua, 231
Ball, Joseph, 277
Ballinger's Creek, 30
Balguoer, Le Bruce de, 19
Bamber (Lacey, Ferrago, "Frago"), 169, 174
Bamhast, 168
Bar Sedge, 17
Barber, John, 59
Bargaintown Circuit, 86, 238

Barnegat, 29, 101, 137, 142, 171, 172, 185, 200, 206
Barnegat Bay, xiii
Barnegat Light, 184
Barnett, Dan, 296
Bartlet. Capt. James, 273; Oswald Good, 282
Barton, Willis, 249
Bass River (New Gretna), 30, 31, 55, 75, 77, 79, 86, 93, 94, 109, 149, 192, 210
Basse, Jeremiah, 106
Bass's Place, 39
Bathsheba, Indian queen, xiii
Batsto, 13, 15, 16, 52, 54, 72, 120, 155, 160, 244, 268, 276, 277, 289, 293
Batsto River, 276, 281
Baylin, Capt., 225
Bear Creek, 22, 220
Beard, Billy, 296
Beaver Dam Creek, 176
Becky Lane Creek, 27, 90, 109
Belangee. Evi (Ive), 30; Jene, 28; Dr. Jim, 43; family, 6, 30, 111
Bell. Dwight, 292, 293; James, 239
Bellanger. John, 153; Samuel, 153
Berlin (Long-a-Coming), 290, 293
Bernadon, Kitty, 293
Big Buck Run, 182
Birdsall. Aaron, 133, 136; Jim, 136; Joseph, 137; Robert, 137; William, 133, 134, 135, 137, 142, 195, 196, 289; William Hazleton (Haze), 42, 132, 133-136, 138-144, 196, 210; family, xiv, 114, 119
Big Sheepshead Creek, 77
Black, T. G., 180
Black Horse (Columbus), 207, 208
Blackman. Leah, 21, 22, 23, 27, 50, 78, 92, 159, 209; Nehemiah, 234; family, 3, 141, 234
Blackman's, 86
Blackman's Mills, 235
Black's Bridge, 180
Blake. Georgianna, 222, 223, 224, 226, 232, 247, 249; Mida, 226, 228, 229; family, 234, 237
Blue Anchor, 118, 219, 291

Bodine. Jean, 97; John, 44
Bond, Mr., 146
Bosen, Lt. Col. the Baron de, 17, 18
Boswell, Mr., 272
Bowdle, Tristram, 294
Bowen. Carrie J., 60, 70, 245; Capt. Jonathan Steelman, 69; Oscar, 64; family, 225, 241, 243
Bowker, Selah, 190
Boyle, Rev., 271, 272
Bozarth. Fire Warden, 244; Flora, 266; family, 198
Bozarthtown, 198
Bradford, William, 66
Brainerd, Rev. John, 223, 235, 237
Branson. Henry, 179; Huds, 179; Jim, 179; Joe, 179; family, 178, 180, 183
Brandywine, Battle of, 8
Breckenridge family, 177
Bricksburg (Lakewood), 171
Bridgeport (Wading River), 30, 55, 78, 120, 161, 168, 190, 198, 205, 208, 264, 268
Bridgeton, 89, 198
Brielle, 76
Brigantine, 54, 66
Brigantine Beach, 52
Briggs, John C., 298
Bristol, 207
Britton family, 178
Broadfield, Mrs., 146
Bromville (Gustav Juliet), 10
Brooks, 266
Brookville (Tattletown, Millville, Headleyville, Tattlertown), 166, 174, 183
Broom. Catherine, 119; Janie, 119; William, 119
Brooms, Abe, 127
Brown, Preserve, 28, 31
Brush, "Granny," 274
Buck Neck Swamp, 202
Buck Neck Swamp Road, 57
Buckshutem, 101
Bull, Richard, 120
Bull Creek, 134
Bulltown, 28, 31, 32, 34, 43, 125, 133, 134, 141, 147, 155, 192, 301, 302

Bunnell, Fred, 169, 170
Burlington, 4, 30, 65, 66, 111
Burlington County, xiii, 6, 15, 22, 31, 47, 53, 59, 60, 62, 98, 99
Burnett. Thomas, 235; family, 234
Burns. Hannah (Cranmer), 30; Joseph, 30, 209; Margaret, 209
Burnside, James, 62
Burnt Bridge, 171
Burr, William, 287
Burton family, 254
Buzby, 167; Jack, 189, 190

Cake family, 234
Cale. Carrie, 31; Capt. Daniel, 31, 273, 275; Franklin, 31; John, 31, 273; Olive, 271; Rebecca, 31; Reuben, 31; Sarah, 31; Capt. Watson, 30, 43, 119, 127, 128, 130; William, 31; family, 31, 273, 275
Camburn. See Cameron
Camden, 192
Camden & Atlantic Railroad, 106
Camden County, 98
Cameron. Daniel, 181; William (Camburn), 181
Campbell, Capt. Duncan, 52, 53
Cape May, 13, 21, 60, 281
Cape May County, 246
Carlisle. Elizabeth, 93, 94; Capt. John, 72, 92-98 passim, 113, 206; Richard Risley, 93, 94; family, 31, 102
Carr family, 254
Cavalier. See Cavileer
Cavileer. Benny, 89; Belsy Lewis, 275; Cale, 89, 249, 267, 268; Charlie, 88-91, 273, 275; Ezekiel, 79; George, 88, 91, 92; Gilbert, 74; Grover Cleveland, 89; Jess, 89, 273; Jim, 89; John, 89, 91, 213, 271; Mary, 89; Nettie, 273; Pedro (Peter), 58, 82, 88, 89; Raymond, 88-92; "Ruby," 88, 89, 273; Sam, 88, 92; Sarah, 89; Walter, 89, 269; William, 89
Cedar Bridge, 26, 174
Cedar Run, 48, 137
Charcoal Point, 31, 34

Charles Landing, 220
Chatsworth, 167, 187, 189
Chestnut Neck, 6-22 passim, 32, 39, 46, 74, 75, 103, 122, 219, 223, 224, 226, 227, 232, 236, 276, 289
Chisler's Club, 178, 179
"Chris" (wheelwright), 296
Christopherson, 170
Cincinnati, Society of, 9
Cinnaminson Township, 78
Clamtown (Tuckerton), 17
Clark. David, 139, 140, 223; Col. Elijah, 15, 75, 139, 140, 219, 222, 238; Hannah, 140; Mrs. J. C., 117; Maj. Lardner, 231; Nehemiah, 282; Parker, 282; Rebecca, 281; Sally, 139, 141; Samuel, 140; Thomas, 138, 139, 140, 222, 234; Thomas, Jr., 140, 141; family, 49, 58, 114, 220, 230, 234
Clarke, James, 220
Clark's Mills, 223
Clark's Landing, 58, 72, 96, 97, 104, 138, 139, 141, 195, 223, 233, 234, 241
Clayton, William, 19
Clevenger, Emma Ford, 144, 158
Clinton, Gen. Sir Henry, 13, 14, 103
Cobb, Alanson ("Lance," "Snapper"), 120, 127, 143, 151-156, 287, 288; Samuel, 287; Thomas, 287
Cochran, George, 293
Coffin. Bodine, 294; Edward Winslow, 292, 294; John Hammond, 59, 292; William, 37, 38, 292, 298; William, Jr., 294
Cohansie, 71
Cold Spring, 125, 282
Collier, Margaret (Mrs. Thomas Leeds), 85
Collins. Anna C., 237; Dr., 225; Capt. Henry, 14, 15; Tilly, 179; Zebulon, 178, 179; family, 3, 7, 282
Collum, William, 31
Columbus (Black Horse), 207, 208
Colwell, Stephen, 44, 107, 292, 293
Committee of Safety, 15
Compton, Mrs. Rhoda Lee, 244

307

Conover, 67
Cook. Maj., 221; family, 221
Cooper, Sam, 231
Copany, 207, 208, 209
Core, Allie, 273
Corliss. Clarence, 185; Vernon, 185
Cornish, Dick, 192
Corrigan, John G., 169
Corson. Edna, 272; Jonas, 272
Corson's Inlet, 212
Cottrell, Alden, 250
Cox. Col. John, 13, 15, 52, 54, 55, 75; Phoebe, 221
Crab Island, 91, 147, 149, 212, 286
Cramer (Crammer, Cranmer). Arthur, 51; Barzillai, 21; Charles, 166, 168; Hezekiah, 21; Horatio B. ("Tater"), 3, 7, 9, 19-24, 46, 57, 70, 254; Isaac, 270; John, 23, 182; Levi, 21; Margaret, 266; Mary Cale ("Mel," "Grannie"), 22, 31, 32, 85, 266, 267, 273; Nicholas, 266, 267; Roy, 22, 28, 32, 36, 40, 72, 77, 273, 289; family, 178, 273
Crammer. See Cramer, Cranmer
Cranberry Inlet, 52
Cranberry Point, 215
Cranmer. Andrew, 27; Asa, 138; Caleb, 79; Hannah, 30; Jacob, 29; John, 22, 27; Joseph, 209; Josiah, 22, 28; Mary, 27, 43; Sarah, 22; Stephen, 22; William, 22, 28, 29. See also Cramer, Crammer
Crate, Gearhart, 60, 175
Crips, 86
Crosswicks Creek, 60
Crowfoot, xii, 59
Crowley. Birdsall, 215, 218, 288; Capt. James, 118; Jesse, 117, 118; Sam, 35, 40, 134, 138, 288; Tom, 40, 283; Sebastian, 117, 118, 283; family, 114
Crowleytown, 7, 22, 28, 30, 31, 32, 33, 38, 39, 120, 155, 280, 281, 302
Cumberland County, 80, 152
Curry. "Doc," 129; Mary, 133

D. S. Road, the, 138

Da Costa, 198
Daniel's Bridge, 174, 181
Dayton. Asa (Aserdaten), 174, 176, 180, 183; Isaiah, 167, 183; Israel, 167
Deep Point, 19, 26, 30, 45
Deerhart, Rev., 271
Delaney, O. J., 213
Delaware Indians, xiii
Delaware River, xii
De Vries, David Pieterzen, 59
Dingee family, 6
Doctor's Point, 11, 46
Doe Hill, 180
Dorsett. Bert, 175; Capt. John L., 175
Double Trouble, 167, 175
Doughty. Gen. Enoch, 282, 292; Salina, 163
Driver, Samuel, 6, 58, 88, 113, 115, 121, 194
Duck Creek, 60
Dunkers, Jasper, 110
Dutch Dock, 75
Dutch Mills, 86

Eagle (stagecoach stop), 168
Eagleswood Township, 169
East Jersey Proprietors, 62
Eastworthy, Ann, 62
Edge, Gov. Walter E., 91
Edwards. Benjamin, 94, 95; James, 94; family, 98
Egbert. Asa, 94; Elizabeth Carlisle, 94
Egg Harbor, 7, 14, 18, 52, 105, 106, 107, 126, 141, 227, 238, 270
Egg Harbor City, 37, 58, 72, 75, 106, 107, 117, 118, 195, 265
Egg Harbor Station, 289
Ellenville, 44
Elton, Thomas, 62
Elwood (Sailor Boy), 120, 161, 198, 276
Endicott family, 282
English's, 86
Enoch family, 222
Eshlow. See Estlow
Estellville, 247, 248
Estelow. See Estlow

308

Estlow. Christopher, 169, 181, 182, 184; Francis Robineau, 182, 184, 189; Godfrey, 166-168, 181, 184; Tilden ("Uncle Till"), 165, 167, 168, 180-184; Willis, 180; family, 168, 177
Ernst, John, 169
Eureka Club, 179
Evelin, Robert, 59
Ewan. Nathaniel R., 98, 99, 100; family, 101, 102
Ewing, John K. M., 207, 208

Falconbre. See Falkinburg
Falkinburg. Henry Jacobs, xiii, 3-6, 109; Henry Jacobs, Jr., 6; Mary, 5
Farrar, Gervas, 68, 238
Fawn Hill, 182
Fenton, Jack, 225
Ferguson, Capt. Patrick, 7, 8, 10, 14-17, 39
Ffaulkinburge, Henry Jacobs, xii, see Falkinburg
Finley, 86
Fitch, John, 229
Fithian, Rev. Philip Vickers, 238-241
Flagler, 79
Florence Station (Guineatown), 300
Ford. Capt. Benny, 130; Constant, 33-35, 38, 40, 41-45, 132; "Fiddler," 215; Jesse, 117, 118; John Wesley ("Jackie"), 43, 120, 143-151, 157, 196, 287; Josiah, 287; "Aunt Hattie," 21, 32, 43, 99, 115, 117, 118, 121, 144, 162, 191, 192, 193, 199, 284, 289; Morris, 118; Sammy, 43, 120, 166, 184-191, 204; Sophie, 214; William, 44, 107
Forked River, 170, 176
Forked River Game Preserve, 173
Forked River Mountains, 167, 172
Forks, The, 12, 16, 38, 39, 62, 86, 116, 160, 192, 215, 223, 225, 228, 276, 277, 282, 286, 289
Forman. Elizabeth Sooy, 114; Ezekiel, 114, 119
Foss, Gus, 125
Fothergill, John, Account of the Life

and Travels in the Work of the Ministry of, 67, 68, 238
Fountain Gale, 302
Fowler, John, 300
Frambese family, 282
Franklin, Gov. William, 54
Franklyn Inn, 236
Freehold, 206
French. Judge, 233; Richard, 74; Sam, 74; family, 55
Friends, Society of, 5
Further Island, 66

Gabeson. See Giberson
Gardner, Rufus, 221
Garrison, Rev. J. Swain (Swayne), 119, 270
Garwood, Alex, 175, 178
Gaskill. Nelson B., 215-217, 229, 243, 303; family, 221
Gauntt, Ann, 6, 43, 253
Giberson. Gideon, 182; John, 178
Giberson's Mills (Keswick), 178
Gibeson. See Giberson
Gifford family, 254
Girard, Stephen, 79
Glass Works, 86
Gloucester, 218, 270, 289
Gloucester County, 25, 59, 62, 66, 67, 99
Gloucester Furnace, 37, 72, 86, 106, 218
Gloucester Land and Town Association, 106, 107
Gloucester Landing, 269
Godfrey, 181
Good Luck, 169
Good Luck Sedge, 19
Goodwater Run, 282
Goose Bay Sedge, 17
Goose Creek Cove, 108
Goshen, 248
Grant. Capt., 53; family, 178
Gratz, Ben, 272
Gravelly Landing, 228, 236
Gray, Mrs. Franklin Adams, 93
Great Bay, 12, 21, 31, 48, 59, 60, 63, 68

Great Egg Harbor, xii, 48, 62, 68, 248, 298
Great Swamp, 202
Green Bank, xiii, 20, 30-32, 38, 43, 50, 70, 86, 92, 112-121, 123, 125, 127, 132, 136, 141, 143, 152, 155, 157, 166, 181, 184, 185, 191-194, 196, 206, 208, 218, 268, 284, 292, 301
Green Bank Rd., 114
Green Bank State Forest, 195
Greenwich, 68
Gregory, George, 248
Griffing, Moses, 221
Griffith, William, 38
Grim, Rev. Harry P., 225, 226, 227, 237
Grover, John, 170
Guiberson. See Giberson
"Guinea George," 130
Guineatown (Florence Station), 300
Gybertson. See Giberson

Haddonfield, 228
Haddonfield Quarterly Meeting, 67
Haines, Jonathan, 37
Hall. Isaiah, 95; John, 274
Halleck, John, 219
Hammonton, 37, 46, 59, 88, 89, 143, 288, 291, 293, 294
Haney, John, 287
Hanover, 246
Hargrove, Squire, 249
Harrisville, 77, 78, 117, 284
Hastings, Capt., 52
Hay. Andrew K., 292, 293, 294, 295; John B., 294
"Haze Crossway," 138
Headleyville (Brookville), 183
Heather Isle, 19
Hedding, Bishop Elijah, 87
Henderson, 31
Hendricks, Jacob, 110
Herman (Hermann, Herman City, Hermantown), 30, 31, 36, 37, 43, 116, 119, 130, 138, 147, 155, 166, 185, 194, 282, 284
Hessians, 9, 10, 11, 15
Heston, Alfred M., 37, 107, 248

Heston's Waggon Jaunts, 225
"Hex," 296
Higbee family, 6, 26, 67, 234
Higbee's, 219
Higbeeville, 25, 26
High Bank, 39, 282
Hilliard family, 178
Hoffner, Hank, 296
Hog Island, 20, 58, 72, 104
Hogback, 182
Hogshutem, 300
Holloway. Arthur, 116; Henry, 38, 285
Horicon, 169, 170
Horn, Wilsey, 38
Horner. Capt., 27; Robert, 94
Horner's House (tavern), 27
Horseshoe, the, 282
Hough, Ed, 174
Howe, Henry, 59
Hughes. Humphrey, 231; Jim, 26; family, 27
Hungry Hill, 198
Hunterdon County, 99
Hurry, Will, 177
Huyler, Adam, 221
Hyson, Ampley, 138

Ingersol family, 67
Indian Mills, 158, 162, 163, 302
Ireland, Mary, 227
Ireland Cove, 38, 39, 281, 282
Island Road, 17, 33, 72

Jackson. Capt., 221; Isaac, 221; Gen. Marcellus L., 42, 45
Jackson (village), 38, 66, 291, 293
Jackson Creek, 281
Jackson Road, 290
Jacksonville (Slabtown), 207, 208
Jacobs, Mary, 253
Jameson, John Franklin, 221
Jenkins, Isaac, 26
Jenkins Neck, 26, 129, 195
Jersey Devil, 65, 191, 204, 215, 239-242, 248
Job's Creek, 111
Johnny Sedge, 19
Johnny's Ditch, 282

Johnson. Ada Hope, 259; Edwin, 194; Capt. Gus, 80, 95, 96, 225, 272; Isaiah, 94; Jess, 275; Jobie, 43; John, 266; Levi, 258, 265, 267, 268, 271, 272, 274; Pulaski, 26; Capt. Mahlon, 267; Will, 116, 119, 120, 193-196, 204; Zaccheus, 267

Johnsontown, 25, 26

Jones' Mill Road, 189

Juliet, Lt. Gustav, 7, 8, 9, 10, 11, 17, 18, 19

Katesputa Pond, 205

Keen, Nicholas, 23

Keith, George, 95

Kell, Mrs. Charles, 158, 160, 161

Kelly. Cornelius, 26; Capt. Manus, 24

Kemble. William Fretz ("Uncle Will"), 71, 125, 192, 255-262, 264, 265, 268, 272; Rev. Samuel T., 258

Keswick (Giberson's Mills), 178

Kettle Run, 197

Kindler, Joseph, 97

King Charles (N. J.), xii

King's Mountain, Battle of, 8

Kirkwood, 299

Knox. Edward P. (Ned), 167, 170, 172-177, 180, 183, 254; Col. John, 276

Koster. Augustus Ernest, 284; Charles, 284; Courtland, 283; Glenden, 283; Hollis, 21, 83, 283, 284; Leon, 116, 149, 194, 284, 286; Rod, 90, 143-145, 151, 155, 185, 282, 283, 285, 289; family, 15, 38, 162

Lacey (Bamber) Twp., 169, 176

Lacey Road, 174, 175

Lacey Station, 176, 179

Lake family, 282

Lakehurst (Manchester), 170

Lamb, Rhoda, 6, 253

Lance, W. L., 170

Lancewood (Whiting), 170

Lane. Hattie, 272; family, 273

Laurel Springs, 36

Lawrence, John, 95

Layer, Mrs. Sam, 241

Leak. See Leek

Leake. Catherine (Mrs. Will), 43; Capt. John, 209; Capt. Will, 43. See also Leek

Lebanon State Forest, 178

Lee, Francis Baizley, 243, 244, 245, 247

Leeds', 86

Leeds. Abraham, 62; Ann, 66; Daniel, 62, 65, 66, 248; Deborah, 62; Dorcas, 235; Elizabeth, 62; Felix, 66, 70; Hannah, 62; Jane, 249; Japheth, 70; Jemima, 62; Jeremiah, 68, 69; Jesse, 70; Mary, 63; Moses, 249, 268; "Mother," 245, 246, 249; Nehemiah, 62; Robert, 94; Robert, Jr., 235; Thomas, 62, 65; Thomas, Jr., 62; Titan, 62; William, 62, 65; family, 60-70, 86, 152

"Leeds Devil." See "Jersey Devil"

Leeds Point, 60-70, 219, 225, 237, 241, 244, 249, 288

Leeds Point Road, 60

Leek. Achsah, 79; "Aunt Beckie," 266, 268, 270, 275; Charles Platt, xiv, 20, 49, 55, 56, 70-81, 82, 84, 86, 103, 108, 254, 280, 289; Elvin, 190; George, 161; Hepsebah, 79; Hezekiah, 79; John, 71, 78, 153, 161, 199; Kesiah, 79; Phoebe, 78; Rosana, 79; William Stafford, 128; family, 70-81

Leektown, 77, 78

Lenni-Lenape Indians, 7

Limmon, Elmer, 190

Lippincott. Gideon, 202; Joseph, 206; Watson, 205, 206, 208, 209, 210; family, 204, 206, 277

Little Buck Run, 182

Little Crab Island, 212

Little Egg Harbor, xii, 5, 10, 11, 13-15, 17, 21, 28, 46, 47, 49, 53, 55, 58, 68, 94, 95, 103, 111, 137, 141, 148, 150, 159, 169, 215, 218, 223, 227, 238, 289

Little Egg Harbor Bay, 111

Little Egg Harbor River, 72

Little Egg Harbor Township, 6

Little Mill, 197
Littles, Mrs., 34, 35, 38, 43, 45
Livingston, 14
Lockwood, Wayne, 190
Long-a-Coming (Berlin), xii, 219, 293
Long Beach, 13, 27
Long Beach Island, 24
Loveland. Catherine, 48, 50; Charles, 30; Capt. Charles, 50, 117; Capt. Sir Charles, 50; Jemima, 48; Mary, 50; family, 21, 29, 30, 48, 49, 79
Loveman, Dr., 174
Lower Bank, 36, 50, 70-81, 81-92, 94, 96-98, 100-103, 105, 112, 113, 119, 139, 147, 155, 171, 191, 195, 196, 198, 206, 215, 260, 261, 265, 289
Lower Dock, 118
Lower Island, 66
Lucas, Rev. Simon, 276

Mahomecum, xii
Manahawkin, 48, 137, 221
Manchester (Lakehurst), 170
Mapes, David, 273
Maple Branch, 197
Marcus Hook, 65
Marks, Louis, 296
Marriner, Capt. William, 221
Marter, Ridgway, 203
Martha, 182, 184, 218
Martha Forge, 181
Martha Furnace, 168
Martha's Vineyard, 14
Mason, Leon, 301
Mathis. Amasa, 51; Arthur, 5; Caleb, 51; Daniel, 55, 65, 236; Elihu, 3, 4, 6, 16, 21, 50, 51, 254; "Great John," 27, 46, 50, 51, 55, 60, 209; Jesse, 60, 61, 63, 66, 249; Job, 65, 78, 111; Micajah, 22; Phoebe, 21; family, 21, 60-70, 79, 88
Mathistown, 195
Matinicunk Island, xii
Matthews. See Mathis
Maurice River, 38
Maxwell. Hannah, 267; Harold, 267; Capt. Joseph Bush, 119; family, 114, 273

Mayberry, Thomas, 277
Mays Landing, 73, 86
Mechescatauxen Creek, 276
Meeting House Road, 26
Merchant, Sam, 206
Micajah Smith's Mills, 223
Mick. Reuben, 288; Steelman, 127
Middle-of-the-Shore (Tuckerton), 5, 14, 17, 26, 141, 160, 290
Middletown, 62, 65
Mill Road, 174, 178
Miller. Gus, 15; John ("Bull"), 302; Mrs. John, 158, 160, 162, 163; Jonas, 236; family, 44
Millville (Brookville), 183
Minicunk Island, 4
Mollicas. See Mullica
Monhunk Island, 4, 17
Monmouth County, 99, 152
Moore, Jerry, 32
Mordecai, 283
Mordecai Swamp, 282, 286
Mordecai's Landing, 39, 283
Morey. Ben, 177; Joe, 177
Morey Lot, 182
Morey Lot Road, 177
Moss (Morse's) Mill, 228
Mott family, 254
Motts' Creek, 25, 57
Mount Holly, 15, 43, 119, 196, 207
Muddy Creek, 60
"Mule Road," 178
Muliicus. See Mullica
Mullica, Eric Palsson, 6, 45, 49, 58, 59, 70, 77, 82, 88, 113, 119
Mullica Hill, 59, 60, 78
Mullica Valley, 13, 111
Mullicus. See Mullica
Mulliner, Joe, 278, 283

McAnniney. See McAnney
McAnney. Jimmy, 142; Capt. John, 90, 199, 200, 204, 210, 211, 212, 214; family, 204
McClellan, Gen. George B., 106
McCloskey, Lou, 296
McCollum, Hugh, 227

312

McConeghy, Laura Larrabee, xiii, 113, 116, 120, 121
McCorey, Mr., 272
McCormack, Mrs., 248
McGraw, "Old Man," 138
McKean, Robert, 209
McKeen, 206. *See also* McKean

Nacote Creek, 74, 86, 215, 219, 223, 225, 228, 234
Naked Creek, 228
Nesco (Wescottville), 36, 38, 143, 195, 286, 292
Nesco Pond, 277
Nescochague Creek, 276
New Brooklyn, 36
New Columbia (Nesco), 155
New Freedom, 197
New Gretna (Bass River), ix, xiii, 20, 21, 30, 46, 58, 75, 86, 93, 149, 192, 195, 198-200, 204, 208
*New Jersey Archives*, 54
*New Jersey Gazette*, 13
Newberry, Dr., 179
Newbould, 31
Newman's Thoroughfares, 19
Nichols. Capt. Abe, 31, 38, 302; Lonzo, 28, 302; Will, 28, 302; family, 44
Nigger Creek, 22, 125
Nigger Island, 273
Noah's Ark, 138
Norcross. Joe, 297; Mrs., 294, 296; Samuel Southard (Sud), 42, 139, 210, 233, 234, 236, 237, 239, 289, 297, 301; Uriah, 297; William, 297. *See also* Norecross
Norecross (Norcross). Charles, 299; Isaiah, 299; John, 299; Job, 299; Joseph, 299; Samuel, 299; Uriah, 299; William, 299
Northfield, 134
Northampton, 60, 62
Noyes, Fred, 70, 84

Oak Island, 46
Oak Knoll, 197
Ocean City, 4

Ocean County, 22, 25, 48, 169, 170
Old Hickory Island, 57
Old Tappan, 11
Oliphant. Eayre, 4; family, 26, 30
Oliver, Edward, 268
Ong, Jacob, 6, 28, 290, 303
Ong's Hat, 6, 26, 215, 289, 302, 303
Osborn. Richard, 4, 6, 17, 18; Thomas, 18, 28; family, 67
Osborn's Creek, 111
Oswego River, 168
Otis, Jim, 147, 213
Oyster Creek, 60, 65, 242

Page, Thomas, 253
Pancake, 177, 182
Parker. Joseph, 4; family, 254
Parks, Johnny, 296
Pasadena (Wheatlands), 174, 177
Patten, Jim, 44
Patton. John, 170; family, 178
Pearce, Joseph, 60
Peck, Benjamin, 62
Pemberton, Israel, 276
Pemberton, 43
Penbryn, 197
Penn Swamp, 198
Pennington family, 282
*Pennsylvania Evening Post*, 13
*Pennsylvania Journal and Weekly Advertiser*, 13
Pennypacker, "Mother," 222
Perce, 294
Perth Amboy, 4
Pestletown, 197
Peterson, Charles, 278, 288
Petticoat Bridge, 207
Pettit. Charles, 54; family, 86
Pharo. Achsah, 268; Joseph, 254; family, 6, 221
Pilesgrove, 68
Pine Coaling, 86
Pitney, Dr. Jonathan, 292
Pleasant Mills (Sweetwater), 20, 38, 77, 86, 116, 120, 160, 198, 264, 268, 276, 277, 299
Pleasantville, 138, 222

313

Plumstead Twp., 169
Pohatcong (Tuckerton) Creek, 111
Point Pleasant, 171
Pole, the, 19
Port Republic (Wrangleboro), 73, 74, 87, 109, 129, 150, 220, 223, 225-228, 232, 233, 237, 239, 241, 278
Porter, Judge Joseph, 282, 292, 293
Potter. Paul, 51; Stephen, 51
Potts, Joseph, 55, 230
Preacher's Hill, 178
Proctor, Tom, 34, 39, 278
Proprietors, Provincial Council of, 4
Pulaski, Count Casimir, 10, 17, 18, 32, 38

Quaker Bridge, 25, 26

Rabbit Island, 125, 282
Radcliffe, Sam, 216, 217, 218
Randolph Township, 7, 193
Rapp. Augusta, 284; John H., 284
Read. Charles, 276, 278; Honoré, 278
Recklesstown, 225
Red Oak Grove, 177
Reeves, Marshall, 187
Revell, Thomas, 66
Richards. Jesse, 274, 286; John, 218, 219, 286; Owen, 292; Samuel, 292; Thomas, 292, 293; William, 218, 277, 292
Ridgway, 6
Ridgway family, 221, 254
Rieck, Dr., 247
Risley, Richard, 95
Riverside, 295
Riverton, 78
Rock (Bass) River, 111
Robinson. Joe, xi-xiv, 103, 280, 281; Johnnie, 266, 282
Rockhill family, 254
Roller, Jake, 296
Rose. Martha, 79; Samuel, 79
Rossel, Hugh, 19
Ryan, Dr., 165
Ryder. Arthur (lightkeeper), 25; Capt. "Jarv," 24

Sailor Boy (Elwood), 120, 161, 276
Salem, 44, 68, 99
Salem County, 152
Salmons, Joel, 203
Sampson, John, 295, 296, 297
Samuel Driver Survey, 195
Salter's Ditch, 302
Sandy Crossing, 197
Sandy Hook, 13, 21
Sandy Ridge, 91
Sawyer family, 254
Schenck, John, 221, 222
Schmoele. Dr. Henry, 106; Dr. William, 106
Schneider. Gus, 3, 6, 7, 8, 9, 20, 21; Mrs., 7
Scott. Andrew, 95; Ellen, 93-97 passim; Robert W., 62, 63, 64
Scull, Joseph, 67
Sears, 3, 37, 50
Seven Islands, 13, 64
Shamong Township, 204
Sheep's Head Creek, 21
Sheep's Head marshes, 16
Shores, Harry, 199, 203
Short Beach, 21
Shourds. Mrs., 242; Cornelius, 244; Samuel, Sr., 248, 249
Shourds' Mill Creek, 111
Shrewsbury, 60, 65, 94
Shrewsbury River, 60
Simm Place, 185
Simpkins, William H. ("Chink"), 120, 121, 127-130, 144, 289
Sims, Emeline, 282; John Clark, 282
Skeekat's Plains, 182
Skin Hill, 300
Skull, John, 68
Slabtown (Jacksonville), 207, 208
Sloop, the, 19
Smallwood. Donny (Frank), 74, 86, 232, 233-236, 238, 239, 254; Sam, 36
Smith. "Uncle Charlie," 296; Capt. Cyrus, 147; Daniel, 30; Capt. Enoch, 150; Evi, 227, 235; F. Hopkinson, 263; Joanna, 31; Capt. Lew, 24; Manuel, 30; Mary, 31; Capt.

Micajah, 226, 229, 230, 232; Robert, 68; Sarah, 235; family, 67, 86
Smithville, 60, 68, 237
Soldiers' Hole, 17
Somers Point, 67
Sommers (Somers), Mary Leeds, 67
Snow family, 206
Sooy. Annie, 116; Asa, 51; Augustus, 49; Billy, 43; Catherine, 50; Cowperthwaite, 50; Damietta, 50; Daniel, 51, 61; Dennis, 138; Capt. Ebeneezer, 48, 50, 55, 56; Ephriam, 114, 116, 119, 195; Ephriam Cline, Jr., 114, 116; Esther, 194, 195; Hannah Lane, 269; Jemima, 114; Joel, 116; Joseph, see Yoos; Capt. Joseph, 52-55; Josephus, 116, 195, 288; Josiah, 50; Kate, 117; Len, 45-47, 48, 50, 57, 58, 79; Lucy Ann Haywood, 114; Lydia, 116; Lucretia, 50; Mary Leek, 79; Nicholas, 113, 114, 115, 119, 120, 194, 195, 282; Nicholas II, 114, 115, 116, 128, 194; Nicholas III, 116; Noah, 138; Raymond, 116; Sabrina, 50; Samuel, 95, 116, 195; Sarah Vanderhoven, 82; Thomas, 117; Watson, 116-119, 269, 272; William, 115-118, 195, 196, 213, 274, 287; Yoos (Yozo, Joseph), 6, 49, 51, 52, 57, 72, 81, 83, 88, 114, 120; Yozo, see Yoos; family, xiv, 3, 7, 88, 98
Springfield, 62
Squan, 48
Stacy. Ann, 66; Robert, 66
Stanley, Jane, 172
Steelman, 67
Stevens, Capt. David, 230, 231
Stewart. Andrew, 287; Frank, 230, 233, 235, 288; John, 143, 287, 288; Robert, 286; Robert Patterson, 277, 285-288 passim
Stoeker, Capt., 221
Stokes, John, 231, 232
Stone Landing, 282
Storer, Capt., 221
Stout (architect), 64
Stoy, James, 298

Strang, Jerry, 296
Strickland, Tom, 64
Stump Creek, 22, 90, 143
Stuyvesant, Rutherford, 179
Sullivan, John, 129
Suse, Aunt, 42, 43
Sutts. "Granny," 294, 295, 296; Manus, 294, 295
Swamp Creek, 60
Swan Bay, 111, 220, 289
Swedesboro, 78, 111
Swedesborough, 4
Sweetwater (Pleasant Mills), 276, 281
Swimming Over Point, 25, 26, 57, 160
Sykes, J., 68, 235

"Ta-Ko-Kan," 121
Tansboro, 36, 291, 297, 298, 300, 301
Tattletown (Brookville), 183
Tattletown (Brookville), 177, 183
Taylor. Christina, 87; Capt. Hen, 128; John M., 231
Ten Mile Hollow, 169, 178
Tennant Church, 208
Terry, Cliff, 71, 115, 215, 273, 284
Thompson, John, 26
Thorne, Henry, 231
Thurston, Harry, 7
Tice Van Horn's Brook, 178
Toms River, 167, 169, 170, 171, 174, 177, 178
Townsend. Daniel, 48; Jemima (Loveland), 48; John, 96
Treen, William, 221
Trenton, 17, 46
Tucker, Ebenezer, 49, 217, 219, 253
Tucker's Beach, 21, 23
Tuckerton (Middle-of-the-Shore), 15, 17, 25, 26, 30, 43, 55, 73, 79, 117, 120, 138, 141, 160, 174, 206, 221, 278, 281
Tuckerton Creek, 111, 221
Tuckerton Railroad, 182
Turkey Point, xiii
Turtle (Turkle) Creek, 79, 88, 152
Turtle Island, 19, 57, 75
Tylertown, 44, 147, 302

315

Underhill. Charles Reginald, 263, 264, 265; Ella, 249, 267, 269, 271-274, 285
Union Clay Works, 179
Updike, Jack, 199-202, 204, 210-212, 214
Upper Bank, 70, 113
Upper Dock, 118

Valiant, George, 213
Valley Forge, Pa., xii, 6
Vandehoven, Cornelius, 82
Van Sant. Isaac, 266, 267; John, 74, 86; Margaret, 266; Mercy Davis, 4; Nathaniel, 266-269, 271; Nicholas, 271; Oscar, 74; Rebecca, 86; Rev. Nicholas, 86; Sam, 74; Sarah Cramer, 266; Stanley, 74; Rev. S. Monroe, 86; family, 73, 74, 79, 86, 114
Vanuxem. James, 282; family, 139
Verrazano, 59
*Vigilant* (ship), 17
Vincentown, 107, 244
Voss, Emma, 117

Wading River (Bridgeport), 30, 55, 57, 77, 78, 103, 109, 111, 120, 161, 168, 190, 198, 205, 208, 212, 264
*Walter Palmer* (ship), 31
Walton, "Uncle Dick," 168, 177, 180
Wapler, Joseph, 32, 37
Ware, Wilmon, xiii
Waretown, 136, 168, 179, 181, 182
Warren Grove, 185, 187
Washington Field, 26
Washington Township, 22, 28, 75, 193
Waterford Township, 137
Watkins, J. Elfreth, 244, 247
Watson. John, 5, 73, 279, 280, 281; Tom, 27, 28, 135
Weaver, Mrs., 118
Ware. Frank H., 197; Joe, 73, 102, 120, 196-199, 204
Warrington, Rev., 300
Webb. David, 177; Joey, 177; Nate, 177

Webb's Mill, 167, 169, 173, 174, 181
Webb's Mill Road, 178
Webb's Town (Webb Town), 177, 179, 182
Weber. Charlie, 72, 88, 102-113, 125, 197, 198; Charlie, Jr., 102, 103, 109, 112; Ed, 102, 103, 105, 112, 199; Emily, 105; Harry, 105; Lucy, 105; Mary, 105; Otto, 105
Wedham, Capt., 14
Weeks. Col. Jim, 129; Dr. Harry, 266; Hannah, 95, 266; Job, 266; Josephus, 266; Louie, 266; Sam, 266, 270-274; family, 71, 114, 220
Weekstown, 105, 106, 120, 192, 201, 215, 220, 277
Weeksville, 105, 120, 217
Wells Mills, 166, 167, 168, 177, 180, 184
Wescoat's, 86
Wescott (Westcott, Wescoat), Col. Richard, 15, 62, 75, 220, 227, 230
Wescottville (Nesco), 286
West Mill Creek, 281
Westcoatville, 36, 195. *See also* Wescottville
West Jersey, 65
West New Jersey Society of London, 106
West Point Pleasant, 175
West's, 86
Weyman, Ducky, 44
Weymouth, 86, 218, 287, 292, 293, 302
Wharton, Joseph, 37, 77, 91, 146, 148, 213, 263, 277, 285, 286
Wharton Estate, 281
White. Emmaline, 152; George, 152; Mary, 152; Peter, 67; Philip, 152; Samuel, 152; family, 156
White Frost Cove, 57
White Horse Pike, 112
Whitetown, 152, 155
Whiting, Mr., 170
Whiting (Lancewood), 167, 169, 170, 174
Wigwam Creek, 60

Will Hurry (station), 177
Williamstown, 44, 45, 291
Willis, 86
Willits. Ann, 6; Deliverance, 137; Esther Matilda, 94; James, 17; Joseph, 6, 137; Richard, 47; Stephen, 254; Timothy, 48; Wyllis, 48; family, 21, 48
Wills. "Aunt Mary," 36, 37; family, 4
Wilson, Billy, 130
Winslow, 34, 36, 38, 44, 291, 293, 295, 297
Winslow Township, 299
Wireless Road, 9
Wobbar. Augusta, 118; Capt. Otto, 128, 288; family, 114
Wolsiffer, P. M., 106
Woodbury, 232

Woodbury-Creek, 68
Woodmansee. Clarence, 103; "Parson," ix, 193
Woolford, Walter, 295, 297
Woolston. Capt. William, 119; Jane Messick, 119; Peter, 119
Wrangleboro (Port Republic), 86, 224, 235
Wright, Thomas, 97
"Weasy," 266

Young, Dorothy, 66

Zare's Bridge, 182
*Zebra* (ship), 17, 19
Zeb's Bridge, 178
Zion, 86
Zimmerman, Mattie, 301